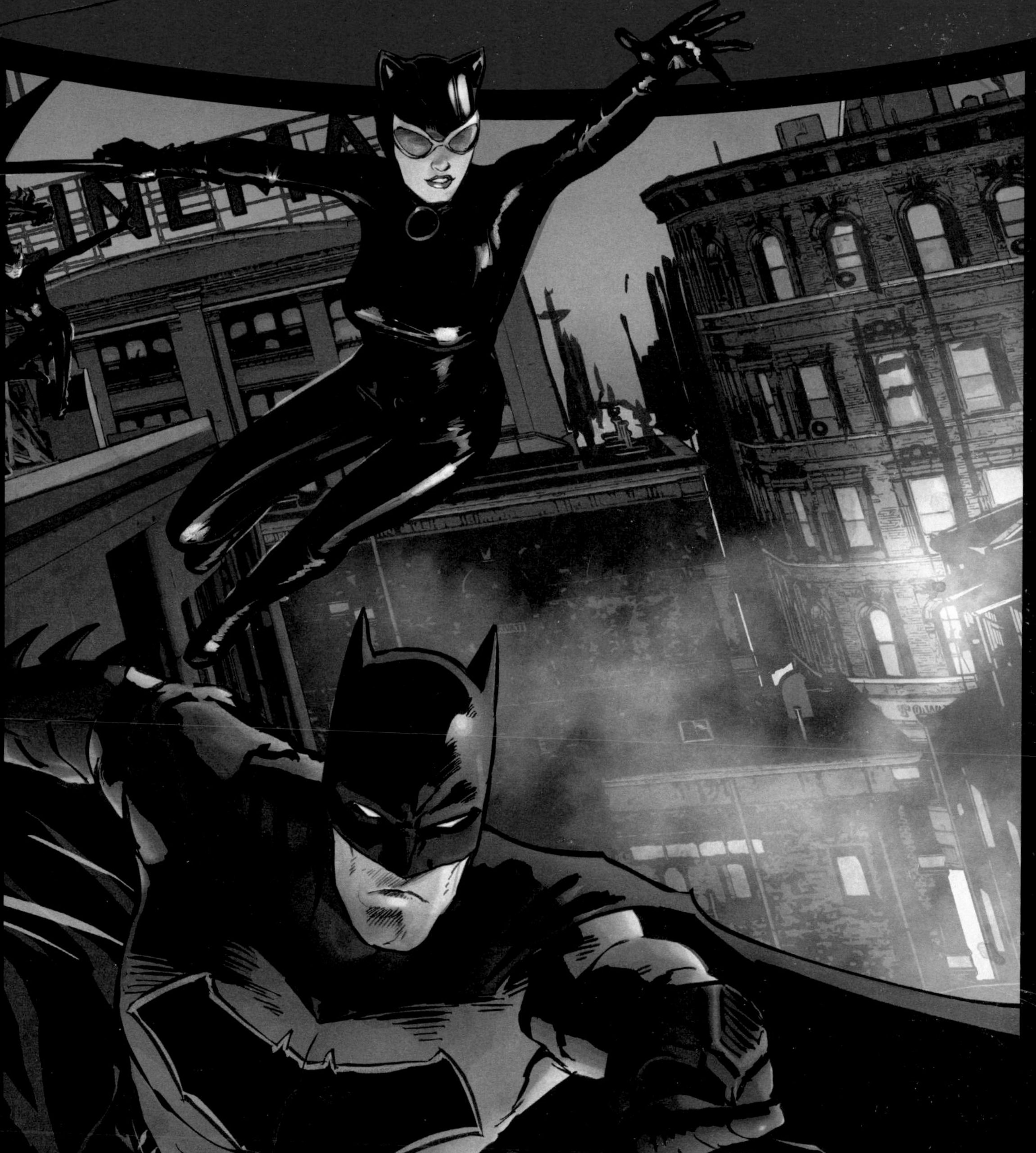

BATMAN

VOL.6 BRIDE OR BURGLAR?

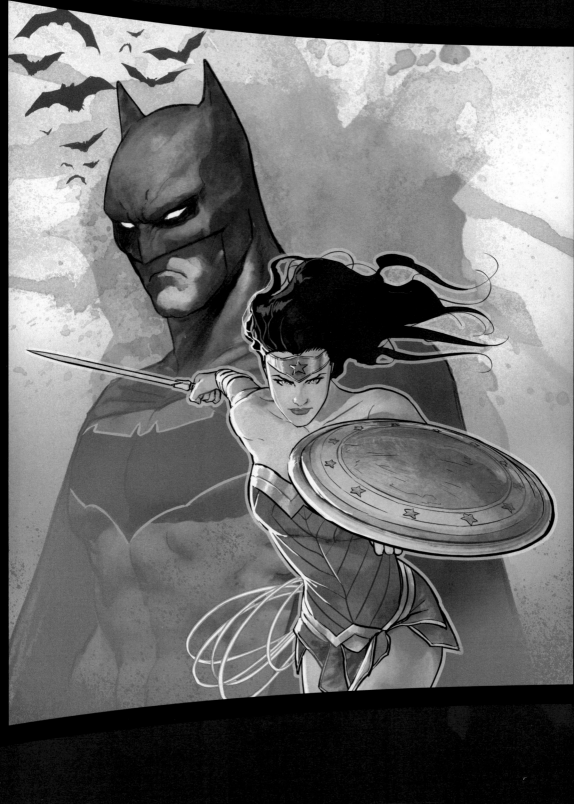

BATMAN

VOL.6 BRIDE OR BURGLAR?

TOM KING
writer

MIKEL JANÍN
JOËLLE JONES
TRAVIS MOORE
HUGO PETRUS
artists

JUNE CHUNG
JORDIE BELLAIRE
GIULIA BRUSCO
colorists

CLAYTON COWLES
letterer

JOËLLE JONES and **JORDIE BELLAIRE**
collection cover artists

BATMAN created by **BOB KANE** with **BILL FINGER**
SUPERMAN created by **JERRY SIEGEL** and **JOE SHUSTER**
SUPERGIRL based on characters created by **JERRY SIEGEL** and **JOE SHUSTER**
By special arrangement with the Jerry Siegel family

JAMIE S. RICH Editor - Original Series * **BRITTANY HOLZHERR** Associate Editor - Original Series * **MAGGIE HOWELL** Assistant Editor - Original Series
JEB WOODARD Group Editor - Collected Editions * **ROBIN WILDMAN** Editor - Collected Edition
STEVE COOK Design Director - Books * **SHANNON STEWART** Publication Design

BOB HARRAS Senior VP - Editor-in-Chief, DC Comics
PAT McCALLUM Executive Editor, DC Comics

DIANE NELSON President * **DAN DiDIO** Publisher * **JIM LEE** Publisher * **GEOFF JOHNS** President & Chief Creative Officer
AMIT DESAI Executive VP - Business & Marketing Strategy, Direct to Consumer & Global Franchise Management
SAM ADES Senior VP & General Manager, Digital Services * **BOBBIE CHASE** VP & Executive Editor, Young Reader & Talent Development
MARK CHIARELLO Senior VP - Art, Design & Collected Editions * **JOHN CUNNINGHAM** Senior VP - Sales & Trade Marketing
ANNE DePIES Senior VP - Business Strategy, Finance & Administration * **DON FALLETTI** VP - Manufacturing Operations
LAWRENCE GANEM VP - Editorial Administration & Talent Relations * **ALISON GILL** Senior VP - Manufacturing & Operations
HANK KANALZ Senior VP - Editorial Strategy & Administration * **JAY KOGAN** VP - Legal Affairs * **JACK MAHAN** VP - Business Affairs
NICK J. NAPOLITANO VP - Manufacturing Administration * **EDDIE SCANNELL** VP - Consumer Marketing
COURTNEY SIMMONS Senior VP - Publicity & Communications * **JIM (SKI) SOKOLOWSKI** VP - Comic Book Specialty Sales & Trade Marketing
NANCY SPEARS VP - Mass, Book, Digital Sales & Trade Marketing * **MICHELE R. WELLS** VP - Content Strategy

BATMAN VOL. 6: BRIDE OR BURGLAR?

DC Comics, 2900 West Alameda Ave., Burbank, CA 91505
Printed by LSC Communications, Kendallville, IN, USA. 6/22/18. First Printing.
ISBN: 978-1-4012-8027-7

Library of Congress Cataloging-in-Publication Data is available.

PEFC
PEFC/29-31-337
PEFC Certified
Printed on paper from sustainably managed forests, controlled sources
www.pefc.org

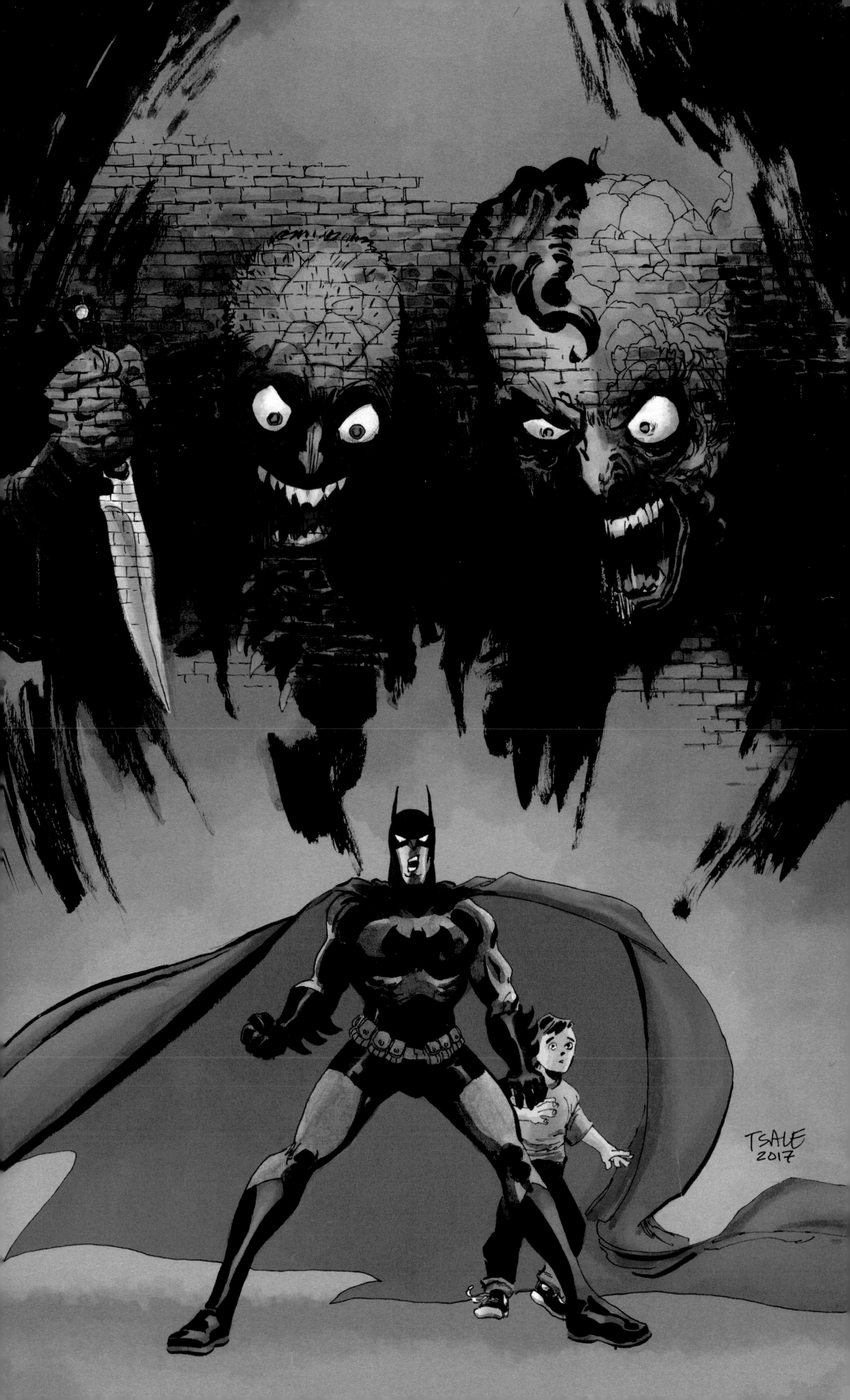
TSALE
2017

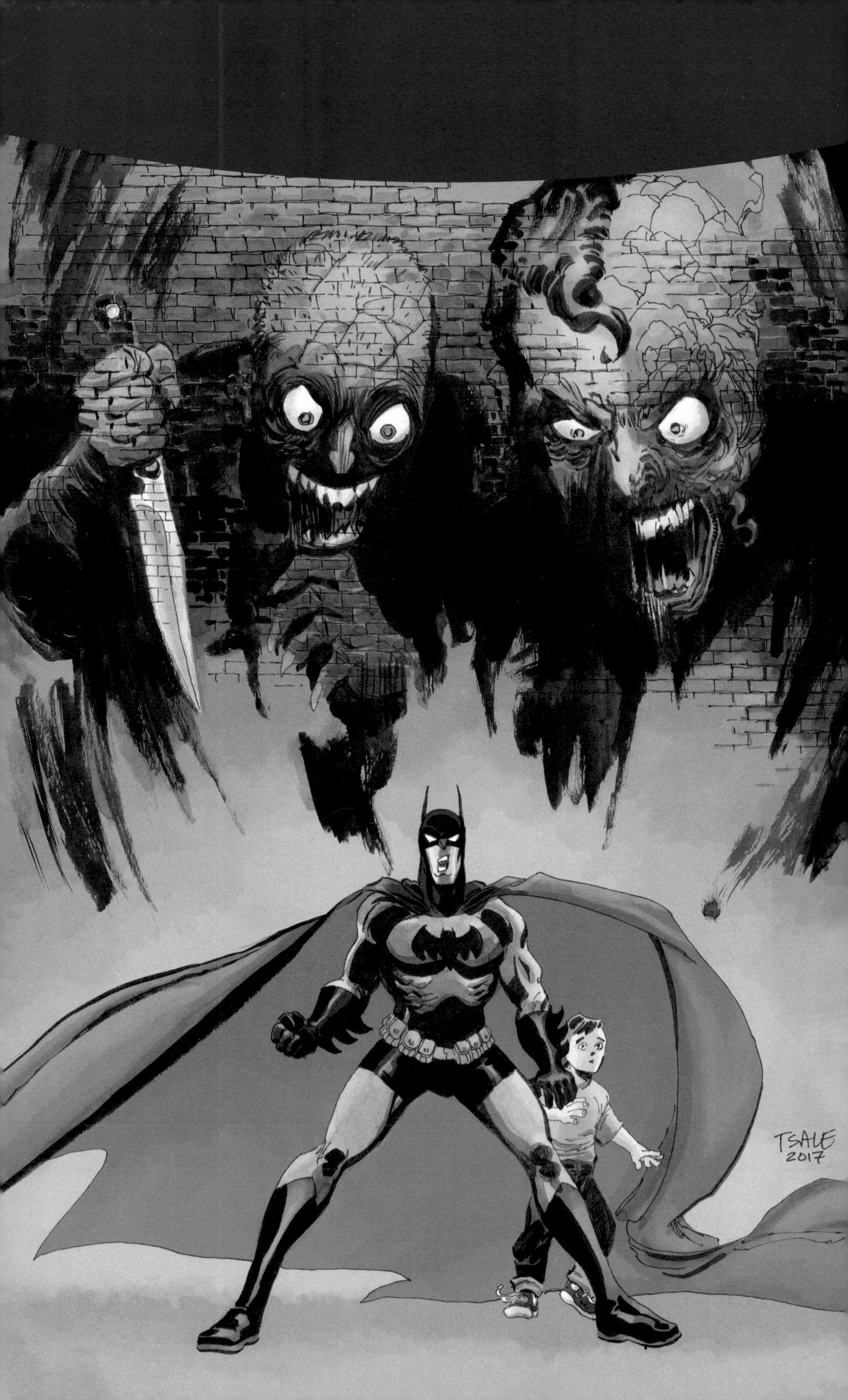
TSALE
2017

"WE JUST CAME HOME."

"I'M SORRY, MATTHEW."

"THEY WERE SUPPOSED TO BE WAITING."

DC COMICS PRESENTS

"I KNOW."

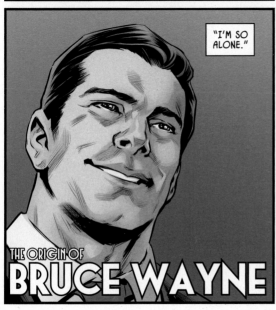

"I'M SO ALONE."

THE ORIGIN OF
BRUCE WAYNE

"YOU'RE NOT ALONE."

TOM KING SCRIPT TRAVIS MOORE PENCILS, INKS
GIULIA BRUSCO COLORS CLAYTON COWLES LETTERS
TIM SALE & DAVE STEWART COVER
MAGGIE HOWELL ASST. EDITOR JAMIE S. RICH EDITOR

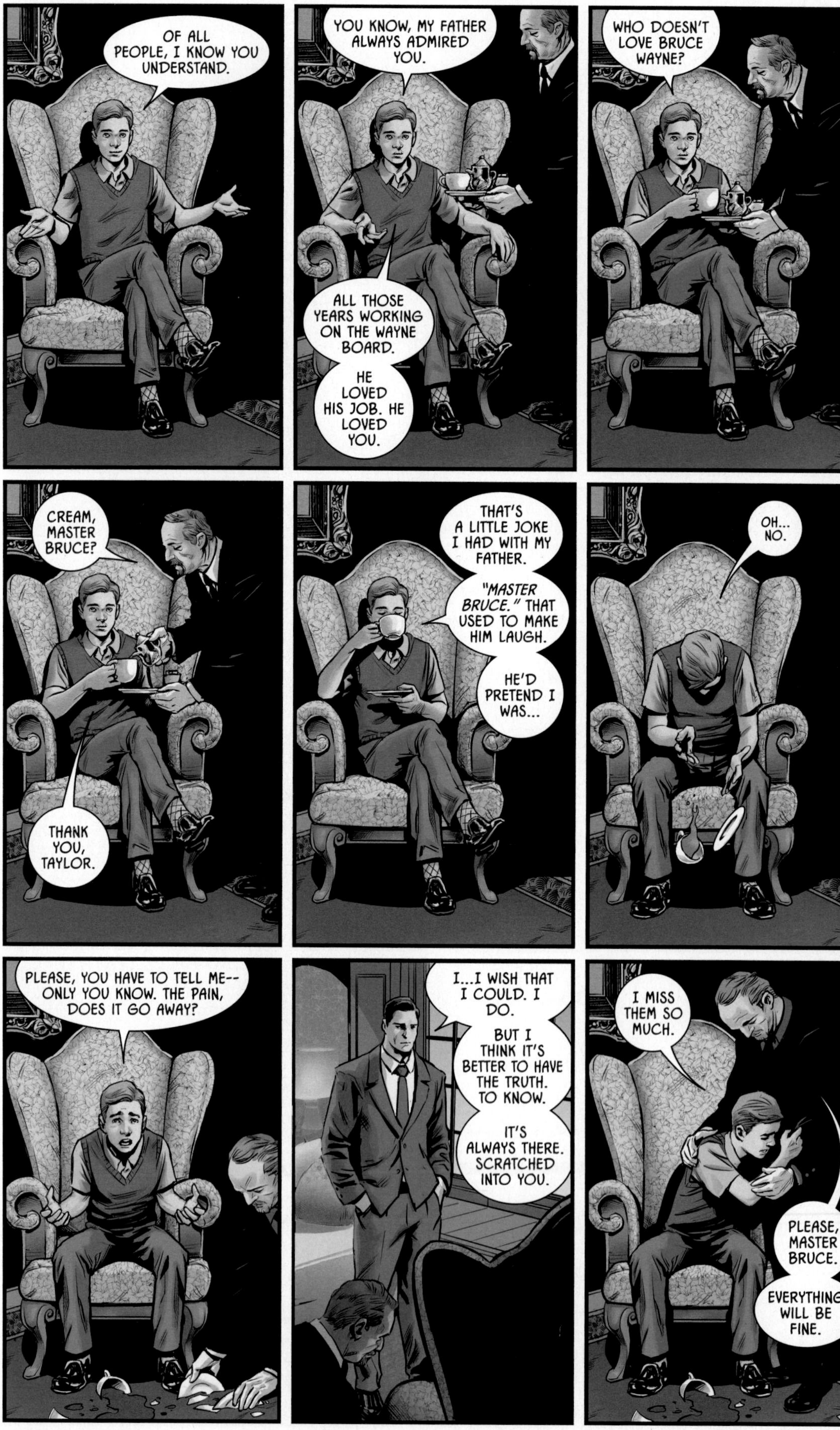
OF ALL PEOPLE, I KNOW YOU UNDERSTAND.
YOU KNOW, MY FATHER ALWAYS ADMIRED YOU.
ALL THOSE YEARS WORKING ON THE WAYNE BOARD.
HE LOVED HIS JOB. HE LOVED YOU.
WHO DOESN'T LOVE BRUCE WAYNE?
CREAM, MASTER BRUCE?
THANK YOU, TAYLOR.
THAT'S A LITTLE JOKE I HAD WITH MY FATHER.
"MASTER BRUCE." THAT USED TO MAKE HIM LAUGH.
HE'D PRETEND I WAS...
OH... NO.
PLEASE, YOU HAVE TO TELL ME-- ONLY YOU KNOW. THE PAIN, DOES IT GO AWAY?
I...I WISH THAT I COULD. I DO.
BUT I THINK IT'S BETTER TO HAVE THE TRUTH. TO KNOW.
IT'S ALWAYS THERE. SCRATCHED INTO YOU.
I MISS THEM SO MUCH.
PLEASE, MASTER BRUCE.
EVERYTHING WILL BE FINE.

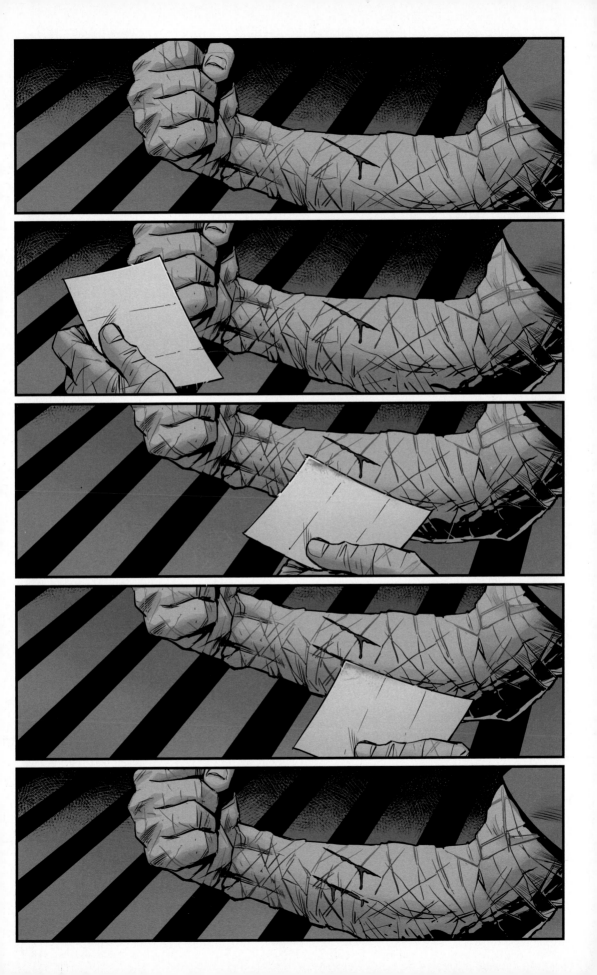

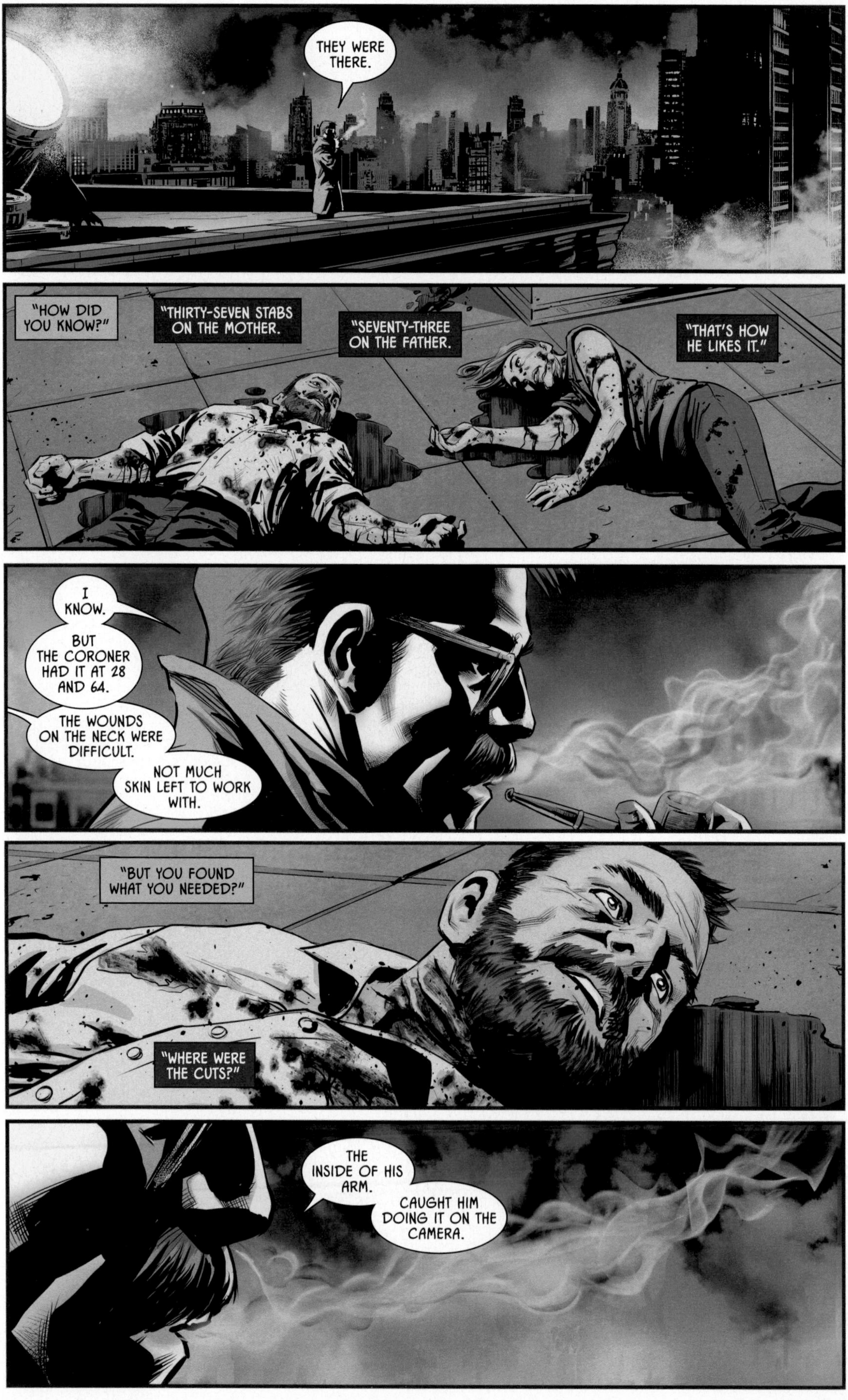
THEY WERE THERE.
"HOW DID YOU KNOW?"
"THIRTY-SEVEN STABS ON THE MOTHER.
"SEVENTY-THREE ON THE FATHER.
"THAT'S HOW HE LIKES IT."
I KNOW.
BUT THE CORONER HAD IT AT 28 AND 64.
THE WOUNDS ON THE NECK WERE DIFFICULT.
NOT MUCH SKIN LEFT TO WORK WITH.
"BUT YOU FOUND WHAT YOU NEEDED?"
"WHERE WERE THE CUTS?"
THE INSIDE OF HIS ARM.
CAUGHT HIM DOING IT ON THE CAMERA.

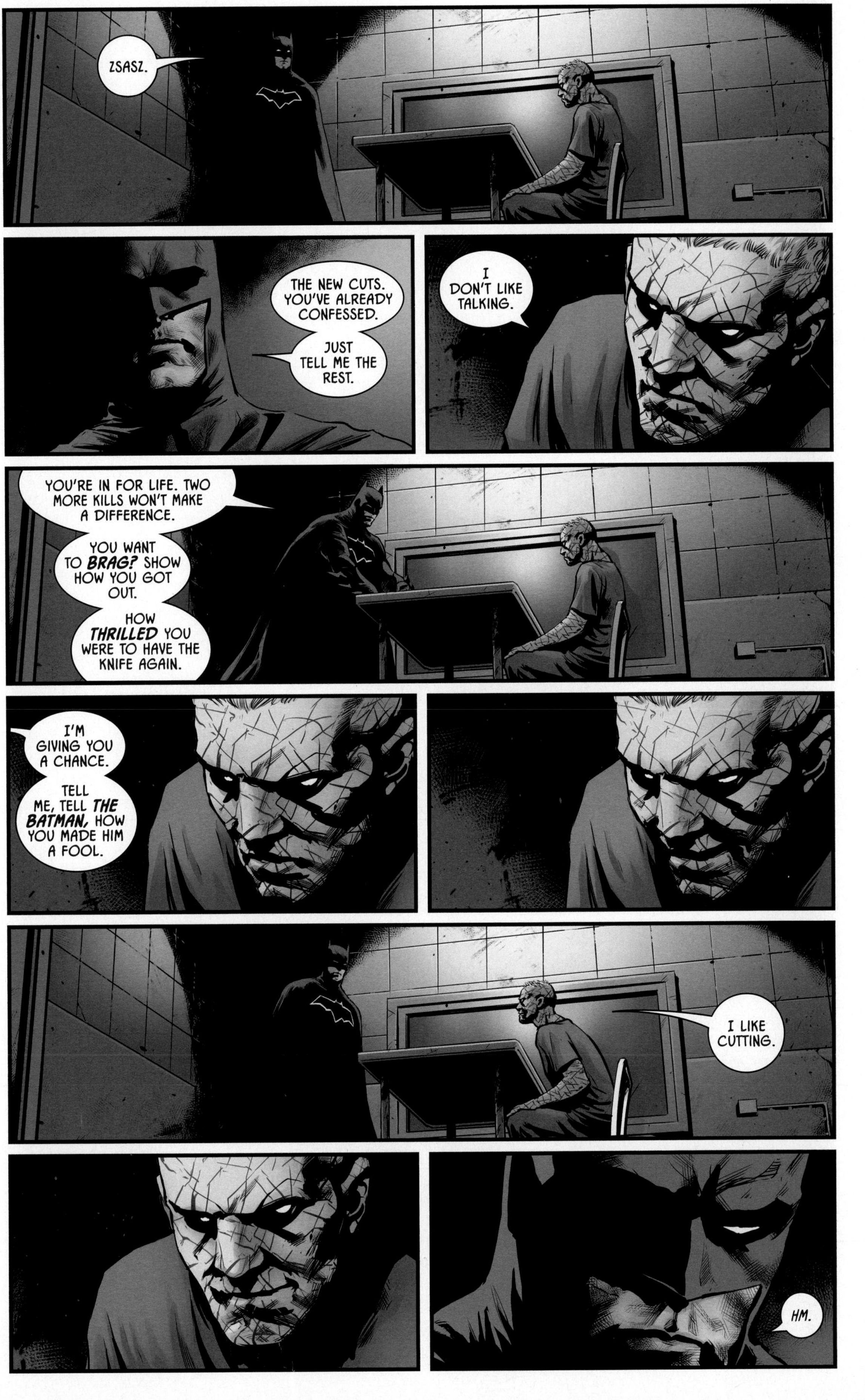
ZSASZ.
THE NEW CUTS. YOU'VE ALREADY CONFESSED.
JUST TELL ME THE REST.
I DON'T LIKE TALKING.
YOU'RE IN FOR LIFE. TWO MORE KILLS WON'T MAKE A DIFFERENCE.
YOU WANT TO BRAG? SHOW HOW YOU GOT OUT.
HOW THRILLED YOU WERE TO HAVE THE KNIFE AGAIN.
I'M GIVING YOU A CHANCE.
TELL ME, TELL THE BATMAN, HOW YOU MADE HIM A FOOL.
I LIKE CUTTING.
HM.

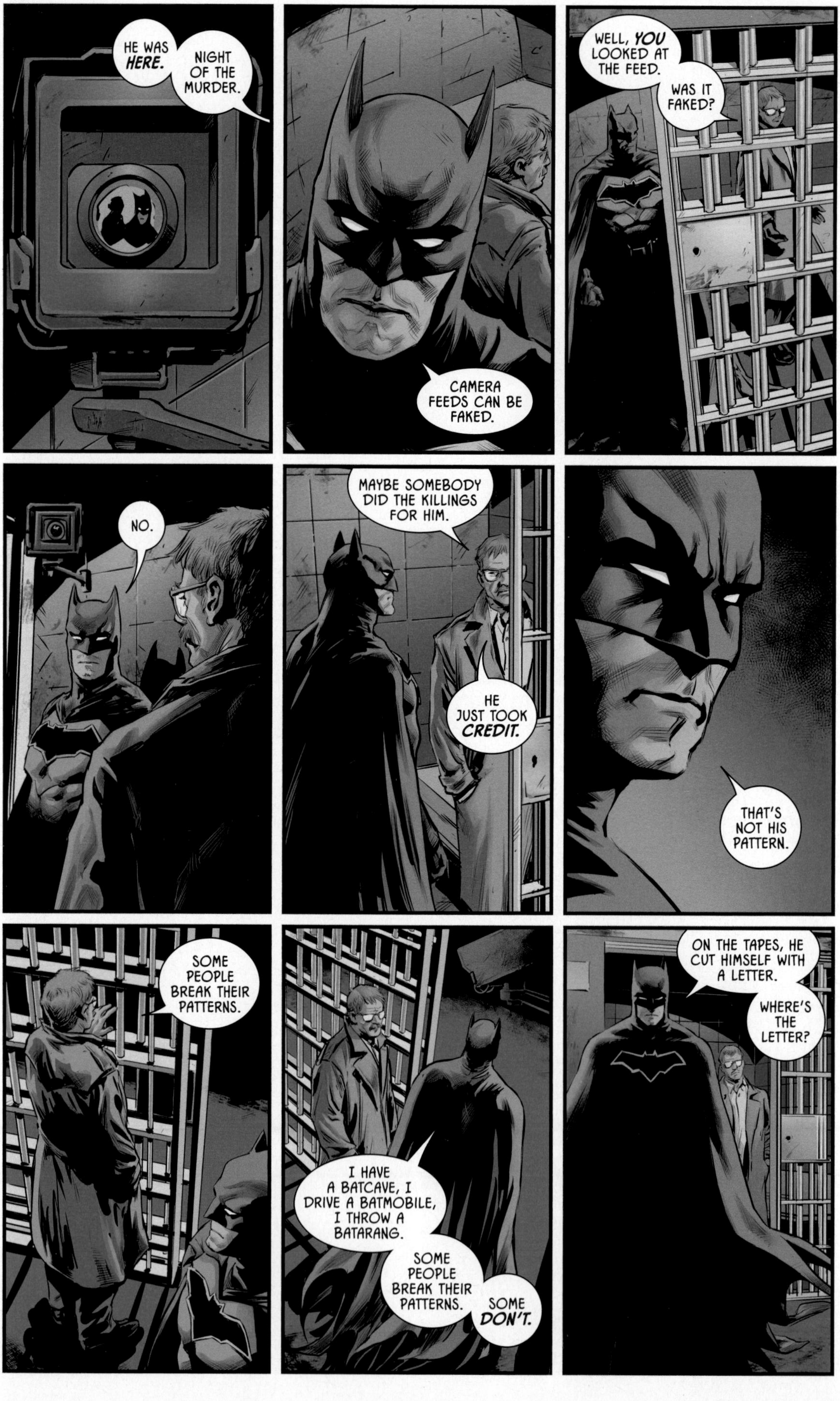
HE WAS HERE.
NIGHT OF THE MURDER.
CAMERA FEEDS CAN BE FAKED.
WELL, YOU LOOKED AT THE FEED.
WAS IT FAKED?
NO.
MAYBE SOMEBODY DID THE KILLINGS FOR HIM.
HE JUST TOOK CREDIT.
THAT'S NOT HIS PATTERN.
SOME PEOPLE BREAK THEIR PATTERNS.
I HAVE A BATCAVE, I DRIVE A BATMOBILE, I THROW A BATARANG.
SOME PEOPLE BREAK THEIR PATTERNS.
SOME DON'T.
ON THE TAPES, HE CUT HIMSELF WITH A LETTER.
WHERE'S THE LETTER?

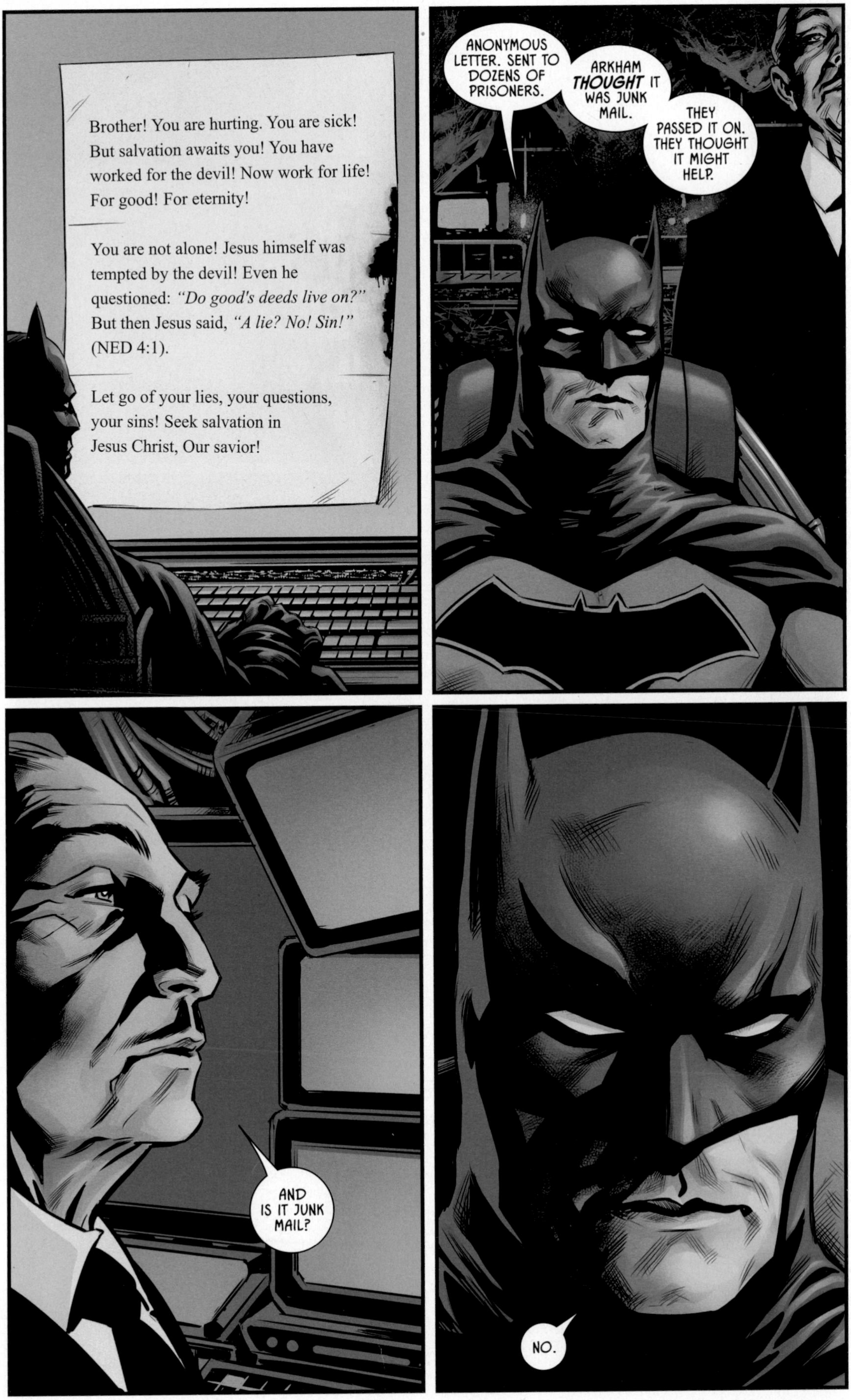
Brother! You are hurting. You are sick! But salvation awaits you! You have worked for the devil! Now work for life! For good! For eternity!
You are not alone! Jesus himself was tempted by the devil! Even he questioned: "Do good's deeds live on?" But then Jesus said, "A lie? No! Sin!" (NED 4:1).
Let go of your lies, your questions, your sins! Seek salvation in Jesus Christ, Our savior!
ANONYMOUS LETTER. SENT TO DOZENS OF PRISONERS.
ARKHAM THOUGHT IT WAS JUNK MAIL.
THEY PASSED IT ON. THEY THOUGHT IT MIGHT HELP.
AND IS IT JUNK MAIL?
NO.

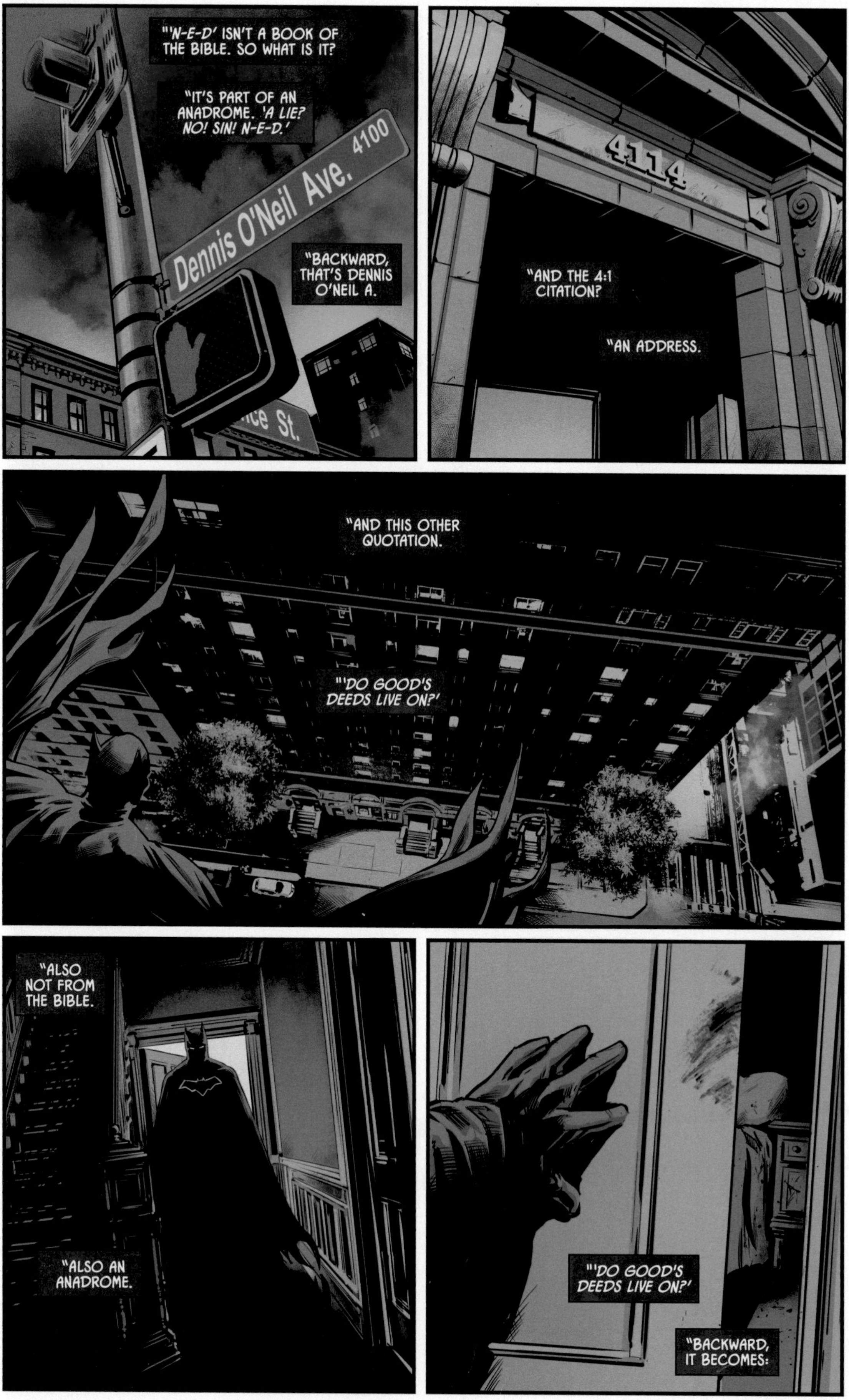
"'N-E-D' ISN'T A BOOK OF THE BIBLE. SO WHAT IS IT?
"IT'S PART OF AN ANADROME. 'A LIE? NO! SIN! N-E-D.'
4100
Dennis O'Neil Ave.
"BACKWARD, THAT'S DENNIS O'NEIL A.
4114
"AND THE 4:1 CITATION?
"AN ADDRESS.
"AND THIS OTHER QUOTATION.
"'DO GOOD'S DEEDS LIVE ON?'
"ALSO NOT FROM THE BIBLE.
"ALSO AN ANADROME.
"'DO GOOD'S DEEDS LIVE ON?'
"BACKWARD, IT BECOMES:

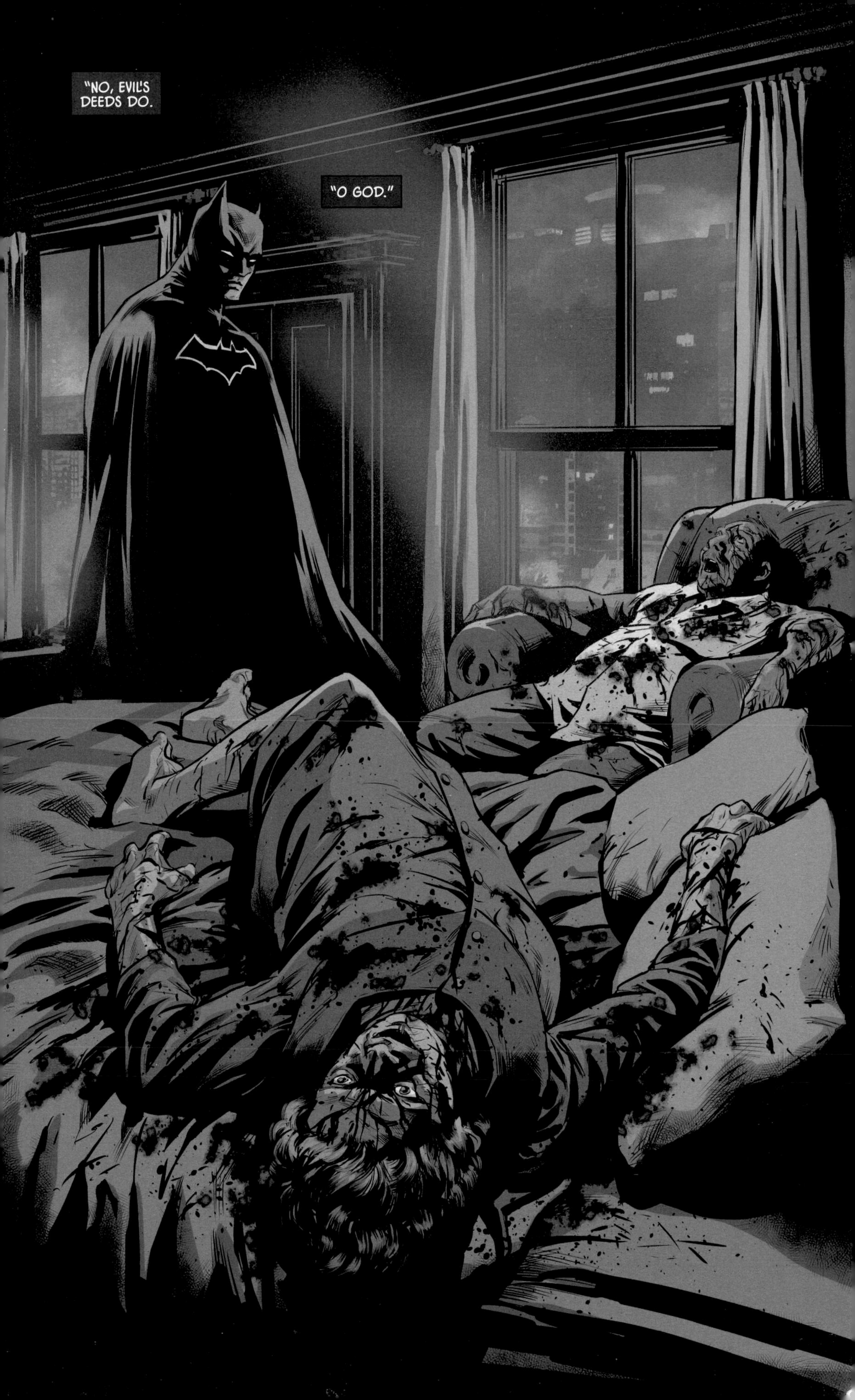
"NO, EVIL'S DEEDS DO.
"O GOD."

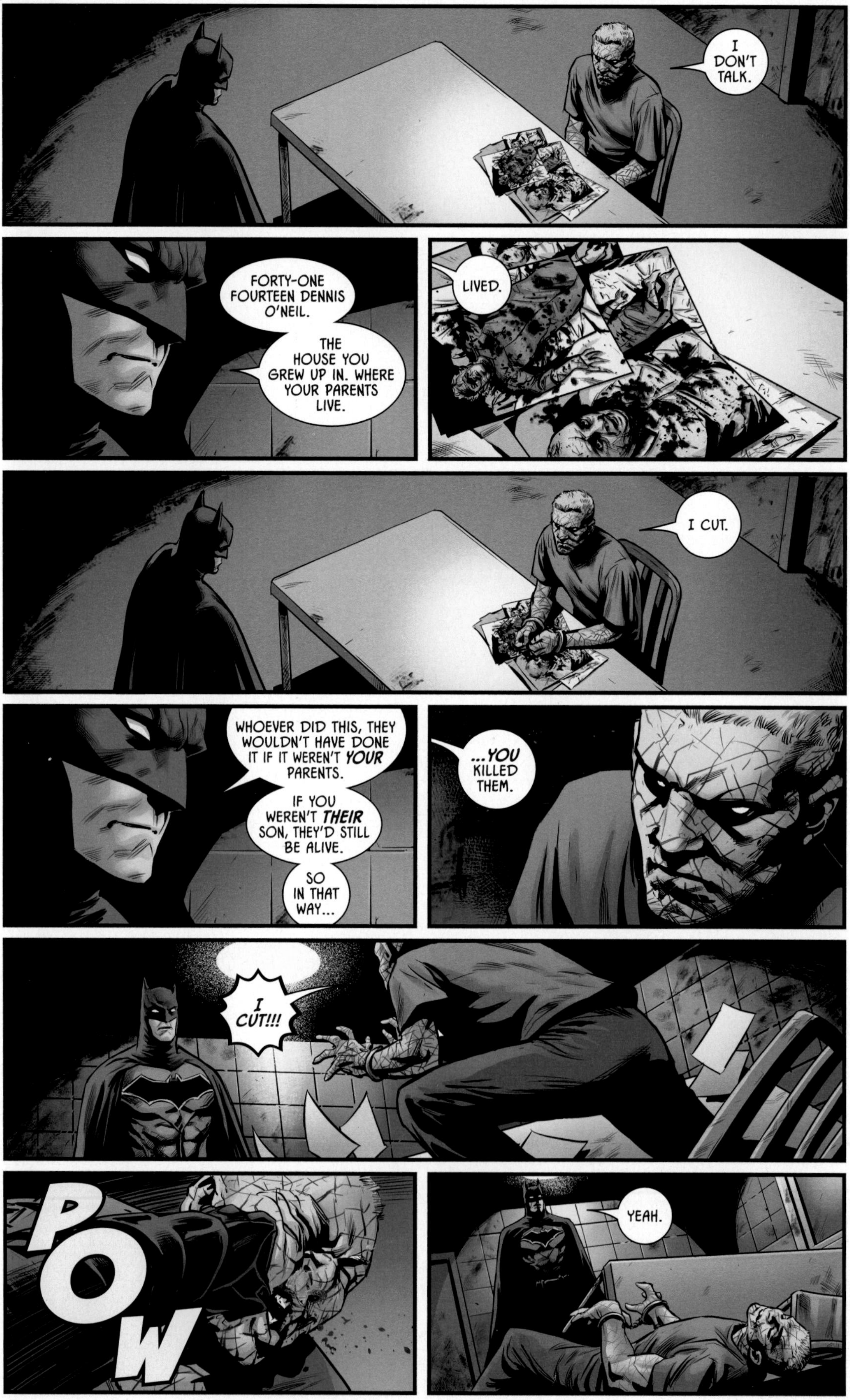
I DON'T TALK.
FORTY-ONE FOURTEEN DENNIS O'NEIL.
THE HOUSE YOU GREW UP IN. WHERE YOUR PARENTS LIVE.
LIVED.
I CUT.
WHOEVER DID THIS, THEY WOULDN'T HAVE DONE IT IF IT WEREN'T YOUR PARENTS.
IF YOU WEREN'T THEIR SON, THEY'D STILL BE ALIVE.
SO IN THAT WAY...
...YOU KILLED THEM.
I CUT!!!
POW
YEAH.

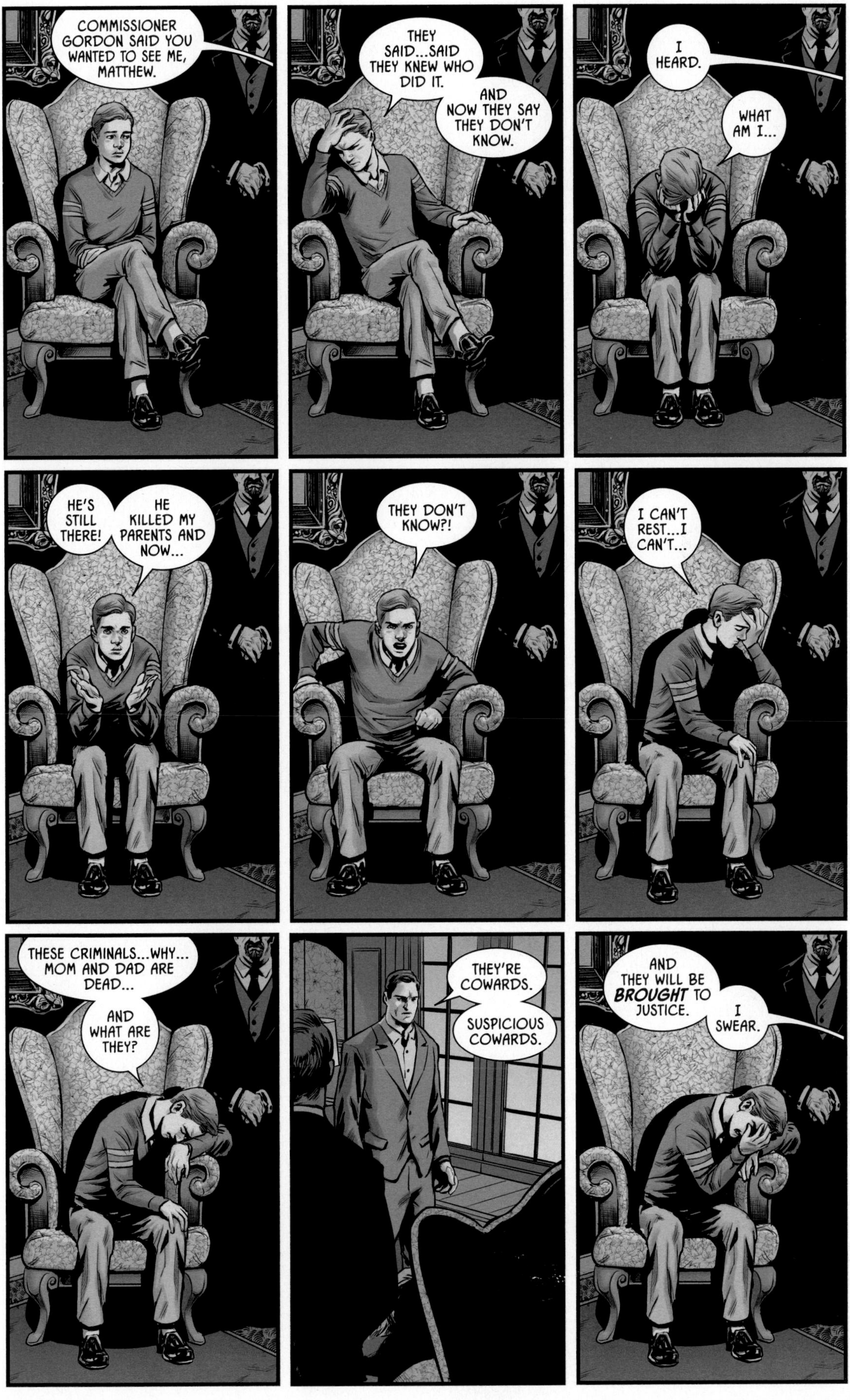
COMMISSIONER GORDON SAID YOU WANTED TO SEE ME, MATTHEW.
THEY SAID...SAID THEY KNEW WHO DID IT.
AND NOW THEY SAY THEY DON'T KNOW.
I HEARD.
WHAT AM I...
HE'S STILL THERE!
HE KILLED MY PARENTS AND NOW...
THEY DON'T KNOW?!
I CAN'T REST...I CAN'T...
THESE CRIMINALS...WHY... MOM AND DAD ARE DEAD...
AND WHAT ARE THEY?
THEY'RE COWARDS.
SUSPICIOUS COWARDS.
AND THEY WILL BE ***BROUGHT*** TO JUSTICE.
I SWEAR.

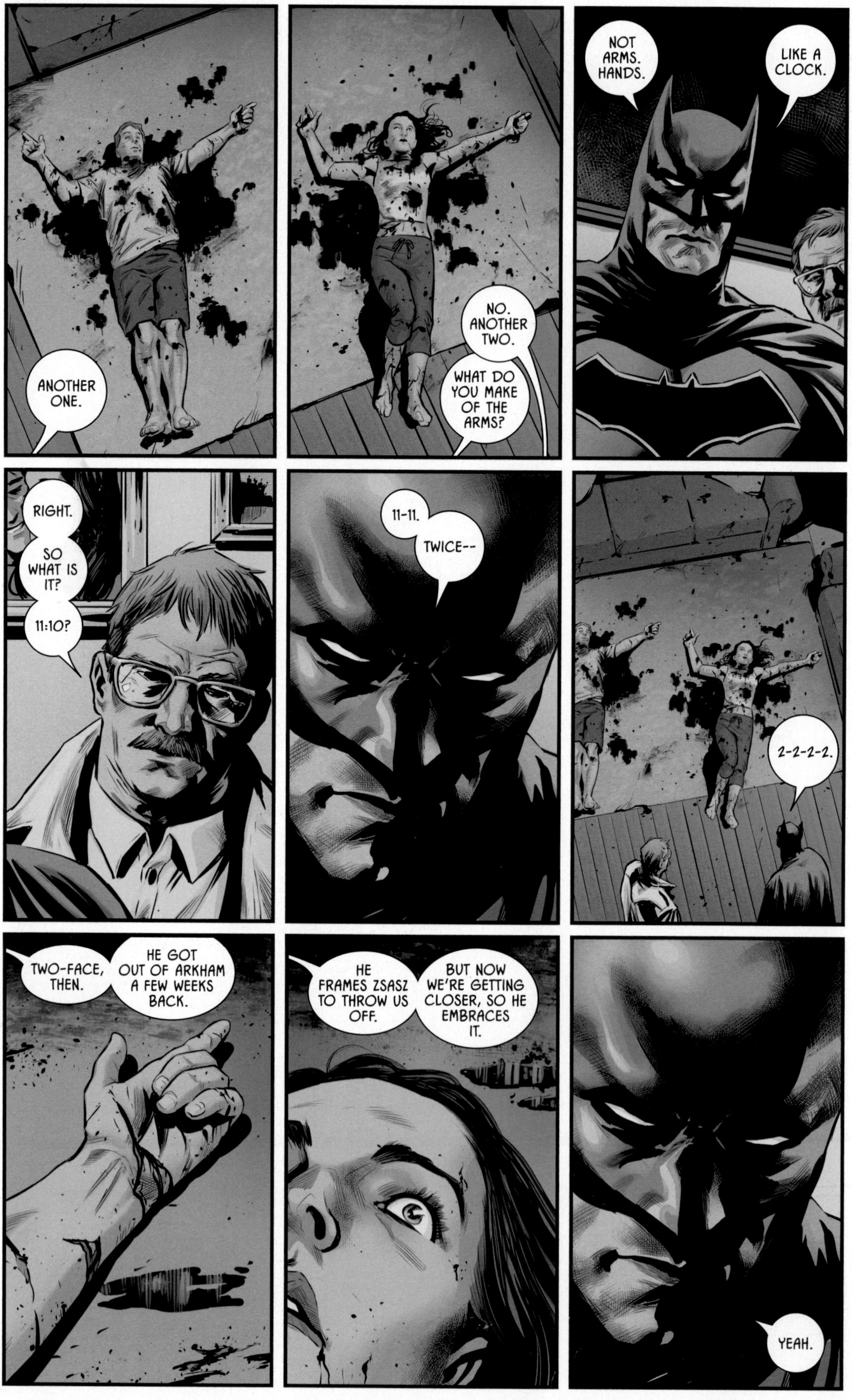
ANOTHER ONE.
NO. ANOTHER TWO.
WHAT DO YOU MAKE OF THE ARMS?
NOT ARMS. HANDS.
LIKE A CLOCK.
RIGHT.
SO WHAT IS IT?
11:10?
11-11.
TWICE--
2-2-2-2.
TWO-FACE, THEN.
HE GOT OUT OF ARKHAM A FEW WEEKS BACK.
HE FRAMES ZSASZ TO THROW US OFF.
BUT NOW WE'RE GETTING CLOSER, SO HE EMBRACES IT.
YEAH.

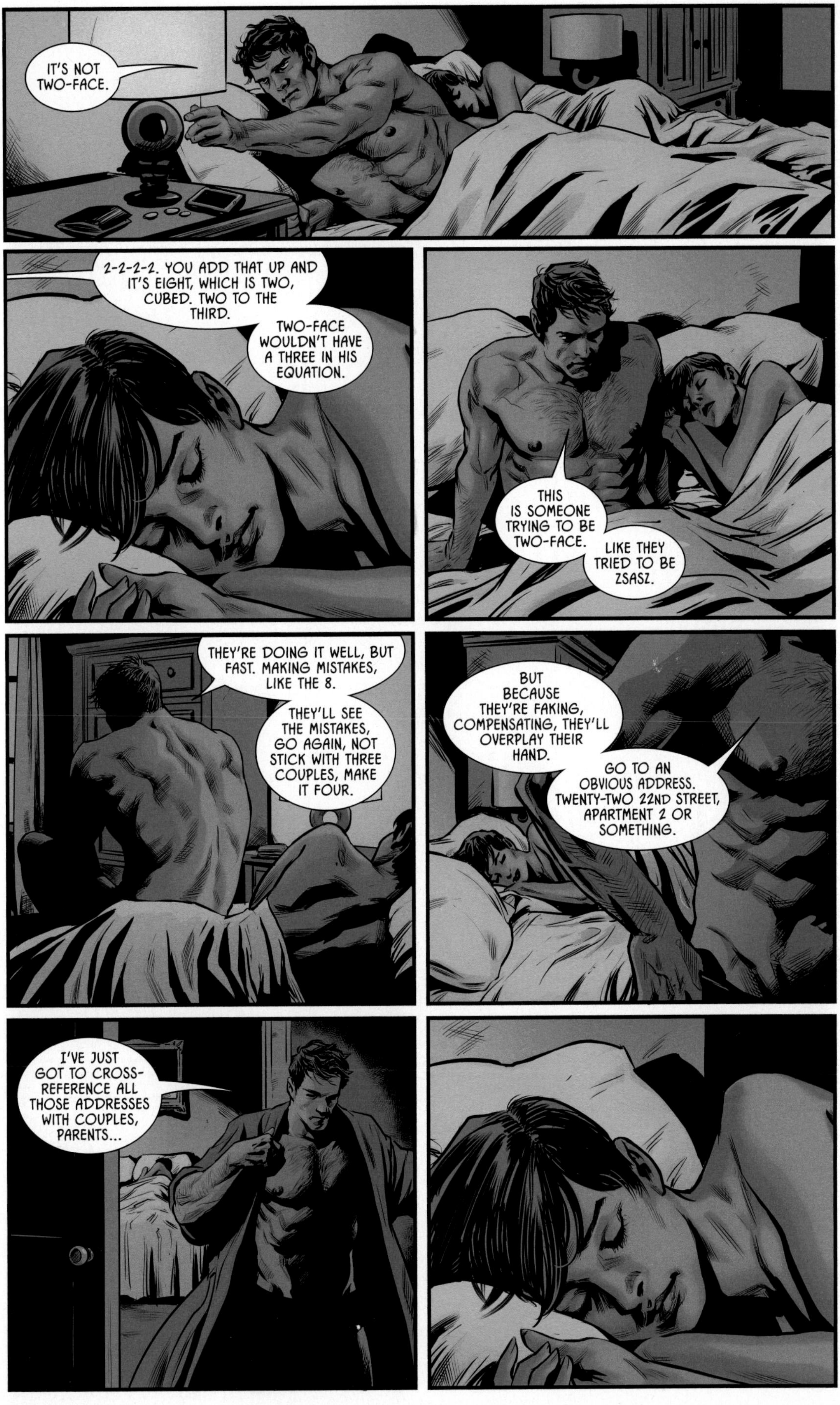
IT'S NOT TWO-FACE.
2-2-2-2. YOU ADD THAT UP AND IT'S EIGHT, WHICH IS TWO, CUBED. TWO TO THE THIRD.
TWO-FACE WOULDN'T HAVE A THREE IN HIS EQUATION.
THIS IS SOMEONE TRYING TO BE TWO-FACE.
LIKE THEY TRIED TO BE ZSASZ.
THEY'RE DOING IT WELL, BUT FAST. MAKING MISTAKES, LIKE THE 8.
THEY'LL SEE THE MISTAKES, GO AGAIN, NOT STICK WITH THREE COUPLES, MAKE IT FOUR.
BUT BECAUSE THEY'RE FAKING, COMPENSATING, THEY'LL OVERPLAY THEIR HAND.
GO TO AN OBVIOUS ADDRESS. TWENTY-TWO 22ND STREET, APARTMENT 2 OR SOMETHING.
I'VE JUST GOT TO CROSS-REFERENCE ALL THOSE ADDRESSES WITH COUPLES, PARENTS...

HELLO.

MR. TAYLOR.

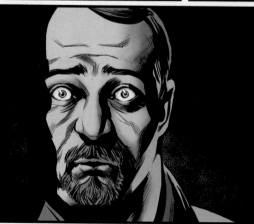

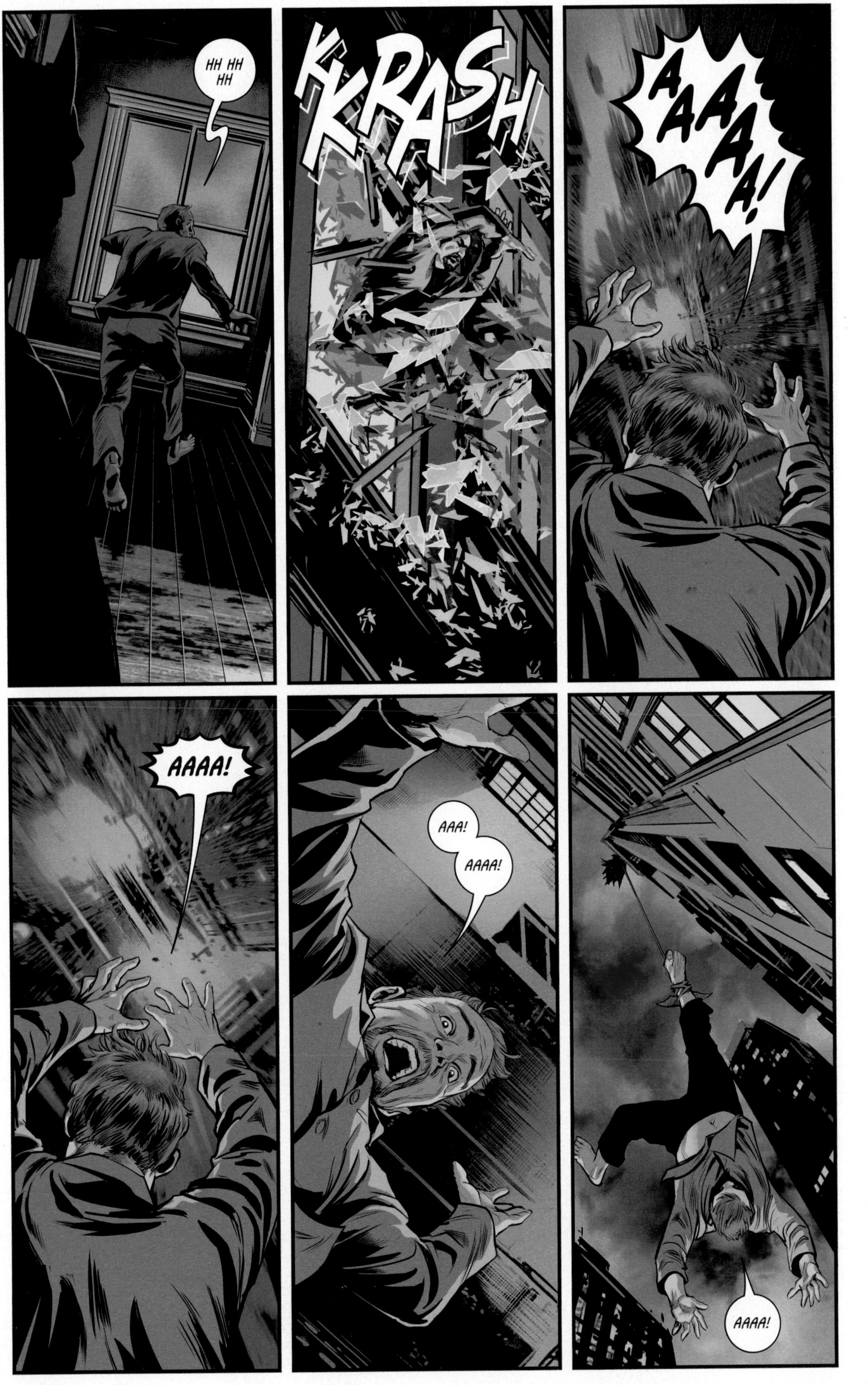
HH HH HH
KKRASH
AAAAA!
AAAA!
AAA!
AAAA!
AAAA!

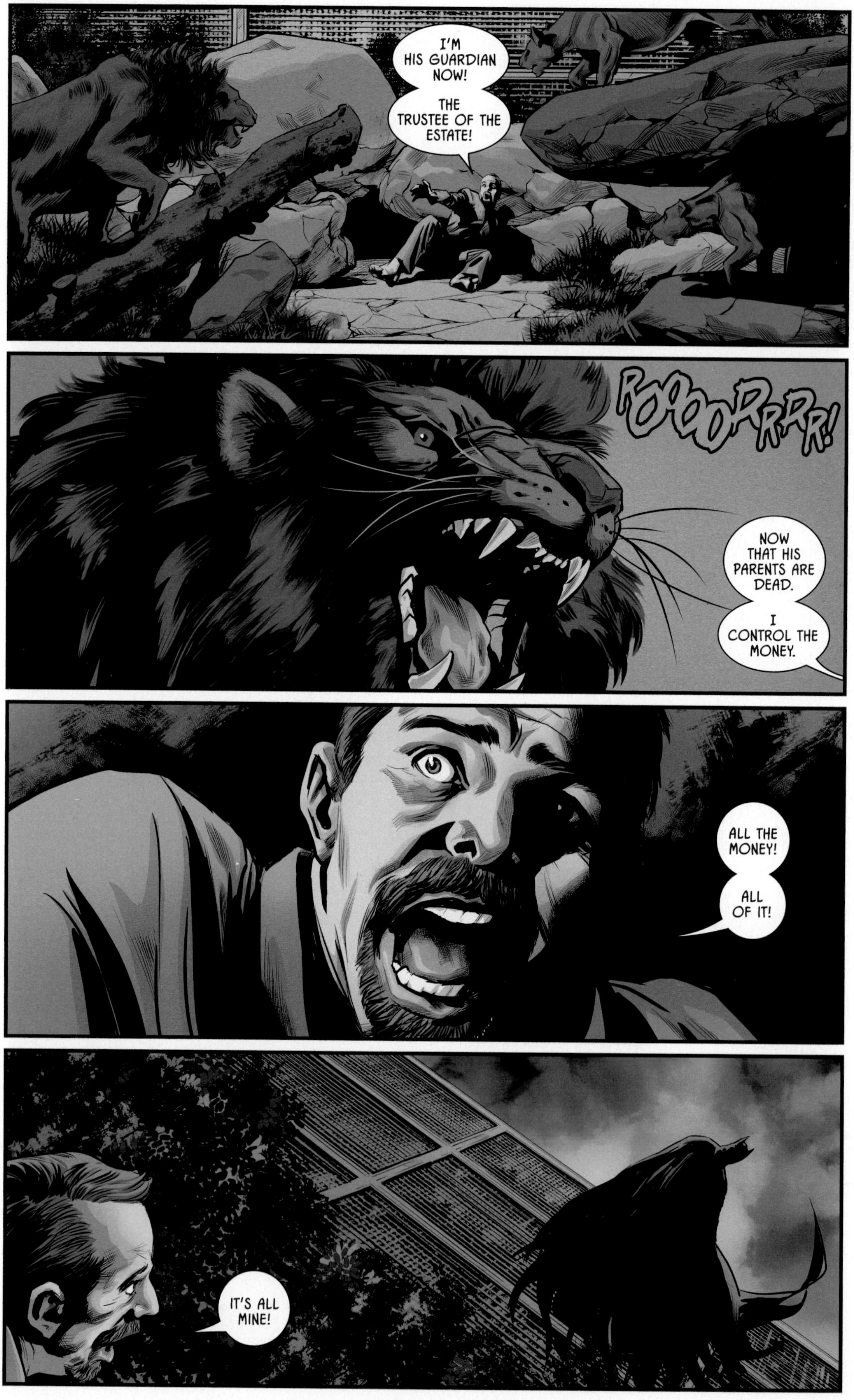

I'M HIS GUARDIAN NOW!
THE TRUSTEE OF THE ESTATE!
ROOOORRRR!
NOW THAT HIS PARENTS ARE DEAD.
I CONTROL THE MONEY.
ALL THE MONEY!
ALL OF IT!
IT'S ALL MINE!

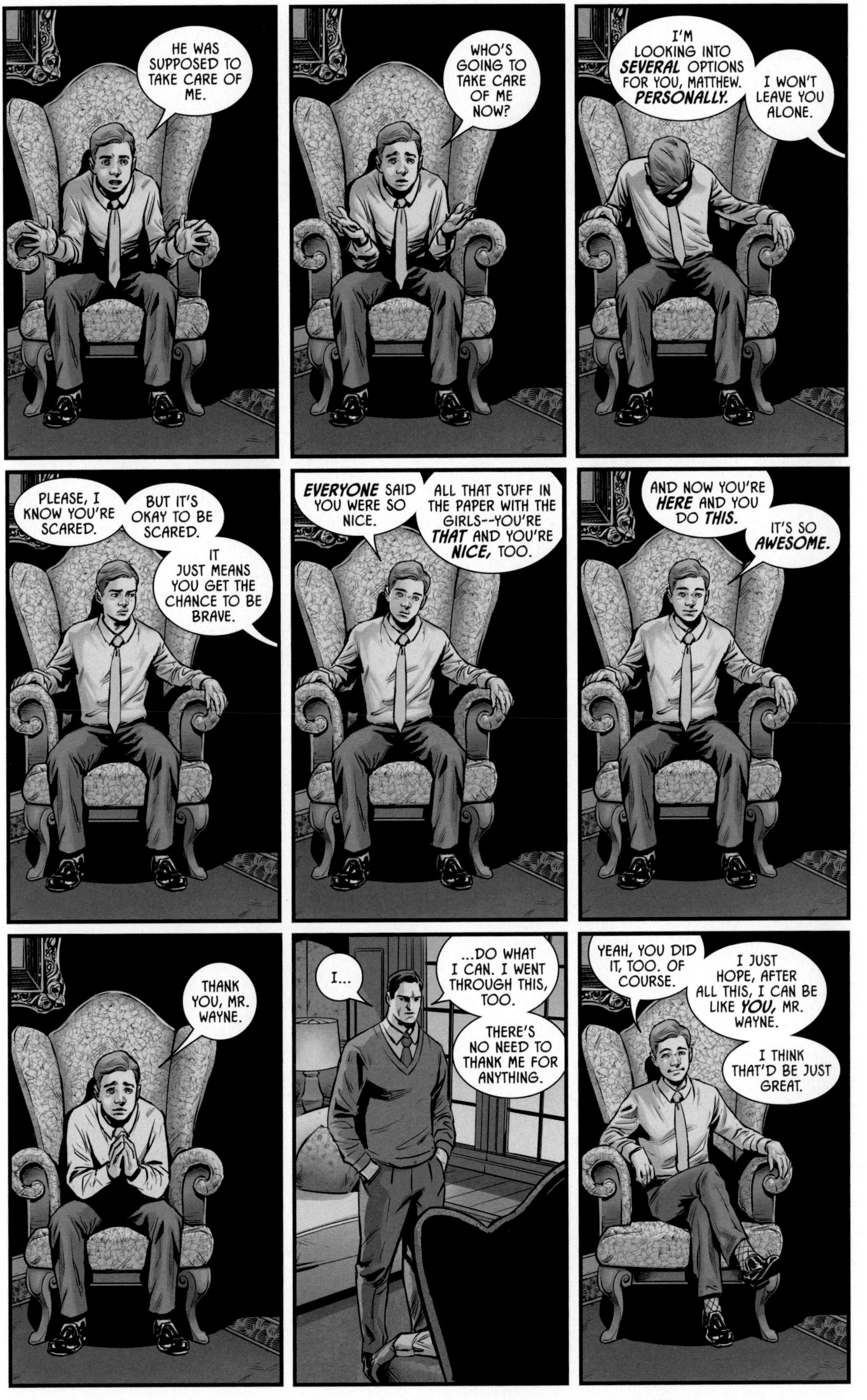

HE WAS SUPPOSED TO TAKE CARE OF ME.
WHO'S GOING TO TAKE CARE OF ME NOW?
I'M LOOKING INTO SEVERAL OPTIONS FOR YOU, MATTHEW. PERSONALLY.
I WON'T LEAVE YOU ALONE.
PLEASE, I KNOW YOU'RE SCARED.
BUT IT'S OKAY TO BE SCARED.
IT JUST MEANS YOU GET THE CHANCE TO BE BRAVE.
EVERYONE SAID YOU WERE SO NICE.
ALL THAT STUFF IN THE PAPER WITH THE GIRLS--YOU'RE THAT AND YOU'RE NICE, TOO.
AND NOW YOU'RE HERE AND YOU DO THIS.
IT'S SO AWESOME.
THANK YOU, MR. WAYNE.
I...
...DO WHAT I CAN. I WENT THROUGH THIS, TOO.
THERE'S NO NEED TO THANK ME FOR ANYTHING.
YEAH, YOU DID IT, TOO. OF COURSE.
I JUST HOPE, AFTER ALL THIS, I CAN BE LIKE YOU, MR. WAYNE.
I THINK THAT'D BE JUST GREAT.

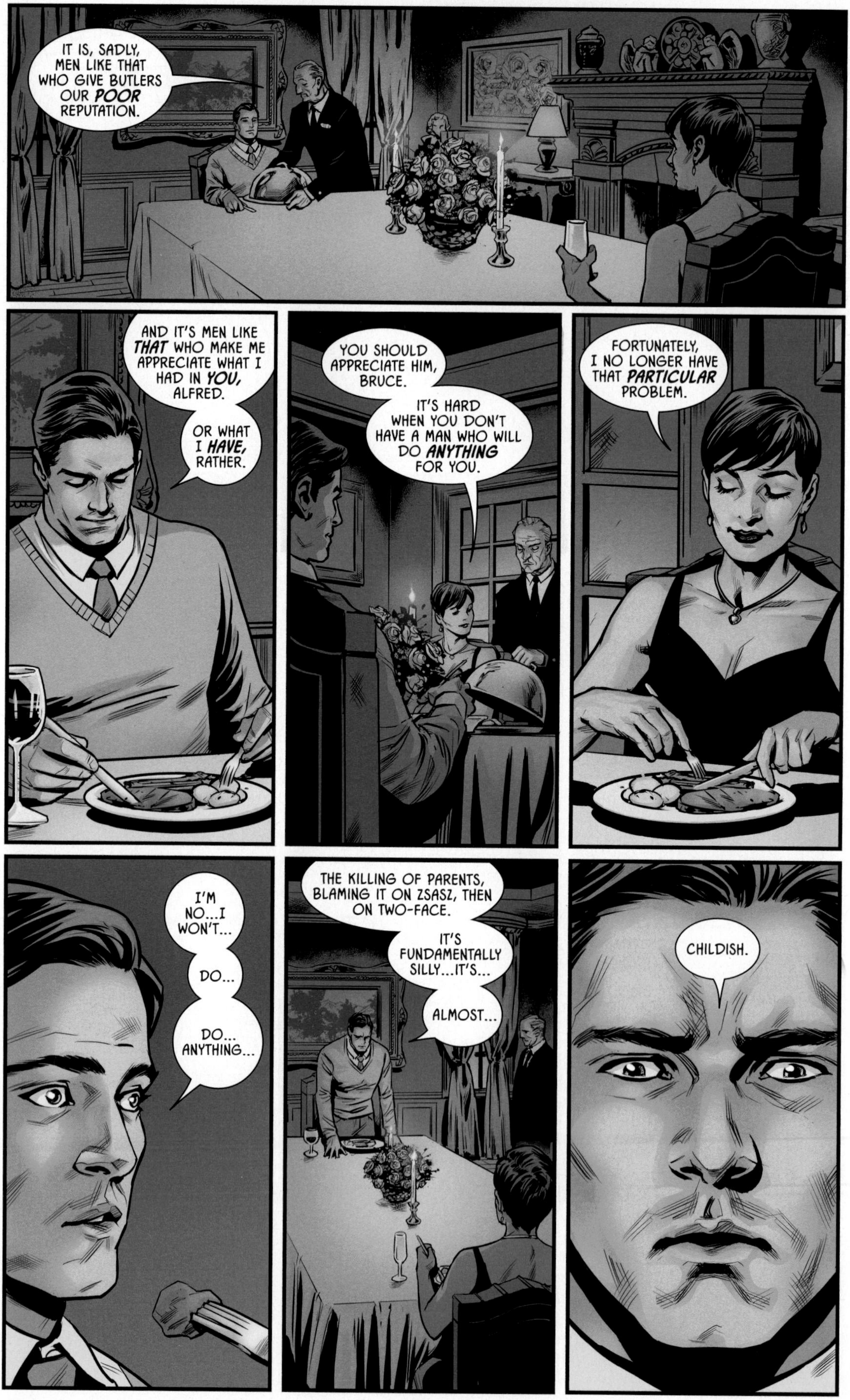
IT IS, SADLY, MEN LIKE THAT WHO GIVE BUTLERS OUR POOR REPUTATION.
AND IT'S MEN LIKE THAT WHO MAKE ME APPRECIATE WHAT I HAD IN YOU, ALFRED.
OR WHAT I HAVE, RATHER.
YOU SHOULD APPRECIATE HIM, BRUCE.
IT'S HARD WHEN YOU DON'T HAVE A MAN WHO WILL DO ANYTHING FOR YOU.
FORTUNATELY, I NO LONGER HAVE THAT PARTICULAR PROBLEM.
I'M NO...I WON'T...
DO...
DO... ANYTHING...
THE KILLING OF PARENTS, BLAMING IT ON ZSASZ, THEN ON TWO-FACE.
IT'S FUNDAMENTALLY SILLY...IT'S...
ALMOST...
CHILDISH.

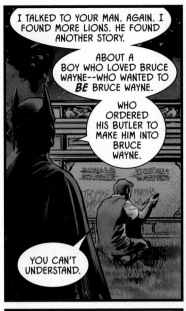

I TALKED TO YOUR MAN. AGAIN. I FOUND MORE LIONS. HE FOUND ANOTHER STORY.

ABOUT A BOY WHO LOVED BRUCE WAYNE--WHO WANTED TO *BE* BRUCE WAYNE.

WHO ORDERED HIS BUTLER TO MAKE HIM INTO BRUCE WAYNE.

YOU CAN'T UNDERSTAND.

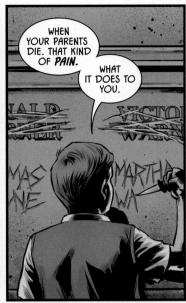

WHEN YOUR PARENTS DIE. THAT KIND OF *PAIN*.

WHAT IT DOES TO YOU.

IT'S ALWAYS THERE.

SCRATCHED INTO YOU.

YOU DON'T UNDERSTAND, *BATMAN,* BECAUSE YOU'RE PART OF THEM.

PART OF THE DARK.

YOU HAVEN'T *SUFFERED* LIKE ME.

I WAS SO SCARED. BUT IT'S OKAY TO BE SCARED.

JUST MEANS YOU GET THE *CHANCE* TO BE *BRAVE*.

MATTHEW, YOU NEED TO COME WITH ME.

I CAN HELP YOU.

DON'T YOU KNOW WHO I AM?

MASTER BRUCE DOESN'T NEED HELP.

I HELP OTHERS. I AM INSPIRED BY MY PARENTS TO SAVE EVERYONE.

LISTEN, YOU'RE SICK.

YOU'RE *SICK.* THE FREAKS ARE *SICK.* GOTHAM IS *SICK.*

MASTER BRUCE IS THE CURE!

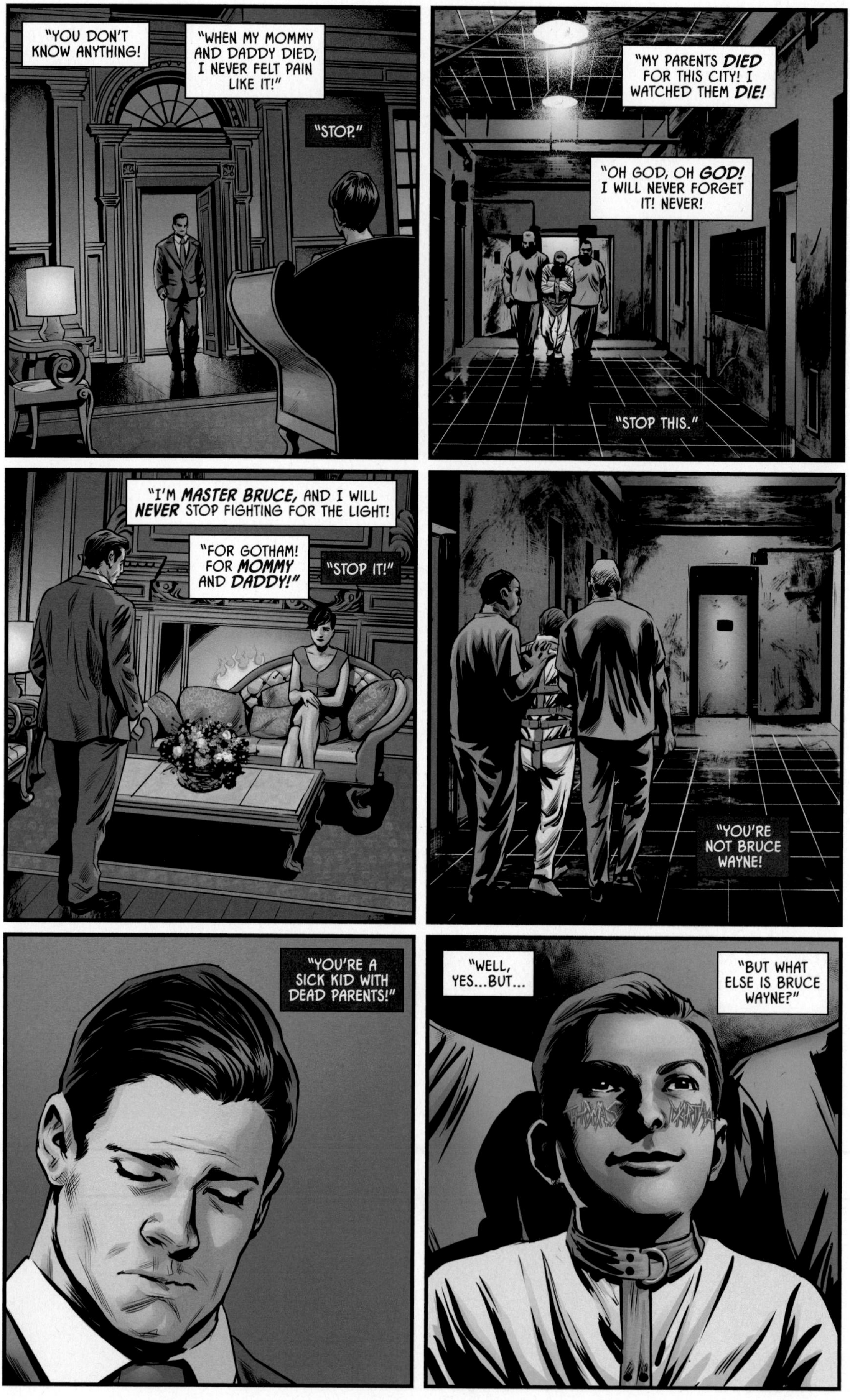
"YOU DON'T KNOW ANYTHING!
"WHEN MY MOMMY AND DADDY DIED, I NEVER FELT PAIN LIKE IT!"
"STOP."
"MY PARENTS DIED FOR THIS CITY! I WATCHED THEM DIE!
"OH GOD, OH GOD! I WILL NEVER FORGET IT! NEVER!
"STOP THIS."
"I'M MASTER BRUCE, AND I WILL NEVER STOP FIGHTING FOR THE LIGHT!
"FOR GOTHAM! FOR MOMMY AND DADDY!"
"STOP IT!"
"YOU'RE NOT BRUCE WAYNE!
"YOU'RE A SICK KID WITH DEAD PARENTS!"
"WELL, YES...BUT...
"BUT WHAT ELSE IS BRUCE WAYNE?"

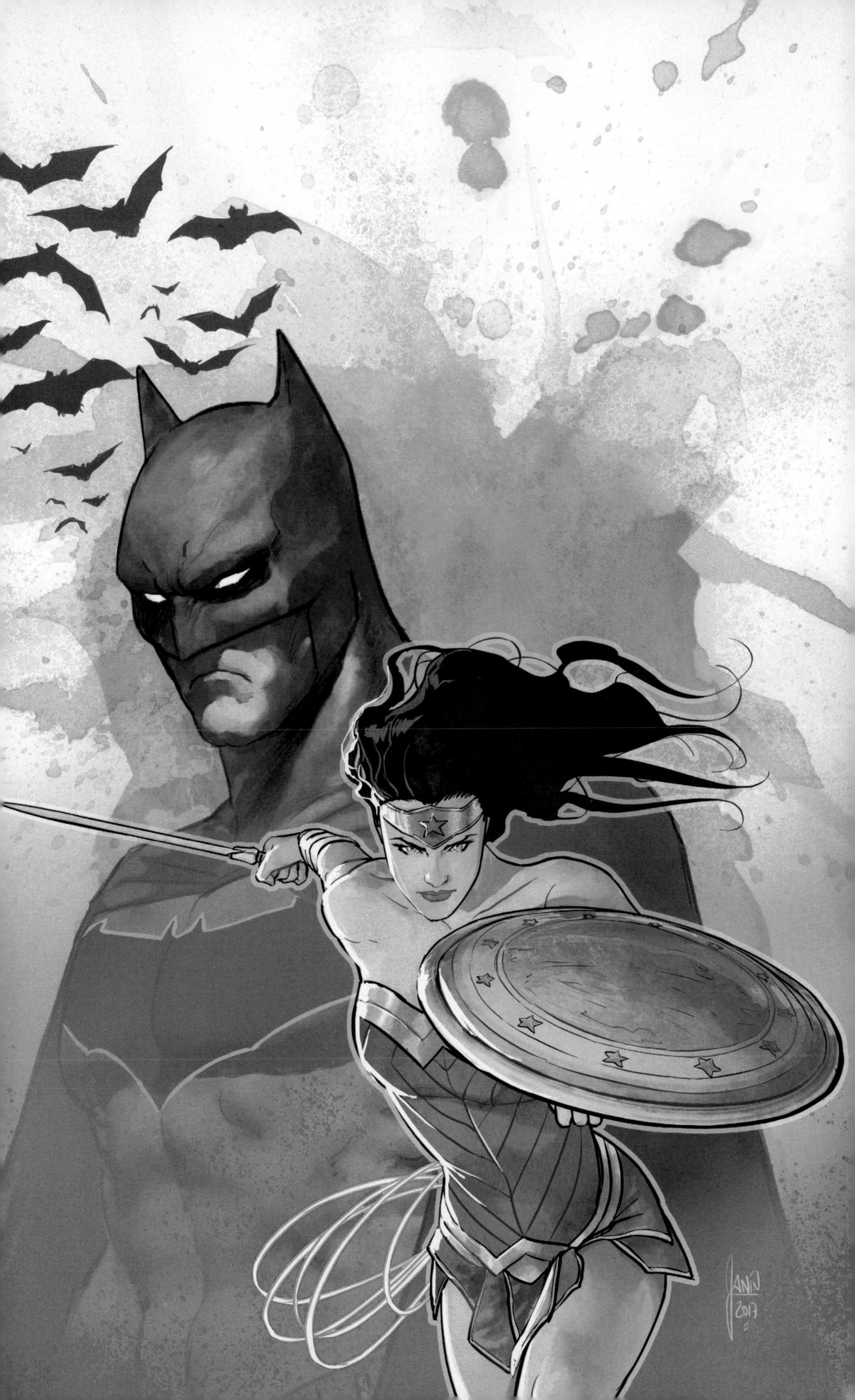
JANÍN
2017

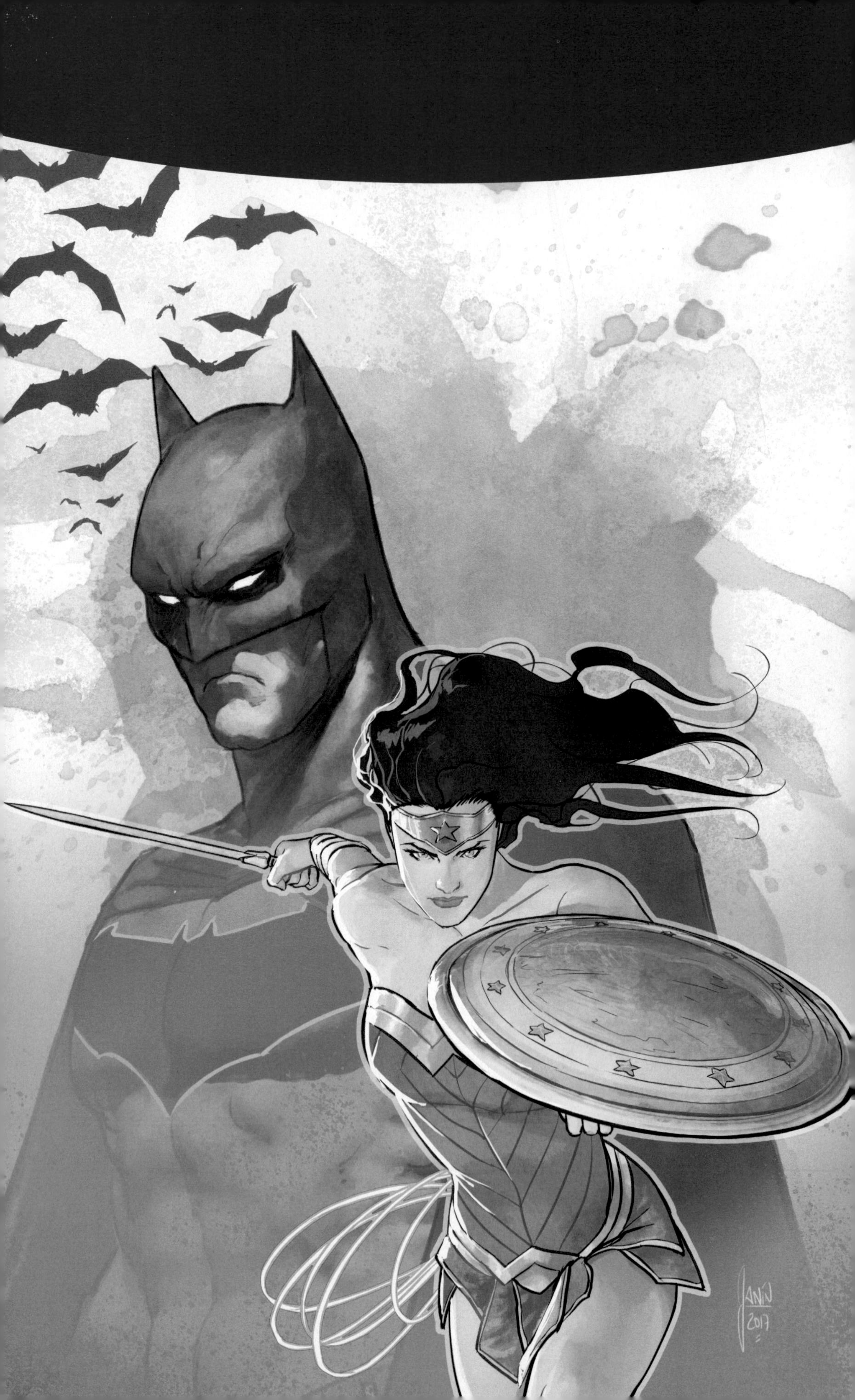
JANIN
2017

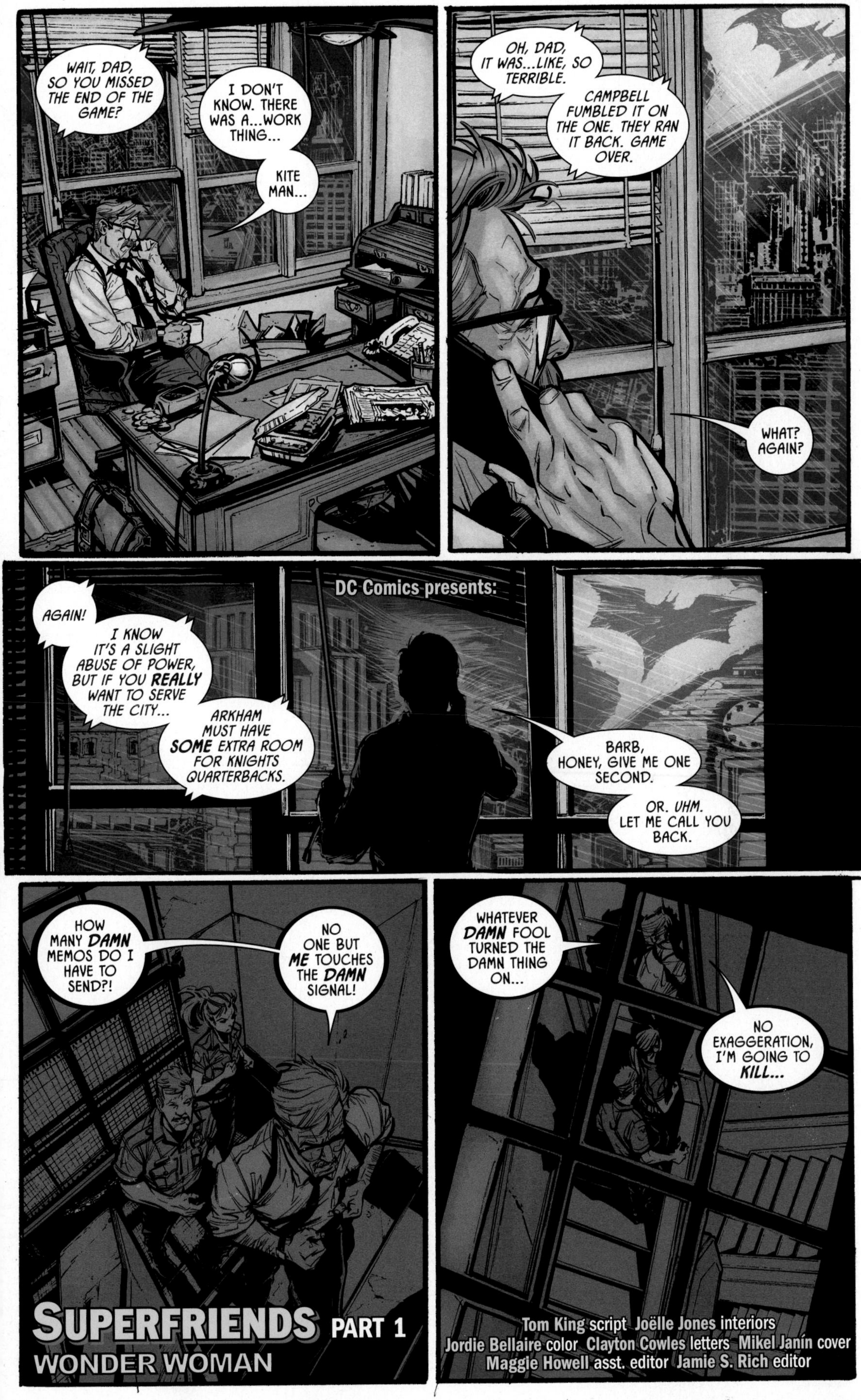

WAIT, DAD, SO YOU MISSED THE END OF THE GAME?
I DON'T KNOW. THERE WAS A...WORK THING...
KITE MAN...
OH, DAD, IT WAS...LIKE, SO TERRIBLE.
CAMPBELL FUMBLED IT ON THE ONE. THEY RAN IT BACK. GAME OVER.
WHAT? AGAIN?
DC Comics presents:
AGAIN!
I KNOW IT'S A SLIGHT ABUSE OF POWER, BUT IF YOU REALLY WANT TO SERVE THE CITY...
ARKHAM MUST HAVE SOME EXTRA ROOM FOR KNIGHTS QUARTERBACKS.
BARB, HONEY, GIVE ME ONE SECOND.
OR. UHM. LET ME CALL YOU BACK.
HOW MANY DAMN MEMOS DO I HAVE TO SEND?!
NO ONE BUT ME TOUCHES THE DAMN SIGNAL!
WHATEVER DAMN FOOL TURNED THE DAMN THING ON...
NO EXAGGERATION, I'M GOING TO KILL...
SUPERFRIENDS PART 1
WONDER WOMAN
Tom King script Joëlle Jones interiors
Jordie Bellaire color Clayton Cowles letters Mikel Janín cover
Maggie Howell asst. editor Jamie S. Rich editor

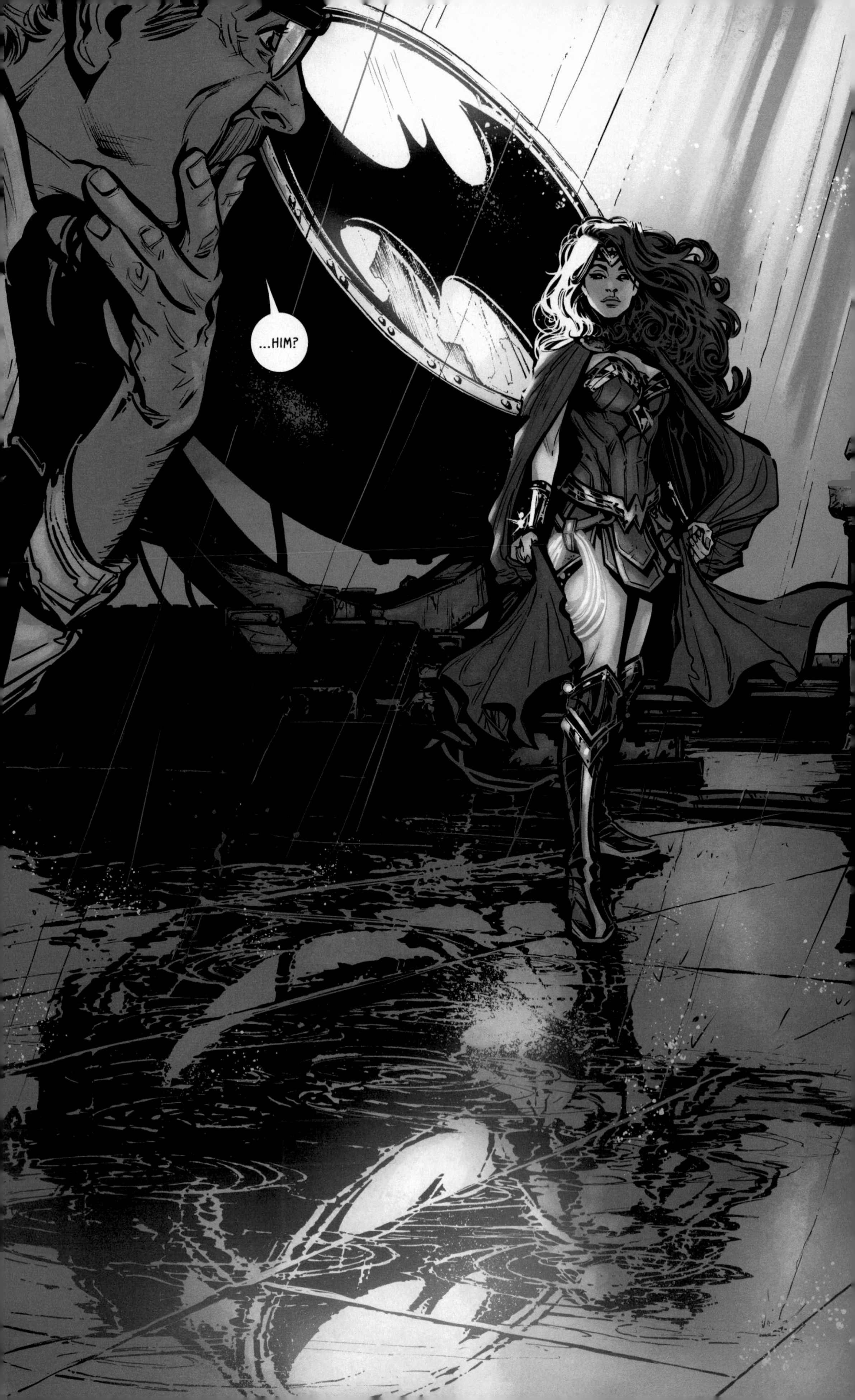
...HIM?

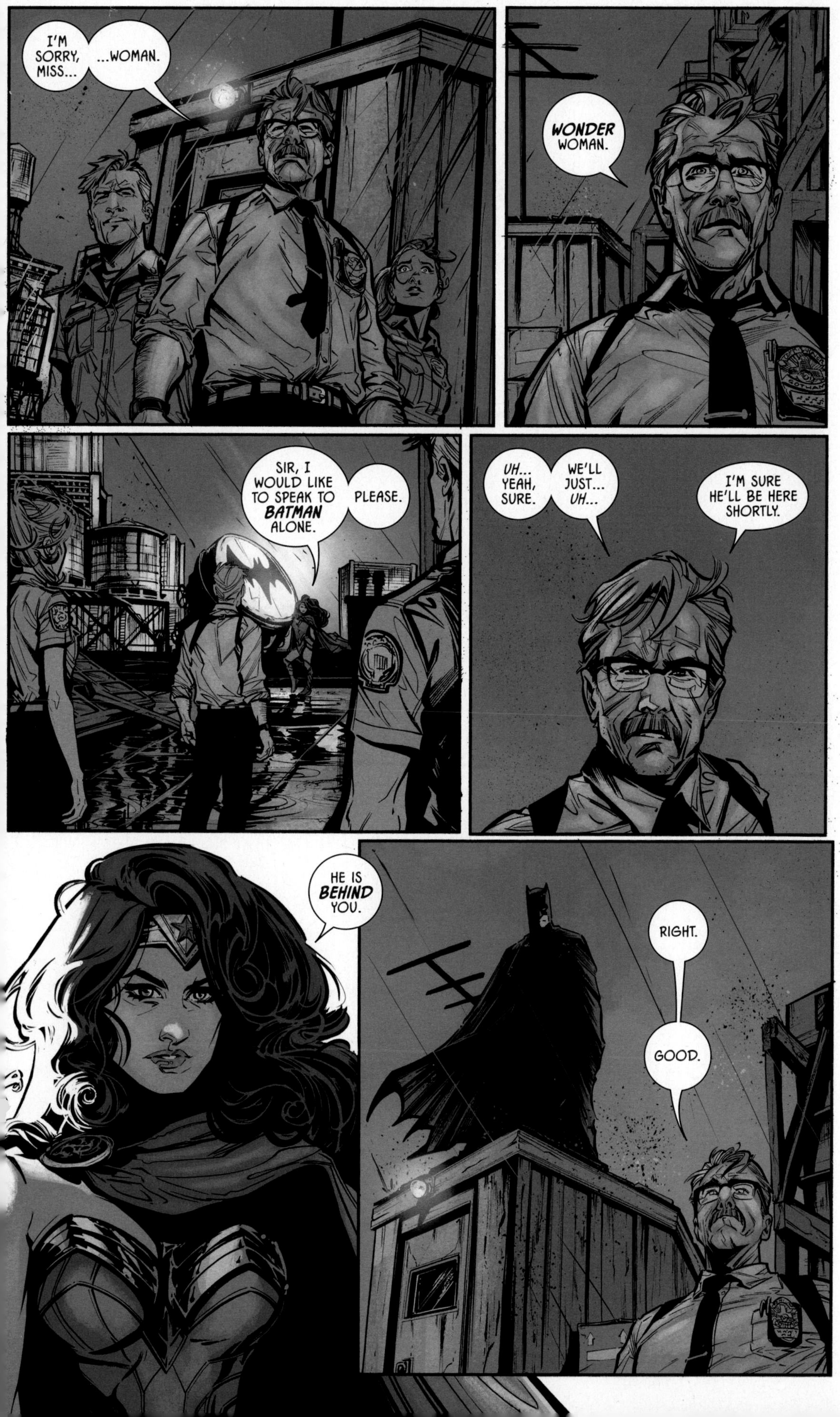

I'M SORRY, MISS...
...WOMAN.
WONDER WOMAN.
SIR, I WOULD LIKE TO SPEAK TO BATMAN ALONE.
PLEASE.
UH... YEAH, SURE.
WE'LL JUST... UH...
I'M SURE HE'LL BE HERE SHORTLY.
HE IS BEHIND YOU.
RIGHT.
GOOD.

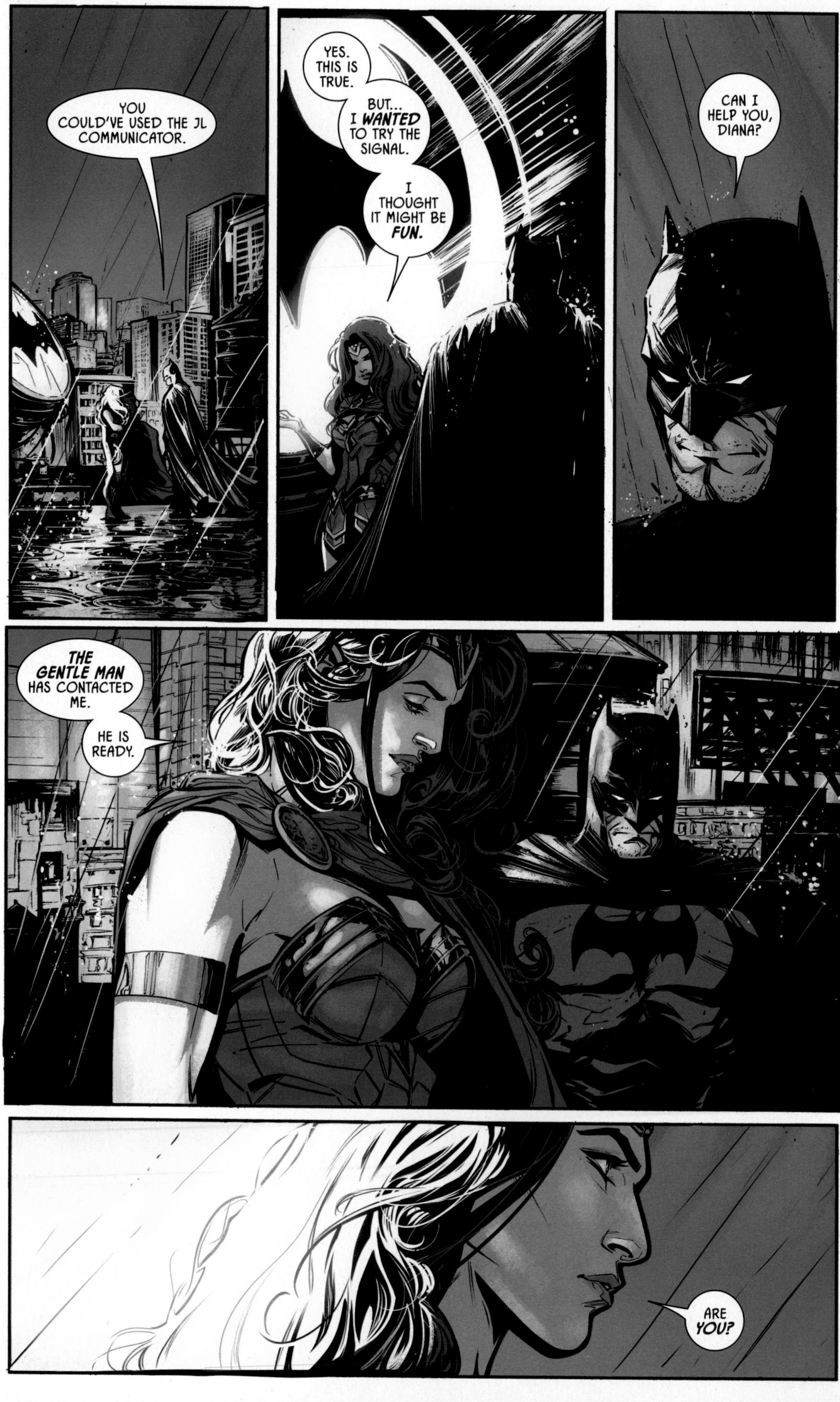

YOU COULD'VE USED THE JL COMMUNICATOR.
YES. THIS IS TRUE.
BUT... I *WANTED* TO TRY THE SIGNAL.
I THOUGHT IT MIGHT BE *FUN.*
CAN I HELP YOU, DIANA?
THE GENTLE MAN HAS CONTACTED ME.
HE IS READY.
ARE *YOU?*

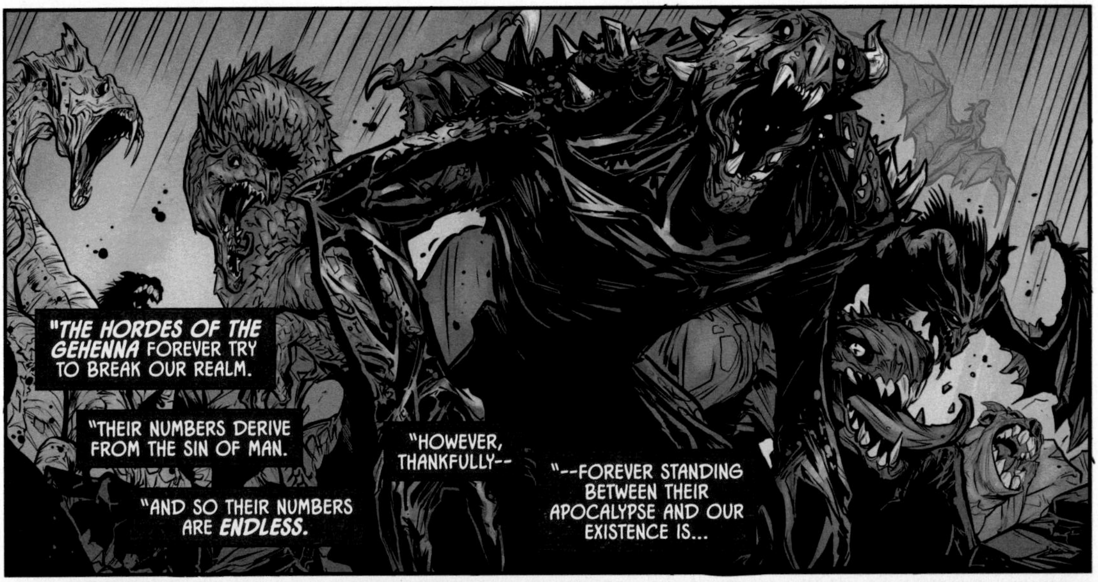
"THE HORDES OF THE GEHENNA FOREVER TRY TO BREAK OUR REALM.
"THEIR NUMBERS DERIVE FROM THE SIN OF MAN.
"AND SO THEIR NUMBERS ARE ENDLESS.
"HOWEVER, THANKFULLY--
"--FOREVER STANDING BETWEEN THEIR APOCALYPSE AND OUR EXISTENCE IS...

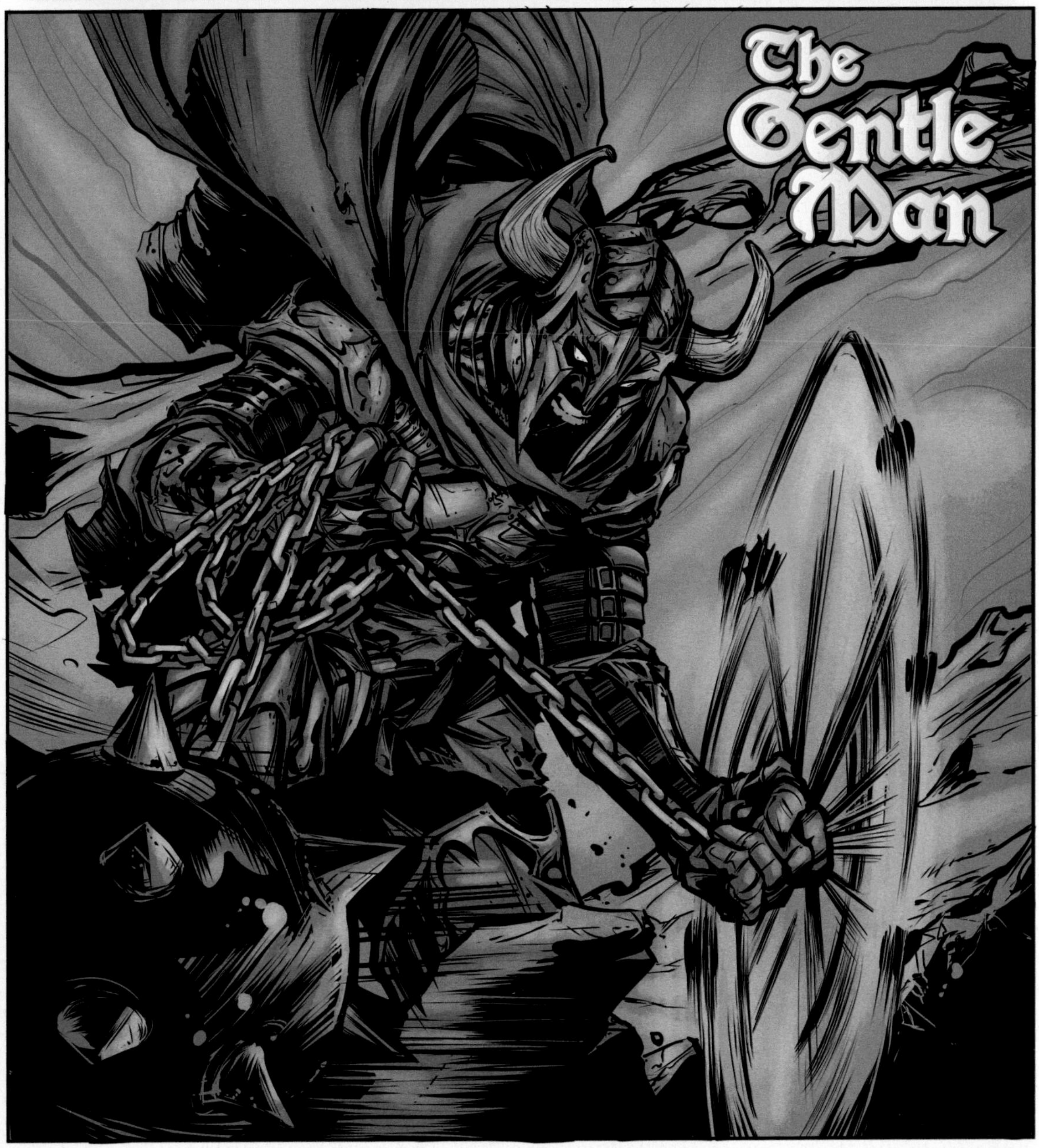
The Gentle Man

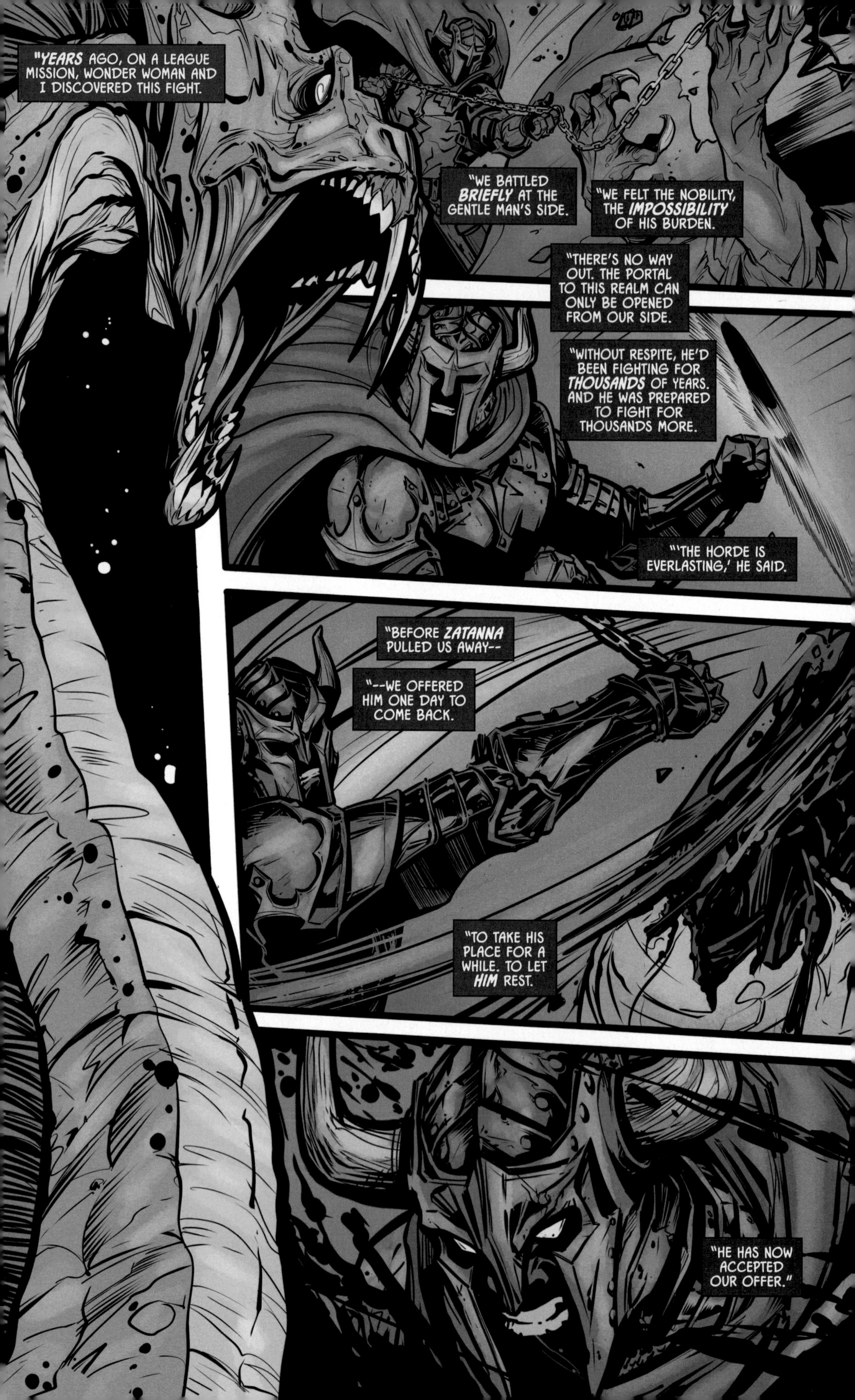
"YEARS AGO, ON A LEAGUE MISSION, WONDER WOMAN AND I DISCOVERED THIS FIGHT.
"WE BATTLED BRIEFLY AT THE GENTLE MAN'S SIDE.
"WE FELT THE NOBILITY, THE IMPOSSIBILITY OF HIS BURDEN.
"THERE'S NO WAY OUT. THE PORTAL TO THIS REALM CAN ONLY BE OPENED FROM OUR SIDE.
"WITHOUT RESPITE, HE'D BEEN FIGHTING FOR THOUSANDS OF YEARS. AND HE WAS PREPARED TO FIGHT FOR THOUSANDS MORE.
"'THE HORDE IS EVERLASTING,' HE SAID.
"BEFORE ZATANNA PULLED US AWAY--
"--WE OFFERED HIM ONE DAY TO COME BACK.
"TO TAKE HIS PLACE FOR A WHILE. TO LET HIM REST.
"HE HAS NOW ACCEPTED OUR OFFER."

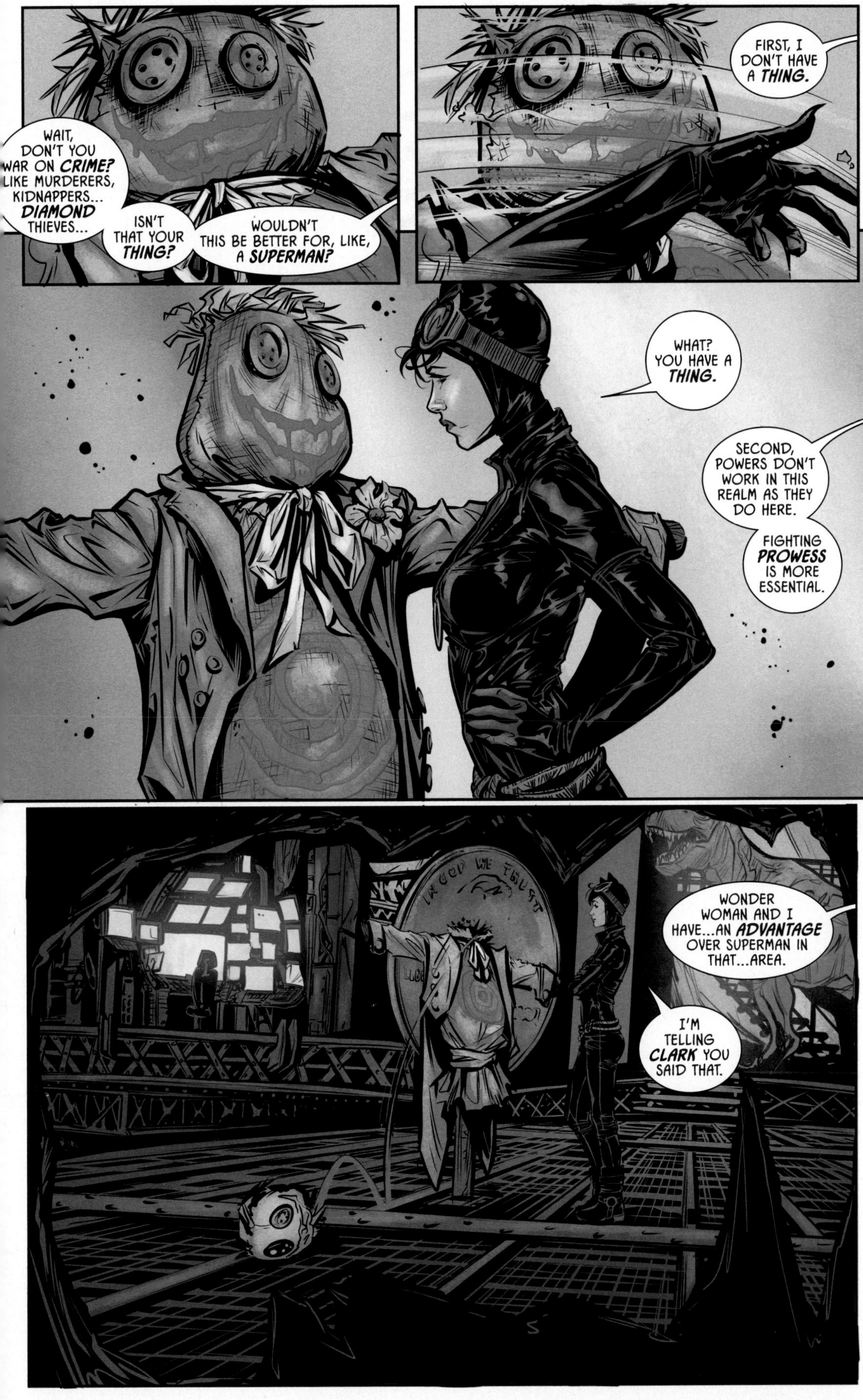

WAIT, DON'T YOU WAR ON CRIME? LIKE MURDERERS, KIDNAPPERS... DIAMOND THIEVES...
ISN'T THAT YOUR THING?
WOULDN'T THIS BE BETTER FOR, LIKE, A SUPERMAN?
FIRST, I DON'T HAVE A THING.
WHAT? YOU HAVE A THING.
SECOND, POWERS DON'T WORK IN THIS REALM AS THEY DO HERE.
FIGHTING PROWESS IS MORE ESSENTIAL.
WONDER WOMAN AND I HAVE...AN ADVANTAGE OVER SUPERMAN IN THAT...AREA.
I'M TELLING CLARK YOU SAID THAT.

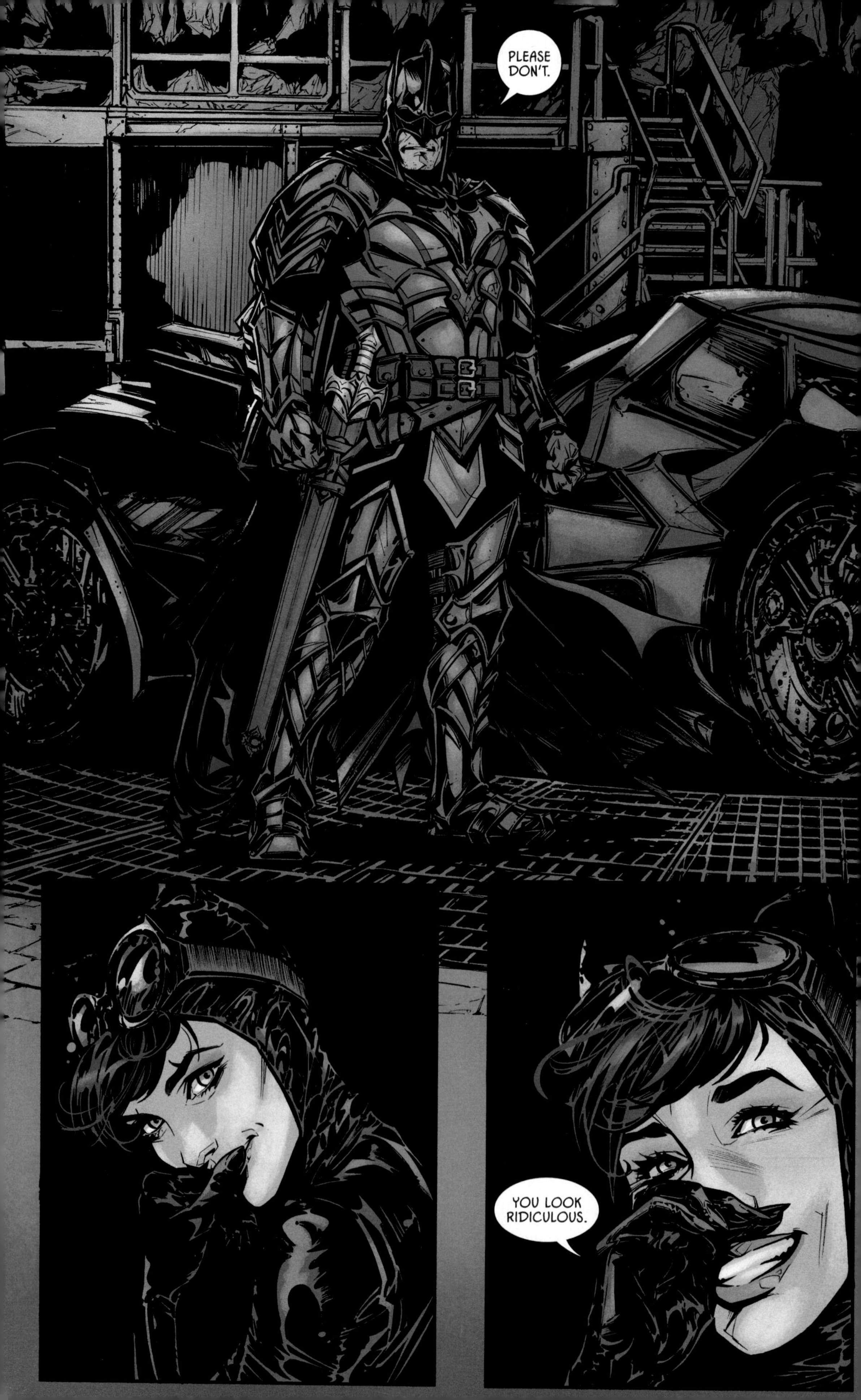
PLEASE DON'T.
YOU LOOK RIDICULOUS.

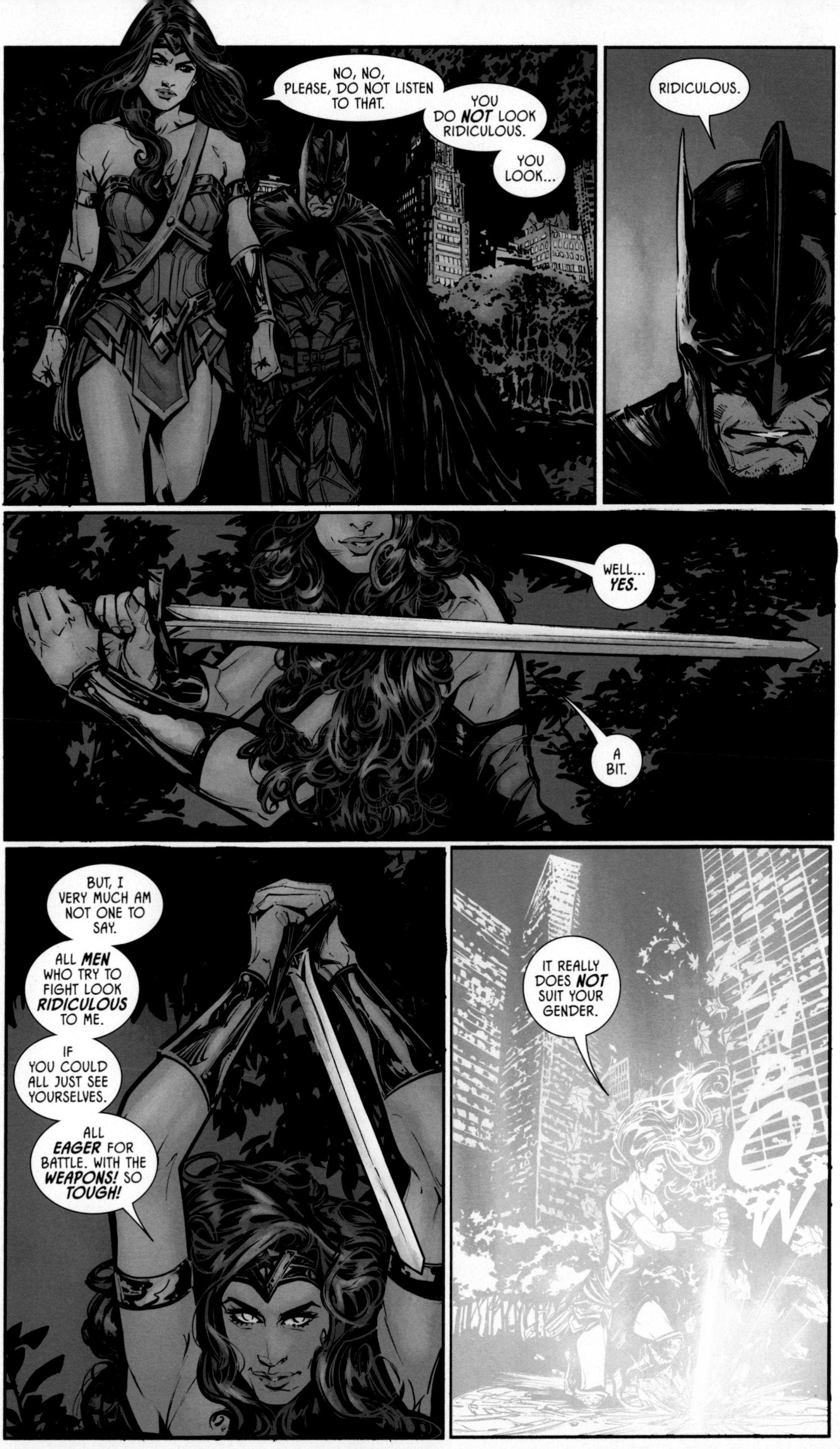
NO, NO, PLEASE, DO NOT LISTEN TO THAT.
YOU DO **NOT** LOOK RIDICULOUS.
YOU LOOK...
RIDICULOUS.
WELL... ***YES.***
A BIT.
BUT, I VERY MUCH AM NOT ONE TO SAY.
ALL ***MEN*** WHO TRY TO FIGHT LOOK ***RIDICULOUS*** TO ME.
IF YOU COULD ALL JUST SEE YOURSELVES.
ALL ***EAGER*** FOR BATTLE. WITH THE ***WEAPONS!*** SO ***TOUGH!***
IT REALLY DOES ***NOT*** SUIT YOUR GENDER.

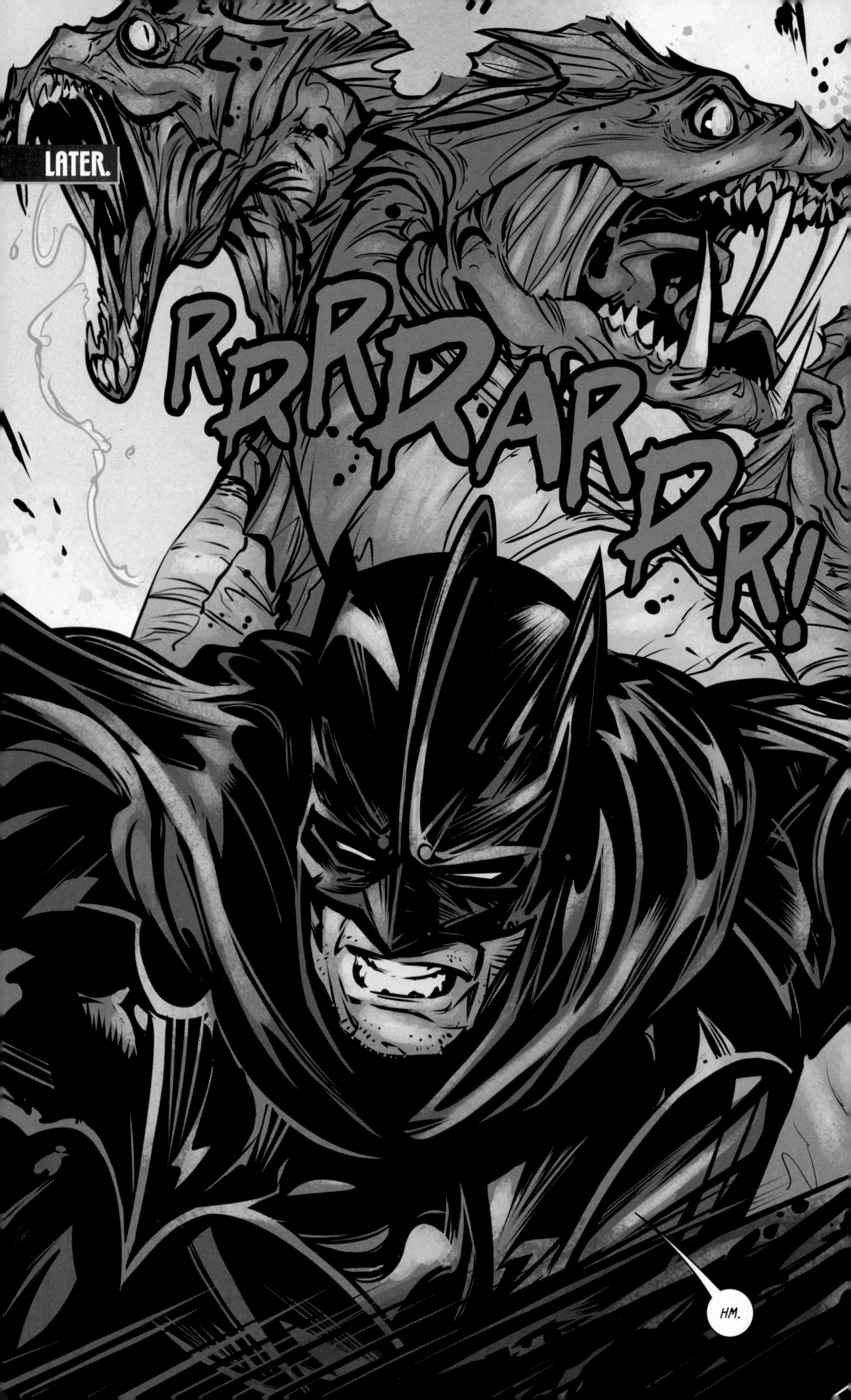
LATER.
RRRRARRRR!
HM.

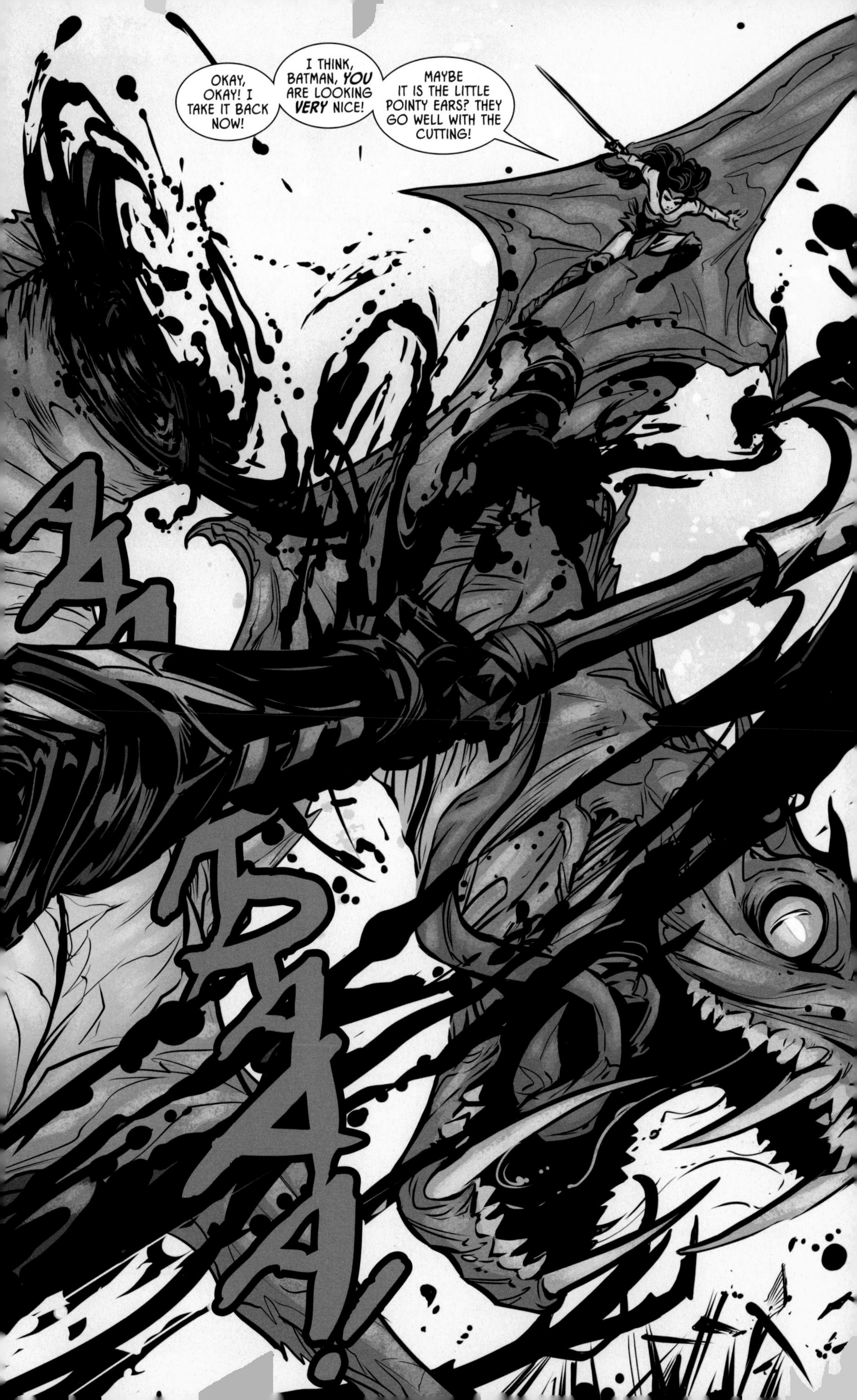
OKAY, OKAY! I TAKE IT BACK NOW!
I THINK, BATMAN, YOU ARE LOOKING VERY NICE!
MAYBE IT IS THE LITTLE POINTY EARS? THEY GO WELL WITH THE CUTTING!

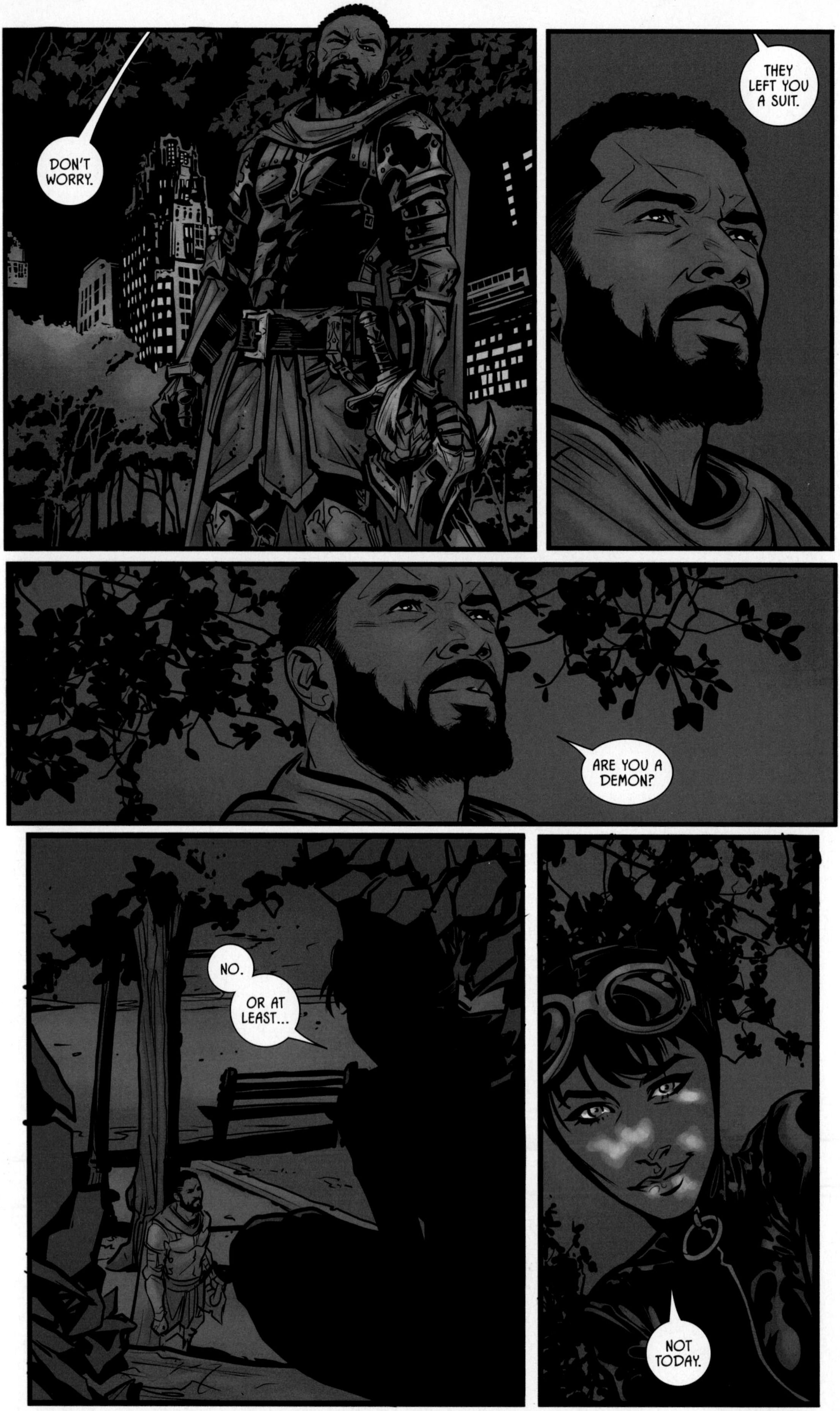
DON'T WORRY.
THEY LEFT YOU A SUIT.
ARE YOU A DEMON?
NO.
OR AT LEAST...
NOT TODAY.

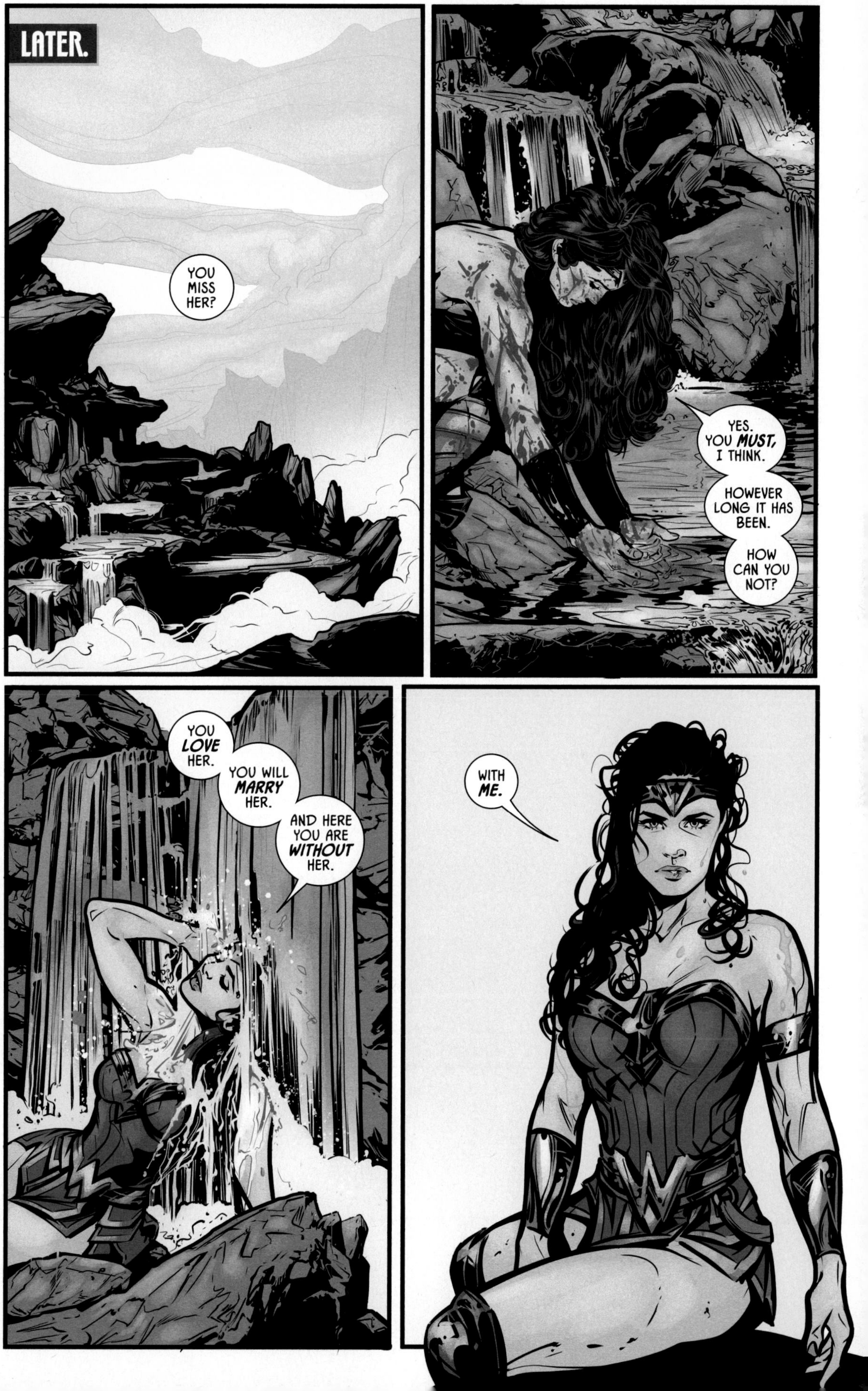
LATER.
YOU MISS HER?
YES. YOU MUST, I THINK.
HOWEVER LONG IT HAS BEEN.
HOW CAN YOU NOT?
YOU LOVE HER.
YOU WILL MARRY HER.
AND HERE YOU ARE WITHOUT HER.
WITH ME.

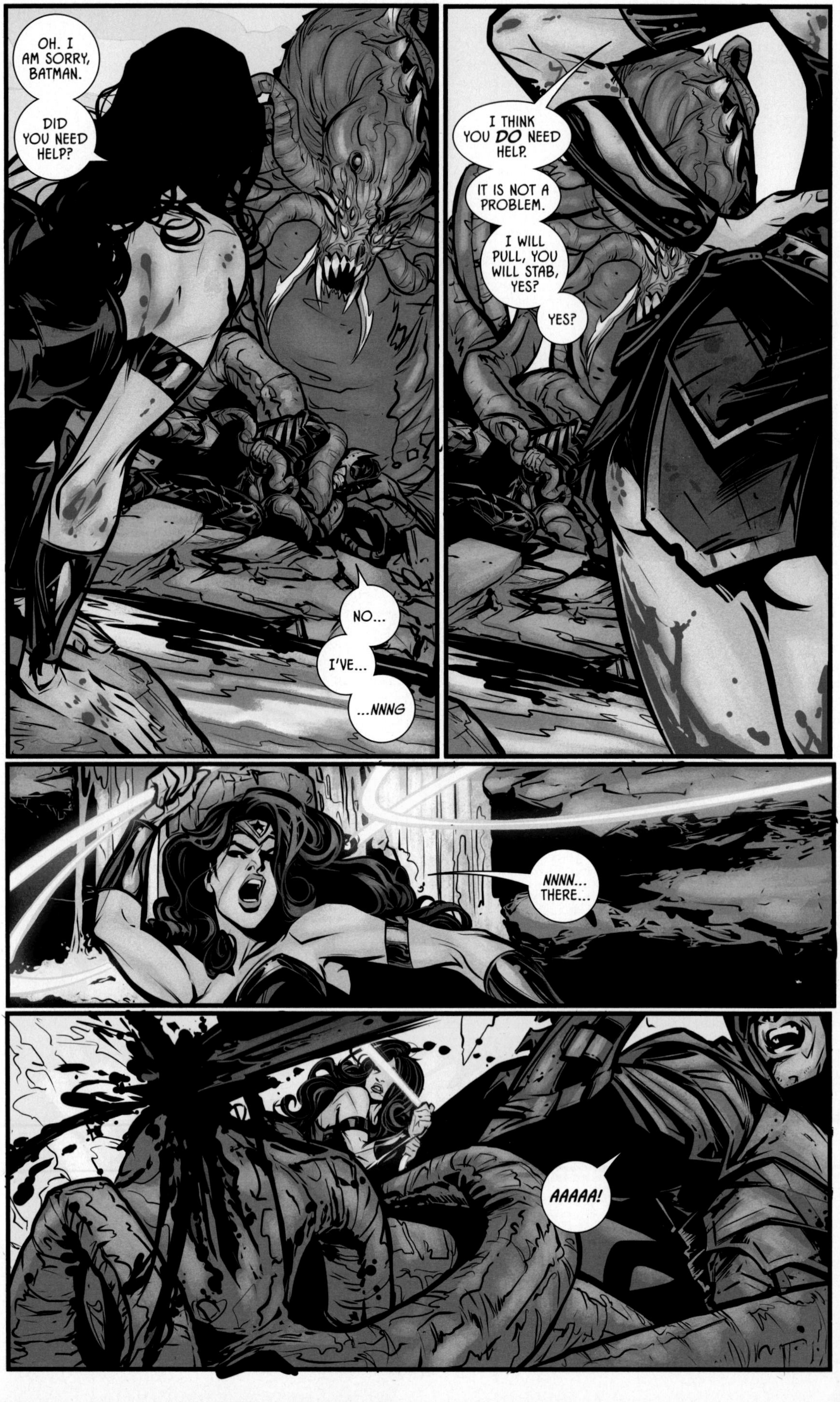
OH. I AM SORRY, BATMAN.
DID YOU NEED HELP?
NO...
I'VE...
...NNNG
I THINK YOU DO NEED HELP.
IT IS NOT A PROBLEM.
I WILL PULL, YOU WILL STAB, YES?
YES?
NNNN... THERE...
AAAAA!

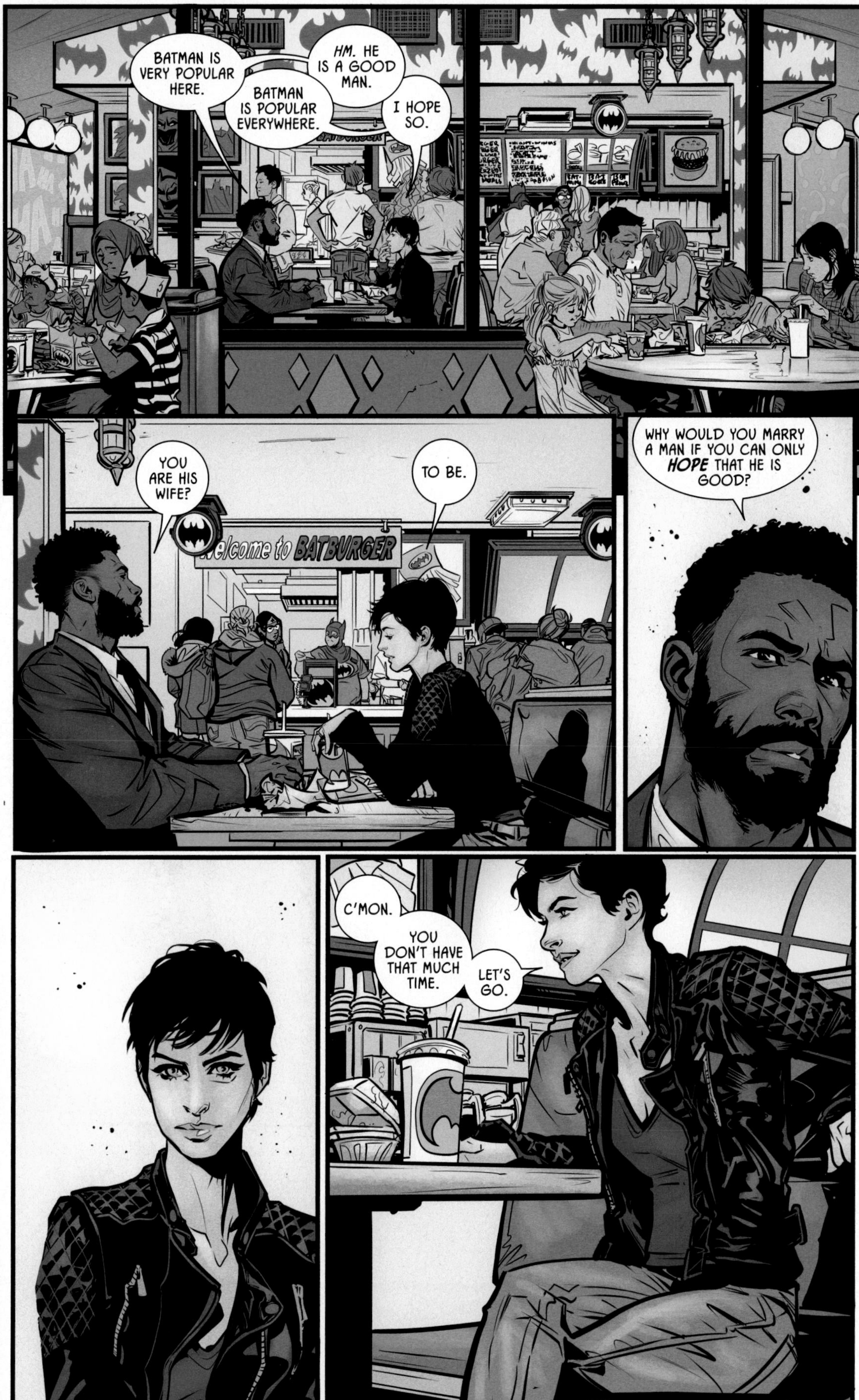
BATMAN IS VERY POPULAR HERE.
HM. HE IS A GOOD MAN.
BATMAN IS POPULAR EVERYWHERE.
I HOPE SO.
BATBURGER
YOU ARE HIS WIFE?
TO BE.
Welcome to BATBURGER
WHY WOULD YOU MARRY A MAN IF YOU CAN ONLY HOPE THAT HE IS GOOD?
C'MON.
YOU DON'T HAVE THAT MUCH TIME.
LET'S GO.

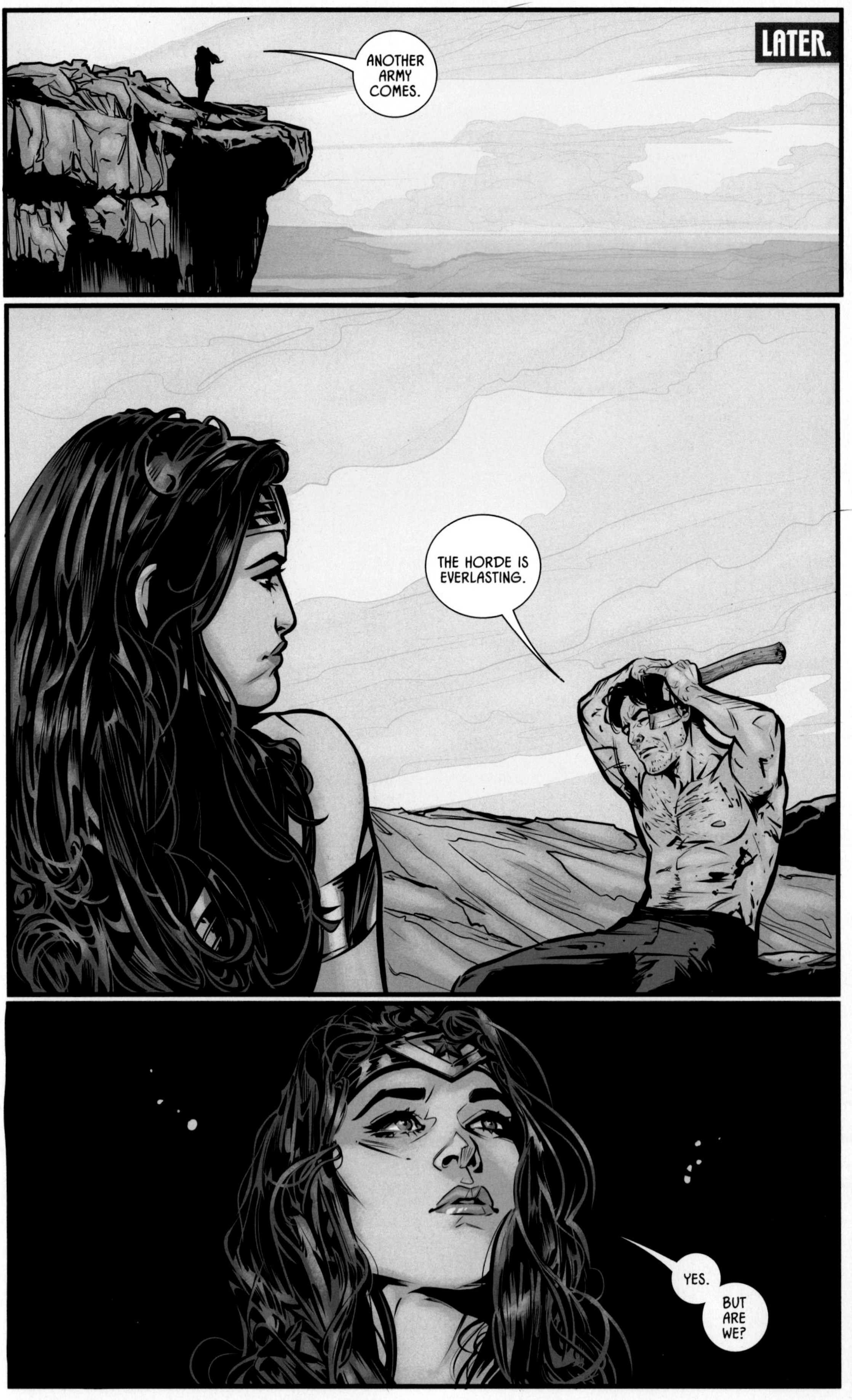
LATER.
ANOTHER ARMY COMES.
THE HORDE IS EVERLASTING.
YES.
BUT ARE WE?

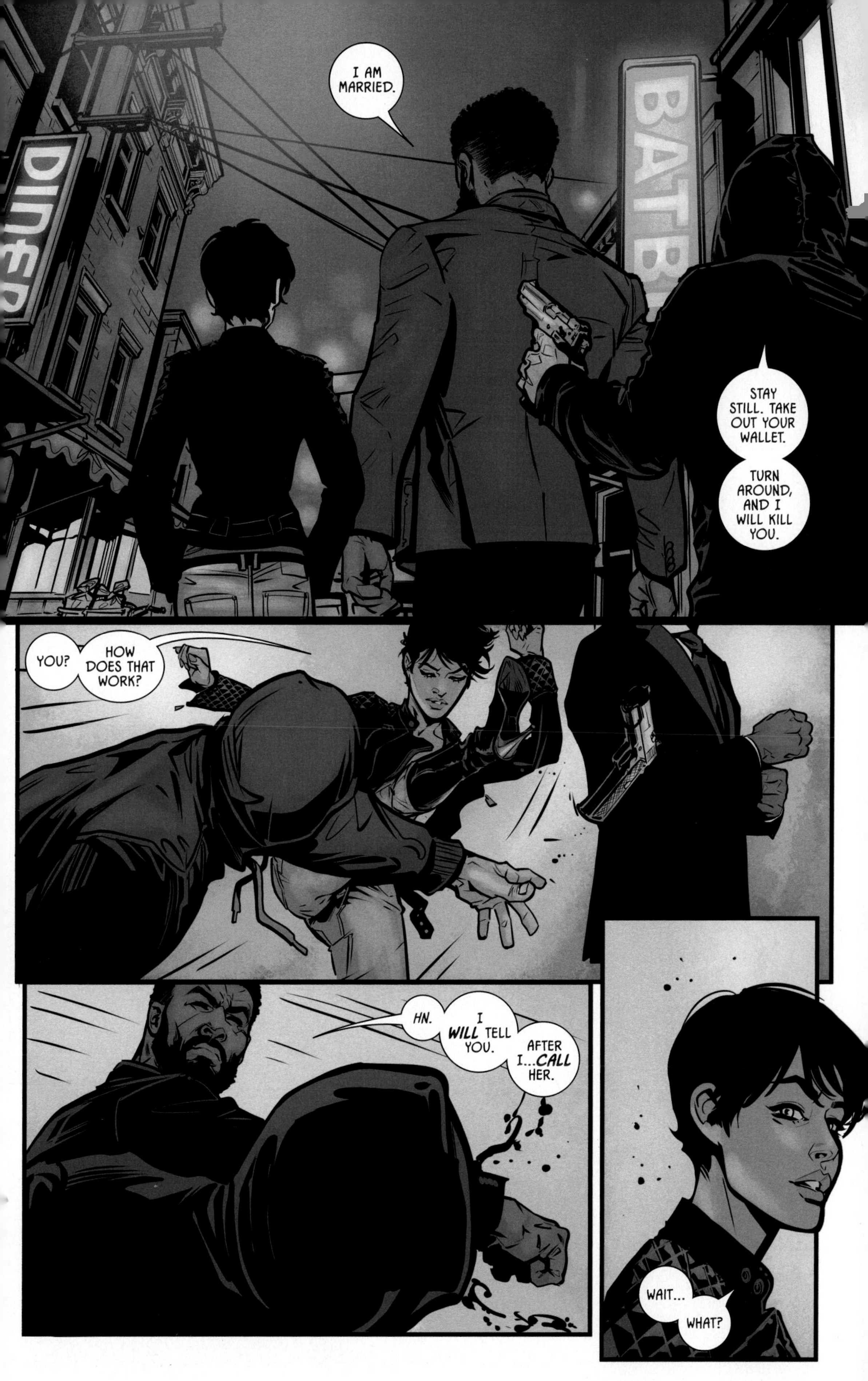

I AM MARRIED.
STAY STILL. TAKE OUT YOUR WALLET.
TURN AROUND, AND I WILL KILL YOU.
YOU?
HOW DOES THAT WORK?
HN.
I *WILL* TELL YOU.
AFTER I...*CALL* HER.
WAIT...
WHAT?

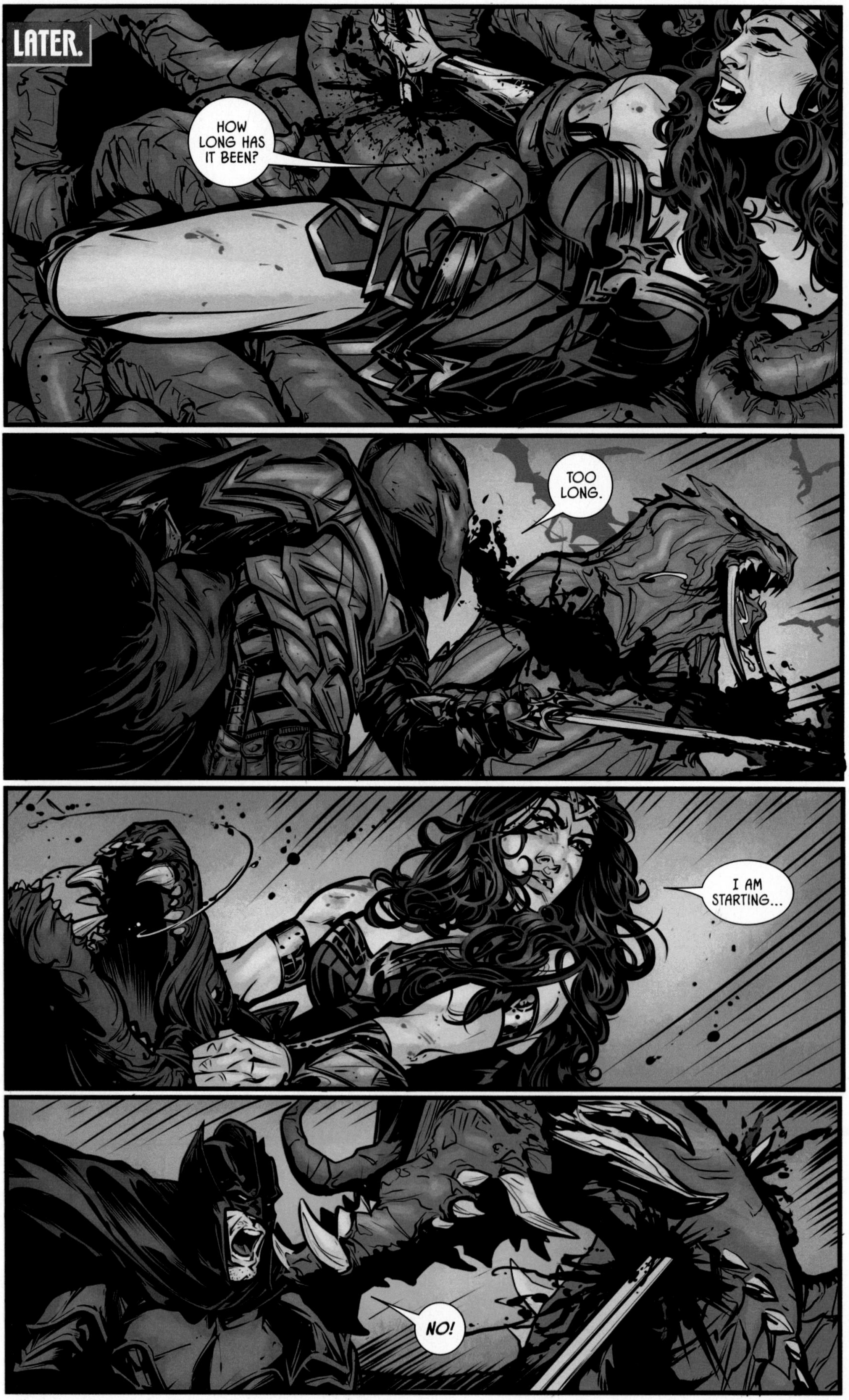
LATER.
HOW LONG HAS IT BEEN?
TOO LONG.
I AM STARTING...
NO!

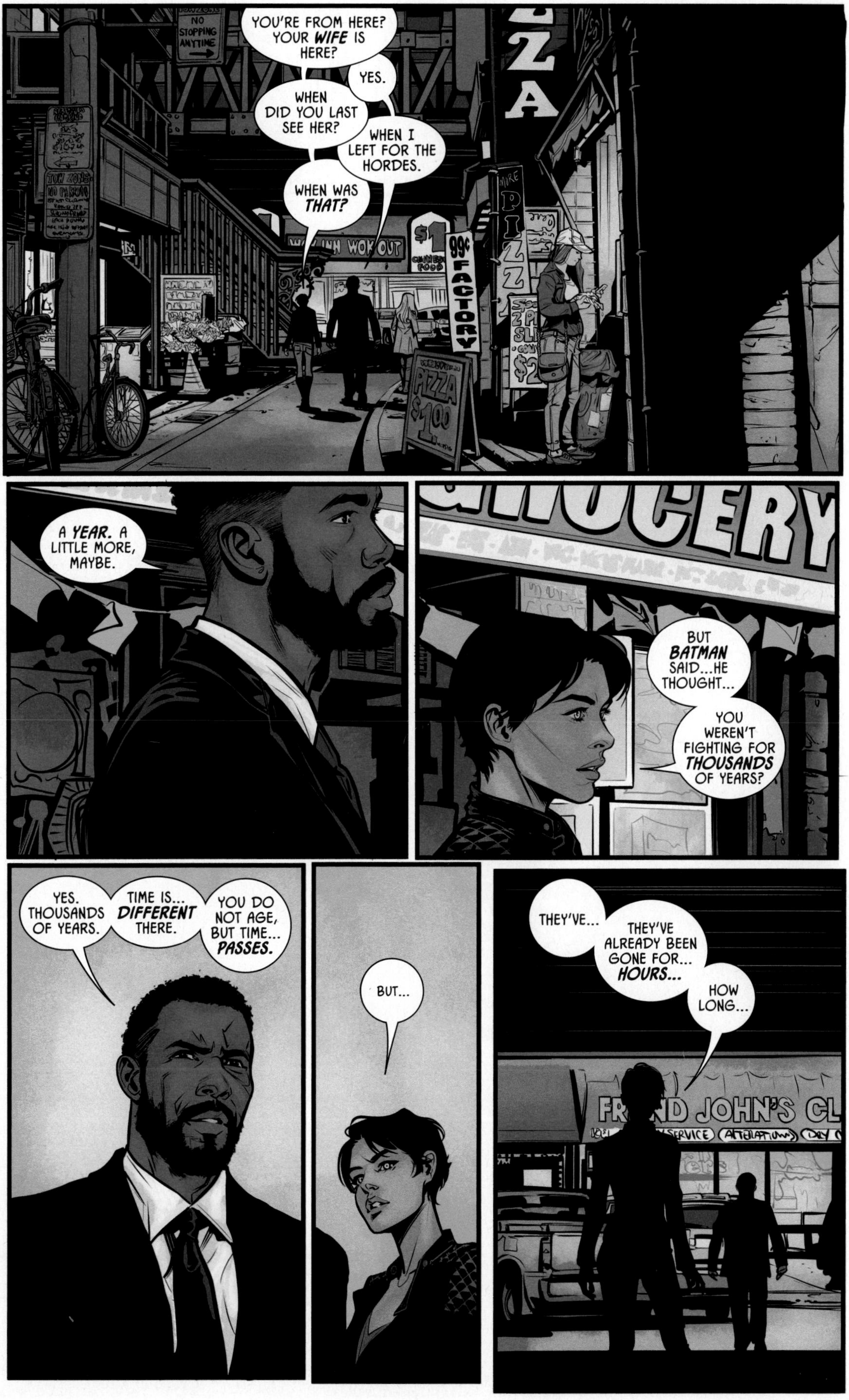
NO STOPPING ANYTIME
YOU'RE FROM HERE? YOUR *WIFE* IS HERE?
YES.
WHEN DID YOU LAST SEE HER?
WHEN I LEFT FOR THE HORDES.
WHEN WAS *THAT?*
PIZZA
WOK OUT
99¢ FACTORY
PIZZA $1.00
A *YEAR.* A LITTLE MORE, MAYBE.
GROCERY
BUT *BATMAN* SAID...HE THOUGHT...
YOU WEREN'T FIGHTING FOR *THOUSANDS* OF YEARS?
YES. THOUSANDS OF YEARS.
TIME IS... *DIFFERENT* THERE.
YOU DO NOT AGE, BUT TIME... *PASSES.*
BUT...
THEY'VE...
THEY'VE ALREADY BEEN GONE FOR... *HOURS...*
HOW LONG...
FR ND JOHN'S CL

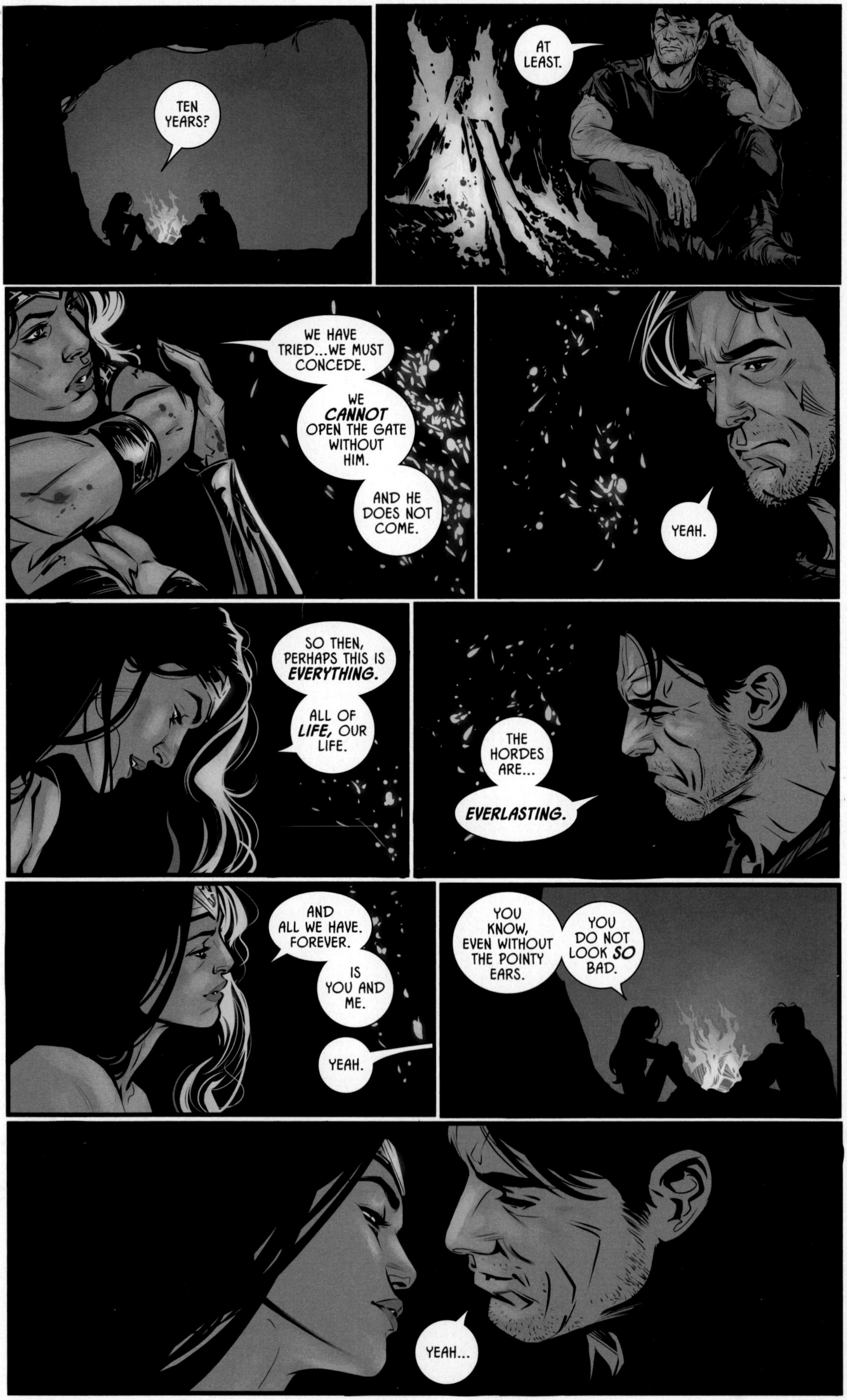
TEN YEARS?
AT LEAST.
WE HAVE TRIED...WE MUST CONCEDE.
WE CANNOT OPEN THE GATE WITHOUT HIM.
AND HE DOES NOT COME.
YEAH.
SO THEN, PERHAPS THIS IS EVERYTHING.
ALL OF LIFE, OUR LIFE.
THE HORDES ARE...
EVERLASTING.
AND ALL WE HAVE. FOREVER.
IS YOU AND ME.
YEAH.
YOU KNOW, EVEN WITHOUT THE POINTY EARS.
YOU DO NOT LOOK SO BAD.
YEAH...

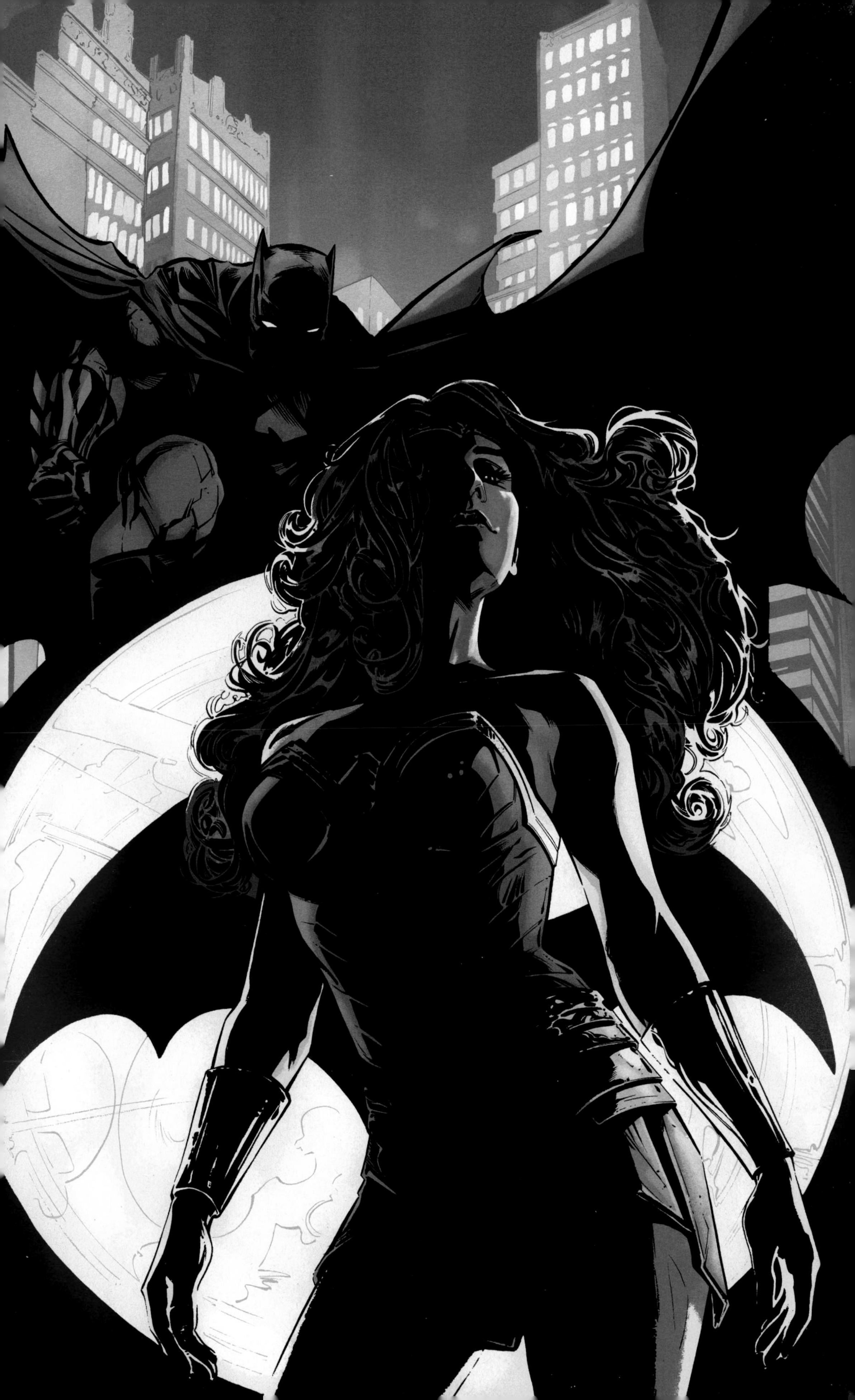

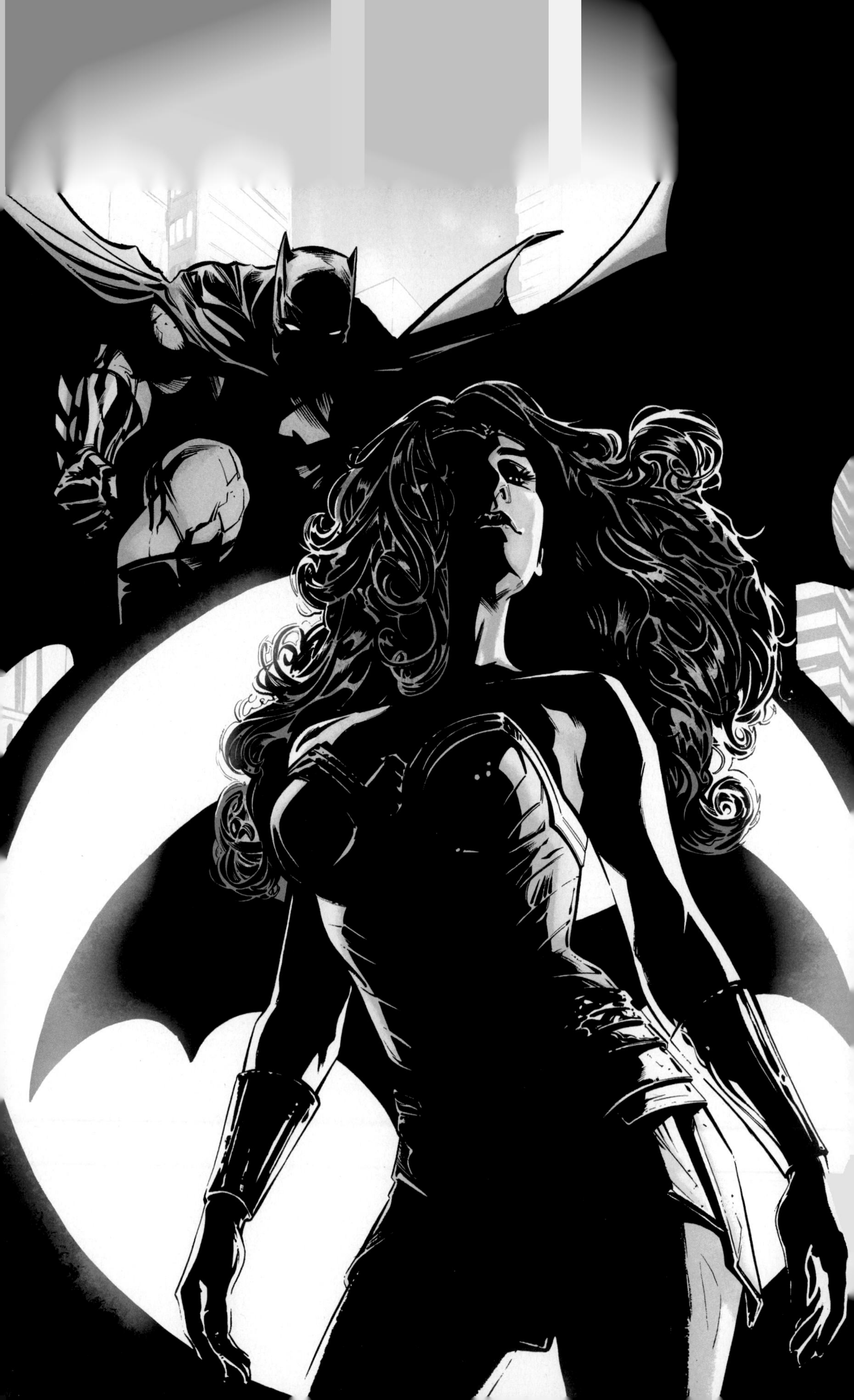

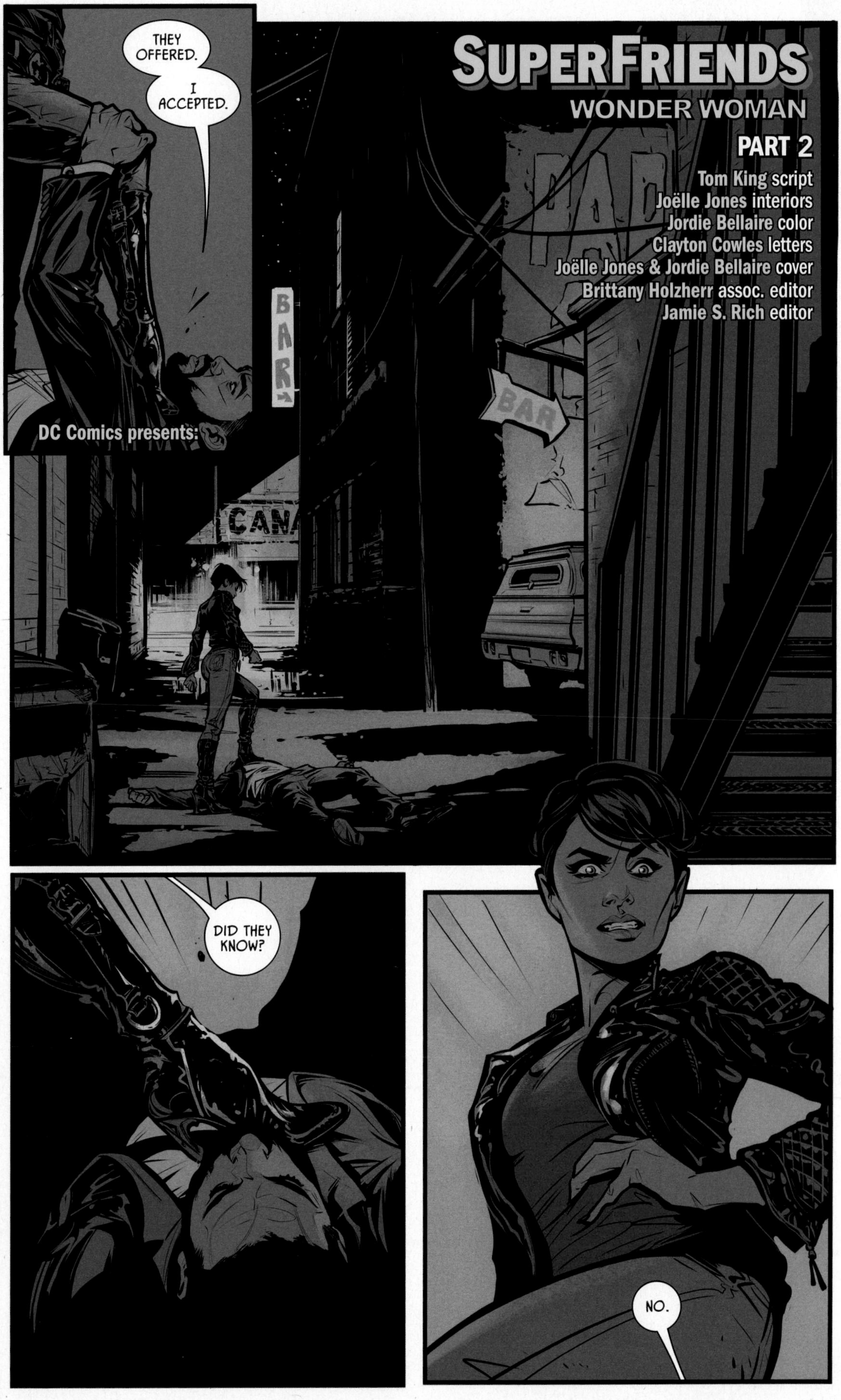
THEY OFFERED.
I ACCEPTED.
DC Comics presents:
SUPERFRIENDS
WONDER WOMAN
PART 2
Tom King script
Joëlle Jones interiors
Jordie Bellaire color
Clayton Cowles letters
Joëlle Jones & Jordie Bellaire cover
Brittany Holzherr assoc. editor
Jamie S. Rich editor
BAR
BAR
DID THEY KNOW?
NO.

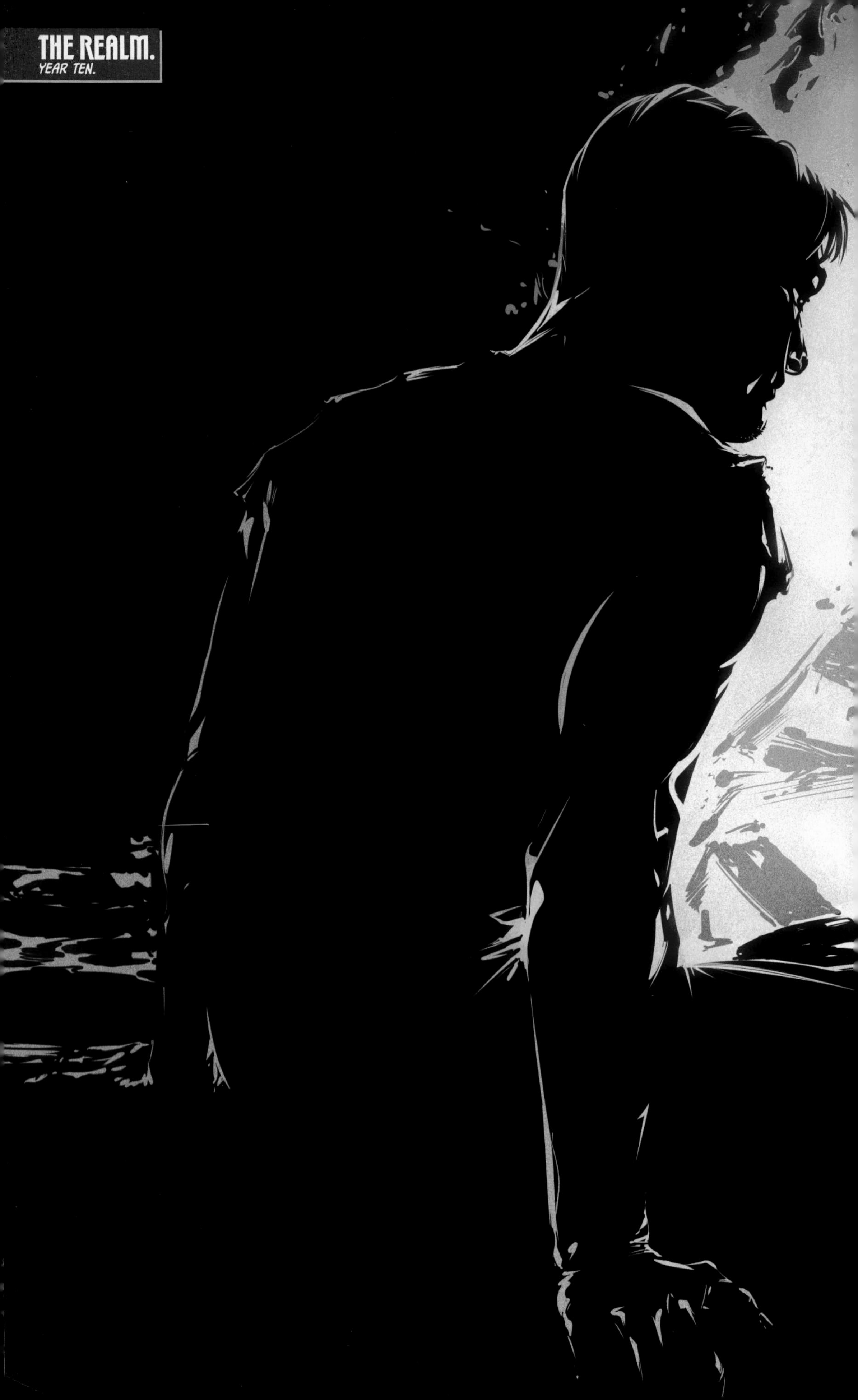
THE REALM.
YEAR TEN.

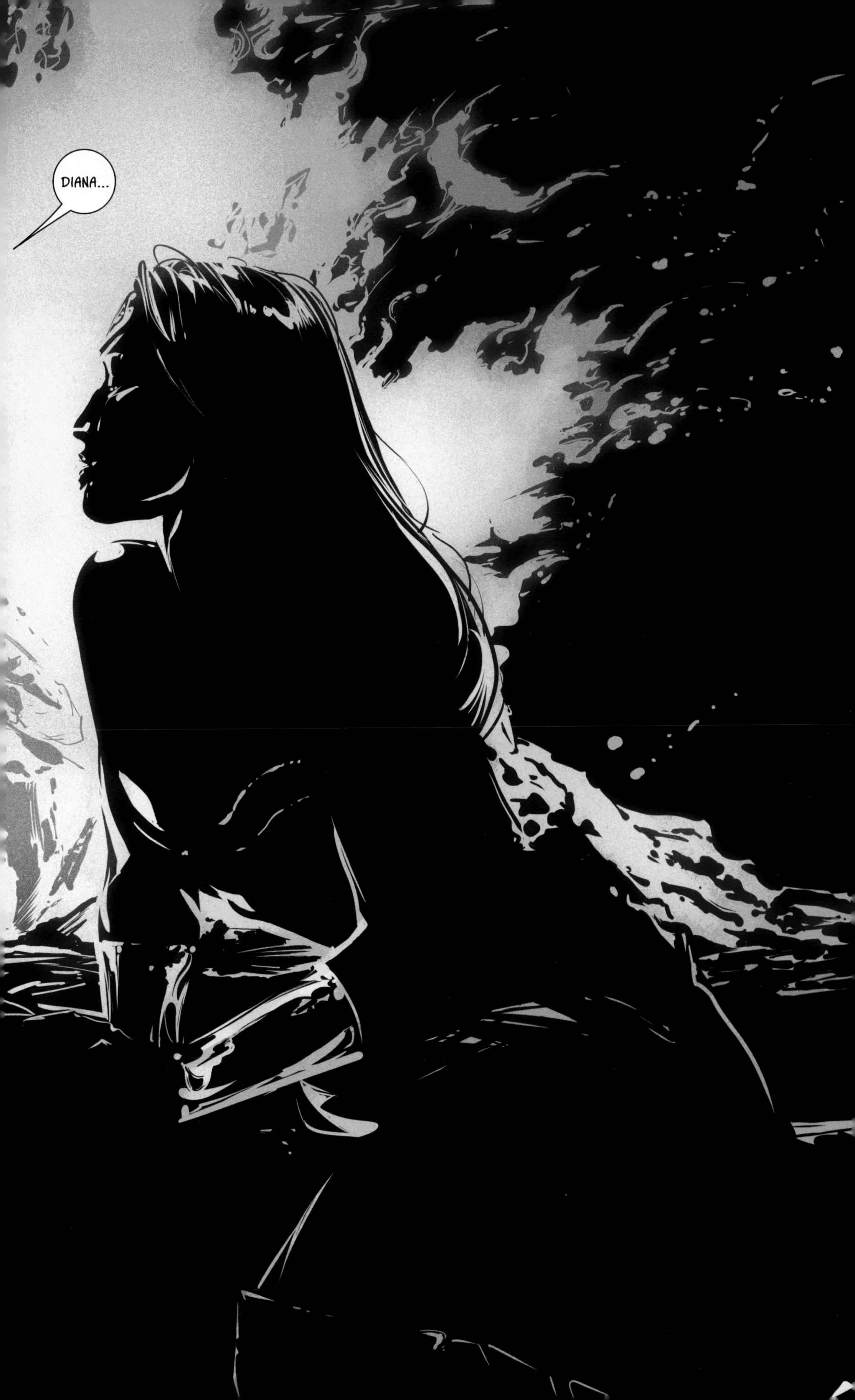
DIANA...

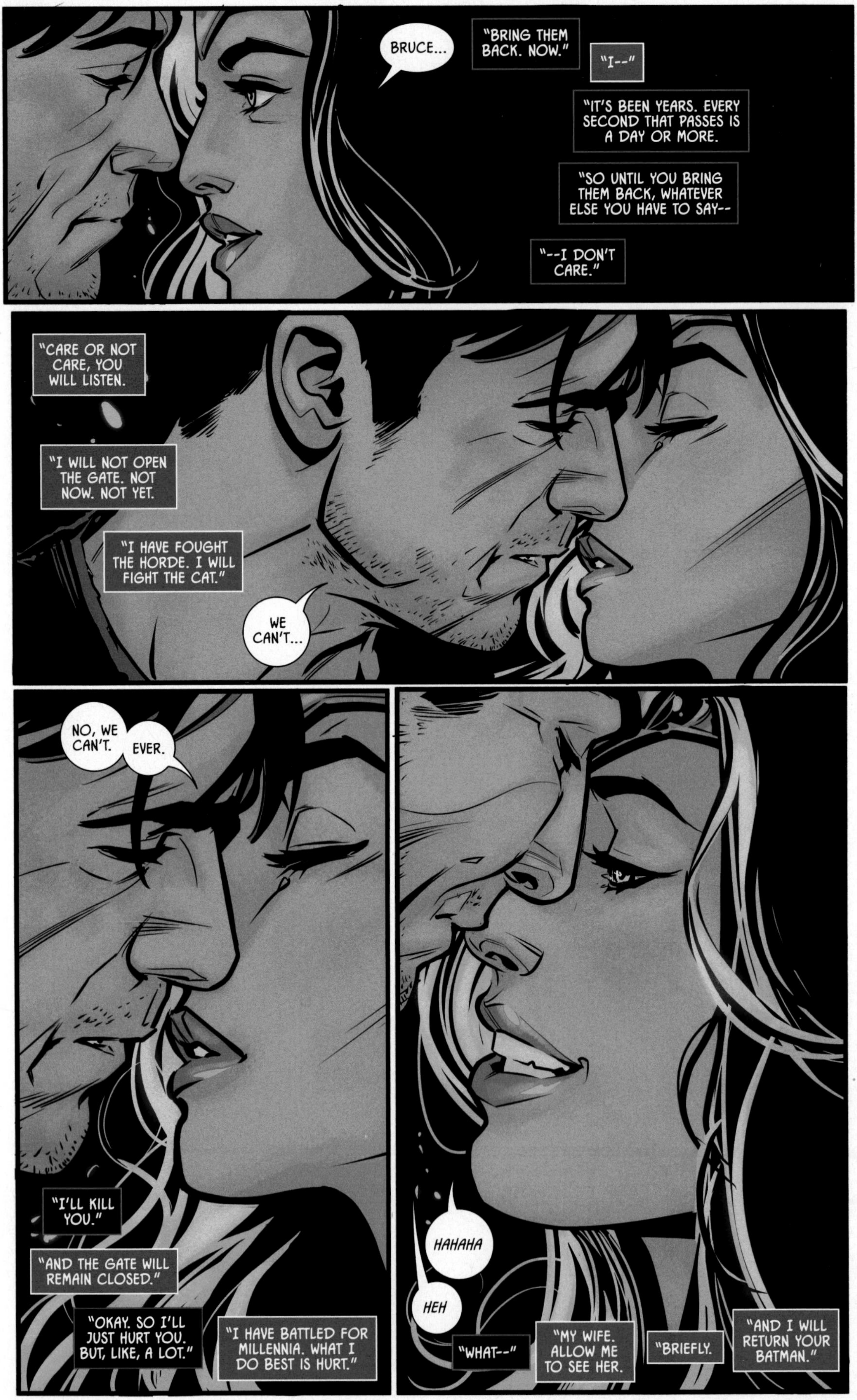
BRUCE...
"BRING THEM BACK. NOW."
"I--"
"IT'S BEEN YEARS. EVERY SECOND THAT PASSES IS A DAY OR MORE.
"SO UNTIL YOU BRING THEM BACK, WHATEVER ELSE YOU HAVE TO SAY--
"--I DON'T CARE."
"CARE OR NOT CARE, YOU WILL LISTEN.
"I WILL NOT OPEN THE GATE. NOT NOW. NOT YET.
"I HAVE FOUGHT THE HORDE. I WILL FIGHT THE CAT."
WE CAN'T...
NO, WE CAN'T.
EVER.
"I'LL KILL YOU."
"AND THE GATE WILL REMAIN CLOSED."
"OKAY. SO I'LL JUST HURT YOU. BUT, LIKE, A LOT."
"I HAVE BATTLED FOR MILLENNIA. WHAT I DO BEST IS HURT."
HAHAHA
HEH
"WHAT--"
"MY WIFE. ALLOW ME TO SEE HER.
"BRIEFLY.
"AND I WILL RETURN YOUR BATMAN."

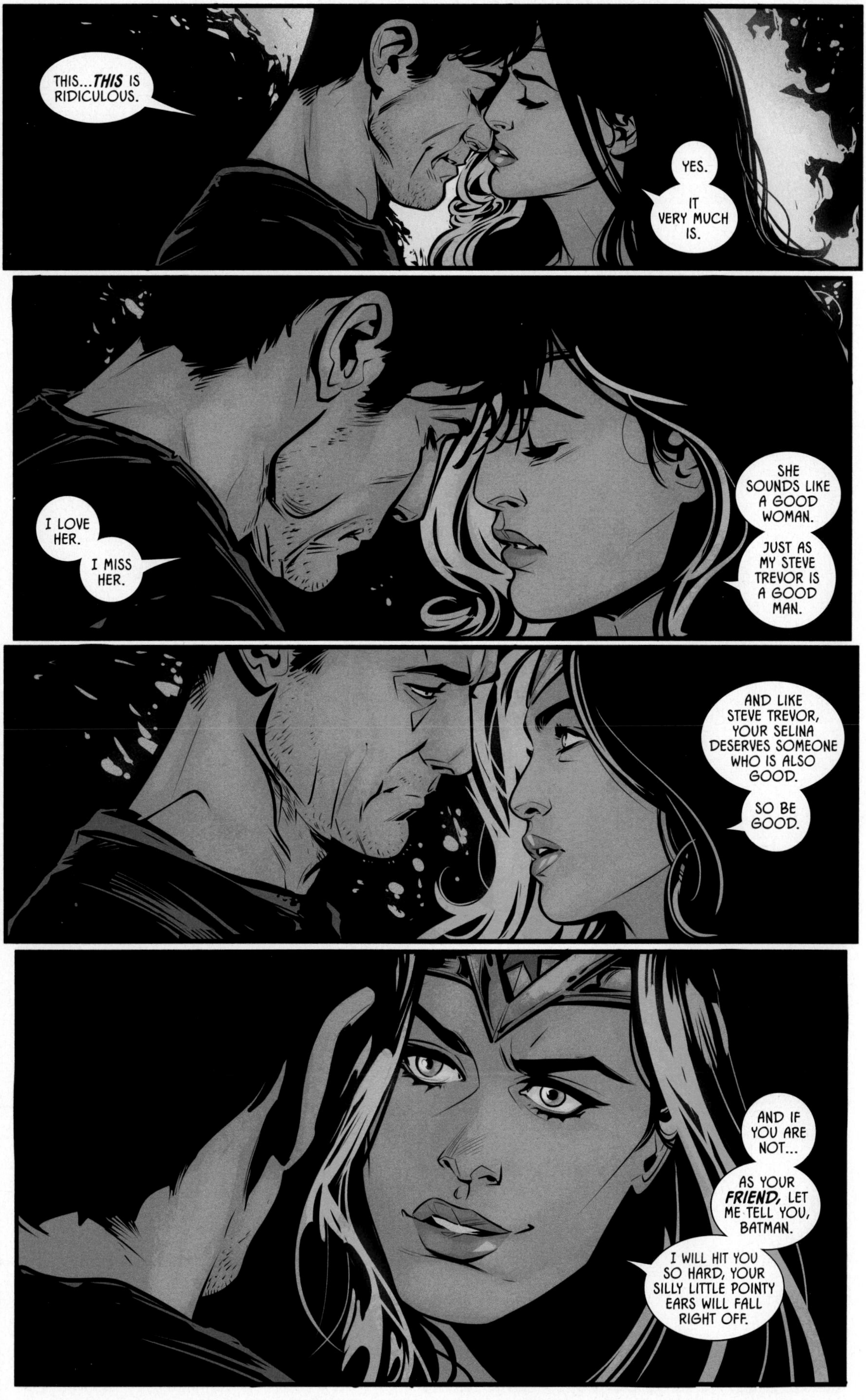
THIS...*THIS* IS RIDICULOUS.
YES.
IT VERY MUCH IS.
I LOVE HER.
I MISS HER.
SHE SOUNDS LIKE A GOOD WOMAN.
JUST AS MY STEVE TREVOR IS A GOOD MAN.
AND LIKE STEVE TREVOR, YOUR SELINA DESERVES SOMEONE WHO IS ALSO GOOD.
SO BE GOOD.
AND IF YOU ARE NOT...
AS YOUR *FRIEND,* LET ME TELL YOU, BATMAN.
I WILL HIT YOU SO HARD, YOUR SILLY LITTLE POINTY EARS WILL FALL RIGHT OFF.

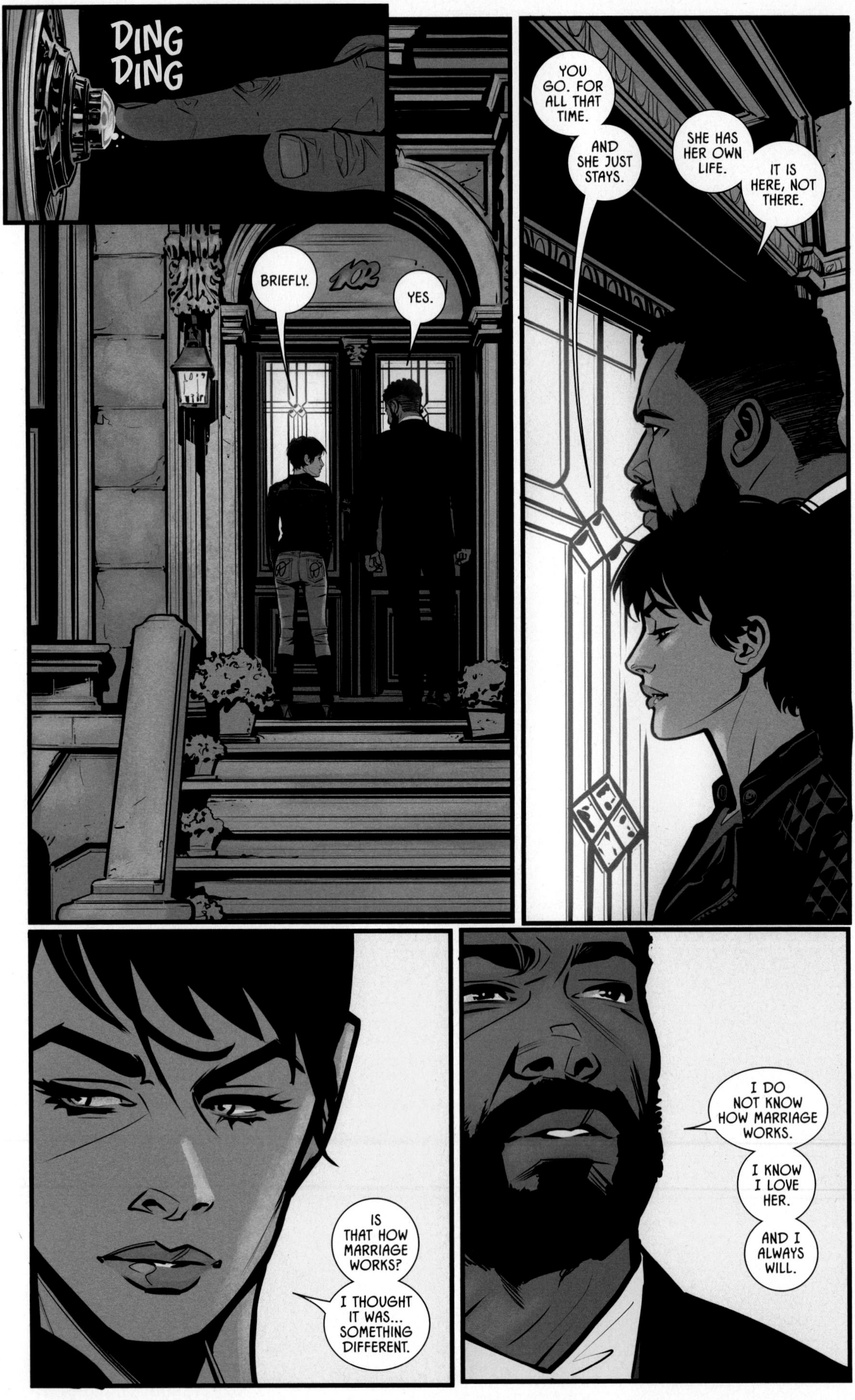
DING DING
BRIEFLY.
YES.
YOU GO. FOR ALL THAT TIME.
AND SHE JUST STAYS.
SHE HAS HER OWN LIFE.
IT IS HERE, NOT THERE.
IS THAT HOW MARRIAGE WORKS?
I THOUGHT IT WAS... SOMETHING DIFFERENT.
I DO NOT KNOW HOW MARRIAGE WORKS.
I KNOW I LOVE HER.
AND I ALWAYS WILL.

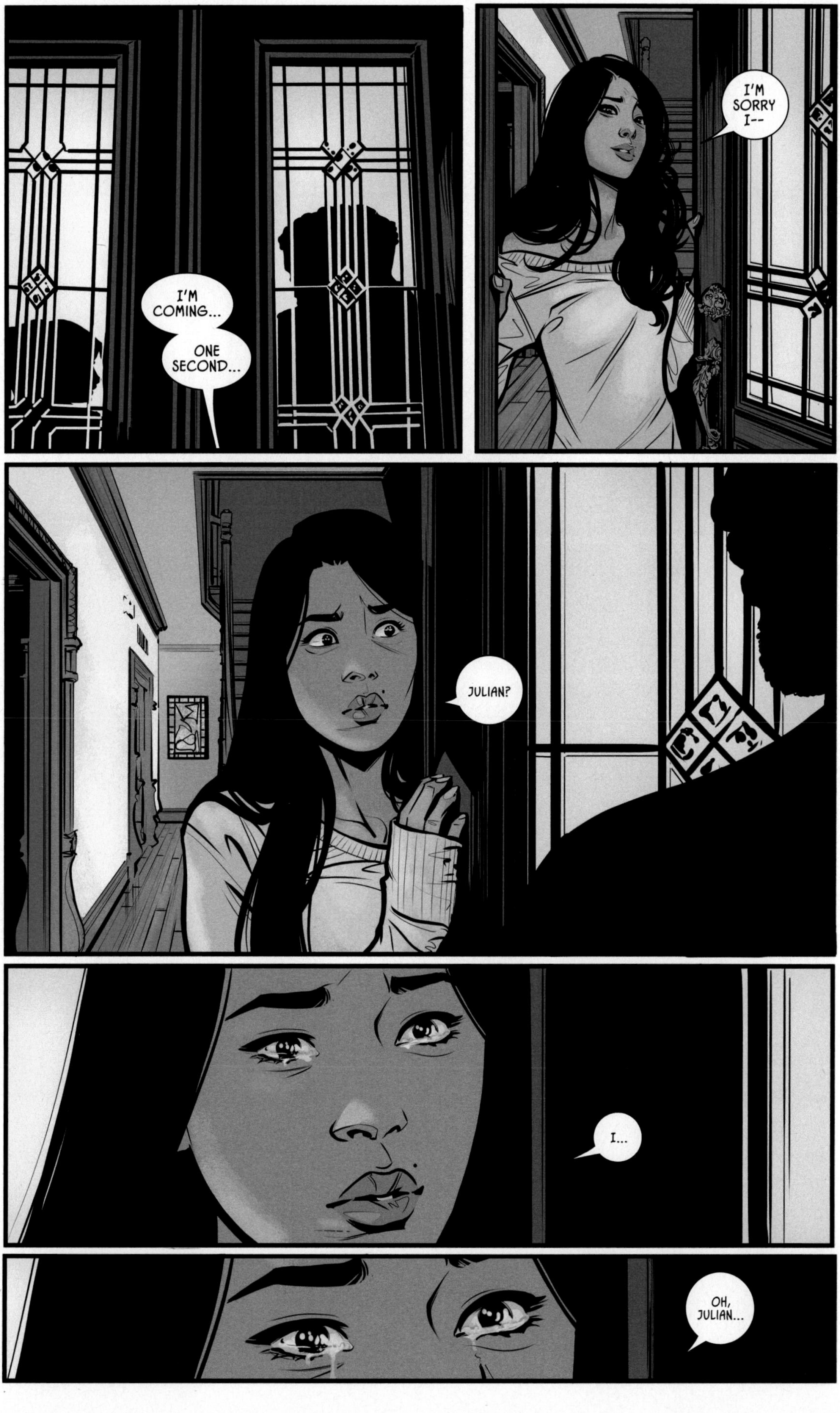
I'M COMING...
ONE SECOND...
I'M SORRY I--
JULIAN?
I...
OH, JULIAN...

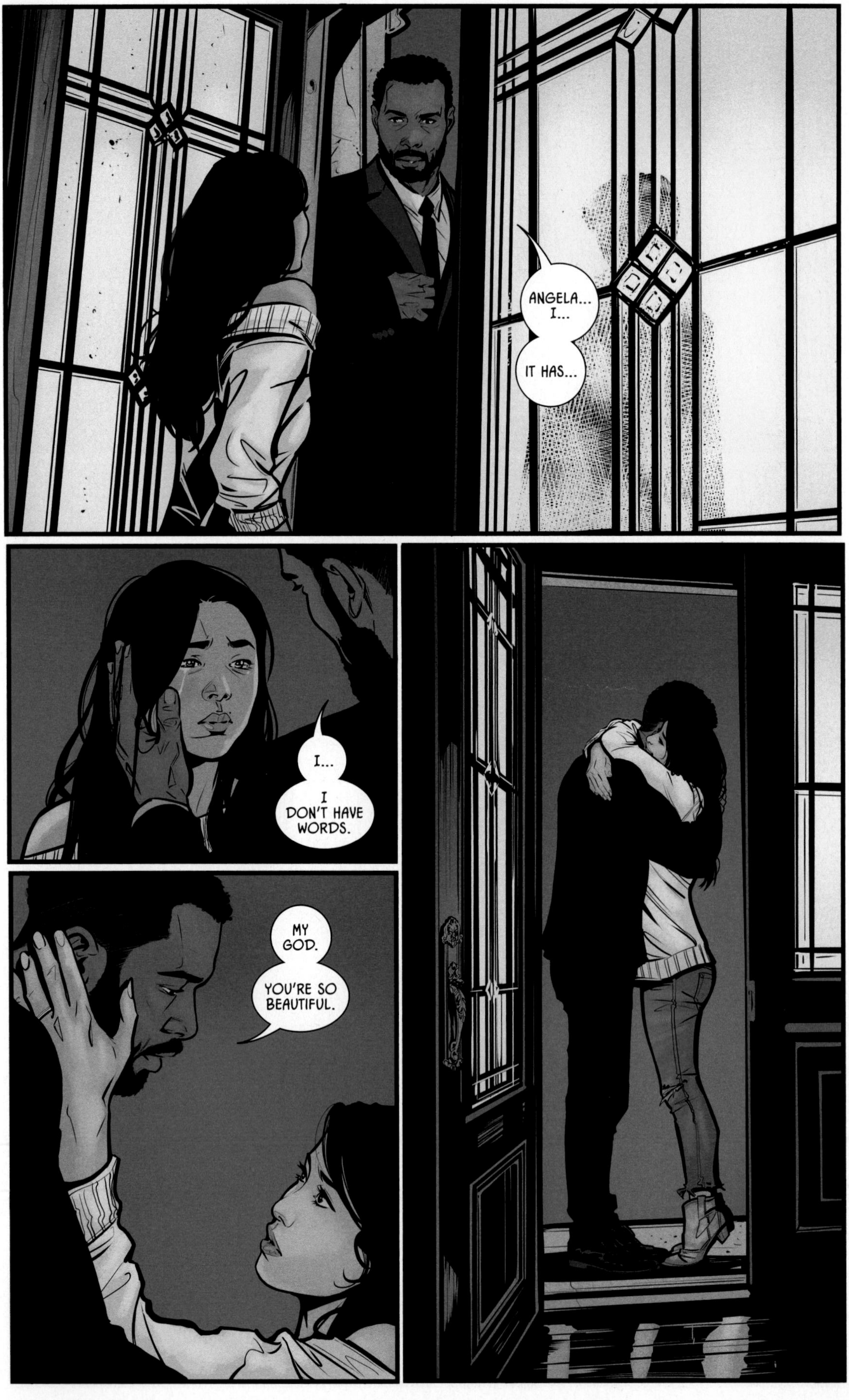
ANGELA... I...
IT HAS...
I...
I DON'T HAVE WORDS.
MY GOD.
YOU'RE SO BEAUTIFUL.

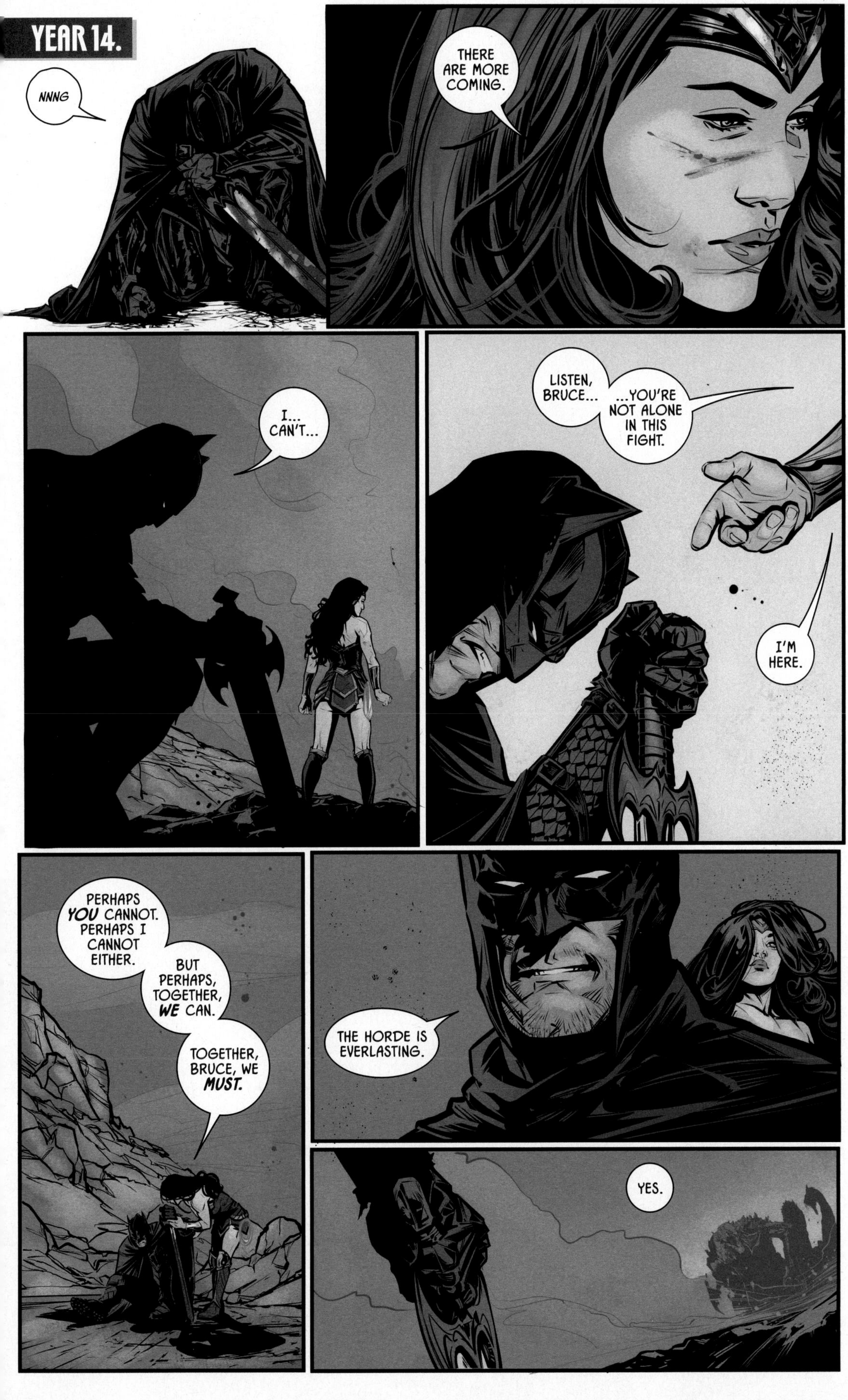
YEAR 14.
NNNG
THERE ARE MORE COMING.
I... CAN'T...
LISTEN, BRUCE...
...YOU'RE NOT ALONE IN THIS FIGHT.
I'M HERE.
PERHAPS *YOU* CANNOT. PERHAPS I CANNOT EITHER.
BUT PERHAPS, TOGETHER, *WE* CAN.
TOGETHER, BRUCE, WE *MUST.*
THE HORDE IS EVERLASTING.
YES.

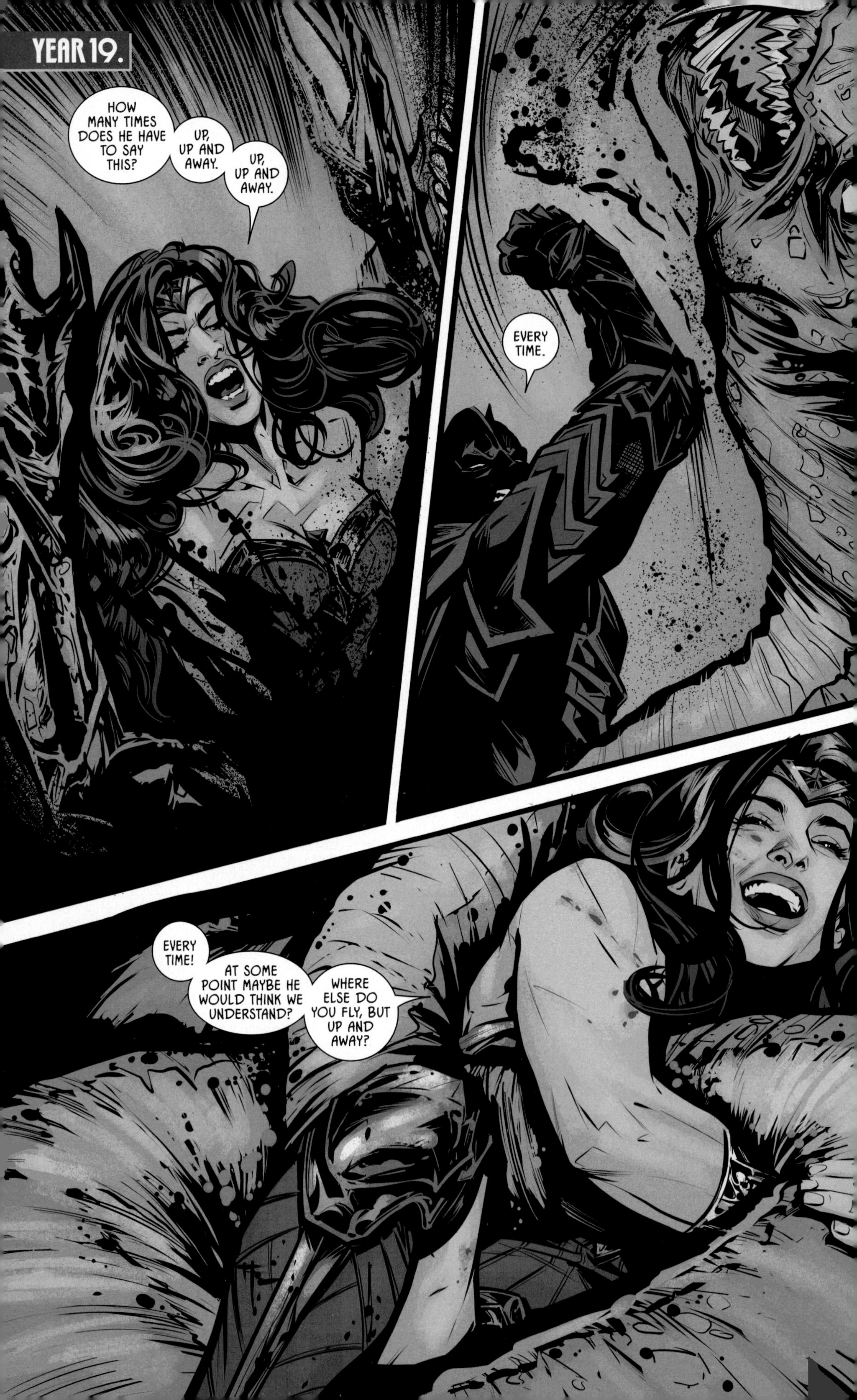
YEAR 19.
HOW MANY TIMES DOES HE HAVE TO SAY THIS?
UP, UP AND AWAY.
UP, UP AND AWAY.
EVERY TIME.
EVERY TIME!
AT SOME POINT MAYBE HE WOULD THINK WE UNDERSTAND?
WHERE ELSE DO YOU FLY, BUT UP AND AWAY?

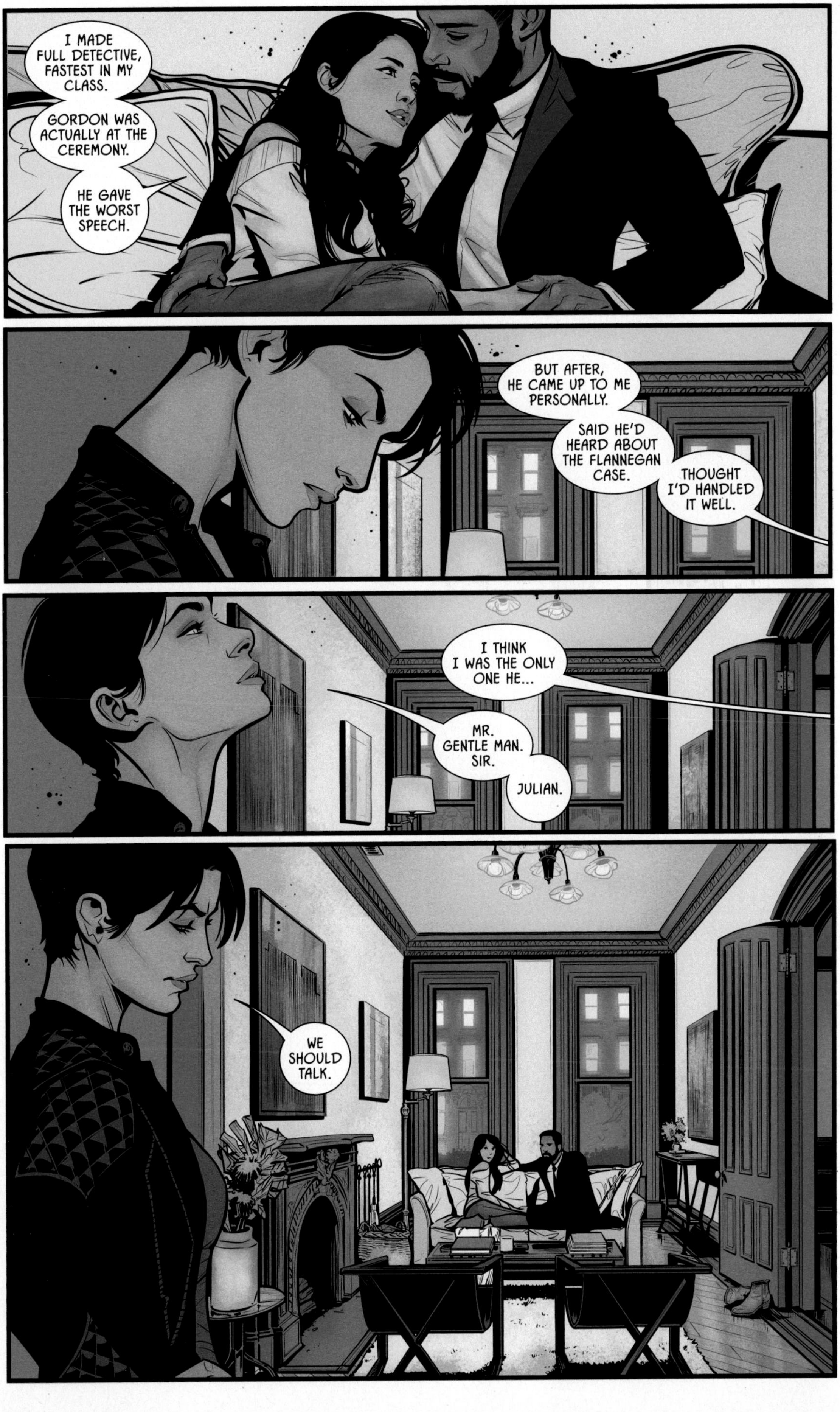
I MADE FULL DETECTIVE, FASTEST IN MY CLASS.
GORDON WAS ACTUALLY AT THE CEREMONY.
HE GAVE THE WORST SPEECH.
BUT AFTER, HE CAME UP TO ME PERSONALLY.
SAID HE'D HEARD ABOUT THE FLANNEGAN CASE.
THOUGHT I'D HANDLED IT WELL.
I THINK I WAS THE ONLY ONE HE...
MR. GENTLE MAN. SIR.
JULIAN.
WE SHOULD TALK.

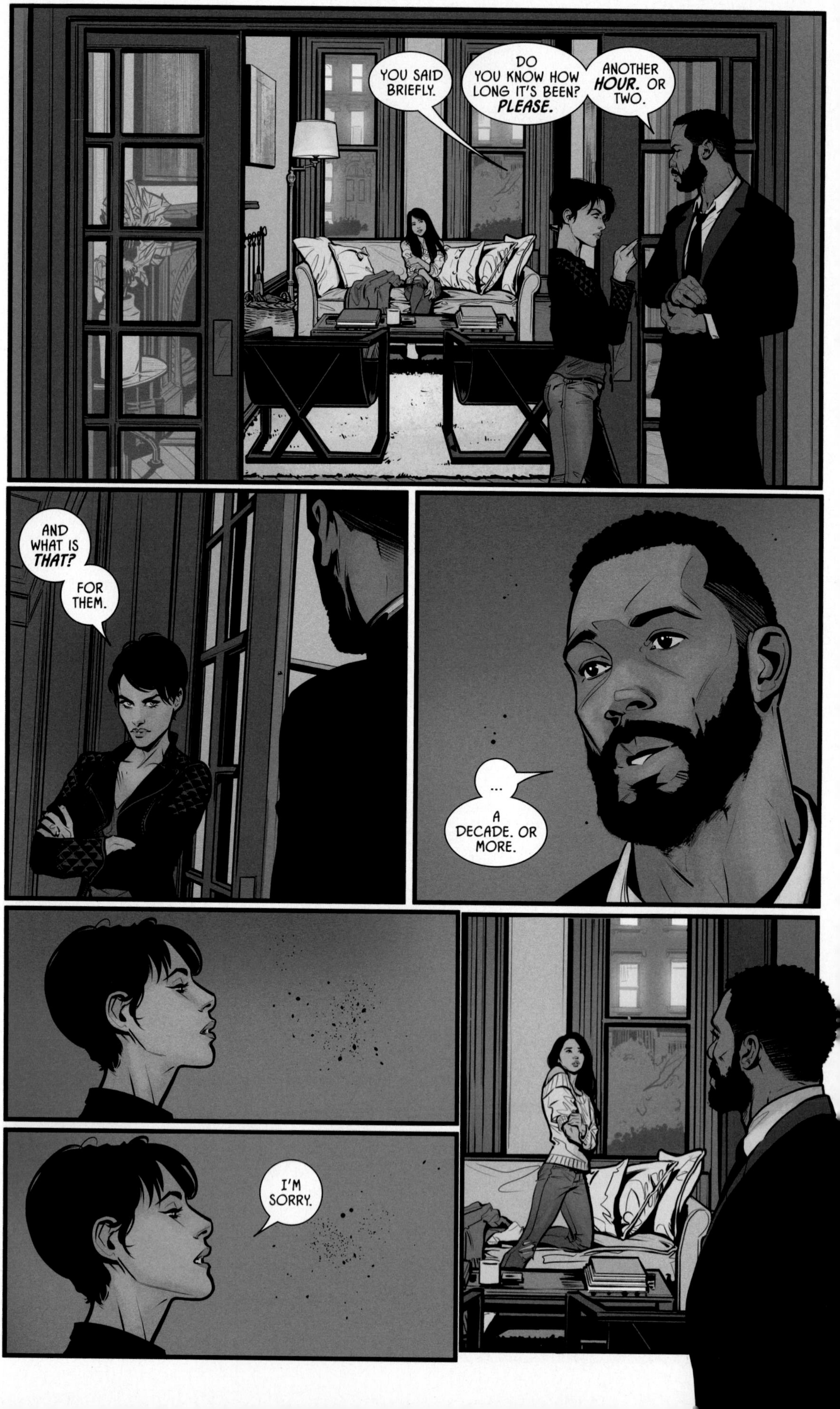
YOU SAID BRIEFLY.
DO YOU KNOW HOW LONG IT'S BEEN? PLEASE.
ANOTHER HOUR. OR TWO.
AND WHAT IS THAT?
FOR THEM.
...
A DECADE. OR MORE.
I'M SORRY.

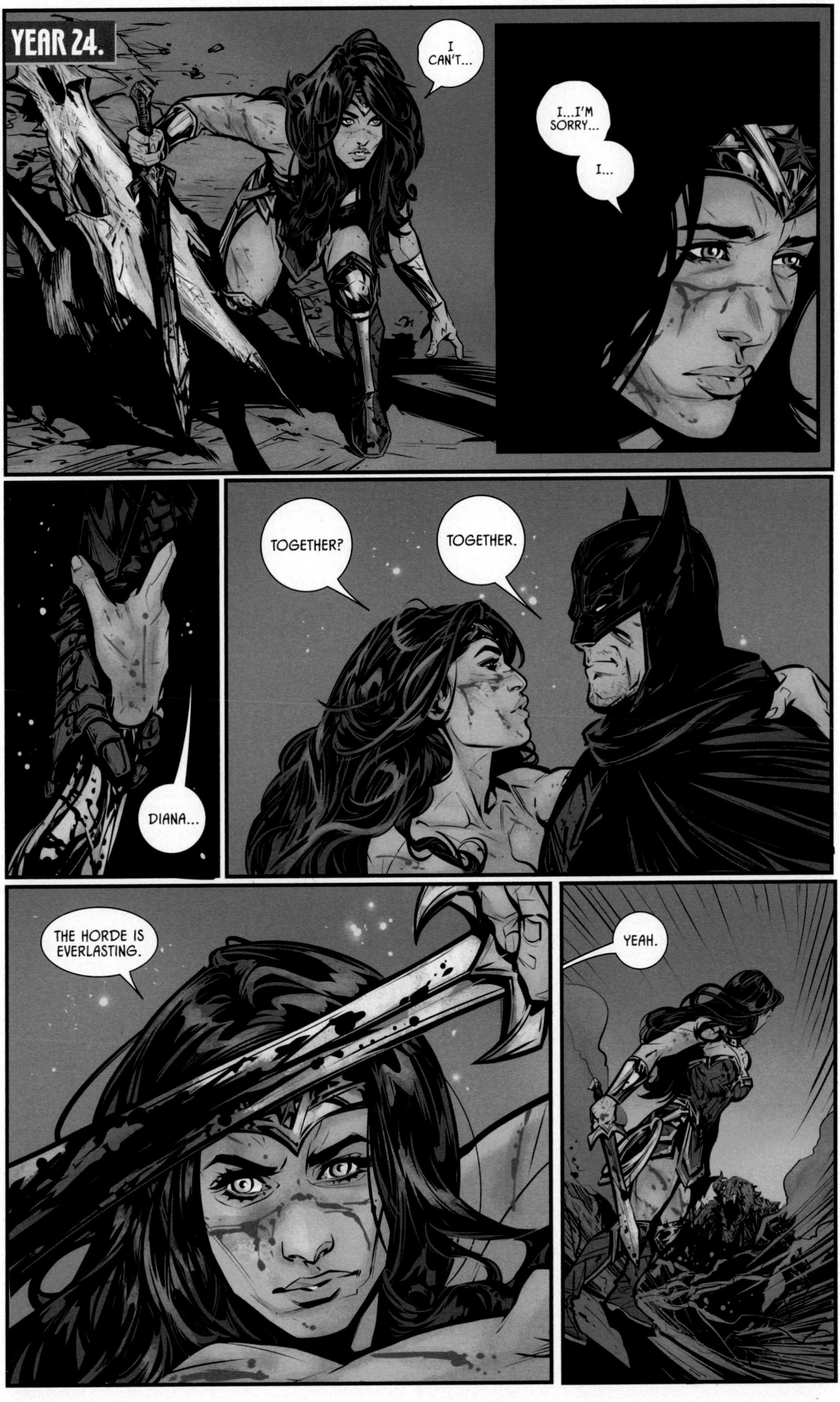
YEAR 24.
I CAN'T...
I...I'M SORRY...
I...
TOGETHER?
TOGETHER.
DIANA...
THE HORDE IS EVERLASTING.
YEAH.

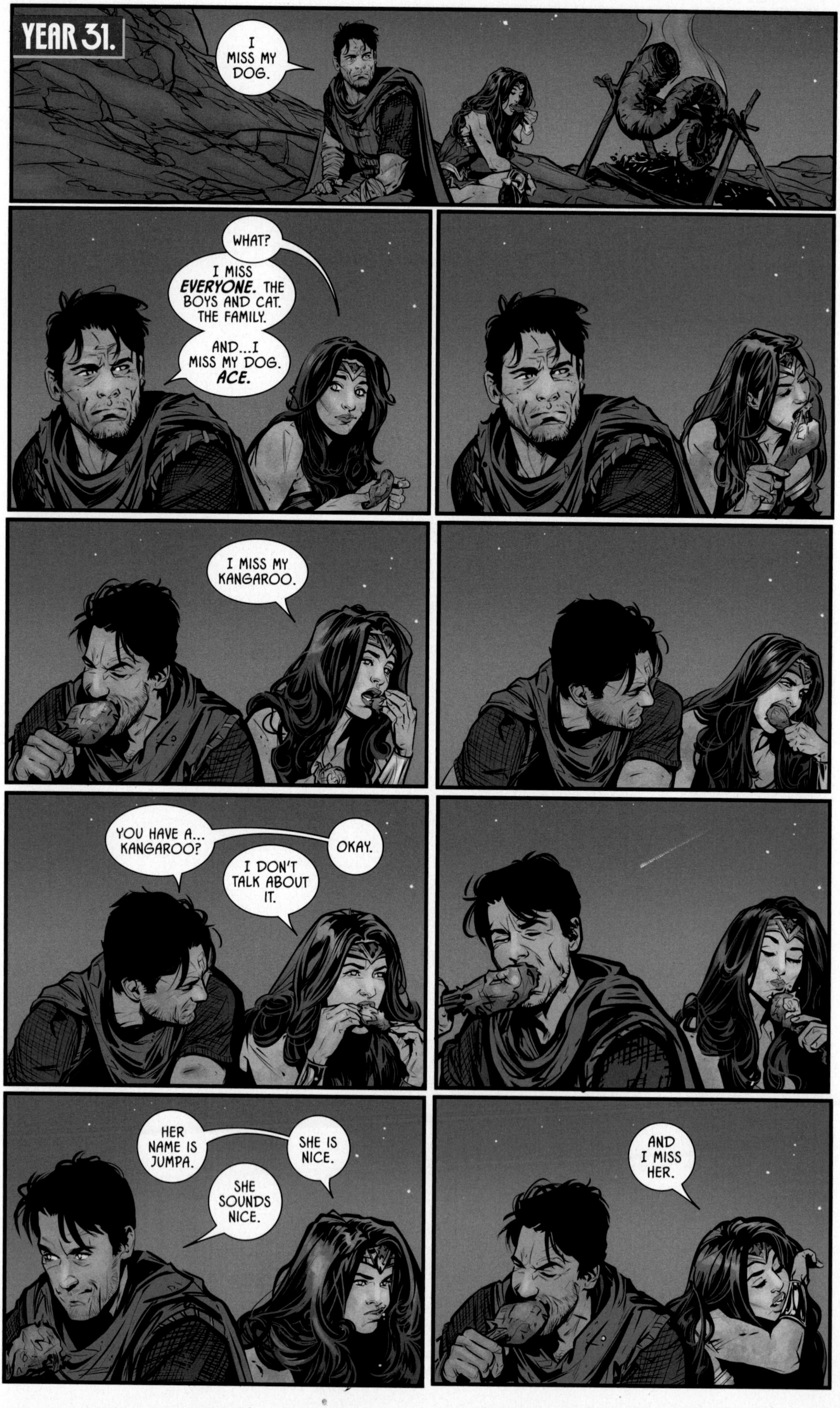
YEAR 31.
I MISS MY DOG.
WHAT?
I MISS *EVERYONE.* THE BOYS AND CAT. THE FAMILY.
AND...I MISS MY DOG. *ACE.*
I MISS MY KANGAROO.
YOU HAVE A... KANGAROO?
I DON'T TALK ABOUT IT.
OKAY.
HER NAME IS JUMPA.
SHE SOUNDS NICE.
SHE IS NICE.
AND I MISS HER.

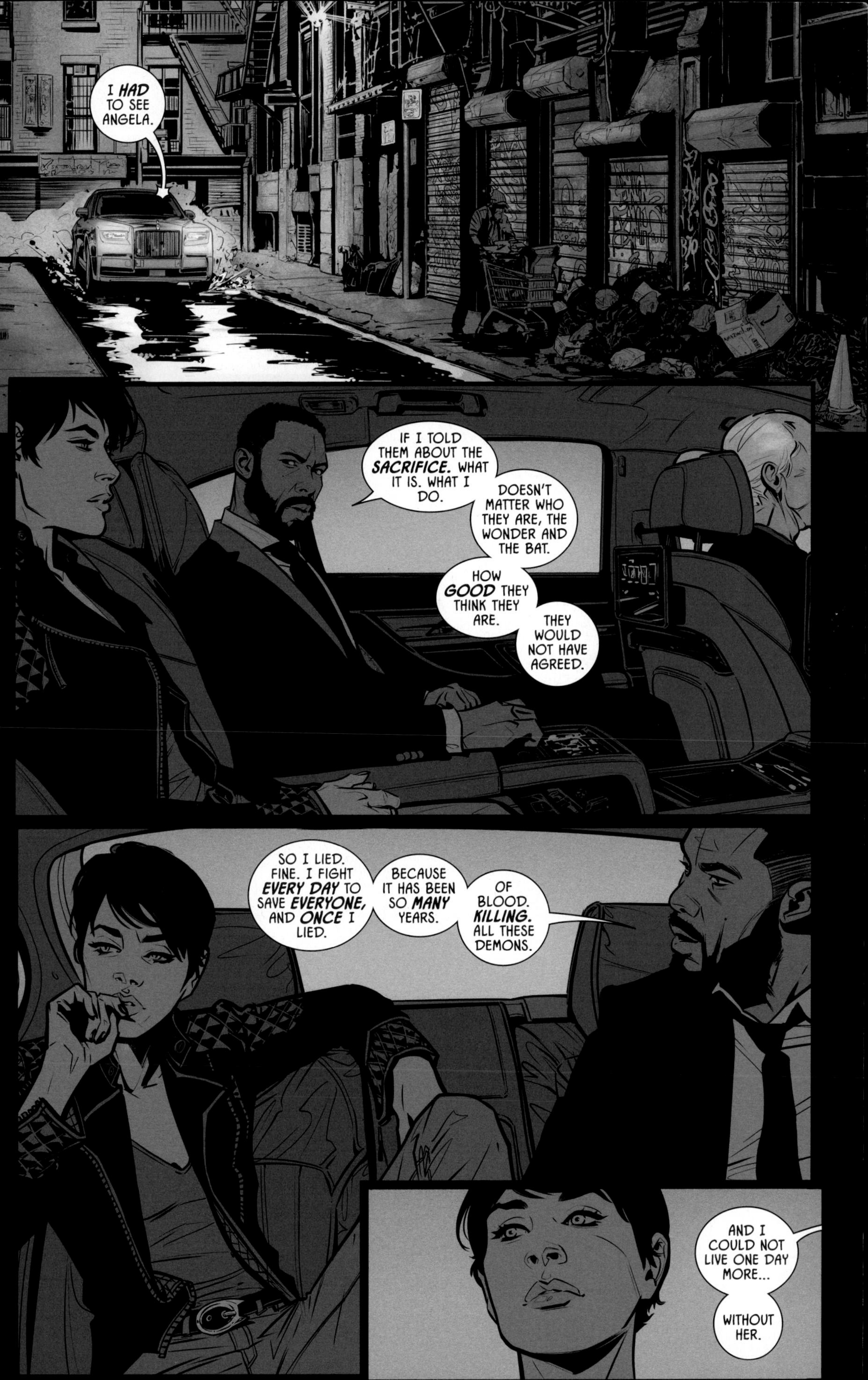

I HAD TO SEE ANGELA.
IF I TOLD THEM ABOUT THE SACRIFICE. WHAT IT IS. WHAT I DO.
DOESN'T MATTER WHO THEY ARE, THE WONDER AND THE BAT.
HOW GOOD THEY THINK THEY ARE.
THEY WOULD NOT HAVE AGREED.
SO I LIED. FINE. I FIGHT EVERY DAY TO SAVE EVERYONE, AND ONCE I LIED.
BECAUSE IT HAS BEEN SO MANY YEARS.
OF BLOOD. KILLING. ALL THESE DEMONS.
AND I COULD NOT LIVE ONE DAY MORE...
WITHOUT HER.

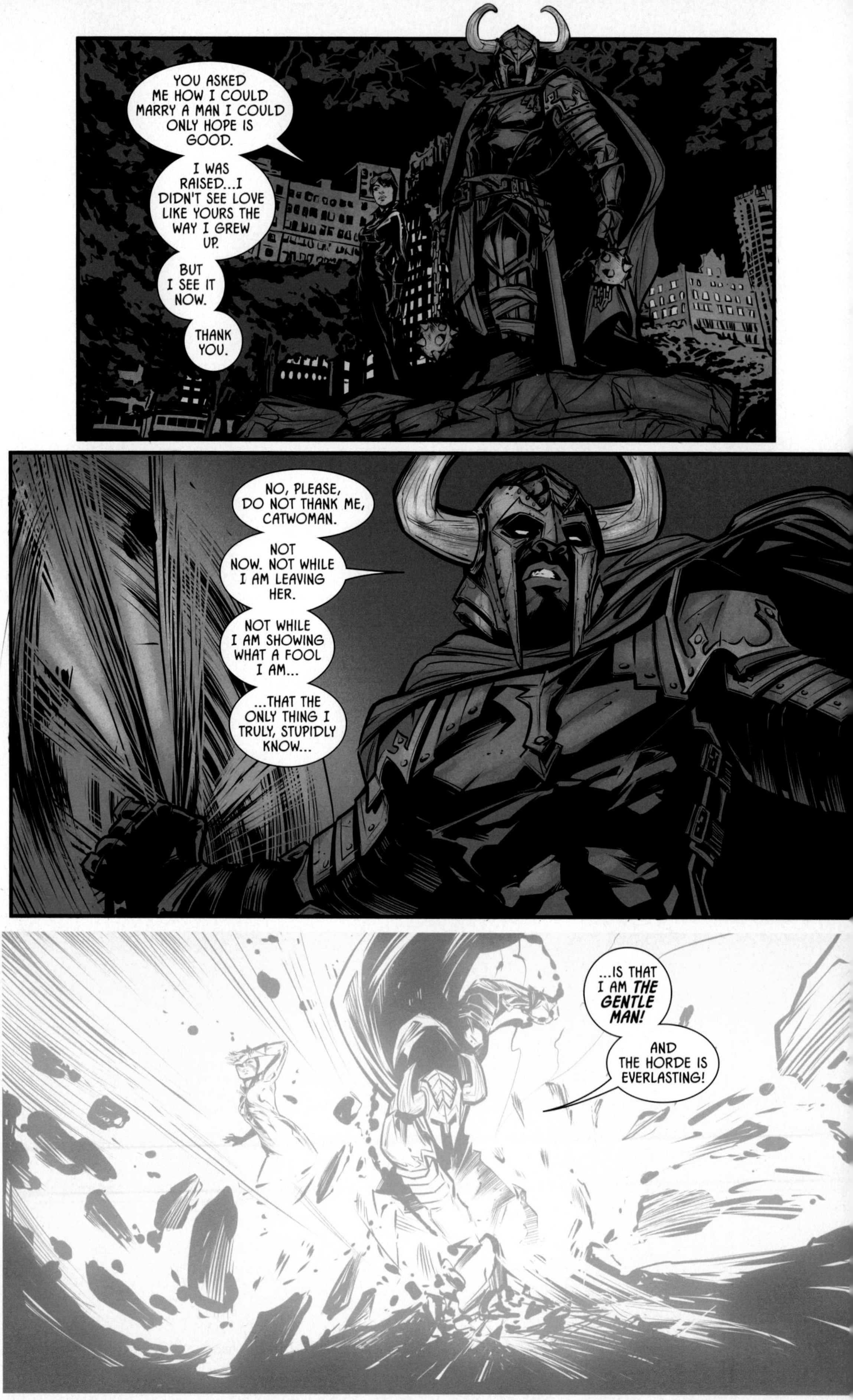
YOU ASKED ME HOW I COULD MARRY A MAN I COULD ONLY HOPE IS GOOD.
I WAS RAISED...I DIDN'T SEE LOVE LIKE YOURS THE WAY I GREW UP.
BUT I SEE IT NOW.
THANK YOU.
NO, PLEASE, DO NOT THANK ME, CATWOMAN.
NOT NOW. NOT WHILE I AM LEAVING HER.
NOT WHILE I AM SHOWING WHAT A FOOL I AM...
...THAT THE ONLY THING I TRULY, STUPIDLY KNOW...
...IS THAT I AM THE GENTLE MAN!
AND THE HORDE IS EVERLASTING!

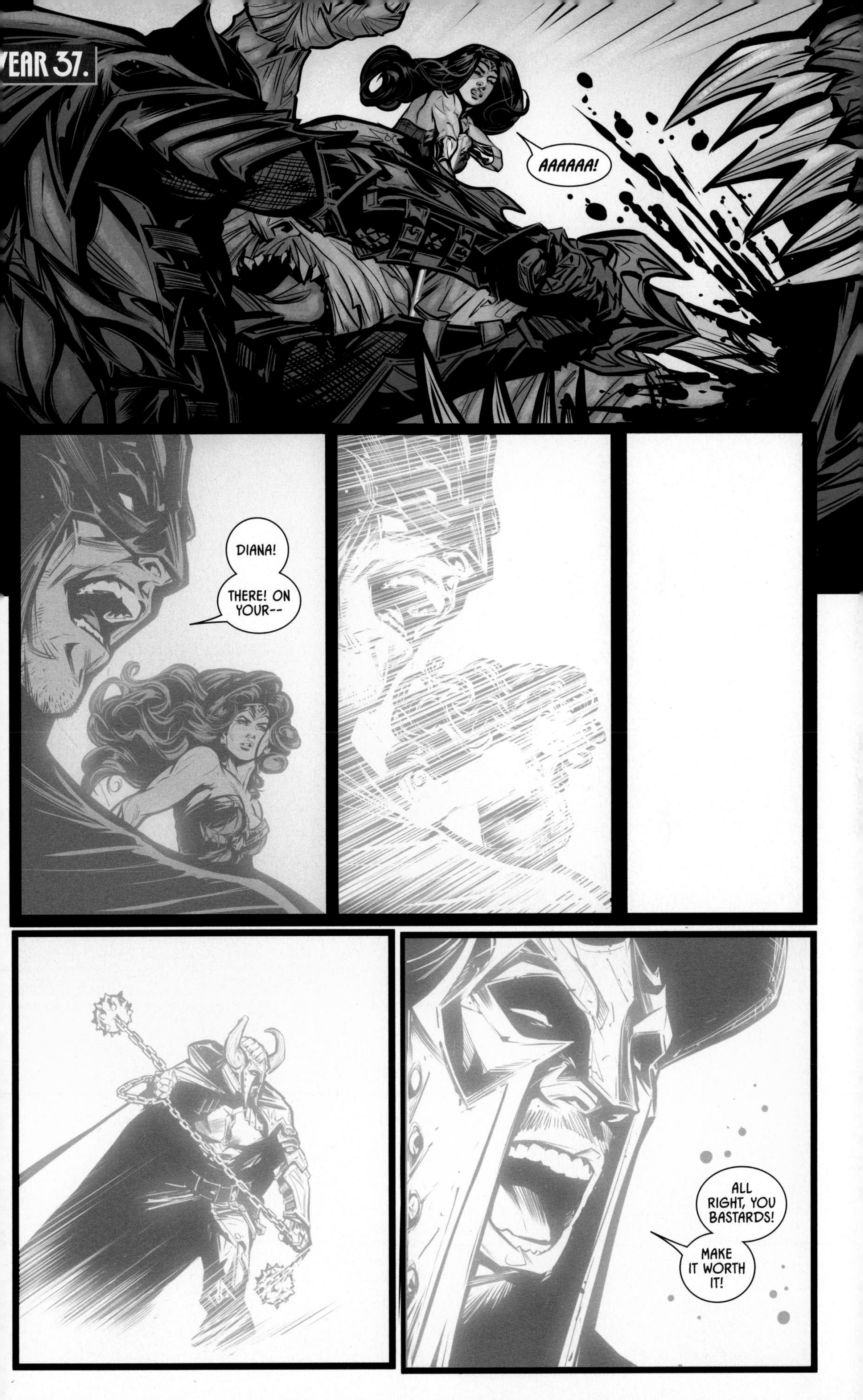
EAR 37.
AAAAAA!
DIANA!
THERE! ON YOUR--
ALL RIGHT, YOU BASTARDS!
MAKE IT WORTH IT!

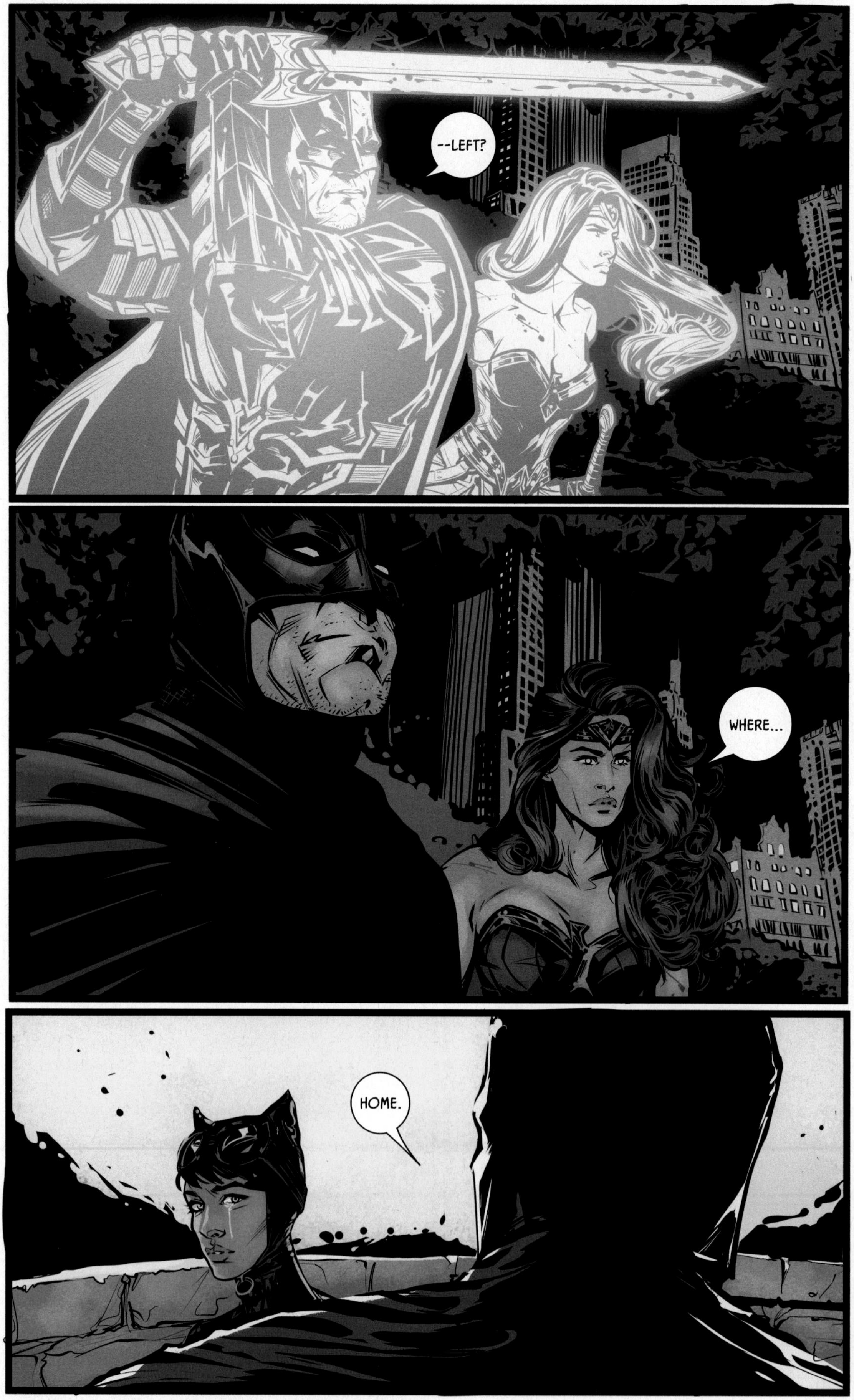
--LEFT?
WHERE...
HOME.

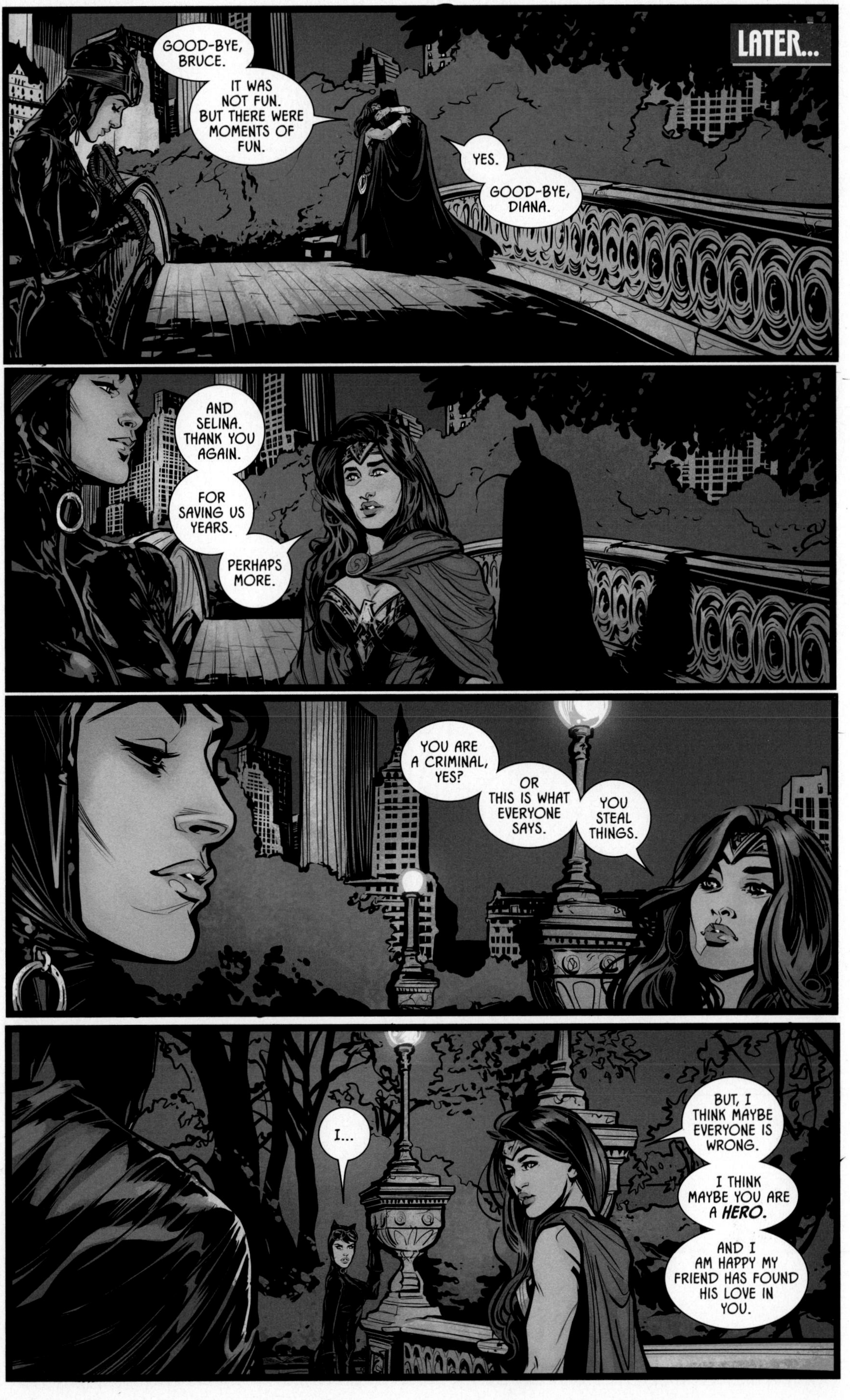
LATER...
GOOD-BYE, BRUCE.
IT WAS NOT FUN. BUT THERE WERE MOMENTS OF FUN.
YES.
GOOD-BYE, DIANA.
AND SELINA. THANK YOU AGAIN.
FOR SAVING US YEARS.
PERHAPS MORE.
YOU ARE A CRIMINAL, YES?
OR THIS IS WHAT EVERYONE SAYS.
YOU STEAL THINGS.
I...
BUT, I THINK MAYBE EVERYONE IS WRONG.
I THINK MAYBE YOU ARE A *HERO.*
AND I AM HAPPY MY FRIEND HAS FOUND HIS LOVE IN YOU.

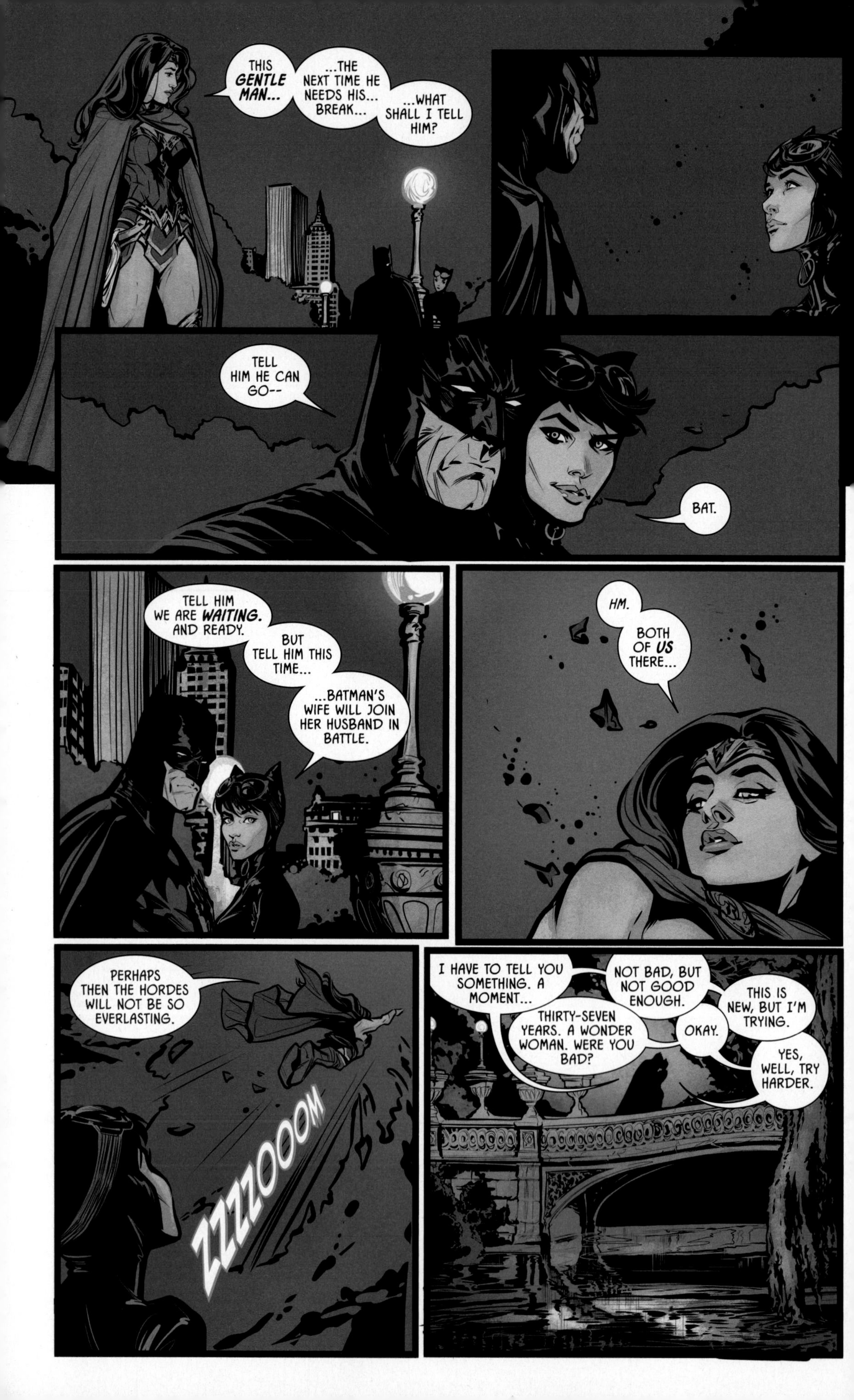
THIS GENTLE MAN...
...THE NEXT TIME HE NEEDS HIS... BREAK...
...WHAT SHALL I TELL HIM?
TELL HIM HE CAN GO--
BAT.
TELL HIM WE ARE WAITING. AND READY.
BUT TELL HIM THIS TIME...
...BATMAN'S WIFE WILL JOIN HER HUSBAND IN BATTLE.
HM.
BOTH OF US THERE...
PERHAPS THEN THE HORDES WILL NOT BE SO EVERLASTING.
ZZZZOOOM
I HAVE TO TELL YOU SOMETHING. A MOMENT...
NOT BAD, BUT NOT GOOD ENOUGH.
THIRTY-SEVEN YEARS. A WONDER WOMAN. WERE YOU BAD?
OKAY.
THIS IS NEW, BUT I'M TRYING.
YES, WELL, TRY HARDER.

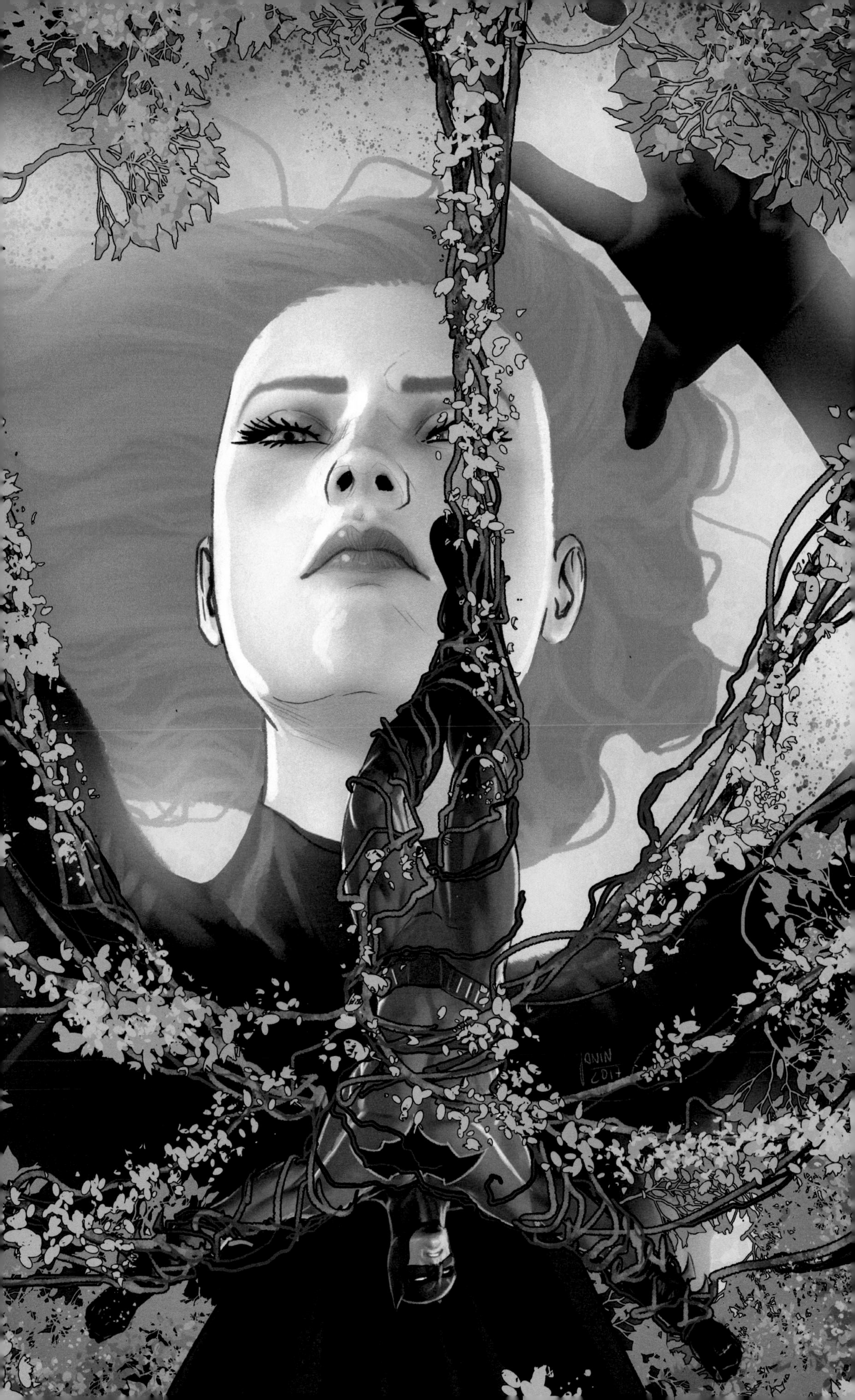
JANIN
2017

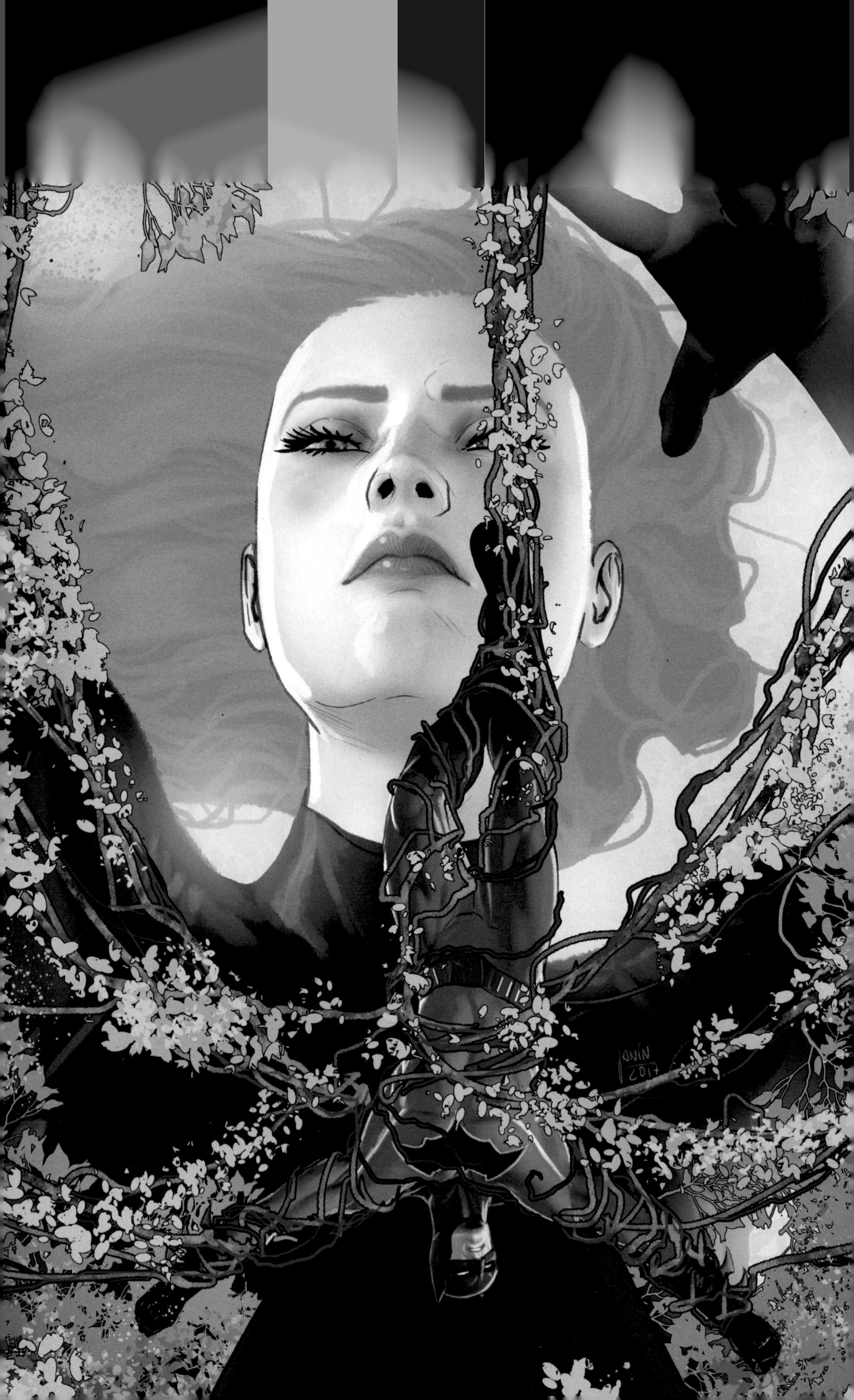
JANÍN
2017

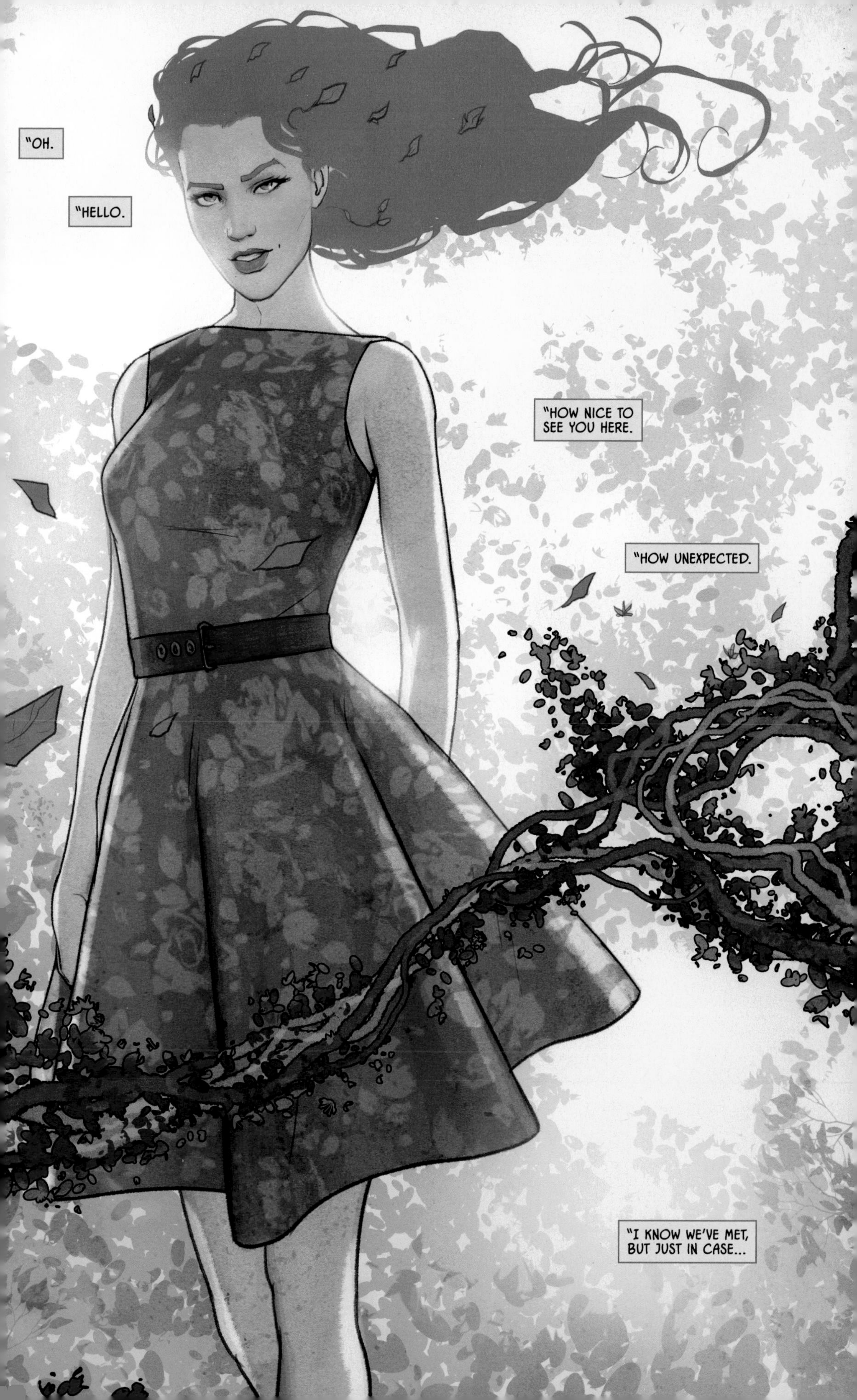
"OH.
"HELLO.
"HOW NICE TO SEE YOU HERE.
"HOW UNEXPECTED.
"I KNOW WE'VE MET, BUT JUST IN CASE...

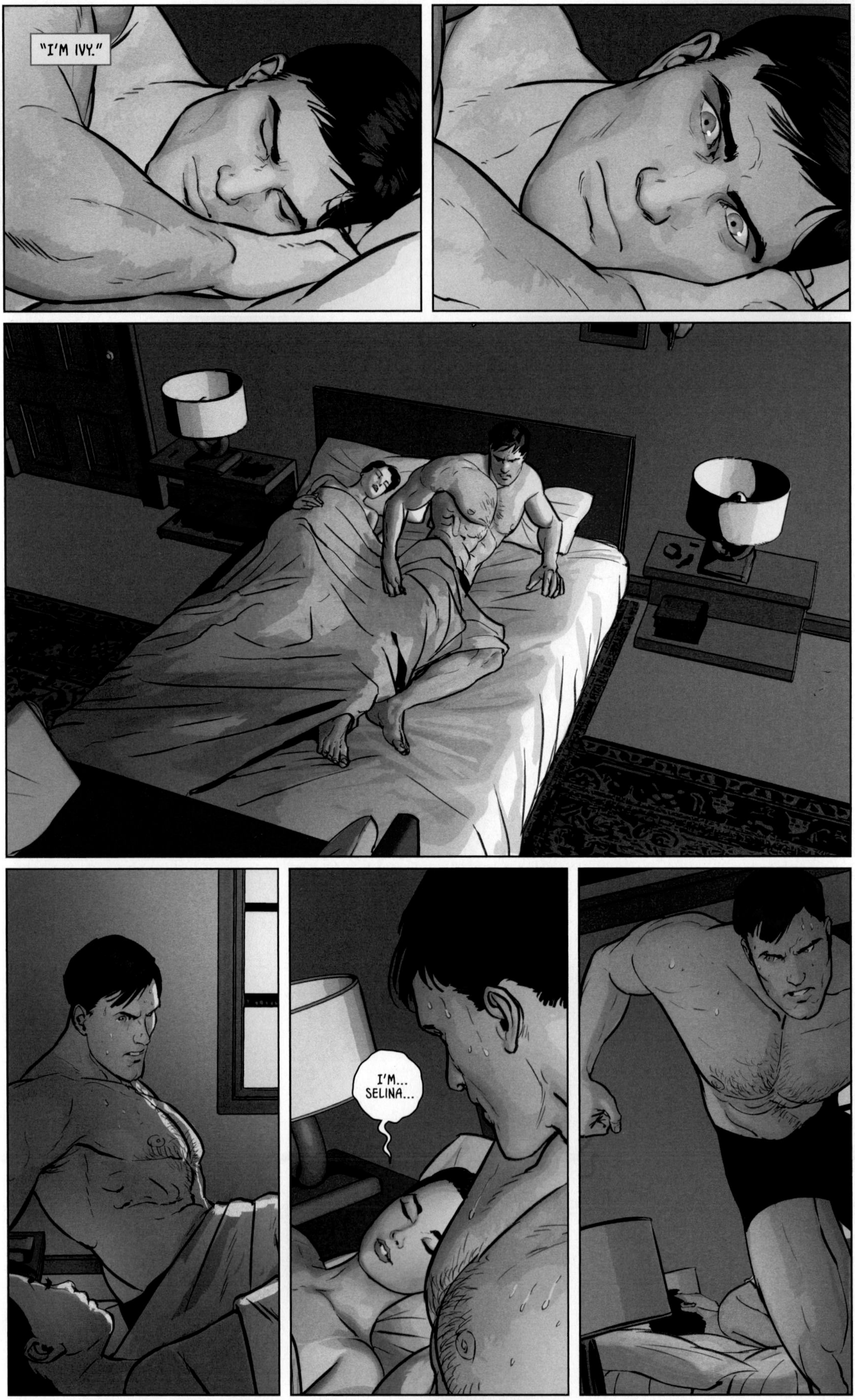
"I'M IVY."
I'M... SELINA...

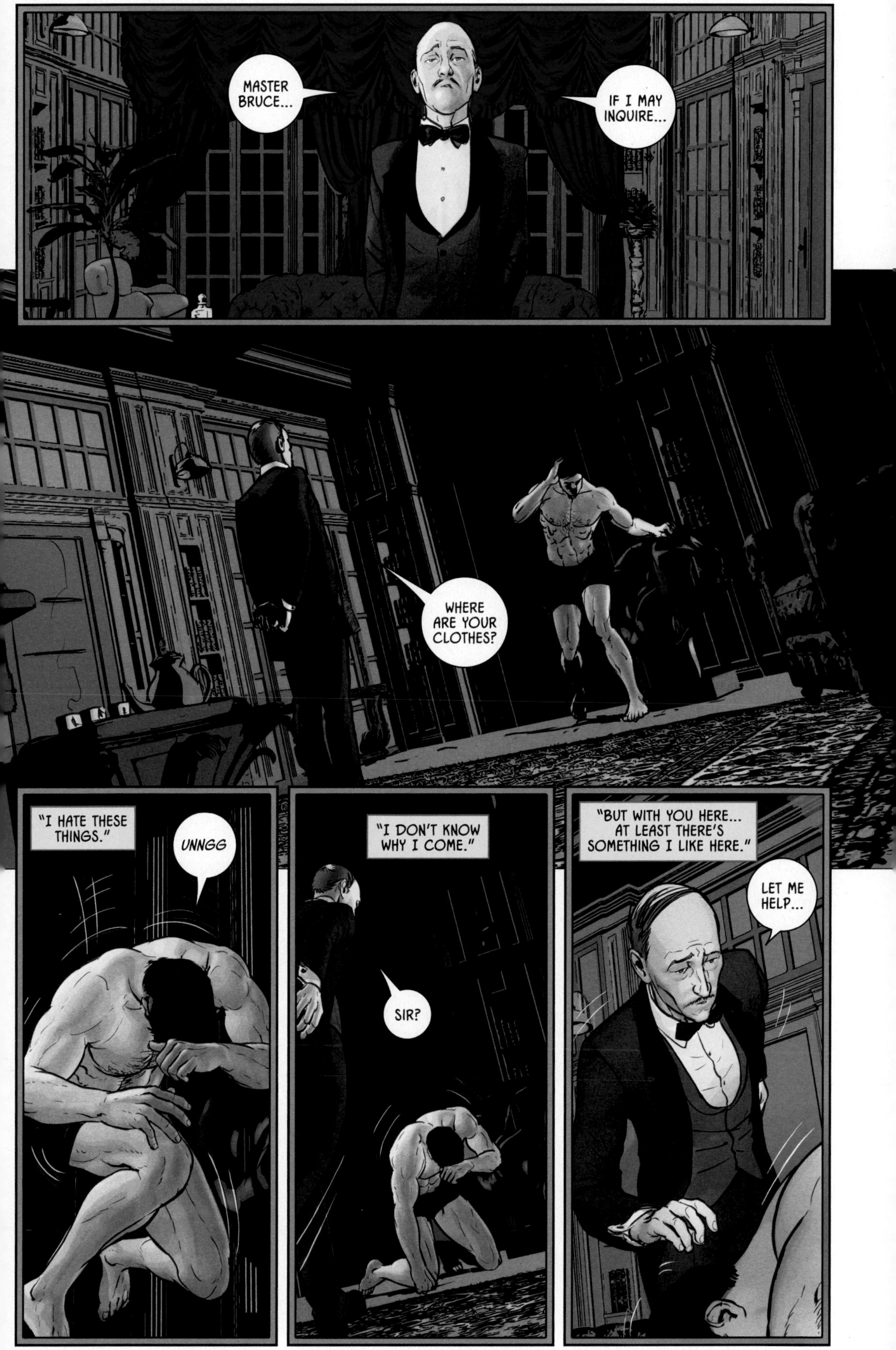
MASTER BRUCE...
IF I MAY INQUIRE...
WHERE ARE YOUR CLOTHES?
"I HATE THESE THINGS."
UNNGG
"I DON'T KNOW WHY I COME."
SIR?
"BUT WITH YOU HERE... AT LEAST THERE'S SOMETHING I LIKE HERE."
LET ME HELP...

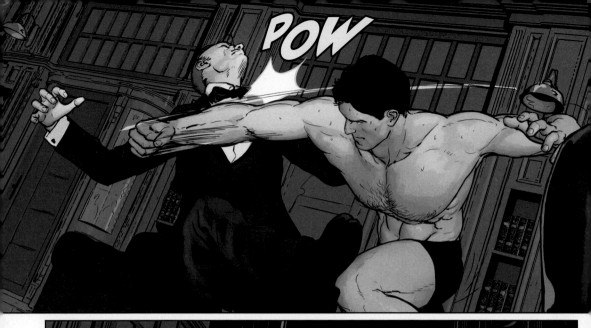

POW

"I SHOULDN'T SAY THIS, BUT YOU LOOK VERY HANDSOME TONIGHT.

"I CAN'T BELIEVE--I SAY I SHOULDN'T SAY THINGS, AND THEN I SAY THEM.

"THAT'S JUST SO ME.

"*AH, WHAT THE HELL, ANYWAY. IT DOESN'T CHANGE ANYTHING.

"I'M ALWAYS ME.

"AND YOU'RE ALWAYS HANDSOME."

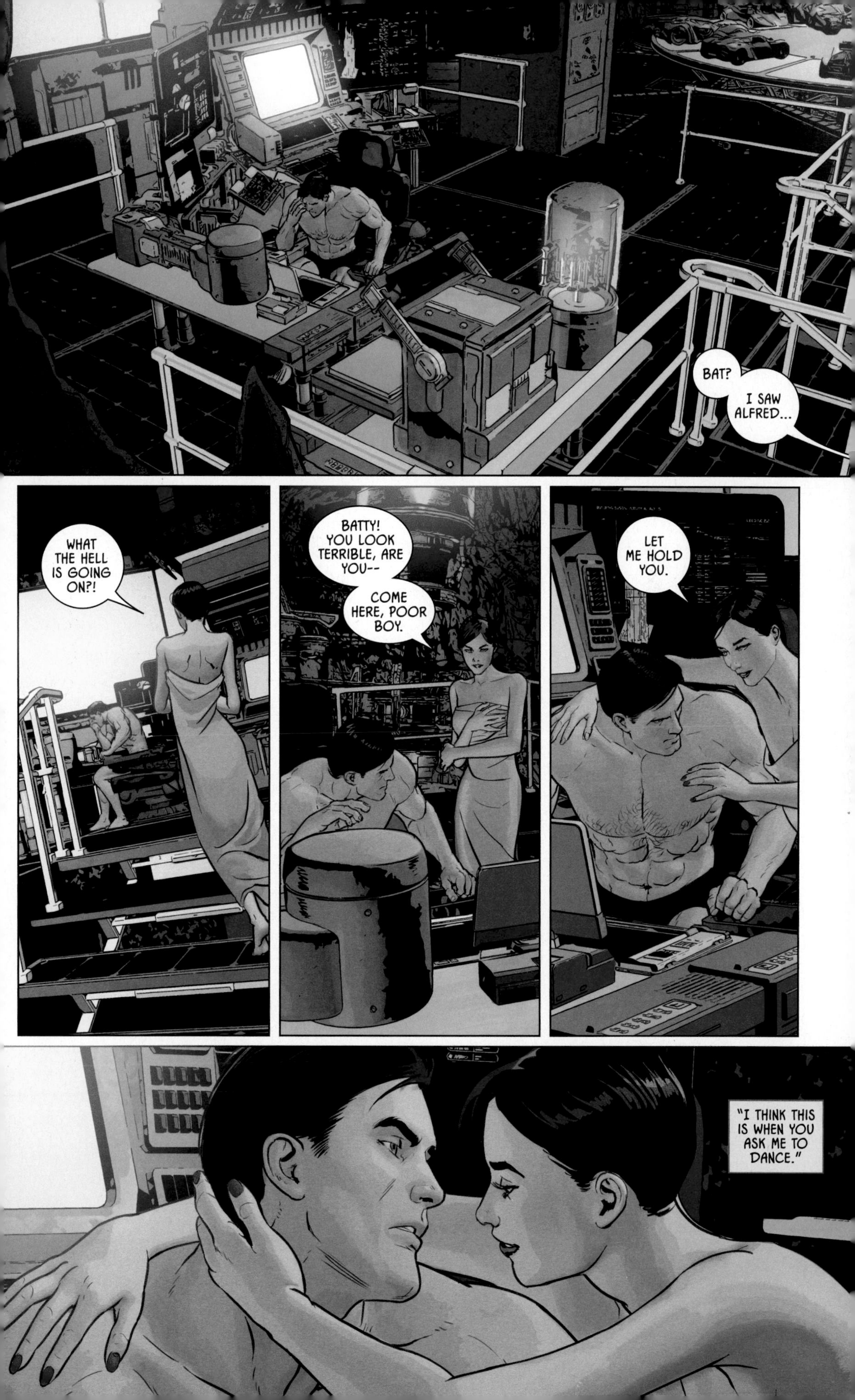
BAT?
I SAW ALFRED...
WHAT THE HELL IS GOING ON?!
BATTY! YOU LOOK TERRIBLE, ARE YOU--
COME HERE, POOR BOY.
LET ME HOLD YOU.
"I THINK THIS IS WHEN YOU ASK ME TO DANCE."

"I LIKE HOW YOU FEEL. I LIKE HOW WE FIT TOGETHER.

"DON'T YOU THINK IT'S NICE?

"HOW WE FIT?

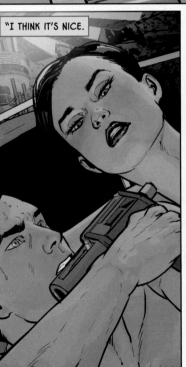

"I THINK IT'S NICE.

"IT'S ALL I THINK ABOUT SOMETIMES."

"I...I'M GOING TO DO IT AGAIN.

"I'M GOING TO SAY WHAT I SHOULDN'T SAY.

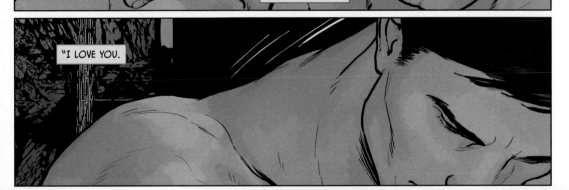

"BUT I...

"I HAVE TO SAY IT.

"I LOVE YOU.

"I LOVE YOU SO MUCH."

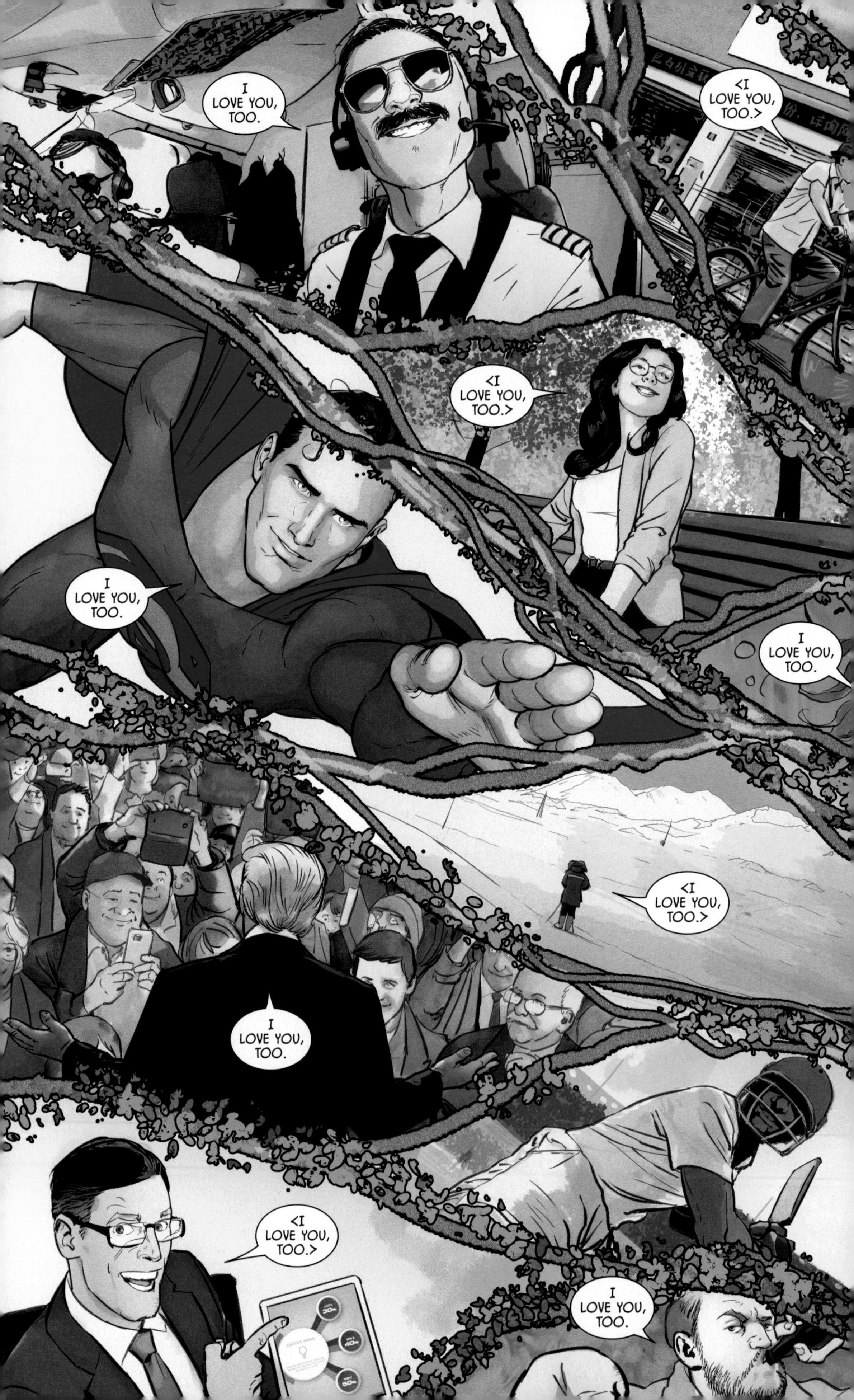
I LOVE YOU, TOO.
<I LOVE YOU, TOO.>
<I LOVE YOU, TOO.>
I LOVE YOU, TOO.
I LOVE YOU, TOO.
<I LOVE YOU, TOO.>
I LOVE YOU, TOO.
<I LOVE YOU, TOO.>
I LOVE YOU, TOO.

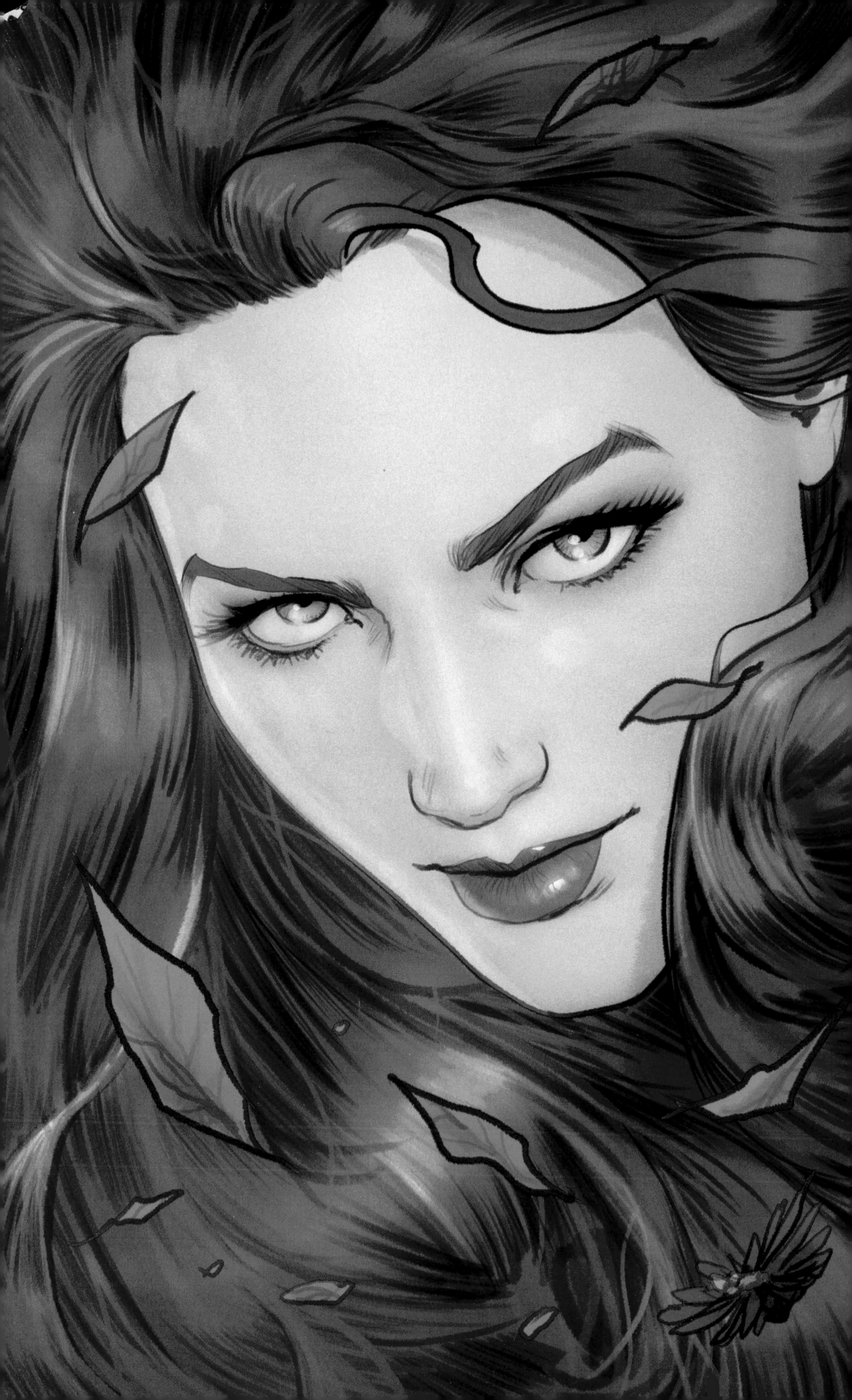

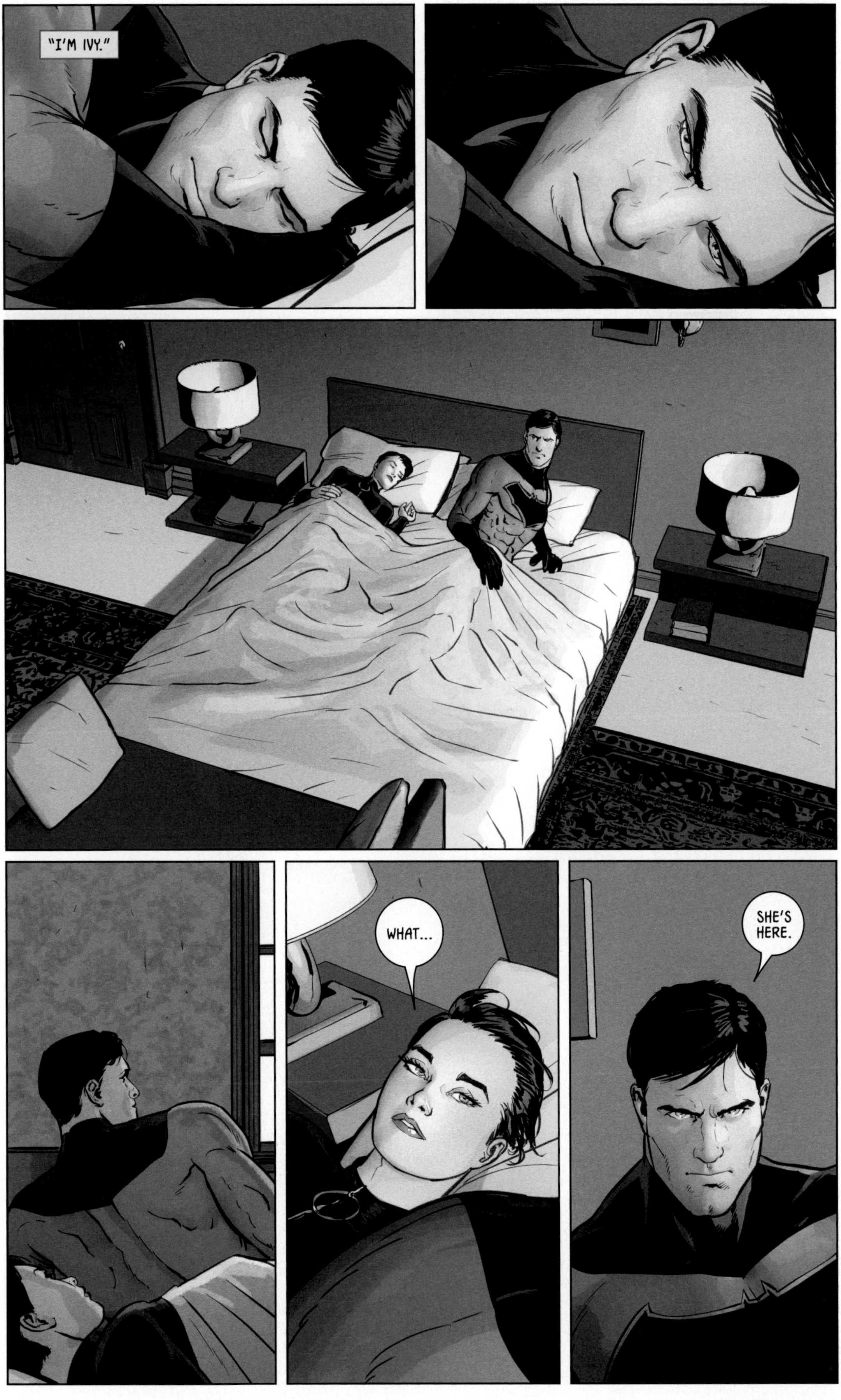
"I'M IVY."
WHAT...
SHE'S HERE.

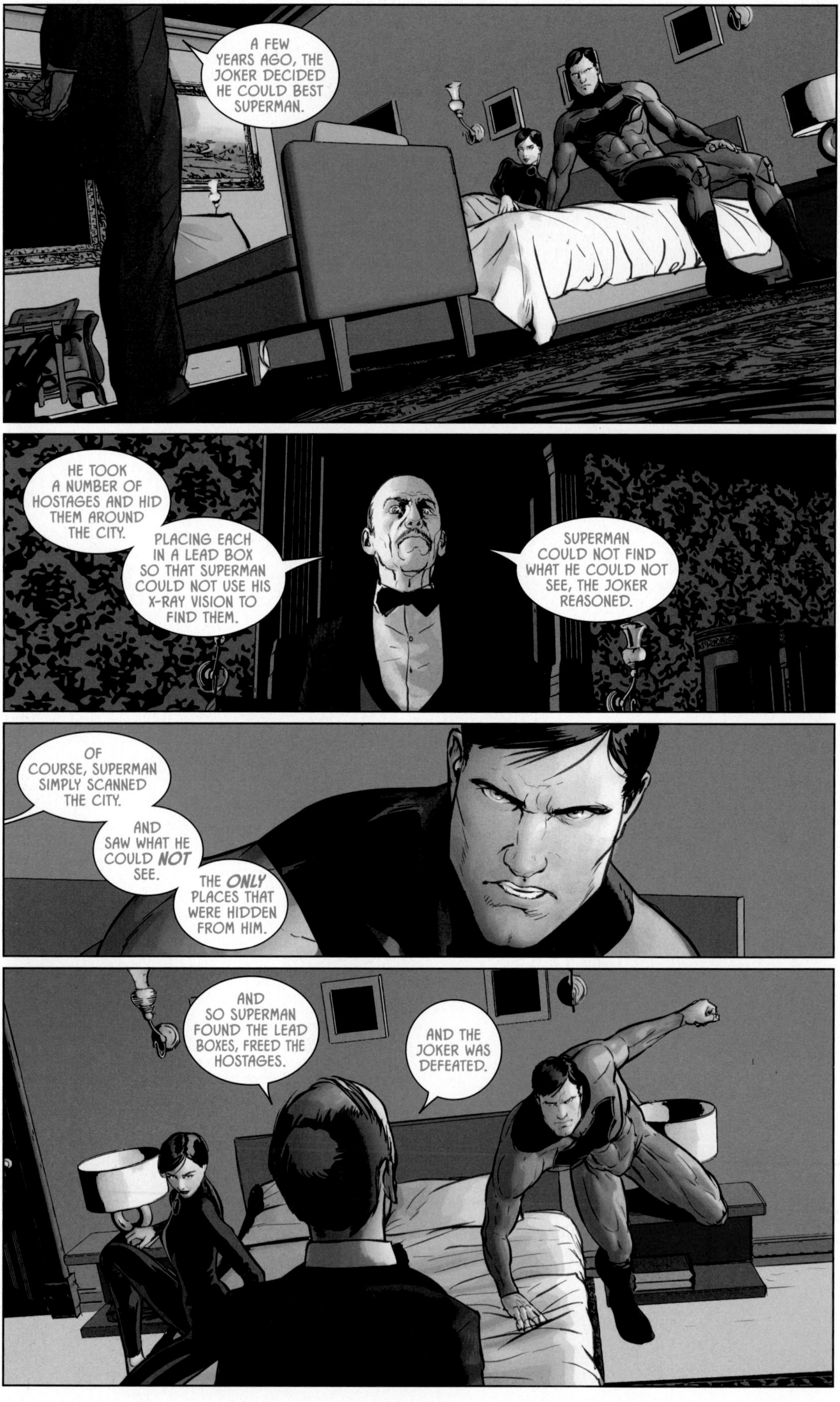
A FEW YEARS AGO, THE JOKER DECIDED HE COULD BEST SUPERMAN.
HE TOOK A NUMBER OF HOSTAGES AND HID THEM AROUND THE CITY.
PLACING EACH IN A LEAD BOX SO THAT SUPERMAN COULD NOT USE HIS X-RAY VISION TO FIND THEM.
SUPERMAN COULD NOT FIND WHAT HE COULD NOT SEE, THE JOKER REASONED.
OF COURSE, SUPERMAN SIMPLY SCANNED THE CITY.
AND SAW WHAT HE COULD *NOT* SEE.
THE *ONLY* PLACES THAT WERE HIDDEN FROM HIM.
AND SO SUPERMAN FOUND THE LEAD BOXES, FREED THE HOSTAGES.
AND THE JOKER WAS DEFEATED.

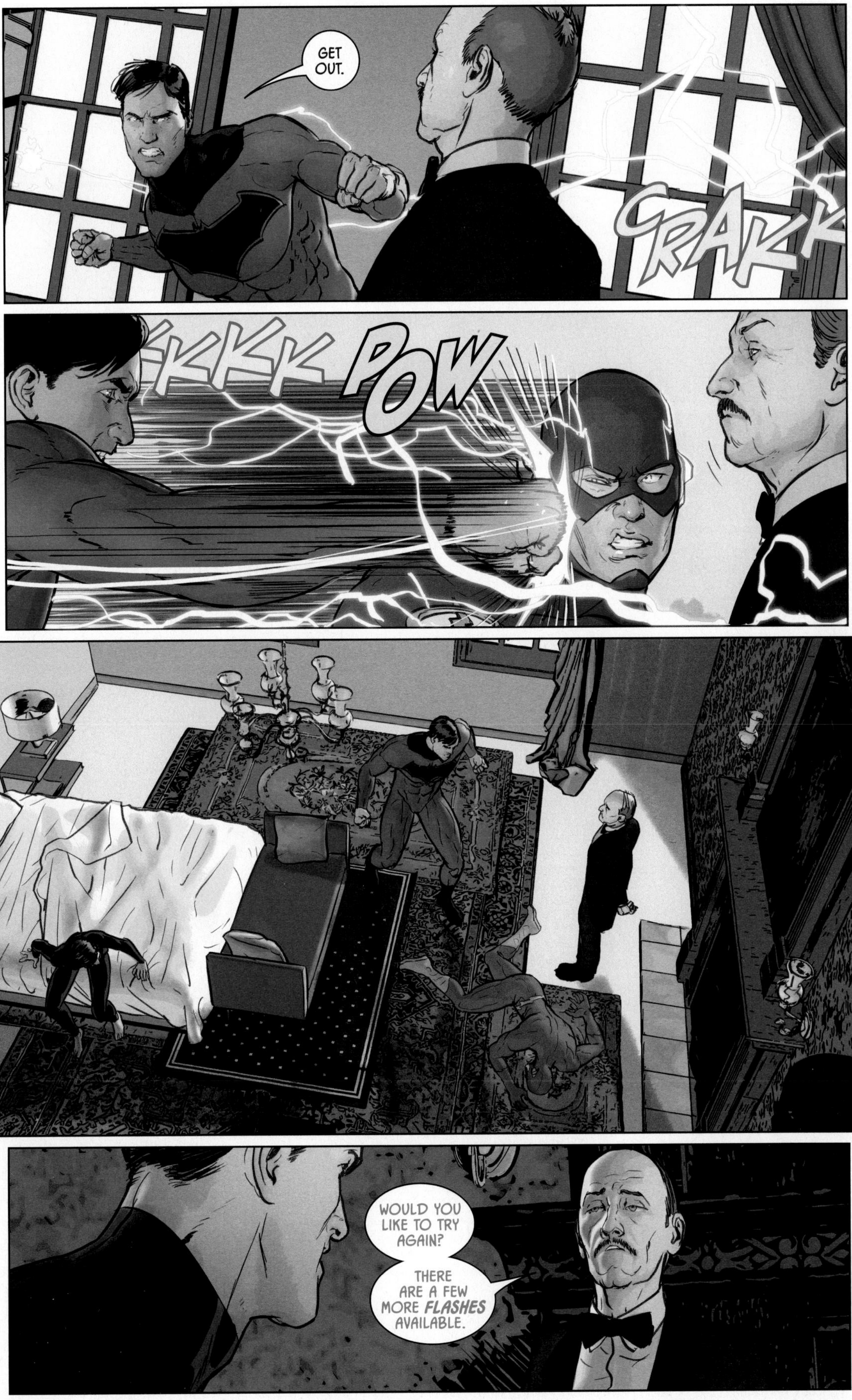
GET OUT.
CRAKK
KKKK POW
WOULD YOU LIKE TO TRY AGAIN?
THERE ARE A FEW MORE FLASHES AVAILABLE.

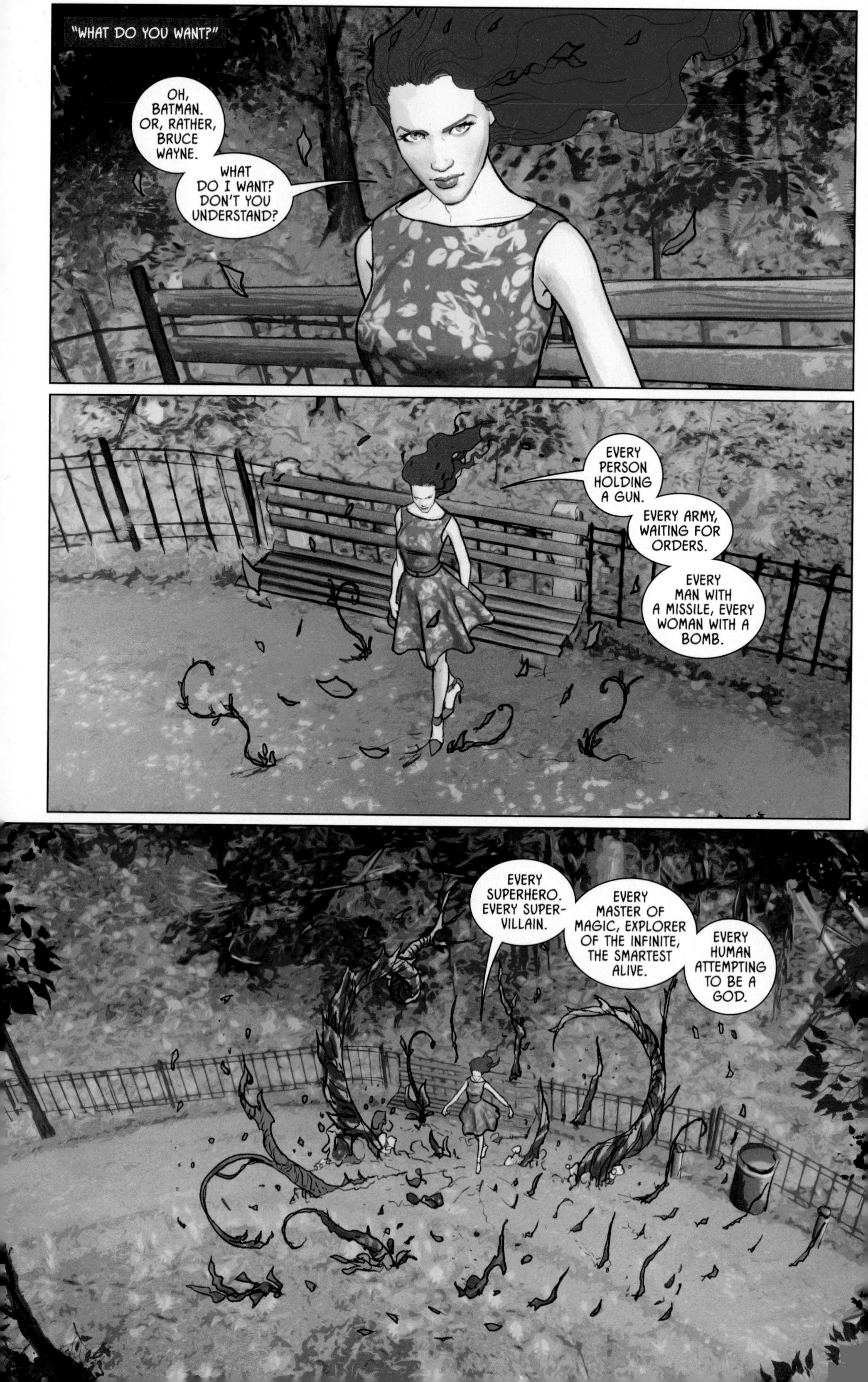
"WHAT DO YOU WANT?"
OH, BATMAN. OR, RATHER, BRUCE WAYNE.
WHAT DO I WANT? DON'T YOU UNDERSTAND?
EVERY PERSON HOLDING A GUN.
EVERY ARMY, WAITING FOR ORDERS.
EVERY MAN WITH A MISSILE, EVERY WOMAN WITH A BOMB.
EVERY SUPERHERO. EVERY SUPER-VILLAIN.
EVERY MASTER OF MAGIC, EXPLORER OF THE INFINITE, THE SMARTEST ALIVE.
EVERY HUMAN ATTEMPTING TO BE A GOD.

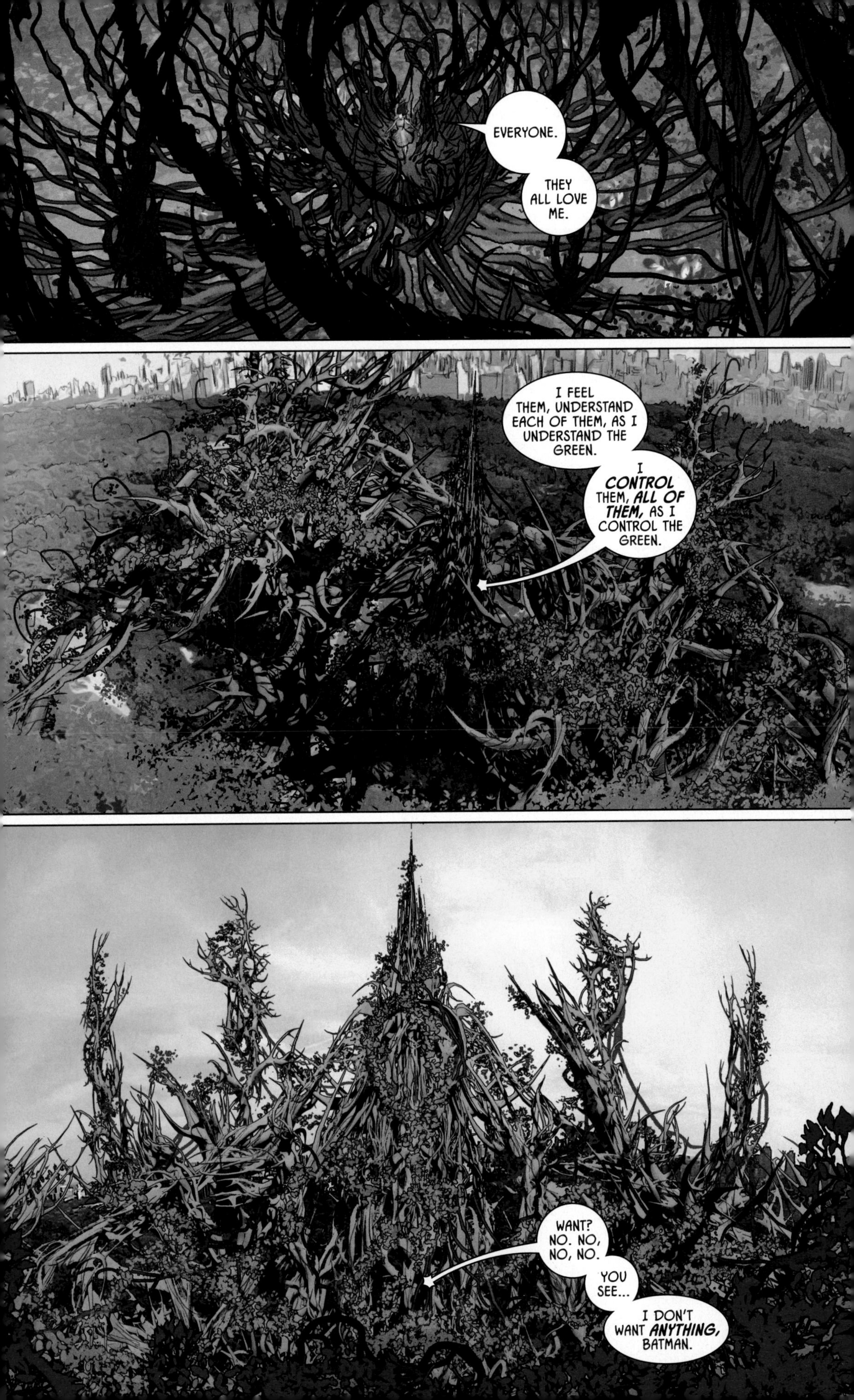
EVERYONE.
THEY ALL LOVE ME.
I FEEL THEM, UNDERSTAND EACH OF THEM, AS I UNDERSTAND THE GREEN.
I **CONTROL** THEM, **ALL OF THEM,** AS I CONTROL THE GREEN.
WANT? NO. NO, NO, NO.
YOU SEE...
I DON'T WANT **ANYTHING,** BATMAN.

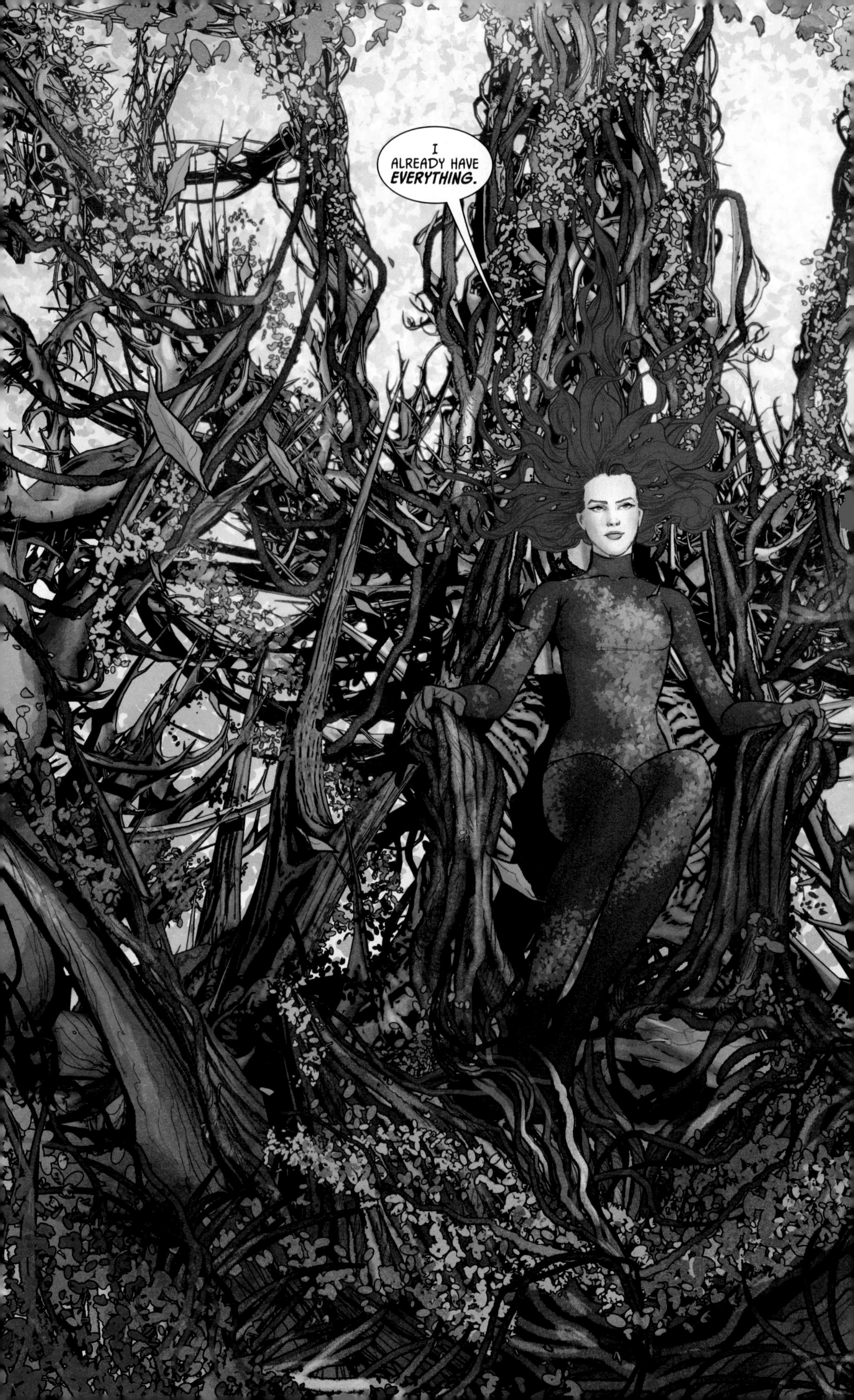
I ALREADY HAVE EVERYTHING.

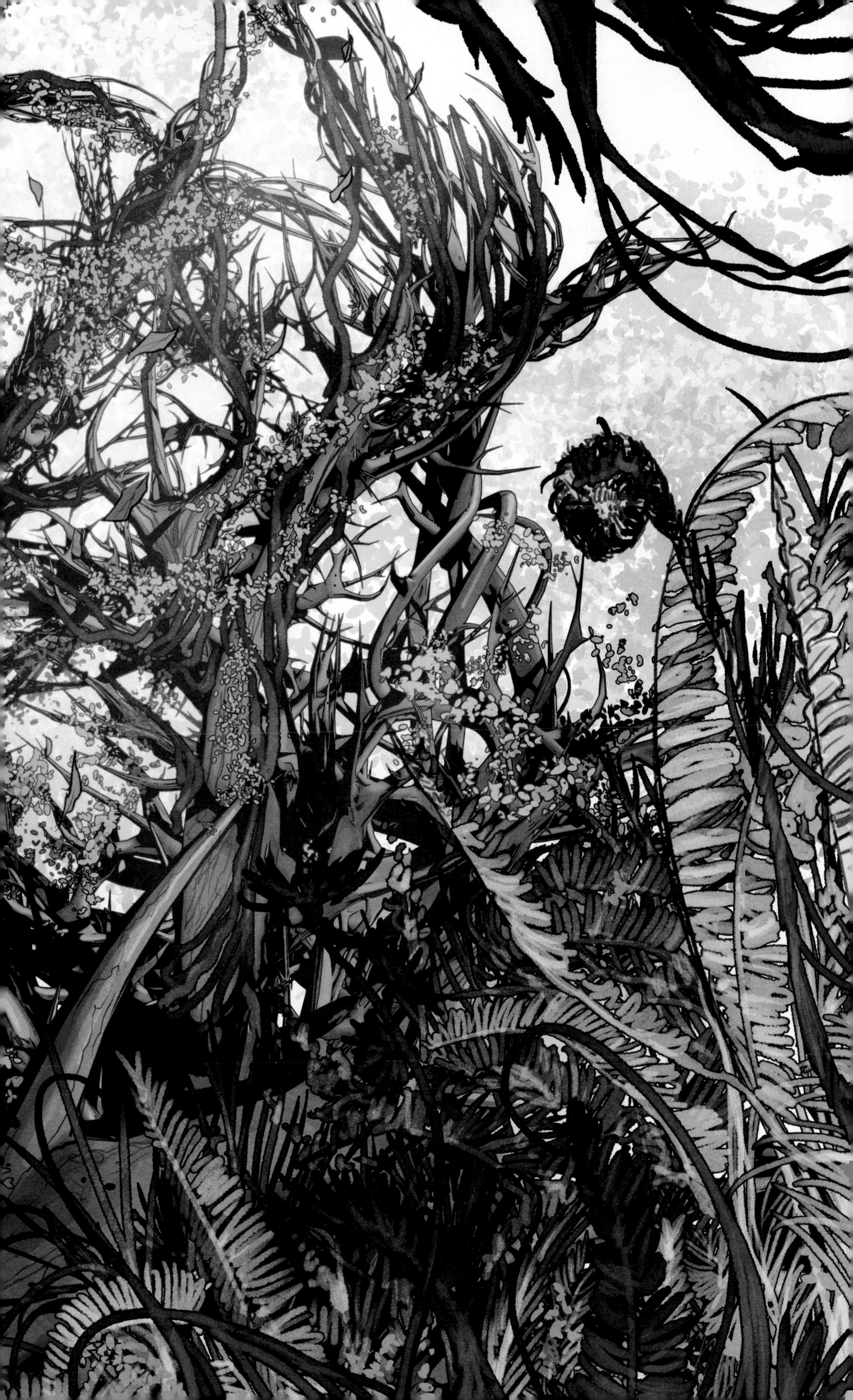

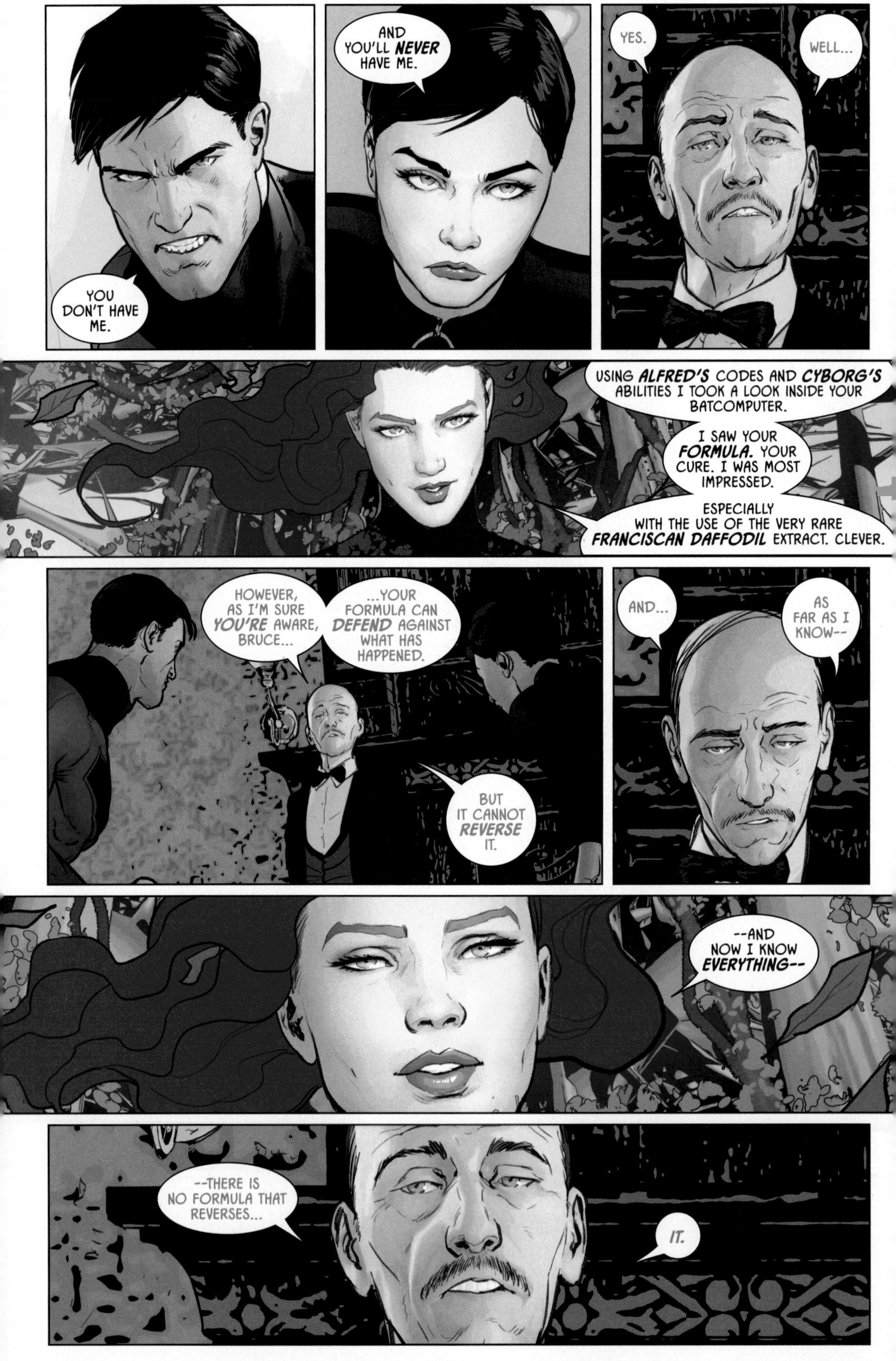
YOU DON'T HAVE ME.
AND YOU'LL NEVER HAVE ME.
YES.
WELL...
USING ALFRED'S CODES AND CYBORG'S ABILITIES I TOOK A LOOK INSIDE YOUR BATCOMPUTER.
I SAW YOUR FORMULA. YOUR CURE. I WAS MOST IMPRESSED.
ESPECIALLY WITH THE USE OF THE VERY RARE FRANCISCAN DAFFODIL EXTRACT. CLEVER.
HOWEVER, AS I'M SURE YOU'RE AWARE, BRUCE...
...YOUR FORMULA CAN DEFEND AGAINST WHAT HAS HAPPENED.
BUT IT CANNOT REVERSE IT.
AND...
AS FAR AS I KNOW--
--AND NOW I KNOW EVERYTHING--
--THERE IS NO FORMULA THAT REVERSES...
IT.

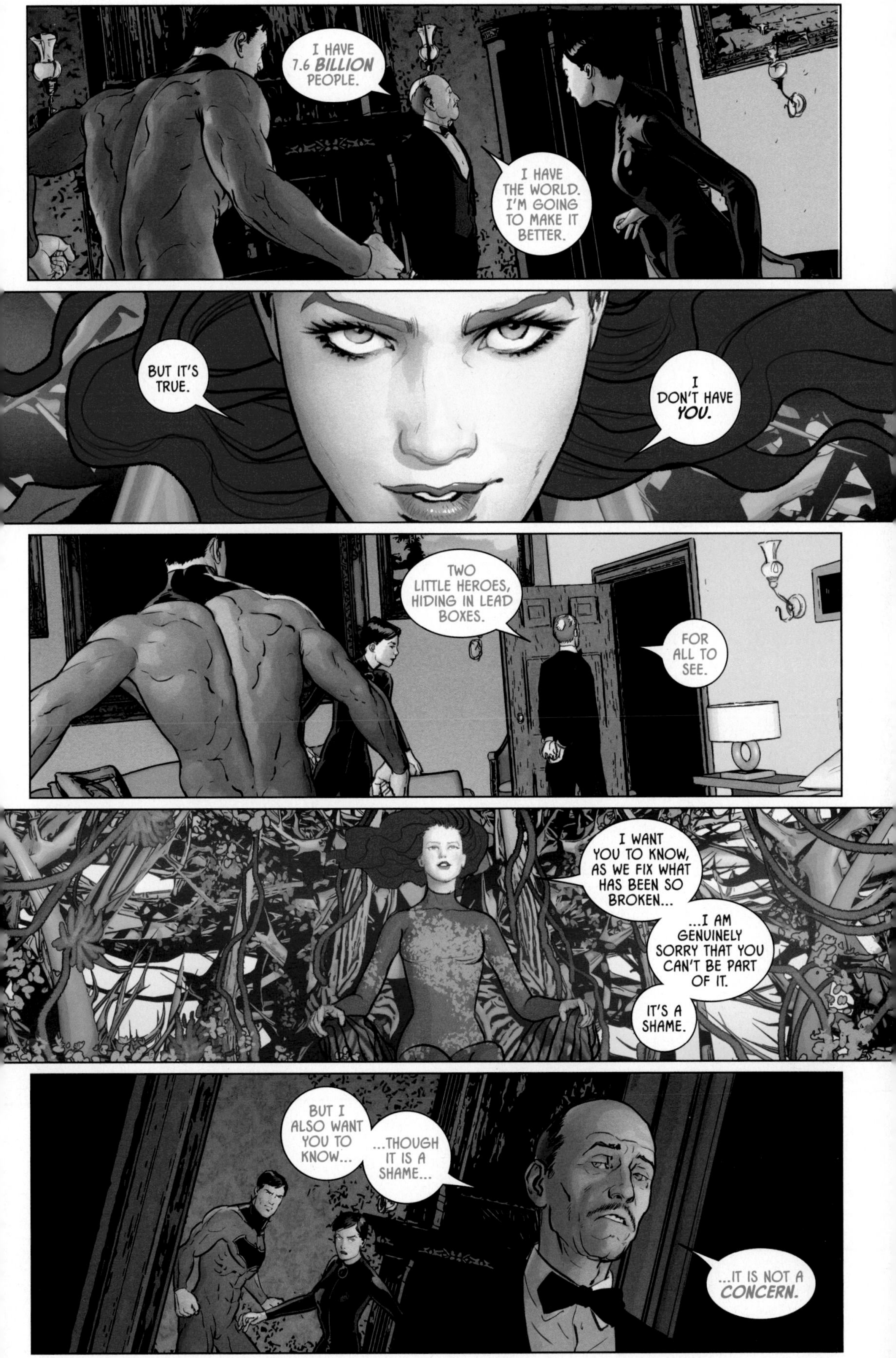
I HAVE 7.6 BILLION PEOPLE.
I HAVE THE WORLD. I'M GOING TO MAKE IT BETTER.
BUT IT'S TRUE.
I DON'T HAVE YOU.
TWO LITTLE HEROES, HIDING IN LEAD BOXES.
FOR ALL TO SEE.
I WANT YOU TO KNOW, AS WE FIX WHAT HAS BEEN SO BROKEN...
...I AM GENUINELY SORRY THAT YOU CAN'T BE PART OF IT.
IT'S A SHAME.
BUT I ALSO WANT YOU TO KNOW...
...THOUGH IT IS A SHAME...
...IT IS NOT A CONCERN.

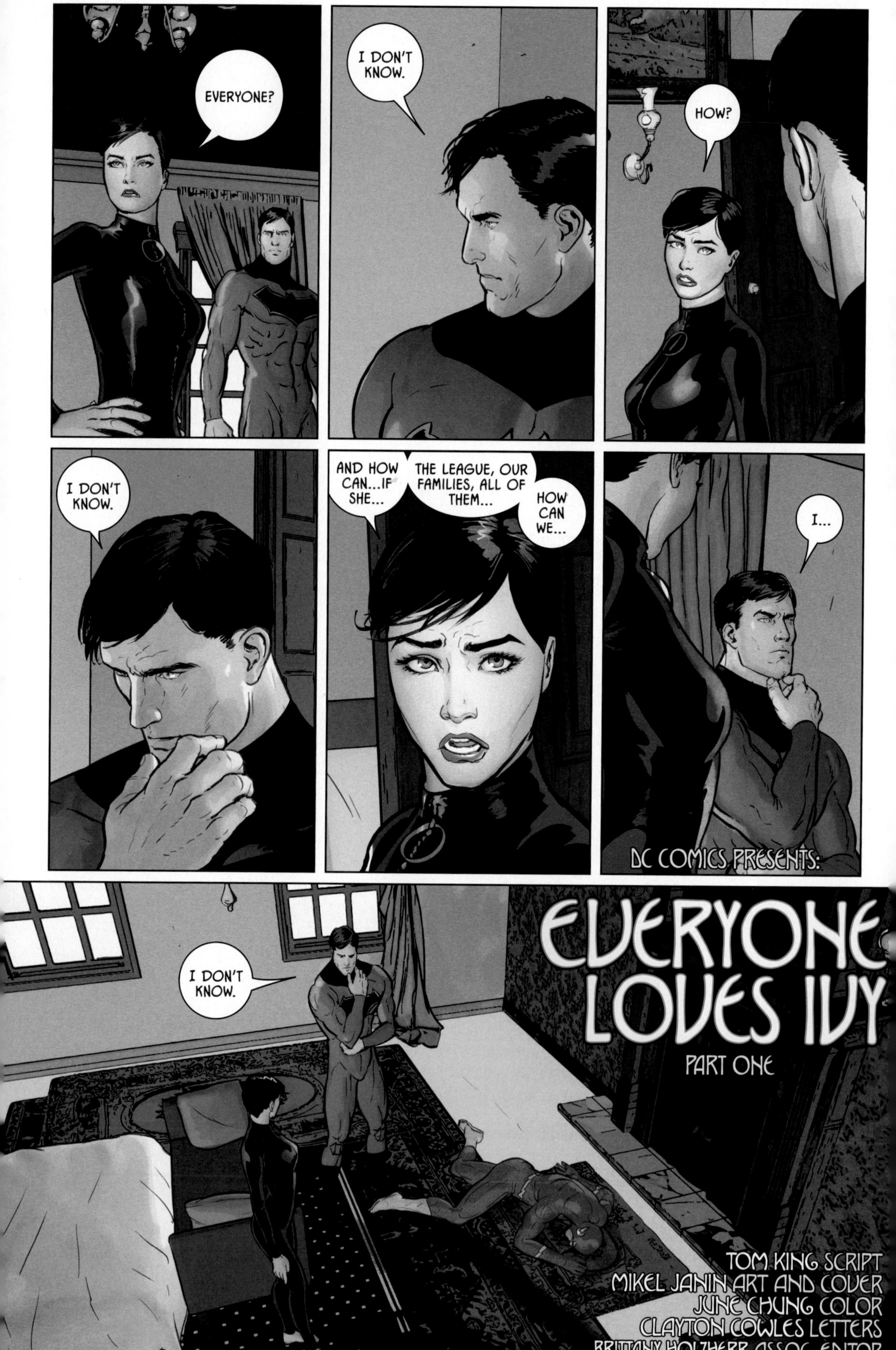
EVERYONE?
I DON'T KNOW.
HOW?
I DON'T KNOW.
AND HOW CAN...IF SHE...
THE LEAGUE, OUR FAMILIES, ALL OF THEM...
HOW CAN WE...
I...
DC COMICS PRESENTS:
I DON'T KNOW.
EVERYONE LOVES IVY
PART ONE
TOM KING SCRIPT
MIKEL JANIN ART AND COVER
JUNE CHUNG COLOR
CLAYTON COWLES LETTERS
BRITTANY HOLZHERR ASSOC. EDITOR
JAMIE S. RICH EDITOR

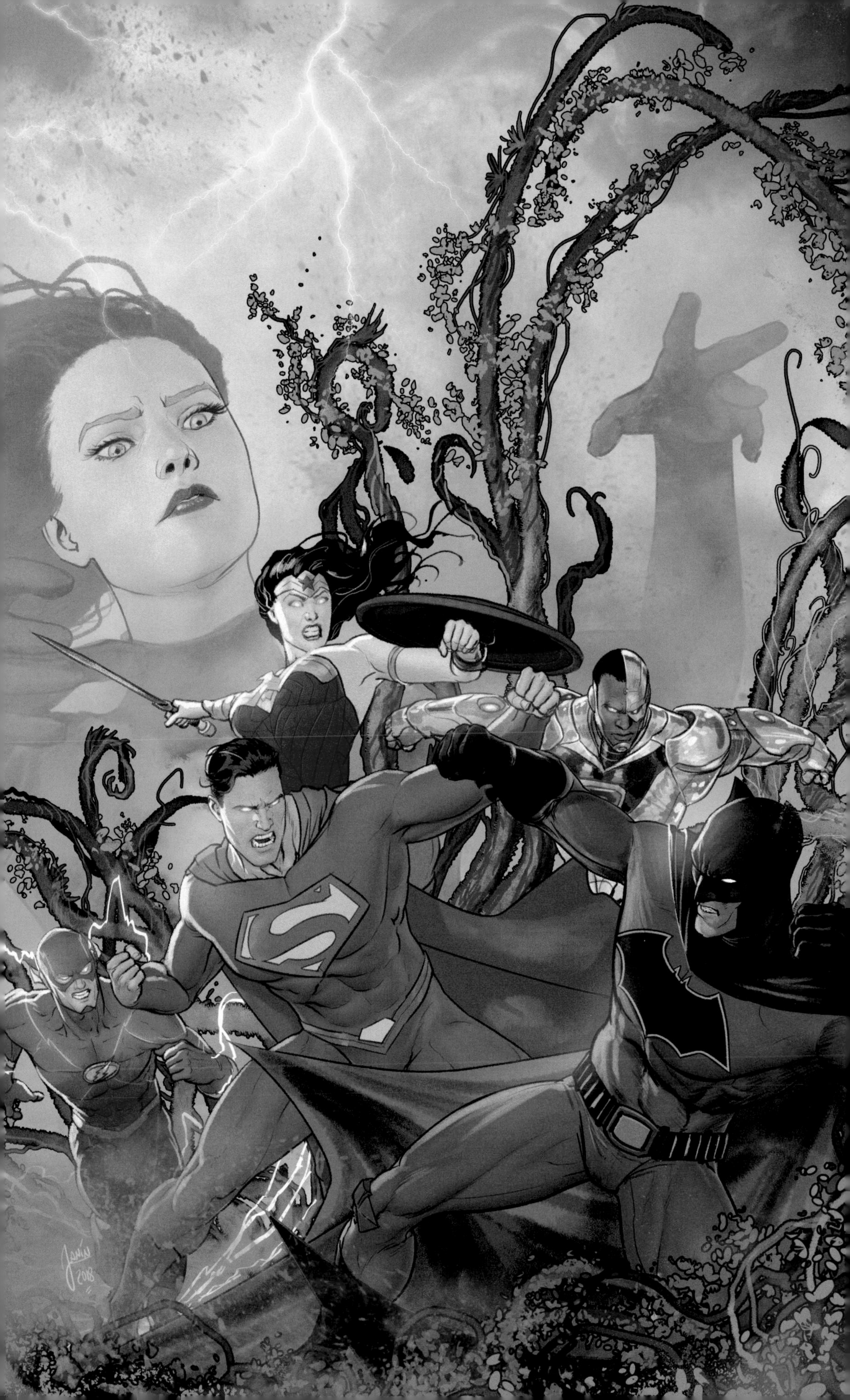

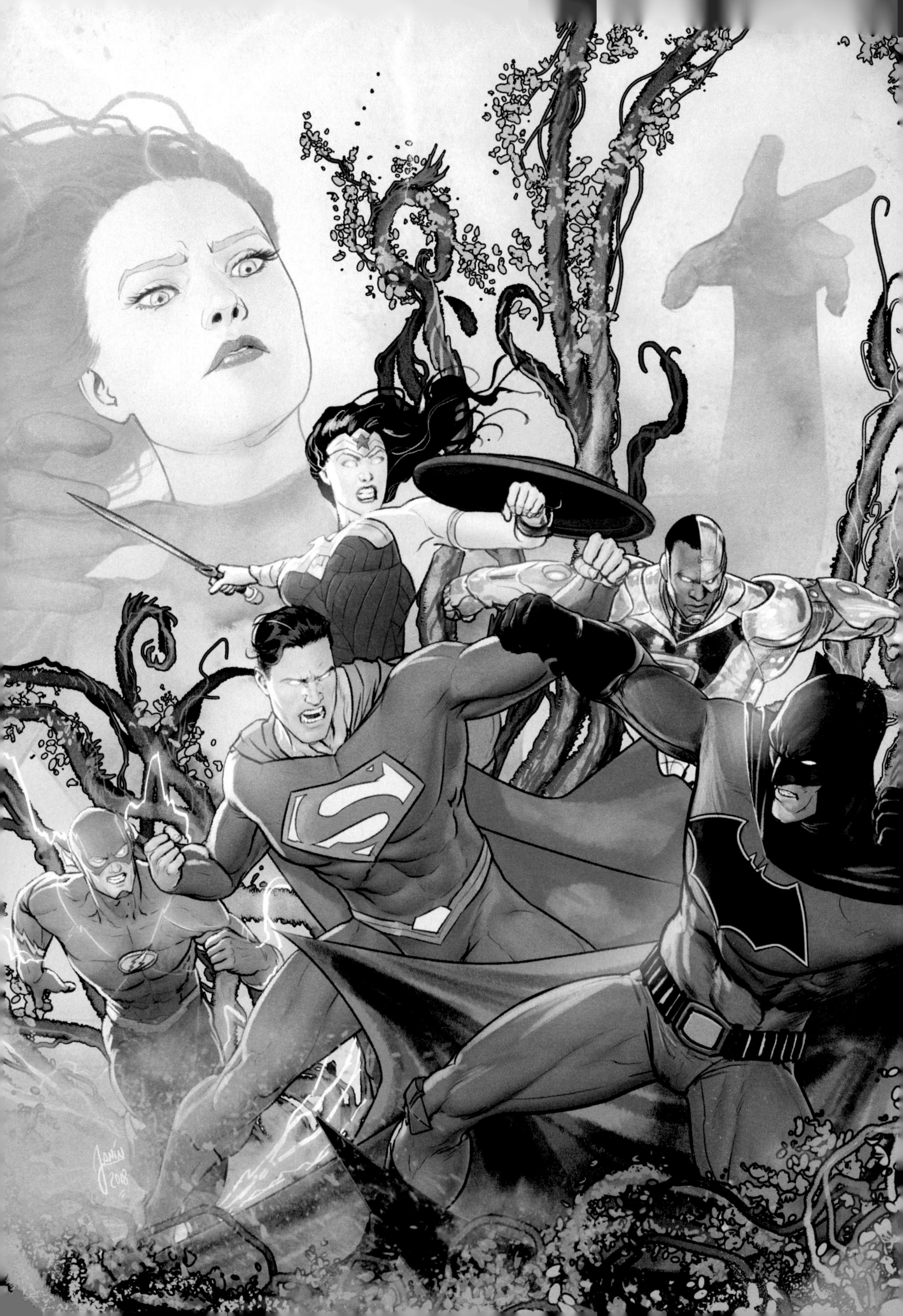
JANIN
2018

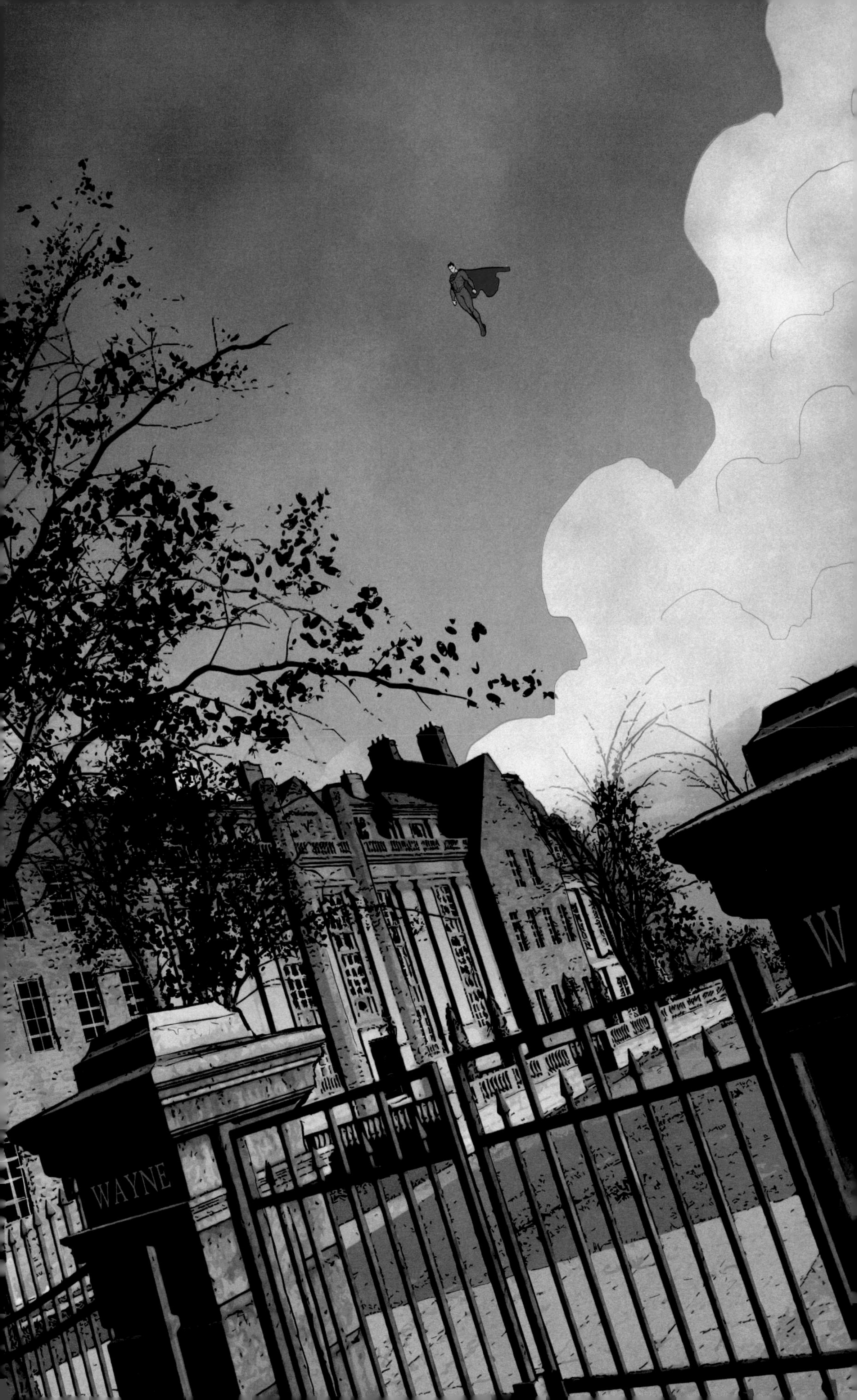
WAYNE

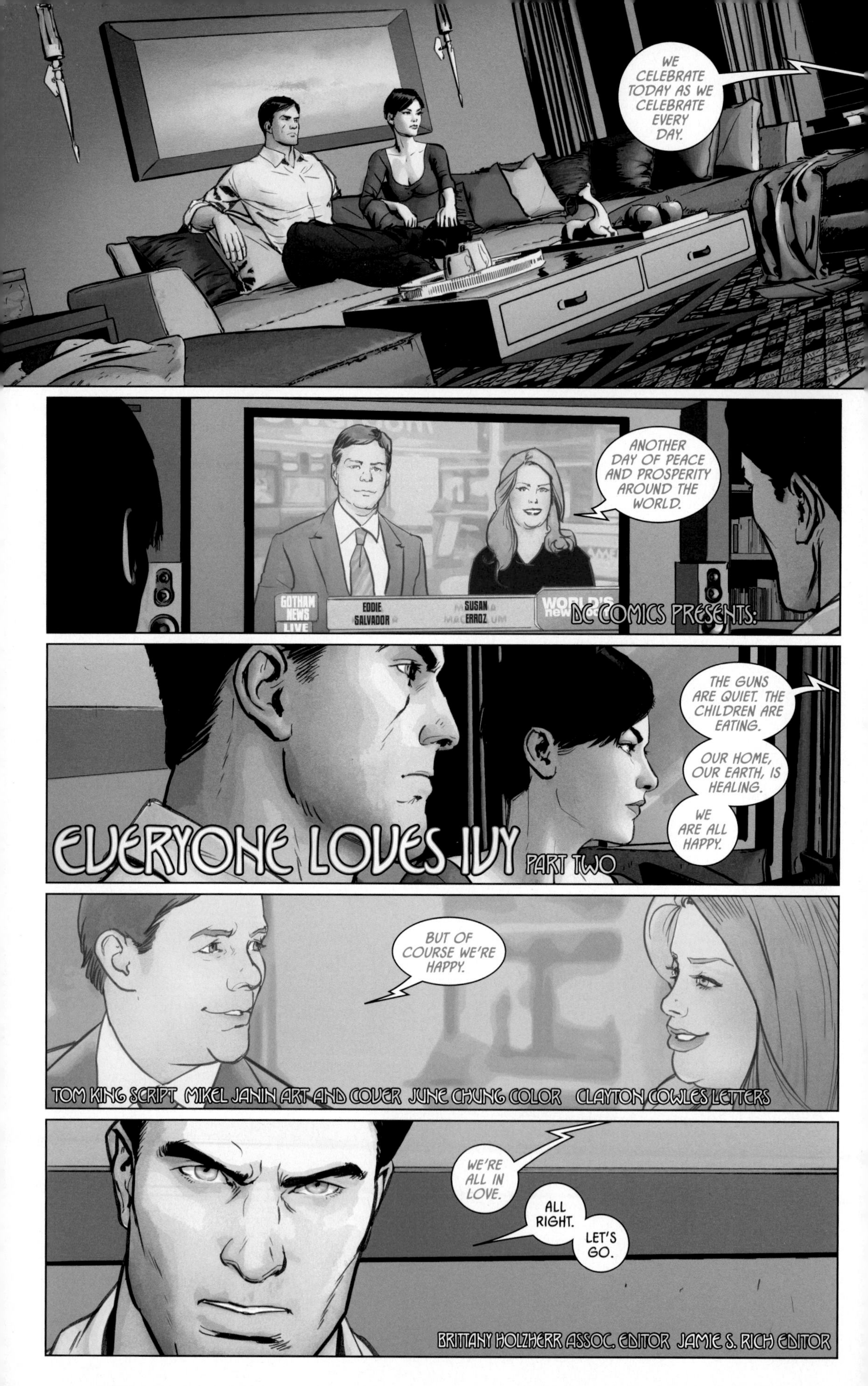
WE CELEBRATE TODAY AS WE CELEBRATE EVERY DAY.
ANOTHER DAY OF PEACE AND PROSPERITY AROUND THE WORLD.
GOTHAM NEWS LIVE
EDDIE SALVADOR
SUSAN ERROZ
DC COMICS PRESENTS:
THE GUNS ARE QUIET. THE CHILDREN ARE EATING.
OUR HOME, OUR EARTH, IS HEALING.
WE ARE ALL HAPPY.
EVERYONE LOVES IVY PART TWO
BUT OF COURSE WE'RE HAPPY.
TOM KING SCRIPT MIKEL JANIN ART AND COVER JUNE CHUNG COLOR CLAYTON COWLES LETTERS
WE'RE ALL IN LOVE.
ALL RIGHT.
LET'S GO.
BRITTANY HOLZHERR ASSOC. EDITOR JAMIE S. RICH EDITOR

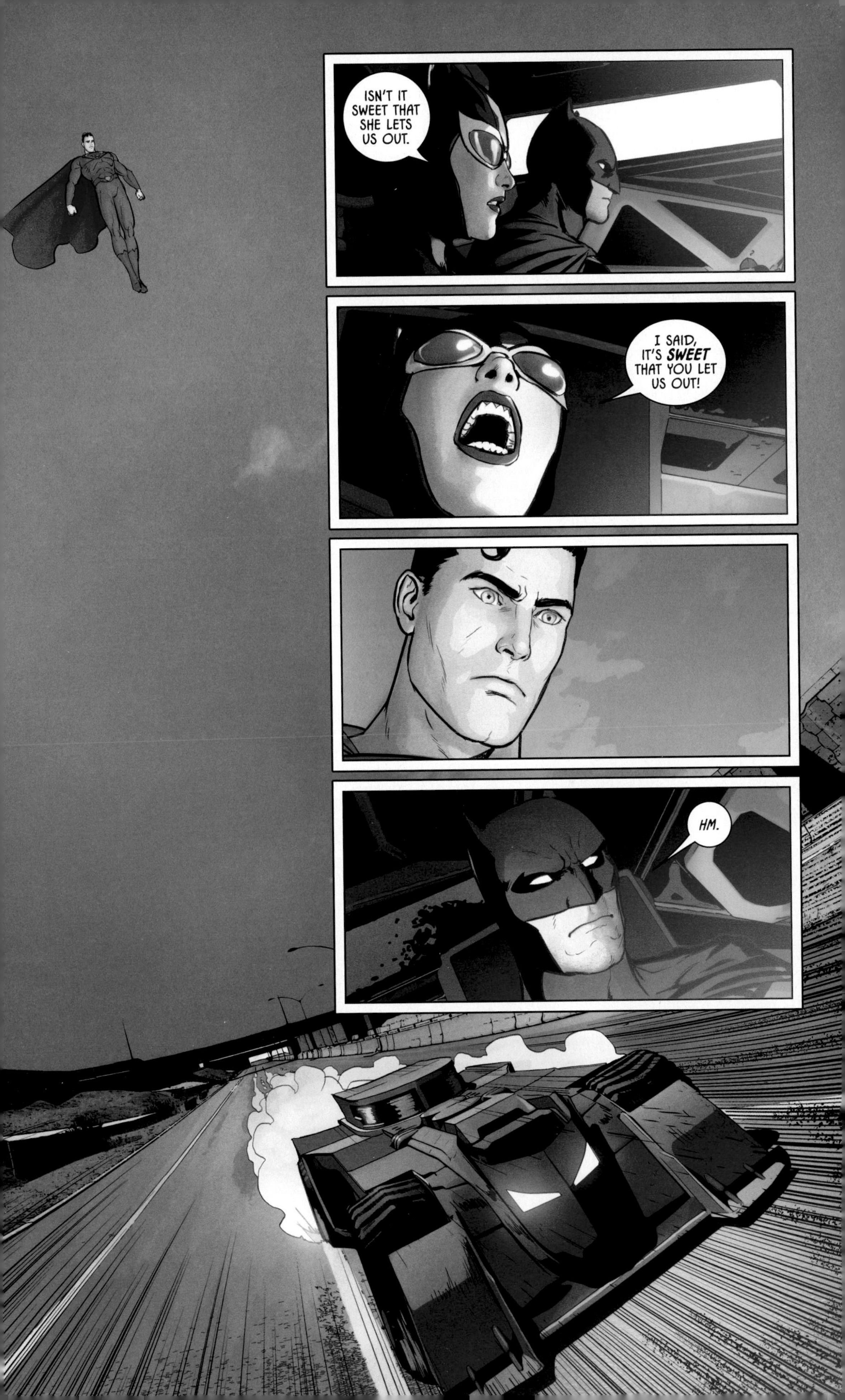
ISN'T IT SWEET THAT SHE LETS US OUT.
I SAID, IT'S **SWEET** THAT YOU LET US OUT!
HM.

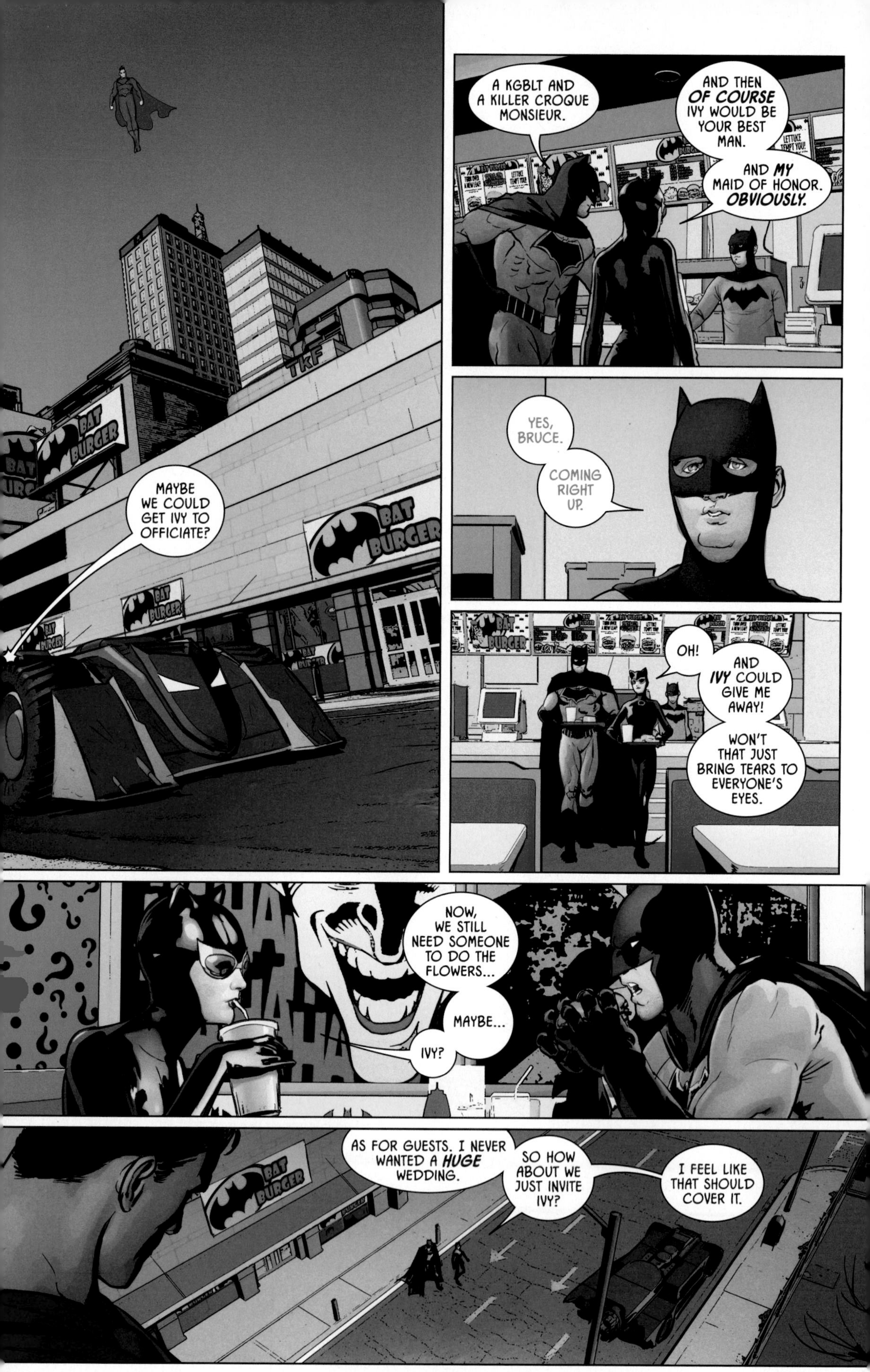
MAYBE WE COULD GET IVY TO OFFICIATE?
A KGBLT AND A KILLER CROQUE MONSIEUR.
AND THEN OF COURSE IVY WOULD BE YOUR BEST MAN.
AND MY MAID OF HONOR. OBVIOUSLY.
YES, BRUCE.
COMING RIGHT UP.
OH!
AND IVY COULD GIVE ME AWAY!
WON'T THAT JUST BRING TEARS TO EVERYONE'S EYES.
NOW, WE STILL NEED SOMEONE TO DO THE FLOWERS...
MAYBE...
IVY?
AS FOR GUESTS. I NEVER WANTED A HUGE WEDDING.
SO HOW ABOUT WE JUST INVITE IVY?
I FEEL LIKE THAT SHOULD COVER IT.

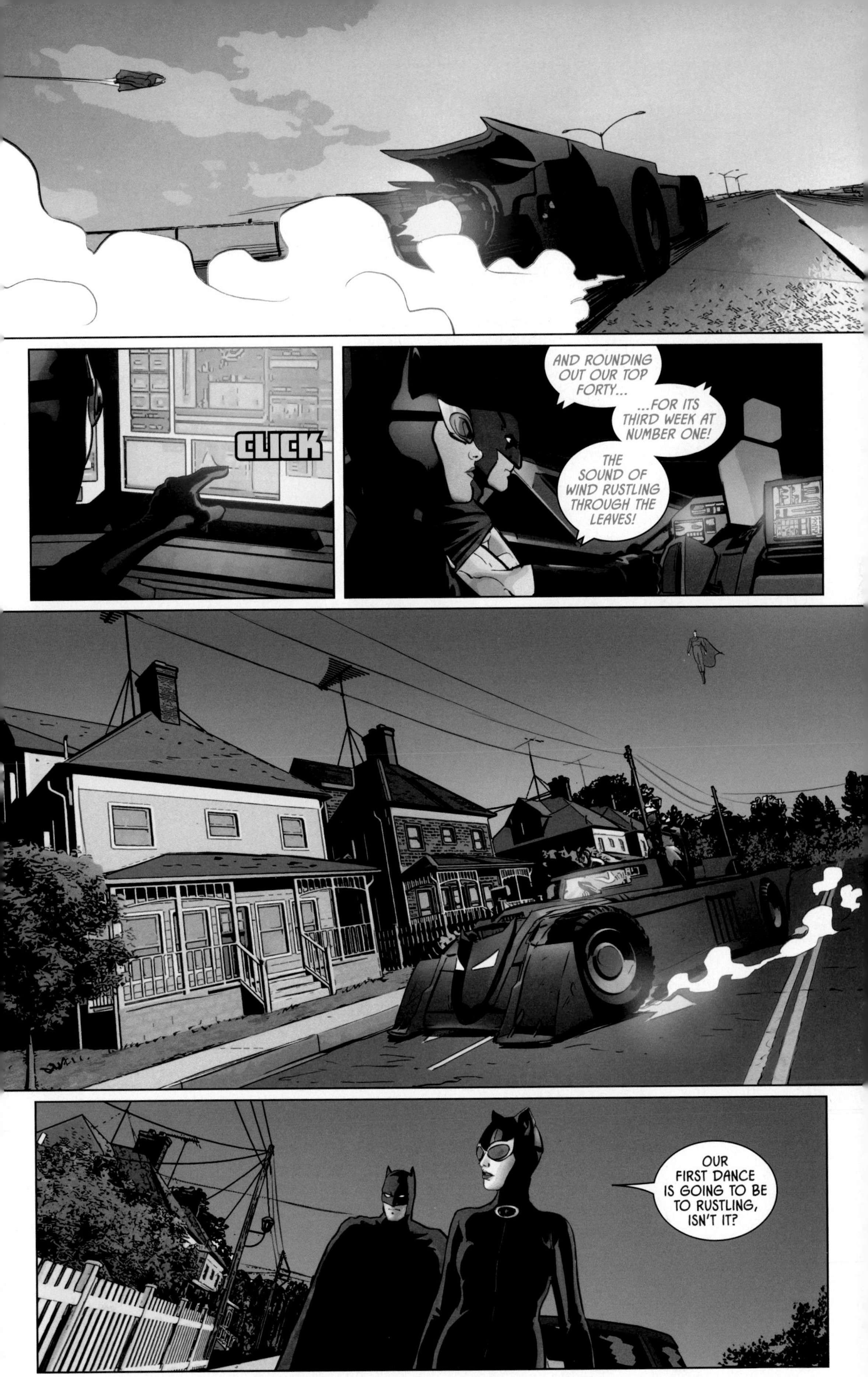
CLICK
AND ROUNDING OUT OUR TOP FORTY...
...FOR ITS THIRD WEEK AT NUMBER ONE!
THE SOUND OF WIND RUSTLING THROUGH THE LEAVES!
OUR FIRST DANCE IS GOING TO BE TO RUSTLING, ISN'T IT?

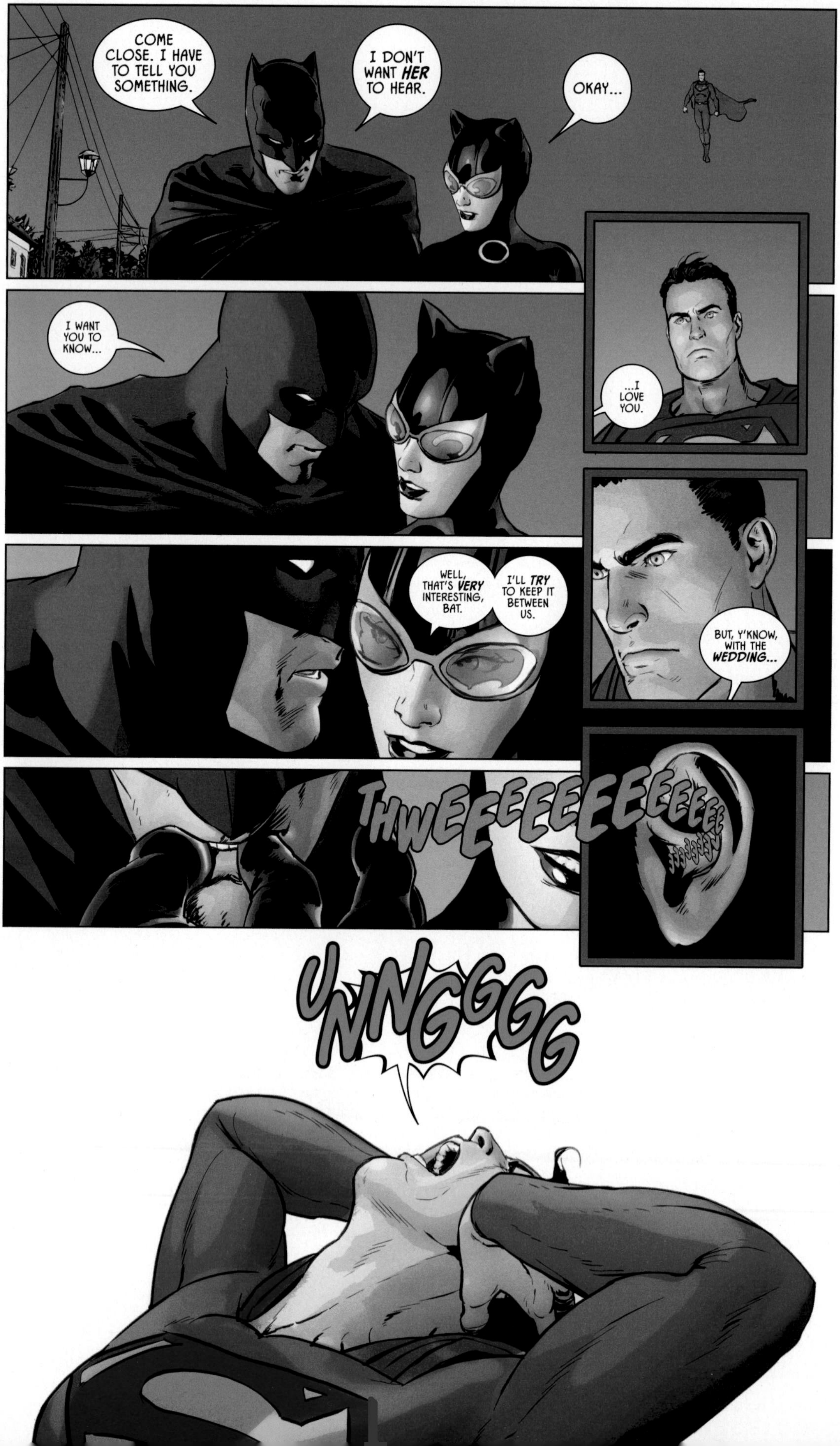
COME CLOSE. I HAVE TO TELL YOU SOMETHING.
I DON'T WANT **HER** TO HEAR.
OKAY...
I WANT YOU TO KNOW...
...I LOVE YOU.
WELL, THAT'S **VERY** INTERESTING, BAT.
I'LL **TRY** TO KEEP IT BETWEEN US.
BUT, Y'KNOW, WITH THE **WEDDING...**
THWEEEEEEEEEEEE
UNNGGGG

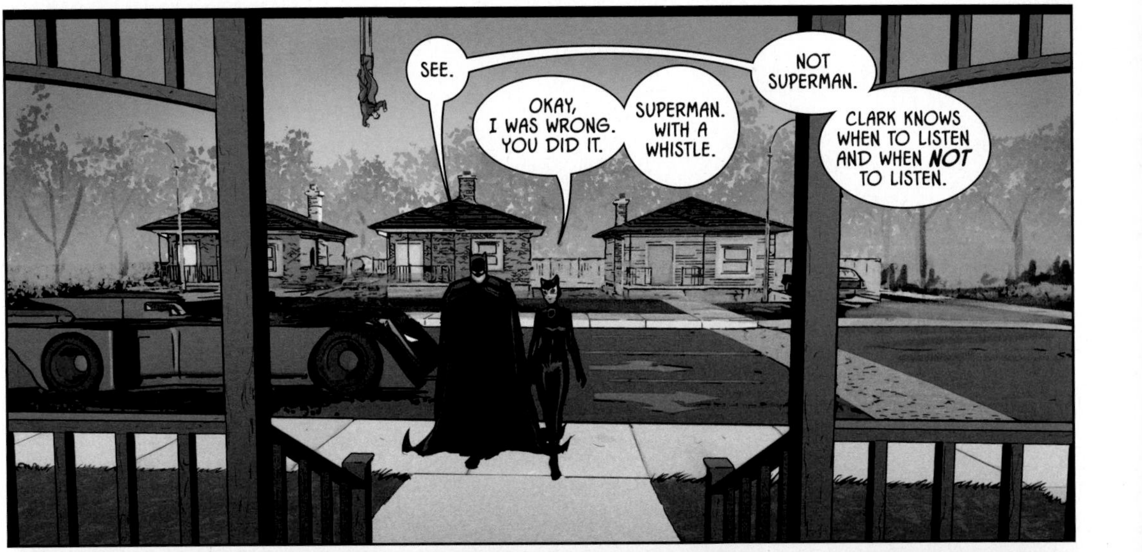
SEE.
OKAY, I WAS WRONG. YOU DID IT.
SUPERMAN. WITH A WHISTLE.
NOT SUPERMAN.
CLARK KNOWS WHEN TO LISTEN AND WHEN ***NOT*** TO LISTEN.

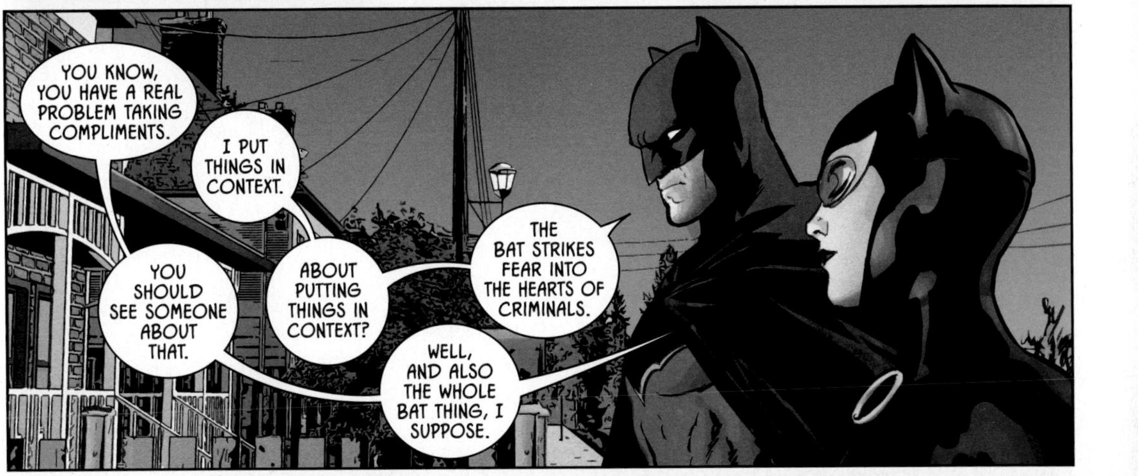
YOU KNOW, YOU HAVE A REAL PROBLEM TAKING COMPLIMENTS.
I PUT THINGS IN CONTEXT.
YOU SHOULD SEE SOMEONE ABOUT THAT.
ABOUT PUTTING THINGS IN CONTEXT?
THE BAT STRIKES FEAR INTO THE HEARTS OF CRIMINALS.
WELL, AND ALSO THE WHOLE BAT THING, I SUPPOSE.

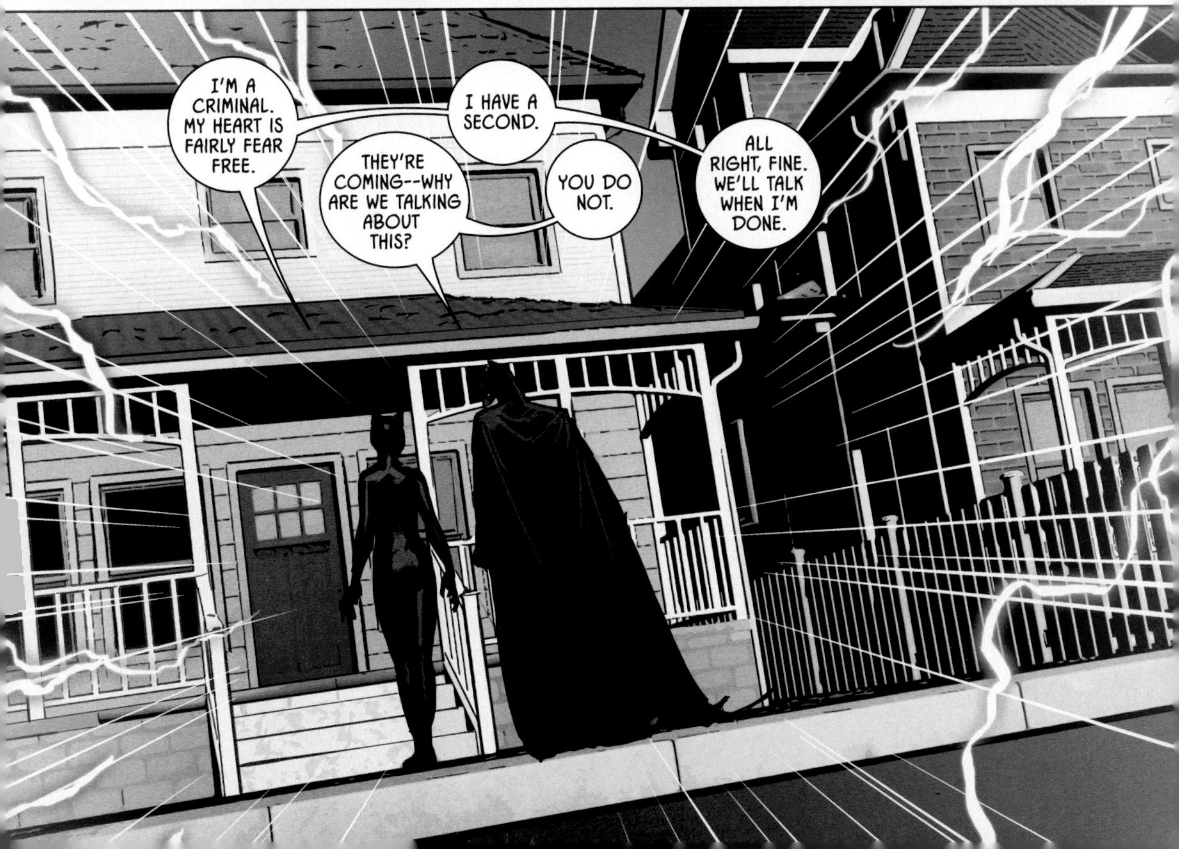
I'M A CRIMINAL. MY HEART IS FAIRLY FEAR FREE.
I HAVE A SECOND.
THEY'RE COMING--WHY ARE WE TALKING ABOUT THIS?
YOU DO NOT.
ALL RIGHT, FINE. WE'LL TALK WHEN I'M DONE.

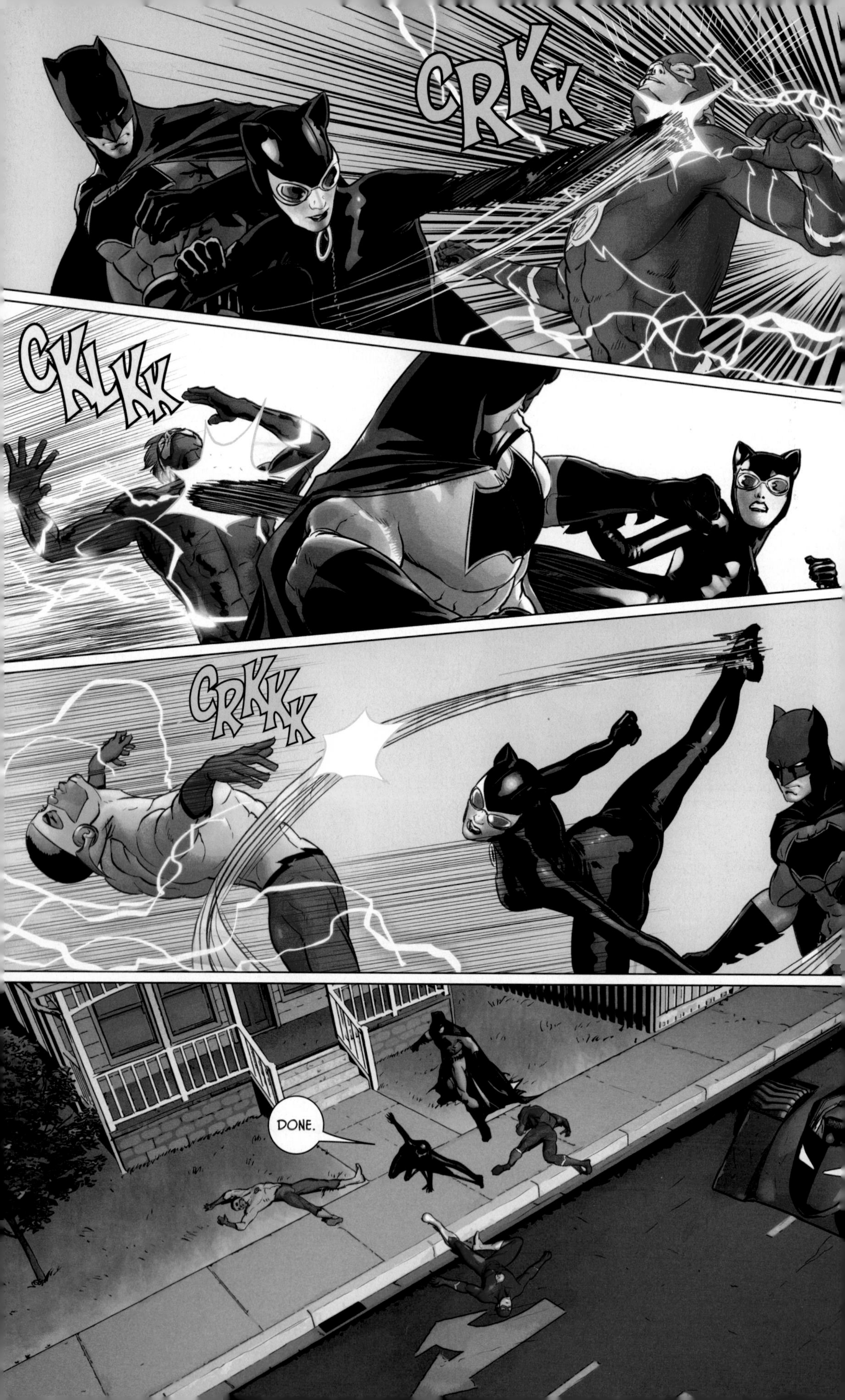
CRKK
CKLKK
CRKKK
DONE.

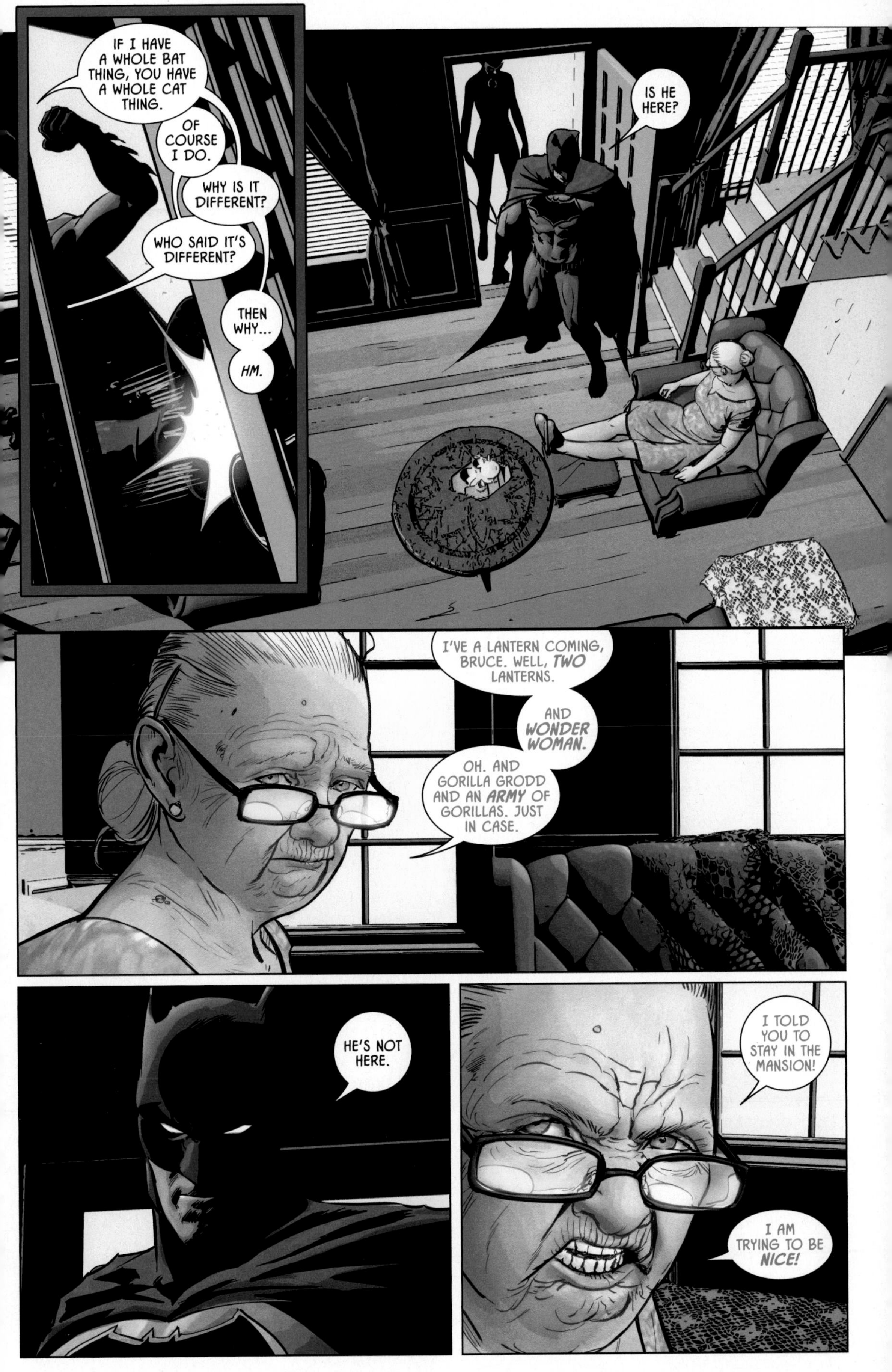
IF I HAVE A WHOLE BAT THING, YOU HAVE A WHOLE CAT THING.
OF COURSE I DO.
WHY IS IT DIFFERENT?
WHO SAID IT'S DIFFERENT?
THEN WHY...
HM.
IS HE HERE?
I'VE A LANTERN COMING, BRUCE. WELL, TWO LANTERNS.
AND WONDER WOMAN.
OH. AND GORILLA GRODD AND AN ARMY OF GORILLAS. JUST IN CASE.
HE'S NOT HERE.
I TOLD YOU TO STAY IN THE MANSION!
I AM TRYING TO BE NICE!

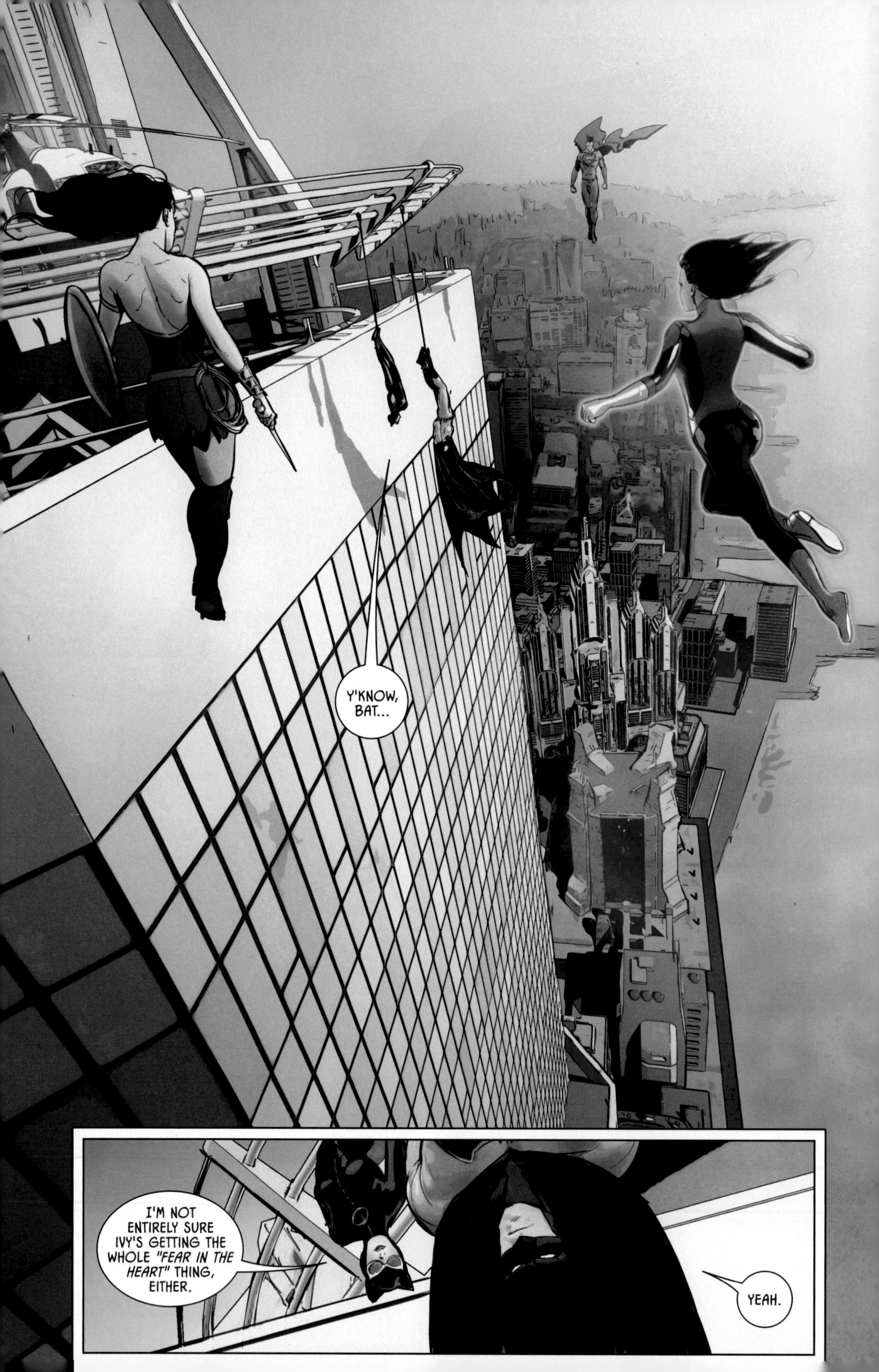
Y'KNOW, BAT...
I'M NOT ENTIRELY SURE IVY'S GETTING THE WHOLE "FEAR IN THE HEART" THING, EITHER.
YEAH.

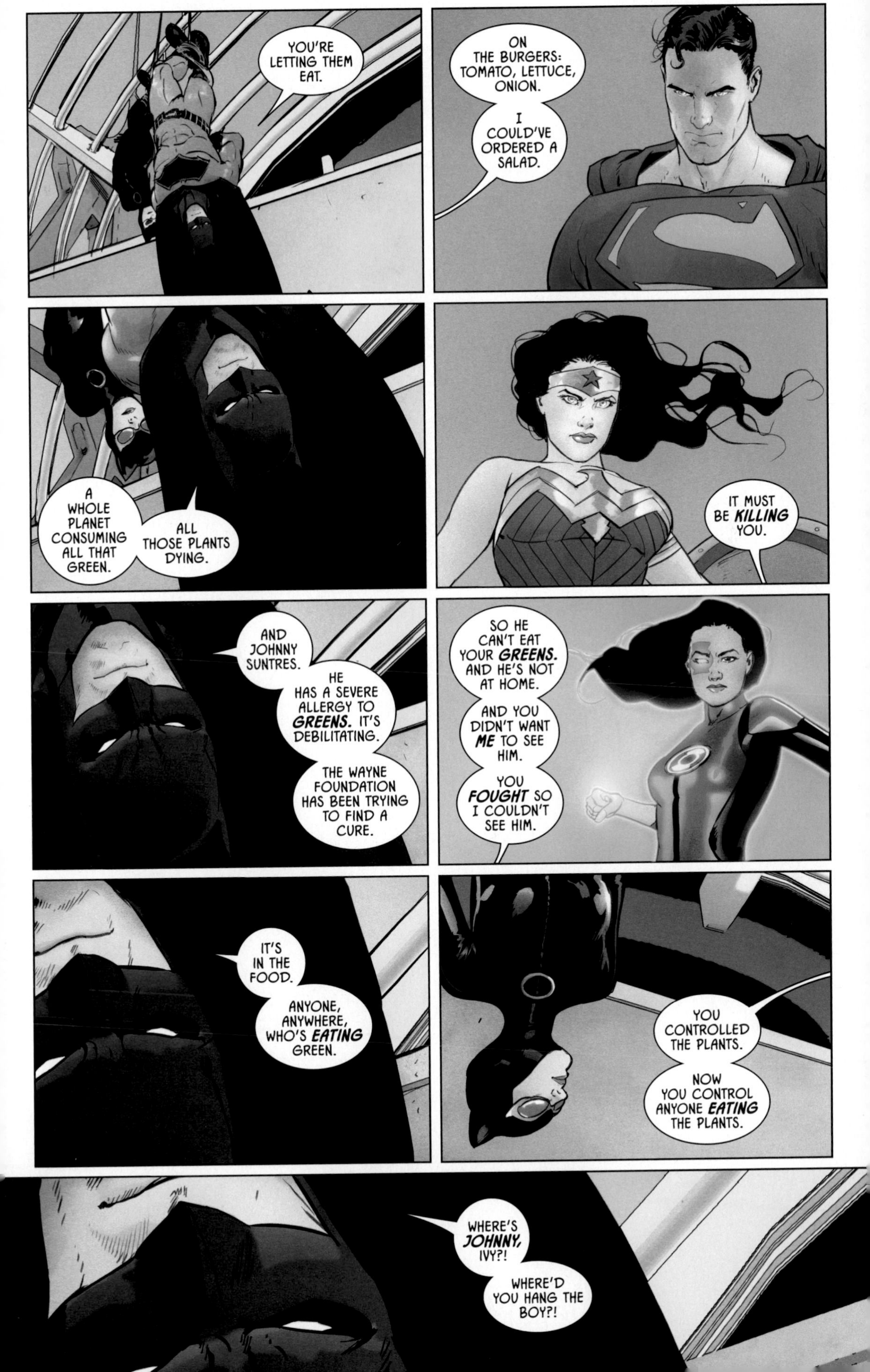
YOU'RE LETTING THEM EAT.
ON THE BURGERS: TOMATO, LETTUCE, ONION.
I COULD'VE ORDERED A SALAD.
A WHOLE PLANET CONSUMING ALL THAT GREEN.
ALL THOSE PLANTS DYING.
IT MUST BE KILLING YOU.
AND JOHNNY SUNTRES.
HE HAS A SEVERE ALLERGY TO GREENS. IT'S DEBILITATING.
THE WAYNE FOUNDATION HAS BEEN TRYING TO FIND A CURE.
SO HE CAN'T EAT YOUR GREENS. AND HE'S NOT AT HOME.
AND YOU DIDN'T WANT ME TO SEE HIM.
YOU FOUGHT SO I COULDN'T SEE HIM.
IT'S IN THE FOOD.
ANYONE, ANYWHERE, WHO'S EATING GREEN.
YOU CONTROLLED THE PLANTS.
NOW YOU CONTROL ANYONE EATING THE PLANTS.
WHERE'S JOHNNY, IVY?!
WHERE'D YOU HANG THE BOY?!

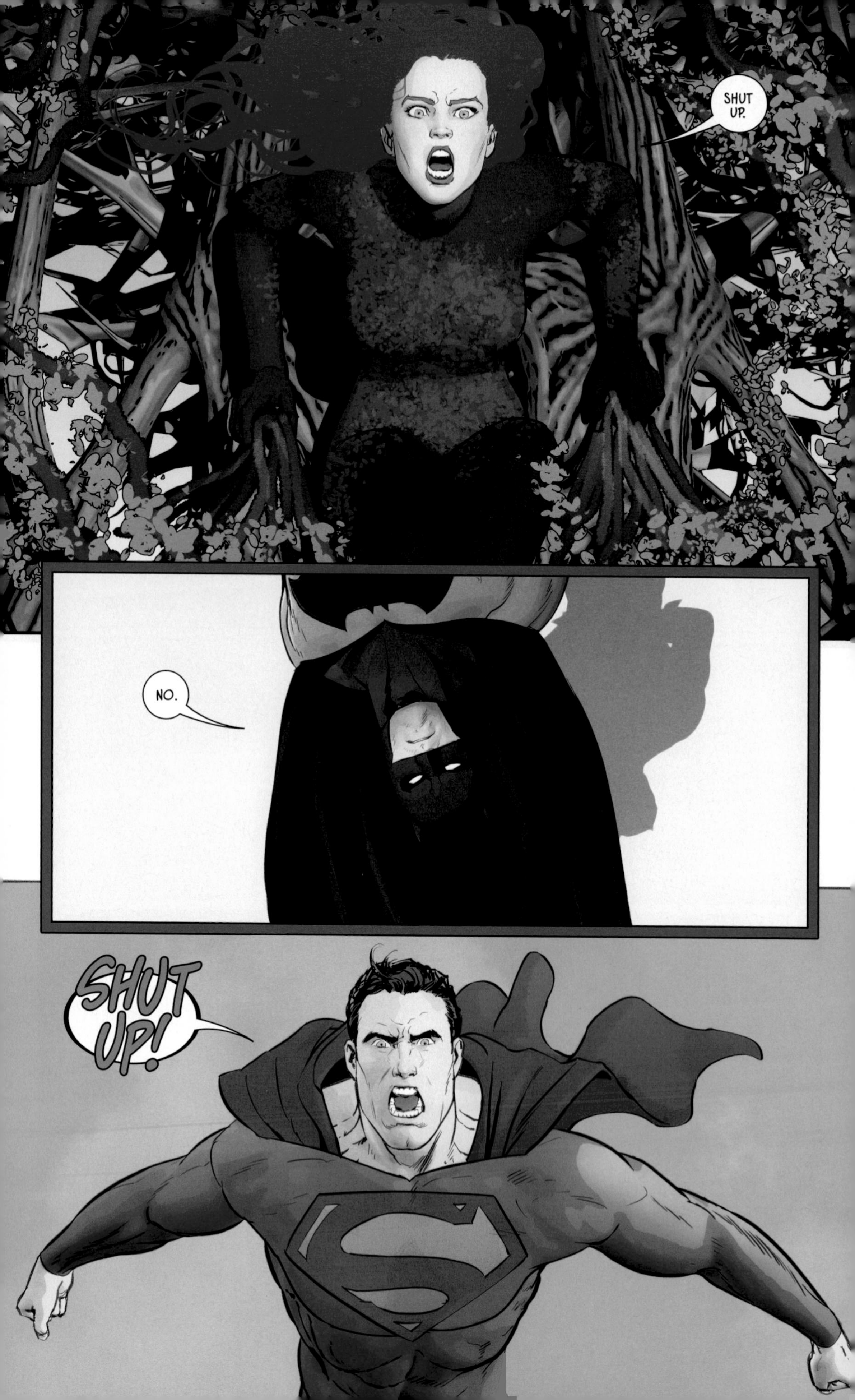
SHUT UP.
NO.
SHUT UP!

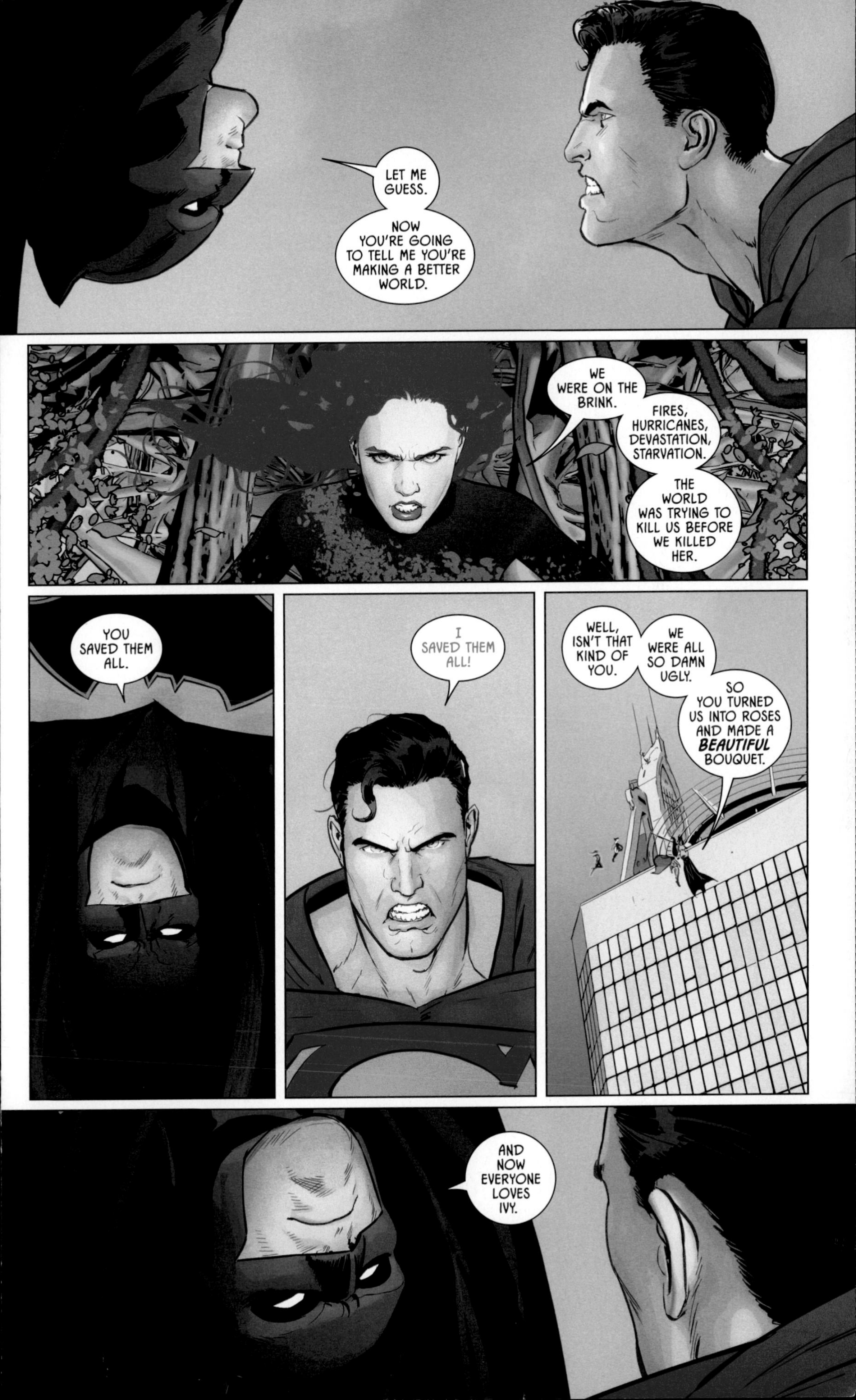
LET ME GUESS.
NOW YOU'RE GOING TO TELL ME YOU'RE MAKING A BETTER WORLD.
WE WERE ON THE BRINK.
FIRES, HURRICANES, DEVASTATION, STARVATION.
THE WORLD WAS TRYING TO KILL US BEFORE WE KILLED HER.
YOU SAVED THEM ALL.
I SAVED THEM ALL!
WELL, ISN'T THAT KIND OF YOU.
WE WERE ALL SO DAMN UGLY.
SO YOU TURNED US INTO ROSES AND MADE A BEAUTIFUL BOUQUET.
AND NOW EVERYONE LOVES IVY.

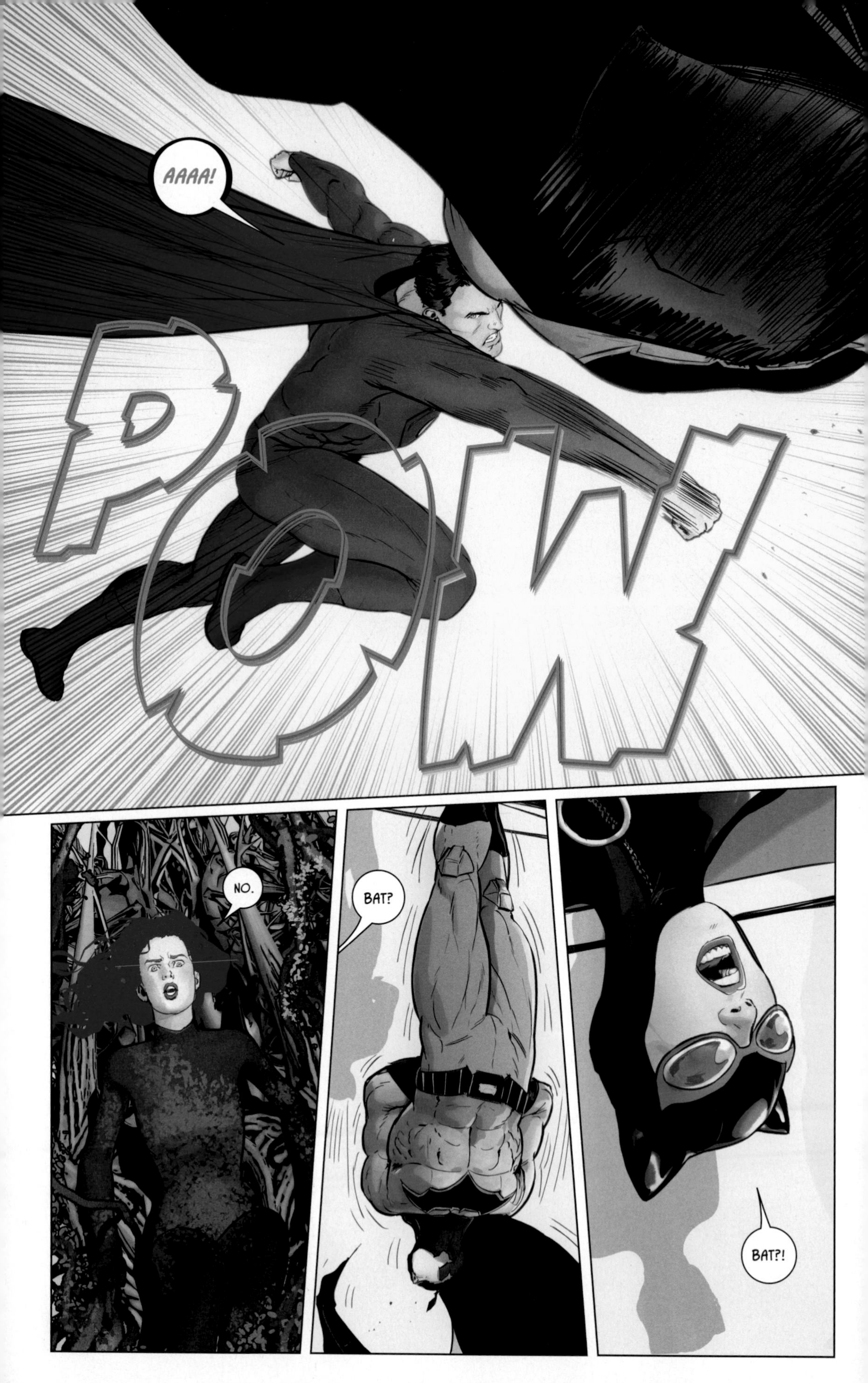
AAAA!
POW
NO.
BAT?
BAT?!

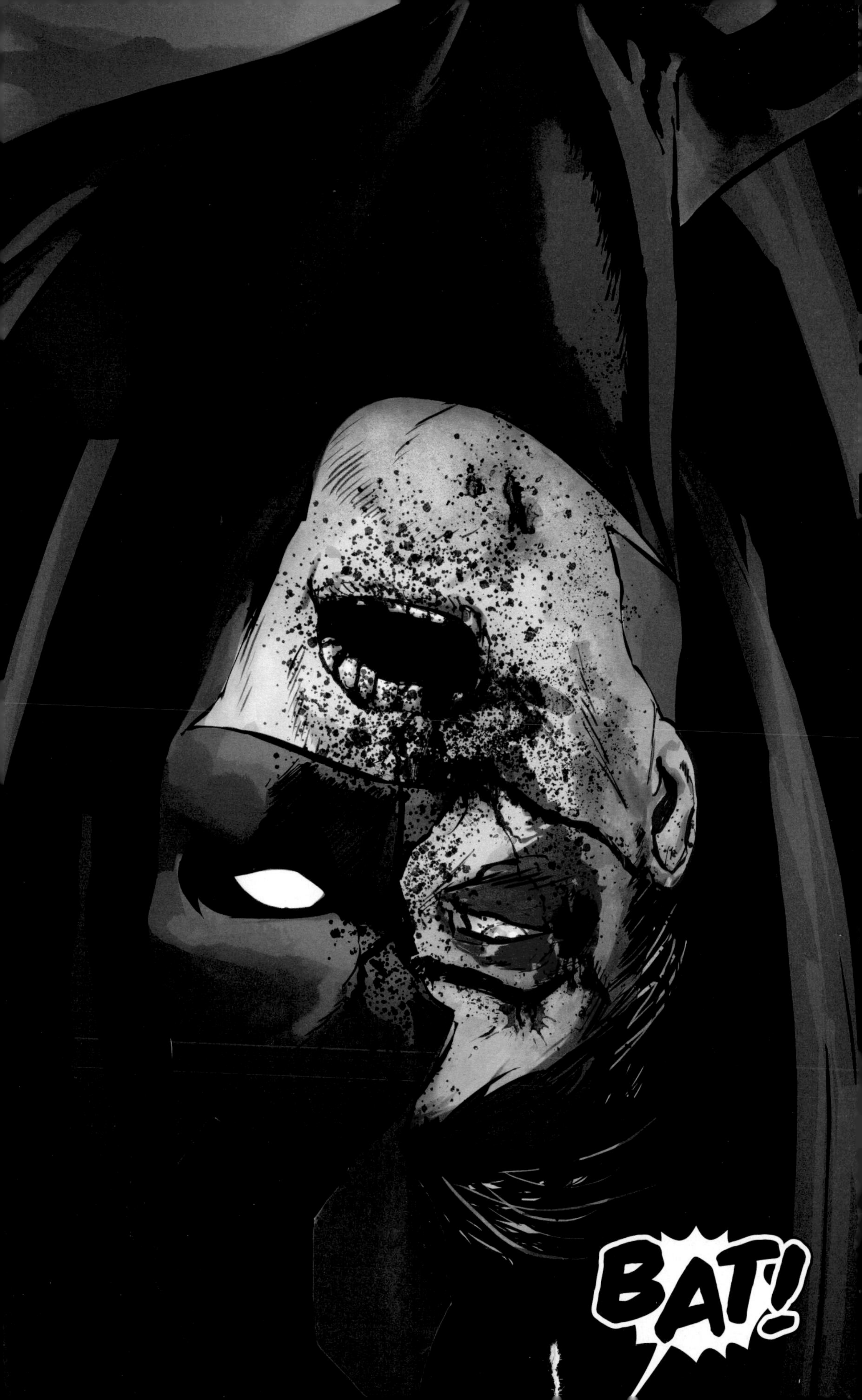
BAT!

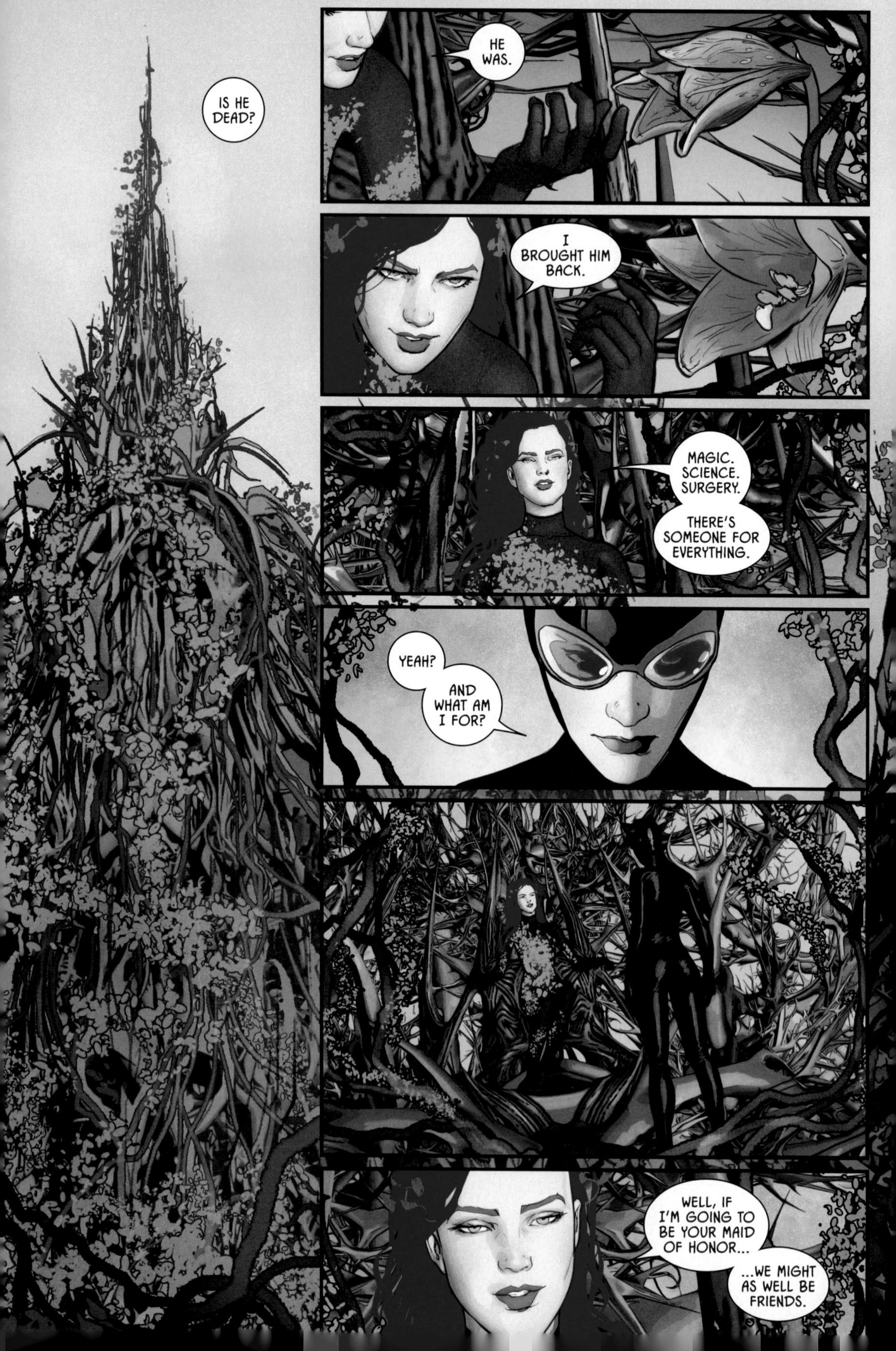
IS HE DEAD?
HE WAS.
I BROUGHT HIM BACK.
MAGIC. SCIENCE. SURGERY.
THERE'S SOMEONE FOR EVERYTHING.
YEAH?
AND WHAT AM I FOR?
WELL, IF I'M GOING TO BE YOUR MAID OF HONOR...
...WE MIGHT AS WELL BE FRIENDS.

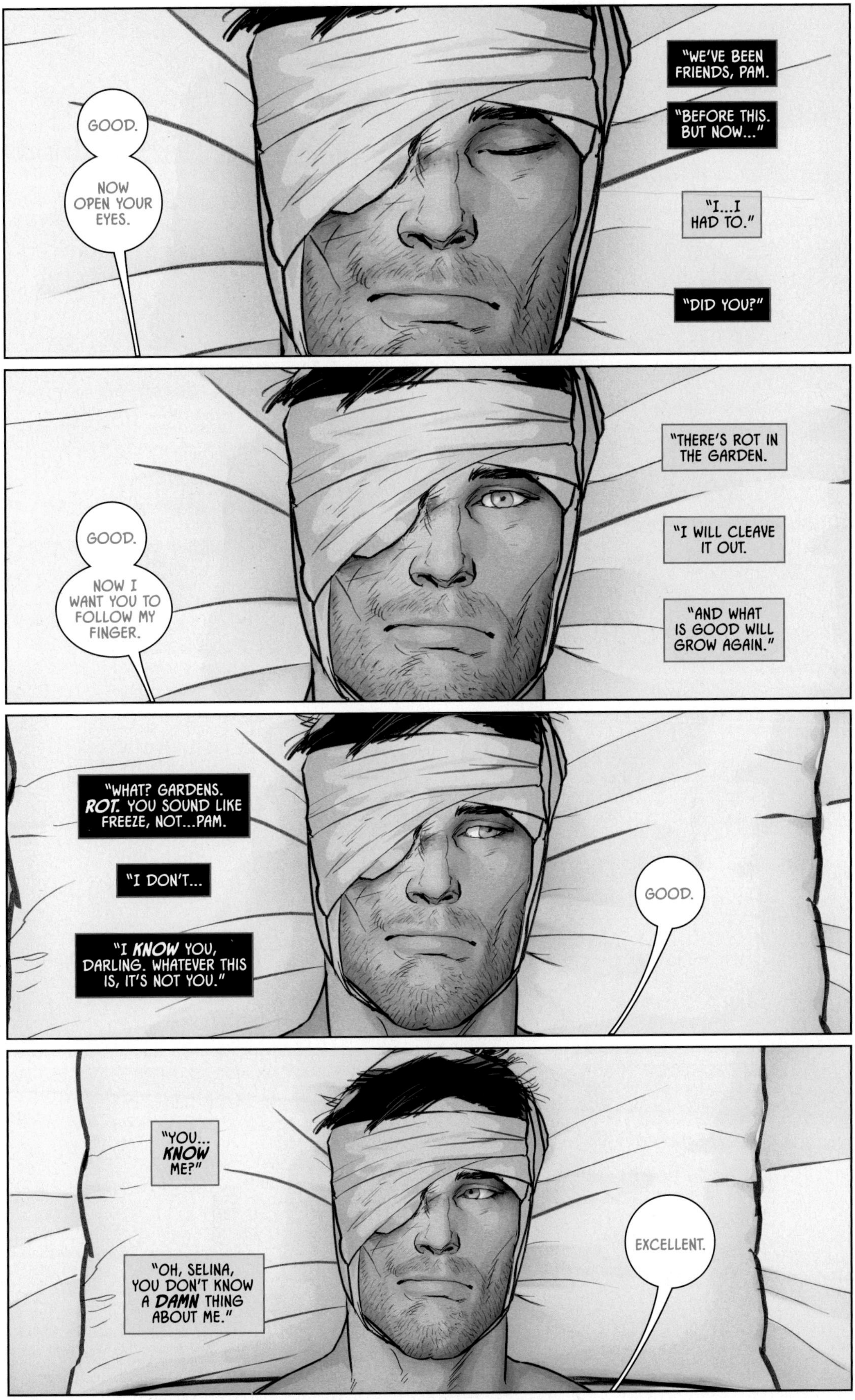
"WE'VE BEEN FRIENDS, PAM.
"BEFORE THIS. BUT NOW..."
GOOD.
NOW OPEN YOUR EYES.
"I...I HAD TO."
"DID YOU?"
"THERE'S ROT IN THE GARDEN.
"I WILL CLEAVE IT OUT.
"AND WHAT IS GOOD WILL GROW AGAIN."
GOOD.
NOW I WANT YOU TO FOLLOW MY FINGER.
"WHAT? GARDENS. ROT. YOU SOUND LIKE FREEZE, NOT...PAM.
"I DON'T...
"I KNOW YOU, DARLING. WHATEVER THIS IS, IT'S NOT YOU."
GOOD.
"YOU... KNOW ME?"
"OH, SELINA, YOU DON'T KNOW A DAMN THING ABOUT ME."
EXCELLENT.

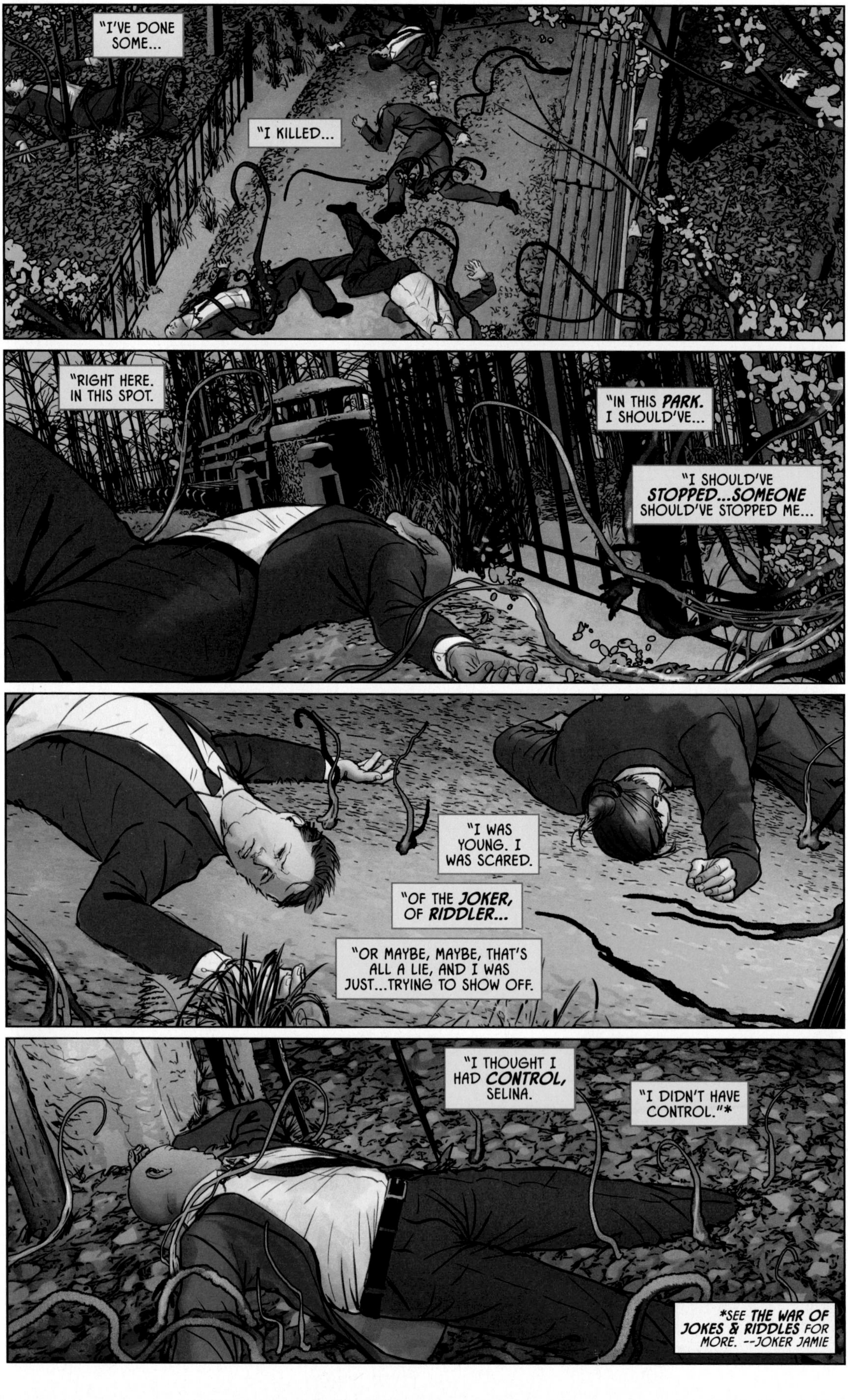
"I'VE DONE SOME...
"I KILLED...
"RIGHT HERE. IN THIS SPOT.
"IN THIS PARK. I SHOULD'VE...
"I SHOULD'VE STOPPED...SOMEONE SHOULD'VE STOPPED ME...
"I WAS YOUNG. I WAS SCARED.
"OF THE JOKER, OF RIDDLER...
"OR MAYBE, MAYBE, THAT'S ALL A LIE, AND I WAS JUST...TRYING TO SHOW OFF.
"I THOUGHT I HAD CONTROL, SELINA.
"I DIDN'T HAVE CONTROL."*
*SEE THE WAR OF JOKES & RIDDLES FOR MORE. --JOKER JAMIE

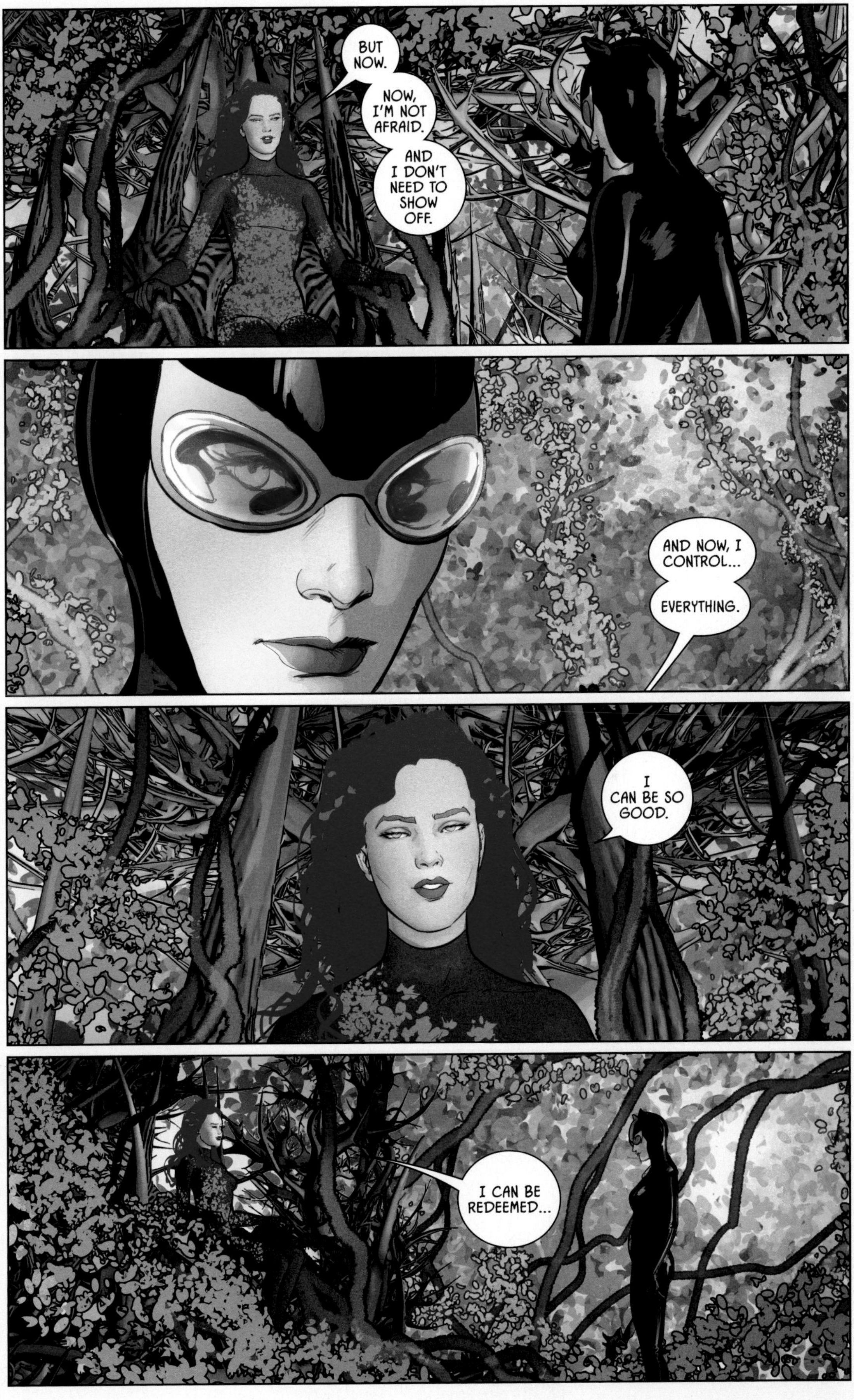
BUT NOW.
NOW, I'M NOT AFRAID.
AND I DON'T NEED TO SHOW OFF.
AND NOW, I CONTROL...
EVERYTHING.
I CAN BE SO GOOD.
I CAN BE REDEEMED...

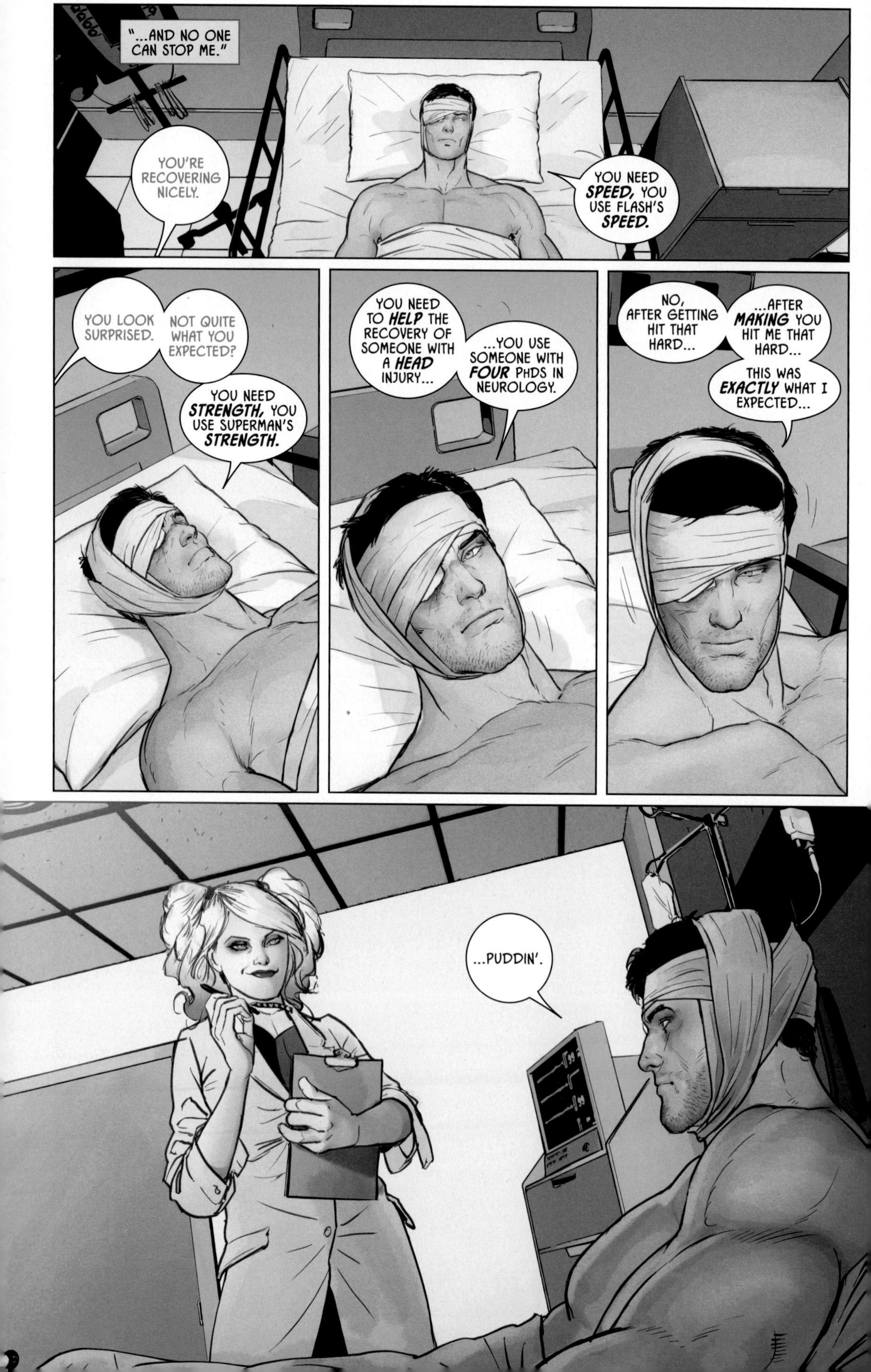
"...AND NO ONE CAN STOP ME."
YOU'RE RECOVERING NICELY.
YOU NEED SPEED, YOU USE FLASH'S SPEED.
YOU LOOK SURPRISED.
NOT QUITE WHAT YOU EXPECTED?
YOU NEED STRENGTH, YOU USE SUPERMAN'S STRENGTH.
YOU NEED TO HELP THE RECOVERY OF SOMEONE WITH A HEAD INJURY...
...YOU USE SOMEONE WITH FOUR PHDS IN NEUROLOGY.
NO, AFTER GETTING HIT THAT HARD...
...AFTER MAKING YOU HIT ME THAT HARD...
THIS WAS EXACTLY WHAT I EXPECTED...
...PUDDIN'.

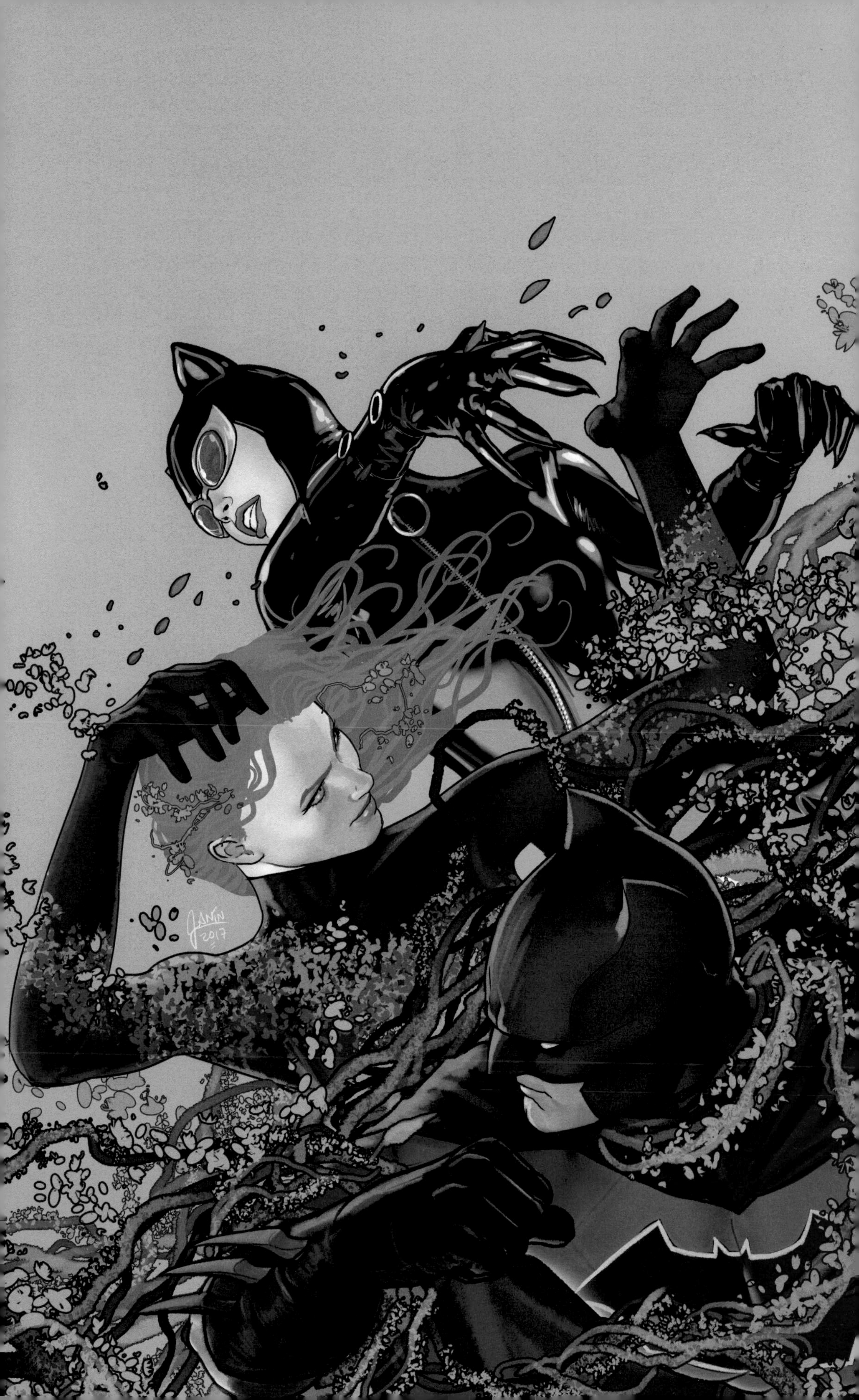
JANIN
2017

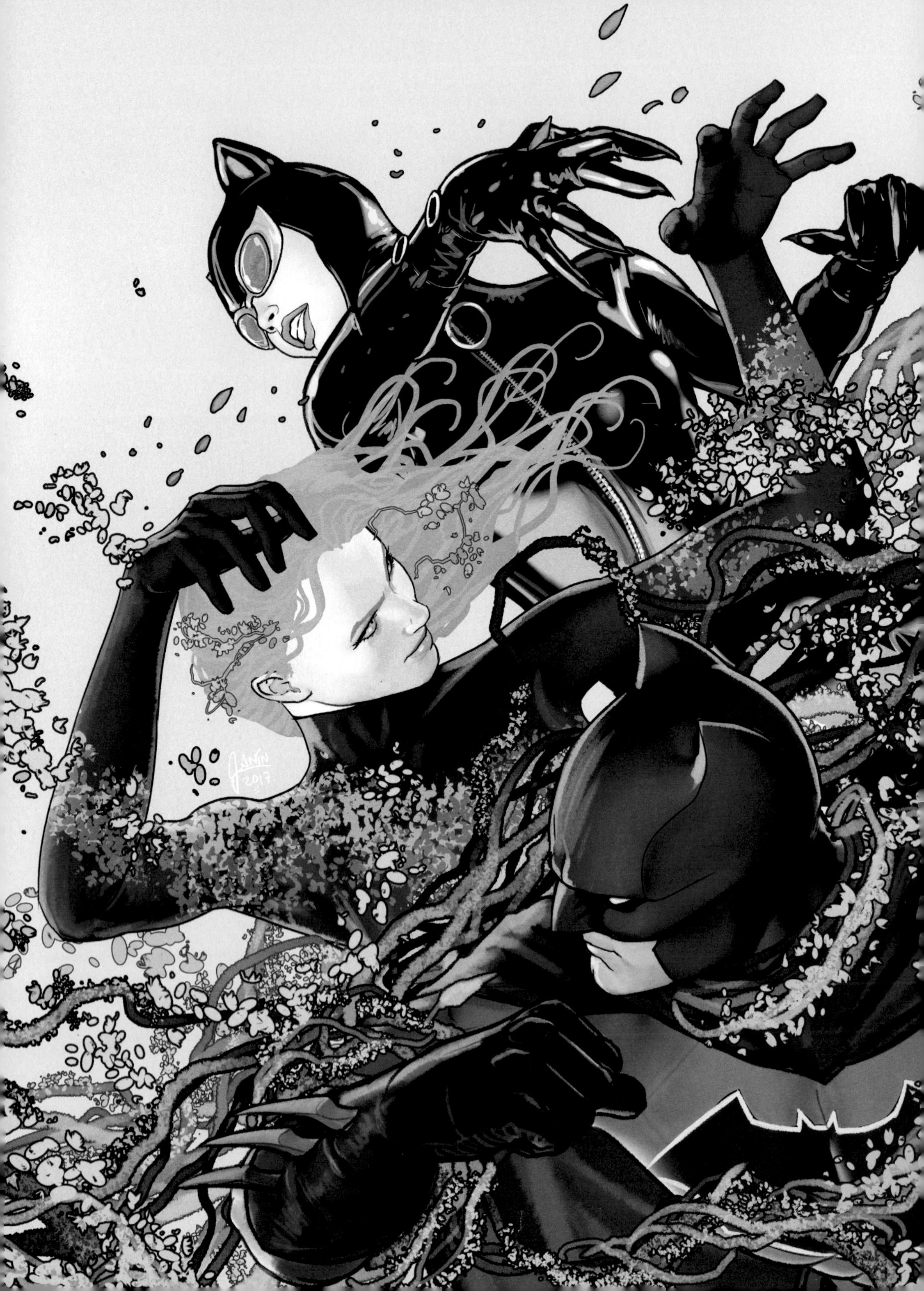
Janin
2017

DC COMICS PRESENTS:

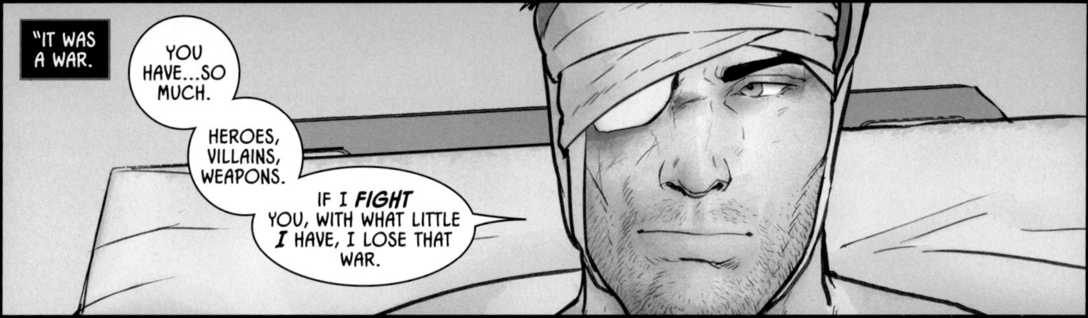
"IT WAS A WAR.
YOU HAVE...SO MUCH.
HEROES, VILLAINS, WEAPONS.
IF I FIGHT YOU, WITH WHAT LITTLE I HAVE, I LOSE THAT WAR.

EVERYONE LOVES IVY
PART THREE

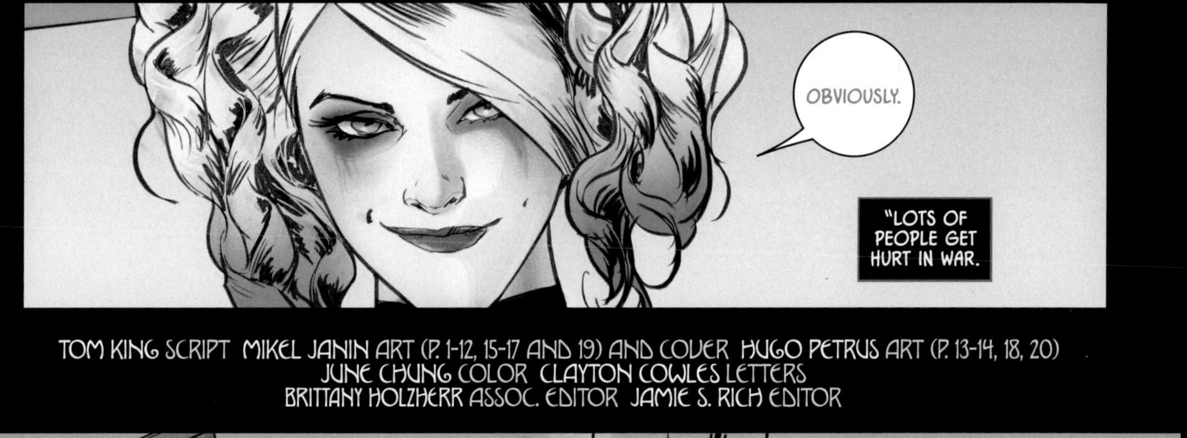
OBVIOUSLY.
"LOTS OF PEOPLE GET HURT IN WAR.

TOM KING SCRIPT MIKEL JANIN ART (P. 1-12, 15-17 AND 19) AND COVER HUGO PETRUS ART (P. 13-14, 18, 20)
JUNE CHUNG COLOR CLAYTON COWLES LETTERS
BRITTANY HOLZHERR ASSOC. EDITOR JAMIE S. RICH EDITOR

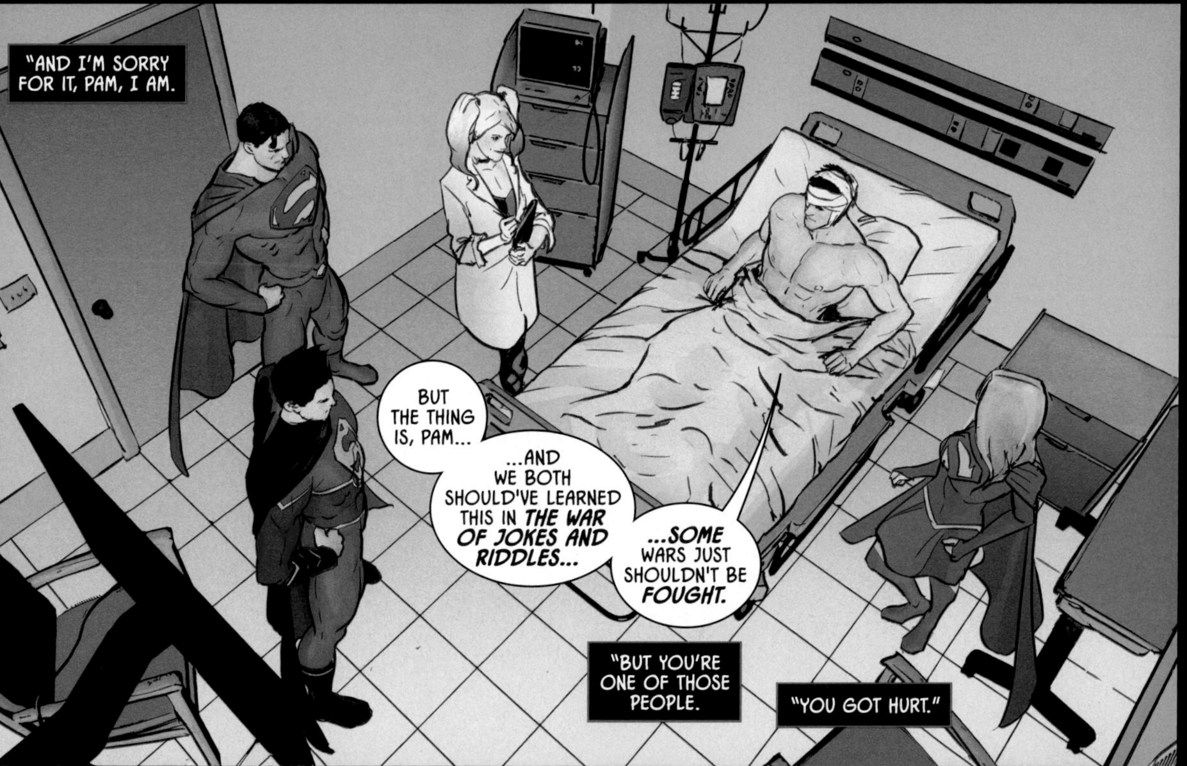
"AND I'M SORRY FOR IT, PAM, I AM.
BUT THE THING IS, PAM...
...AND WE BOTH SHOULD'VE LEARNED THIS IN THE WAR OF JOKES AND RIDDLES...
...SOME WARS JUST SHOULDN'T BE FOUGHT.
"BUT YOU'RE ONE OF THOSE PEOPLE.
"YOU GOT HURT."

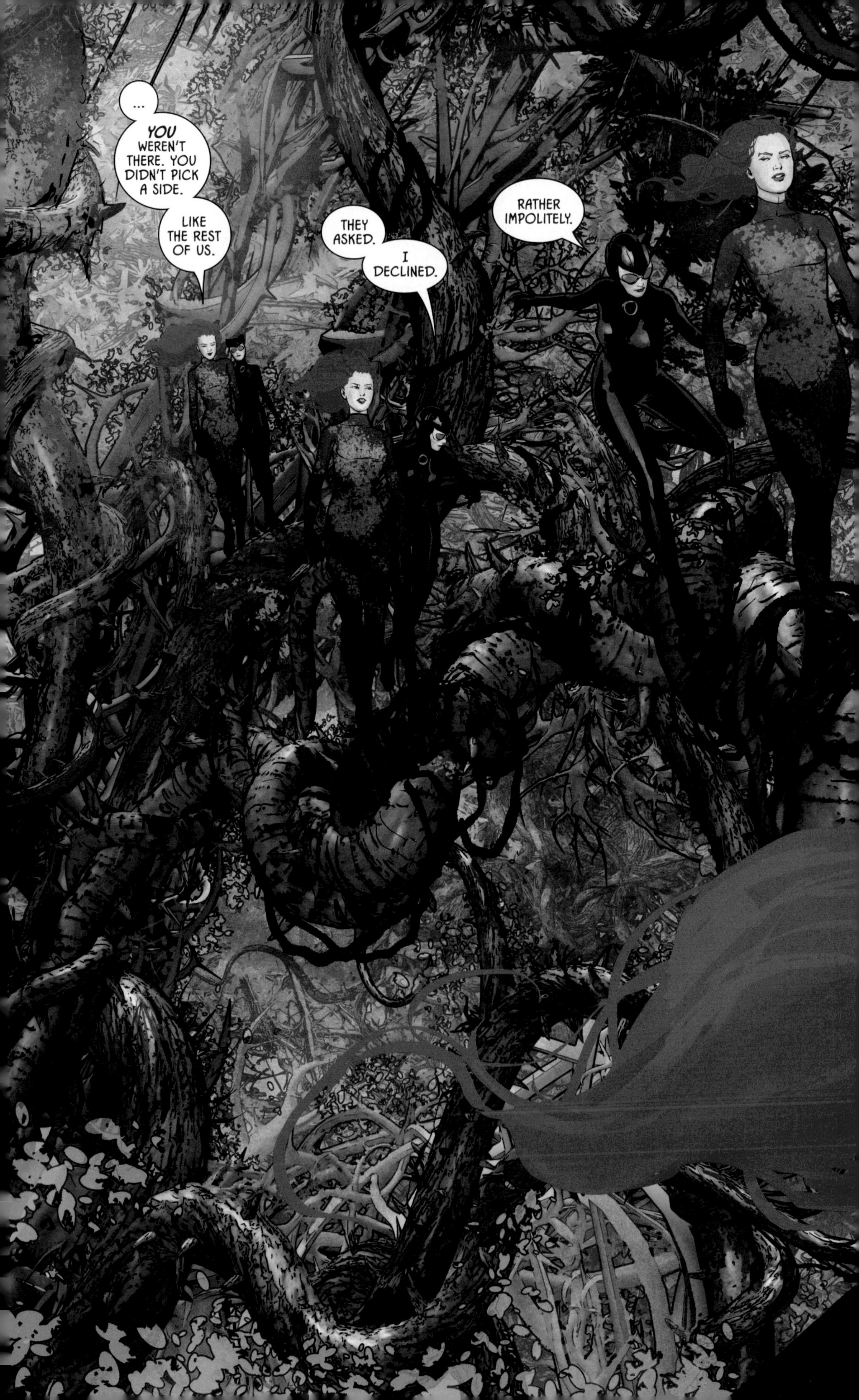
...
YOU WEREN'T THERE. YOU DIDN'T PICK A SIDE.
LIKE THE REST OF US.
THEY ASKED.
I DECLINED.
RATHER IMPOLITELY.

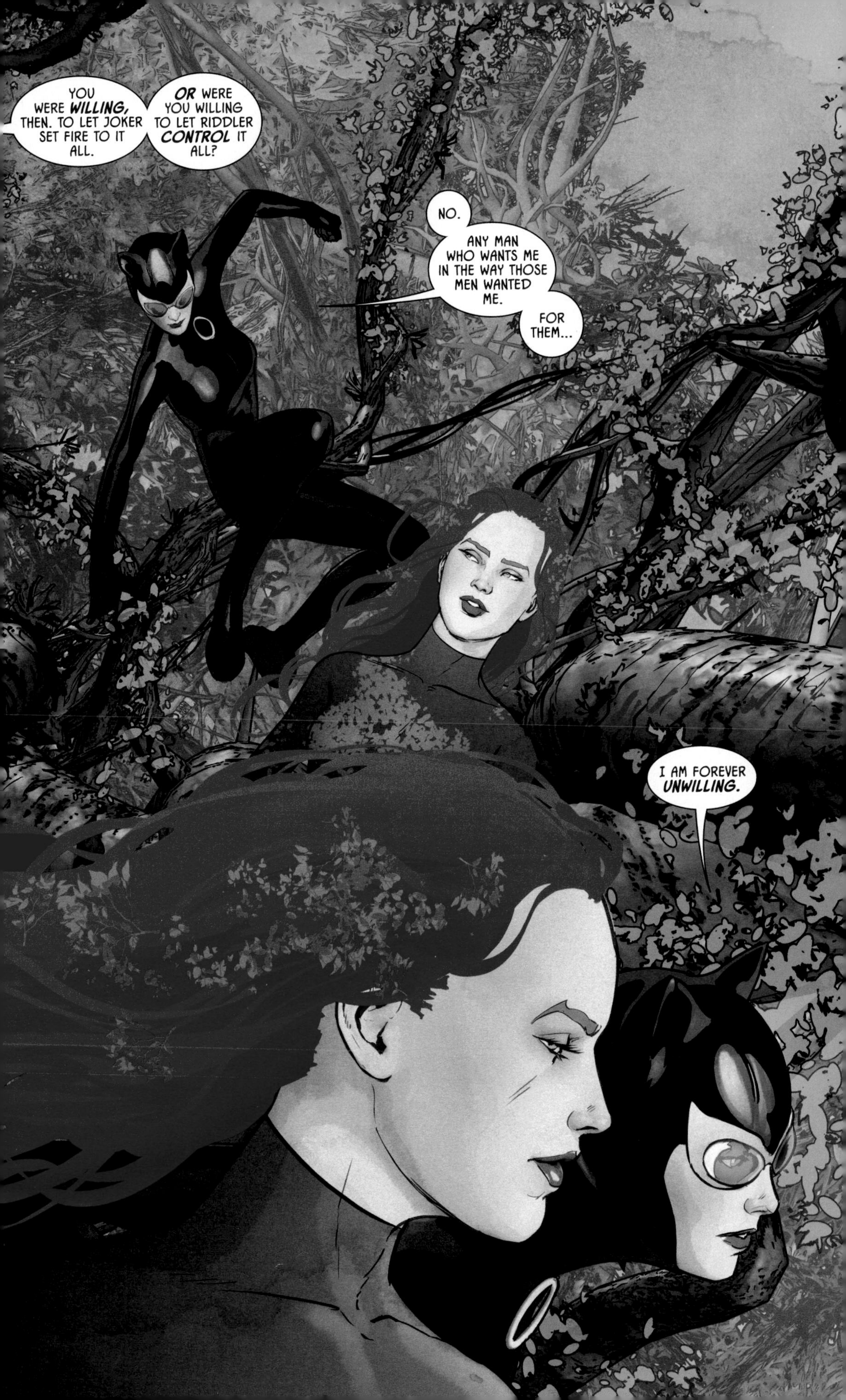
YOU WERE WILLING, THEN. TO LET JOKER SET FIRE TO IT ALL.
OR WERE YOU WILLING TO LET RIDDLER CONTROL IT ALL?
NO.
ANY MAN WHO WANTS ME IN THE WAY THOSE MEN WANTED ME.
FOR THEM...
I AM FOREVER UNWILLING.

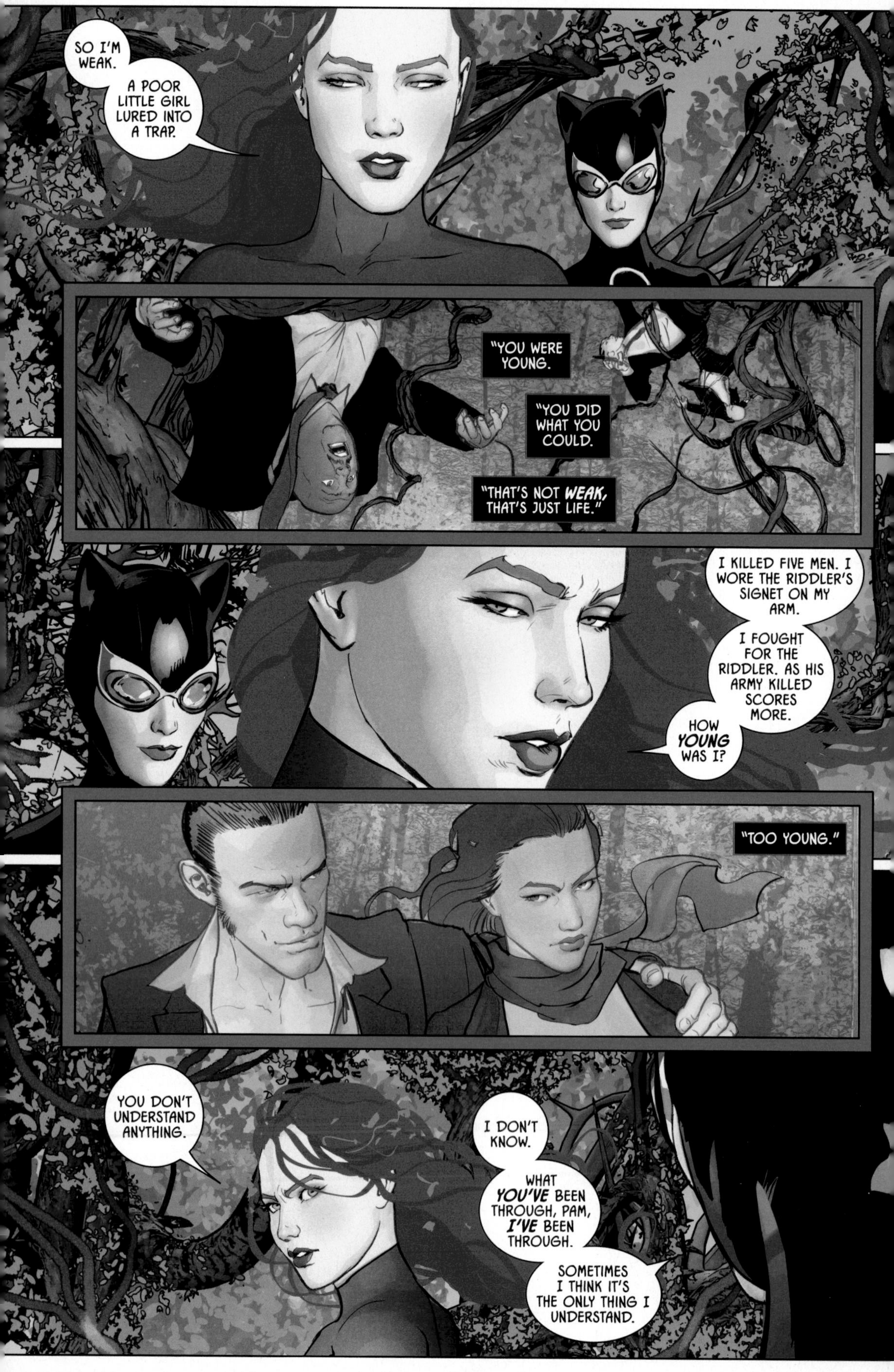
SO I'M WEAK.
A POOR LITTLE GIRL LURED INTO A TRAP.
"YOU WERE YOUNG.
"YOU DID WHAT YOU COULD.
"THAT'S NOT WEAK, THAT'S JUST LIFE."
I KILLED FIVE MEN. I WORE THE RIDDLER'S SIGNET ON MY ARM.
I FOUGHT FOR THE RIDDLER. AS HIS ARMY KILLED SCORES MORE.
HOW YOUNG WAS I?
"TOO YOUNG."
YOU DON'T UNDERSTAND ANYTHING.
I DON'T KNOW.
WHAT YOU'VE BEEN THROUGH, PAM, I'VE BEEN THROUGH.
SOMETIMES I THINK IT'S THE ONLY THING I UNDERSTAND.

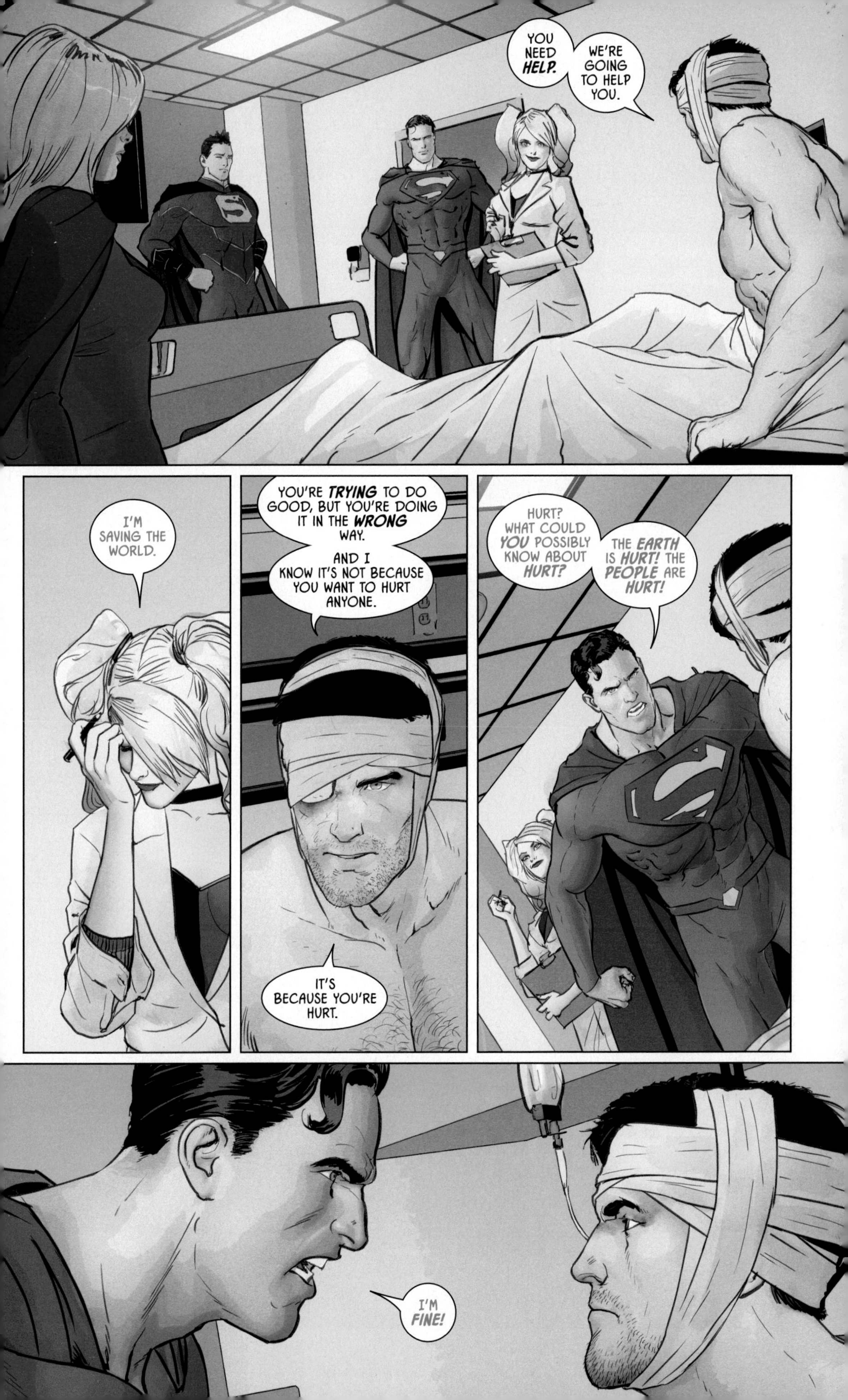
YOU NEED HELP.
WE'RE GOING TO HELP YOU.
I'M SAVING THE WORLD.
YOU'RE TRYING TO DO GOOD, BUT YOU'RE DOING IT IN THE WRONG WAY.
AND I KNOW IT'S NOT BECAUSE YOU WANT TO HURT ANYONE.
IT'S BECAUSE YOU'RE HURT.
HURT? WHAT COULD YOU POSSIBLY KNOW ABOUT HURT?
THE EARTH IS HURT! THE PEOPLE ARE HURT!
I'M FINE!

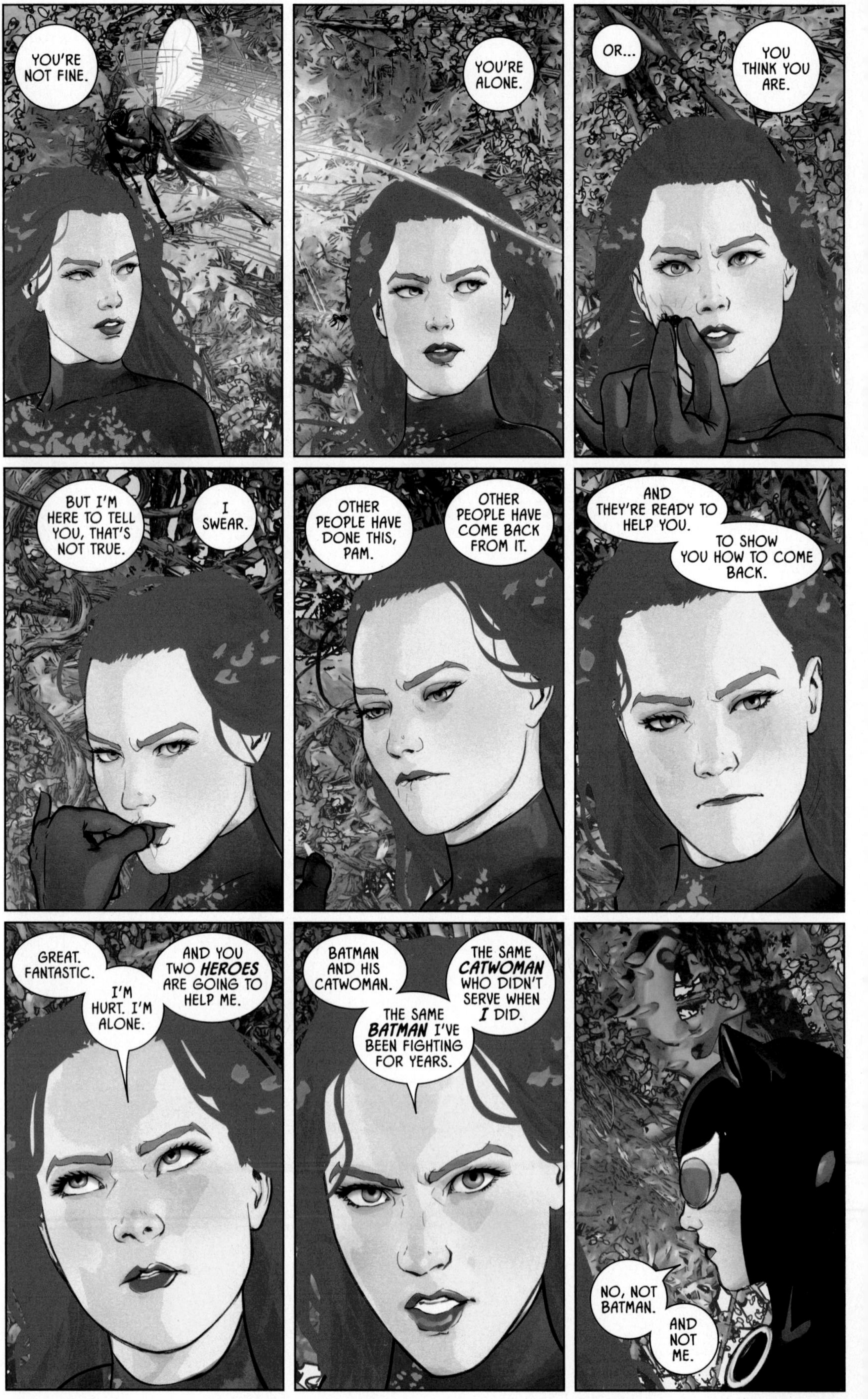
YOU'RE NOT FINE.
YOU'RE ALONE.
OR...
YOU THINK YOU ARE.
BUT I'M HERE TO TELL YOU, THAT'S NOT TRUE.
I SWEAR.
OTHER PEOPLE HAVE DONE THIS, PAM.
OTHER PEOPLE HAVE COME BACK FROM IT.
AND THEY'RE READY TO HELP YOU.
TO SHOW YOU HOW TO COME BACK.
GREAT. FANTASTIC.
I'M HURT. I'M ALONE.
AND YOU TWO HEROES ARE GOING TO HELP ME.
BATMAN AND HIS CATWOMAN.
THE SAME BATMAN I'VE BEEN FIGHTING FOR YEARS.
THE SAME CATWOMAN WHO DIDN'T SERVE WHEN I DID.
NO, NOT BATMAN.
AND NOT ME.

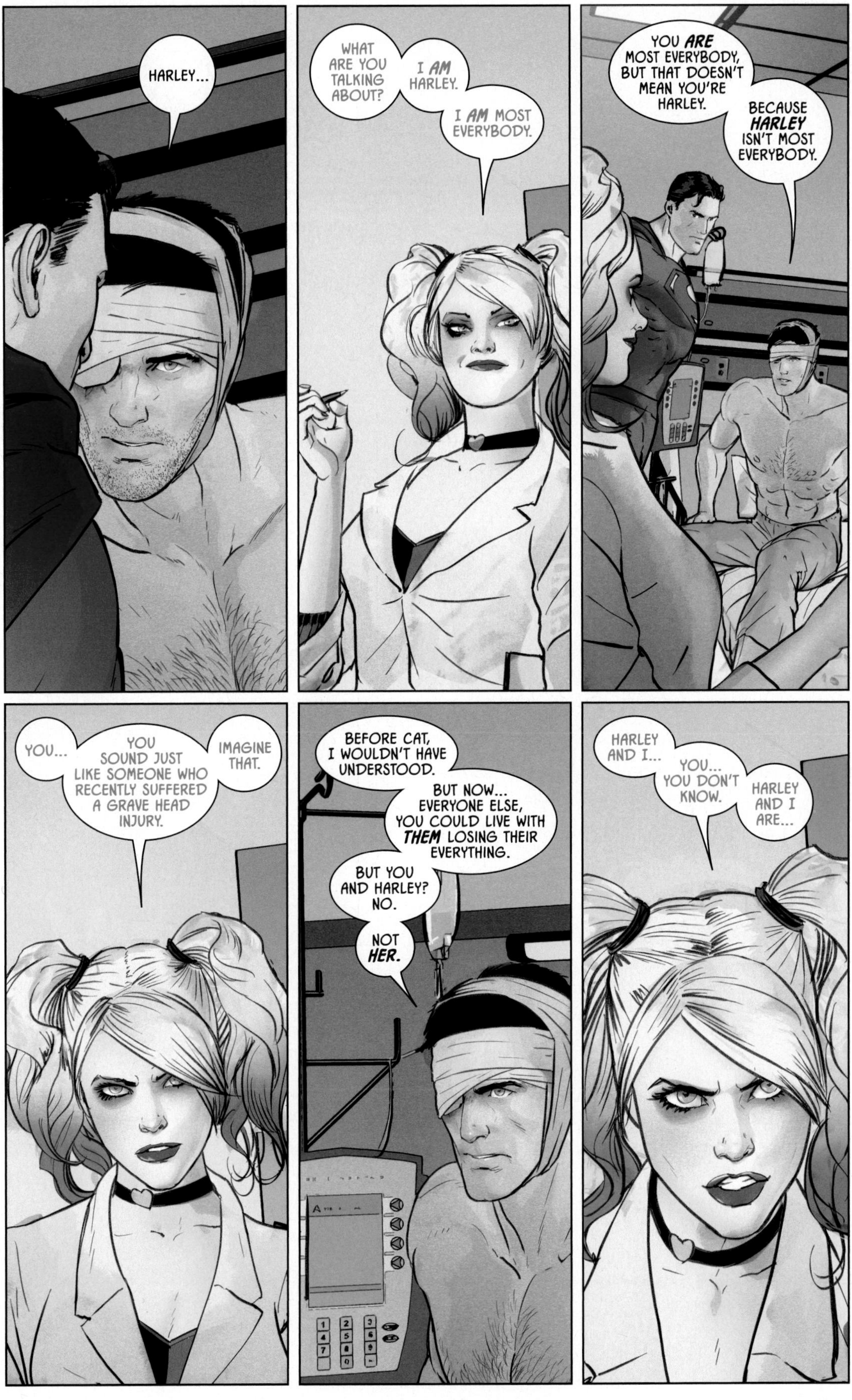
HARLEY...
WHAT ARE YOU TALKING ABOUT?
I AM HARLEY.
I AM MOST EVERYBODY.
YOU ARE MOST EVERYBODY, BUT THAT DOESN'T MEAN YOU'RE HARLEY.
BECAUSE HARLEY ISN'T MOST EVERYBODY.
YOU...
YOU SOUND JUST LIKE SOMEONE WHO RECENTLY SUFFERED A GRAVE HEAD INJURY.
IMAGINE THAT.
BEFORE CAT, I WOULDN'T HAVE UNDERSTOOD.
BUT NOW... EVERYONE ELSE, YOU COULD LIVE WITH THEM LOSING THEIR EVERYTHING.
BUT YOU AND HARLEY? NO.
NOT HER.
HARLEY AND I...
YOU... YOU DON'T KNOW.
HARLEY AND I ARE...

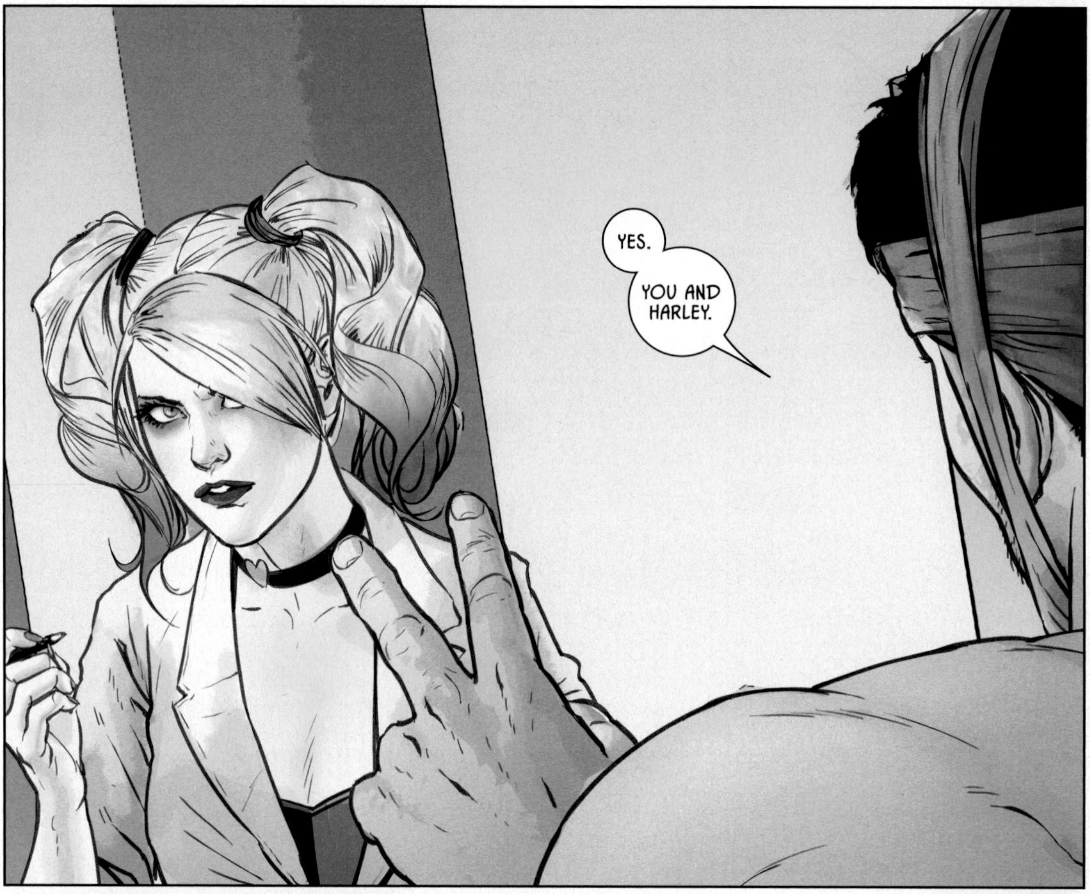
YES.
YOU AND HARLEY.

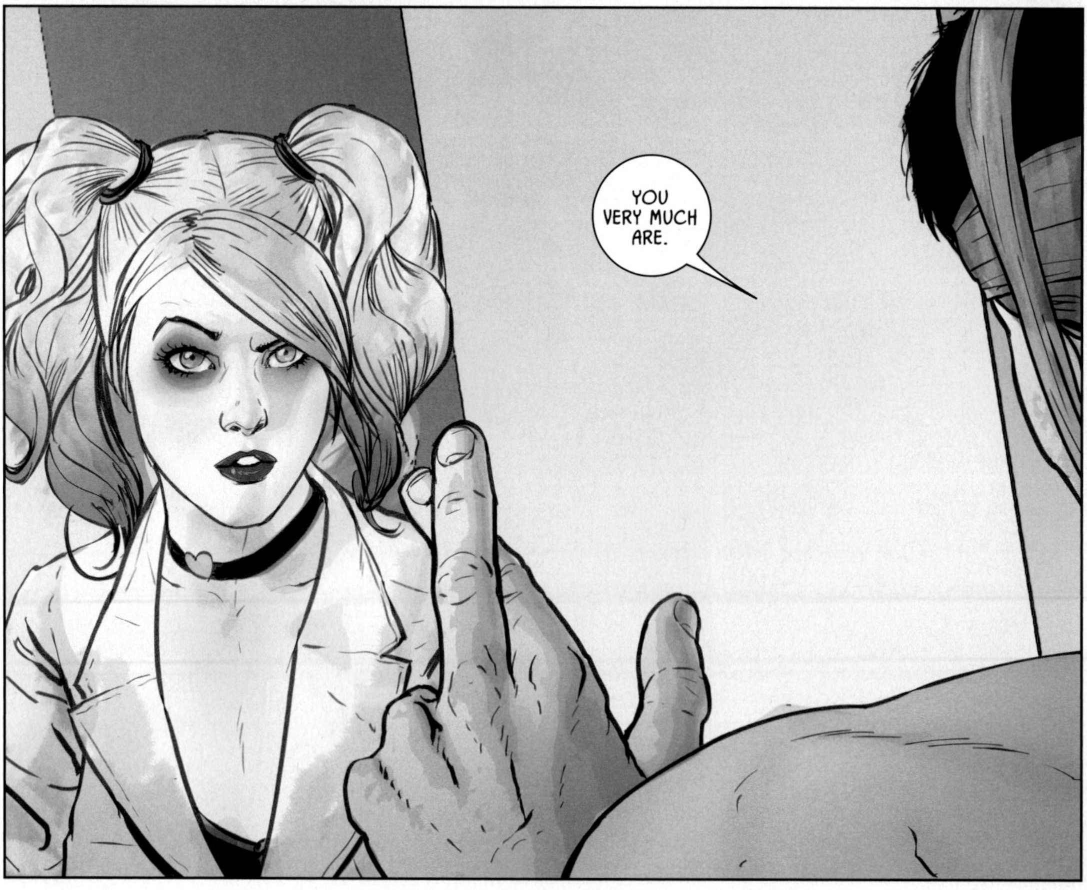
YOU VERY MUCH ARE.

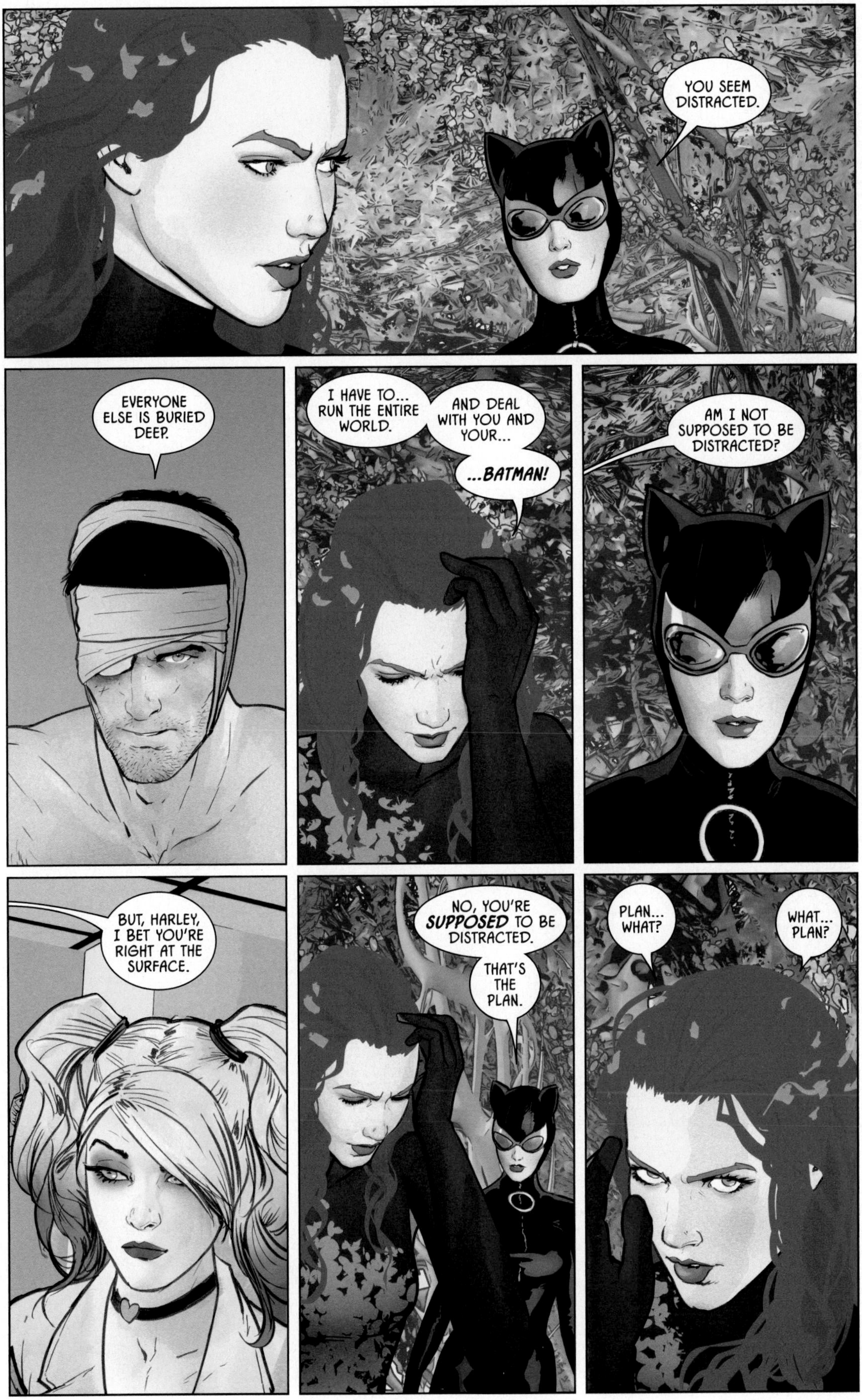
YOU SEEM DISTRACTED.
EVERYONE ELSE IS BURIED DEEP.
I HAVE TO... RUN THE ENTIRE WORLD.
AND DEAL WITH YOU AND YOUR...
...BATMAN!
AM I NOT SUPPOSED TO BE DISTRACTED?
BUT, HARLEY, I BET YOU'RE RIGHT AT THE SURFACE.
NO, YOU'RE SUPPOSED TO BE DISTRACTED.
THAT'S THE PLAN.
PLAN... WHAT?
WHAT... PLAN?

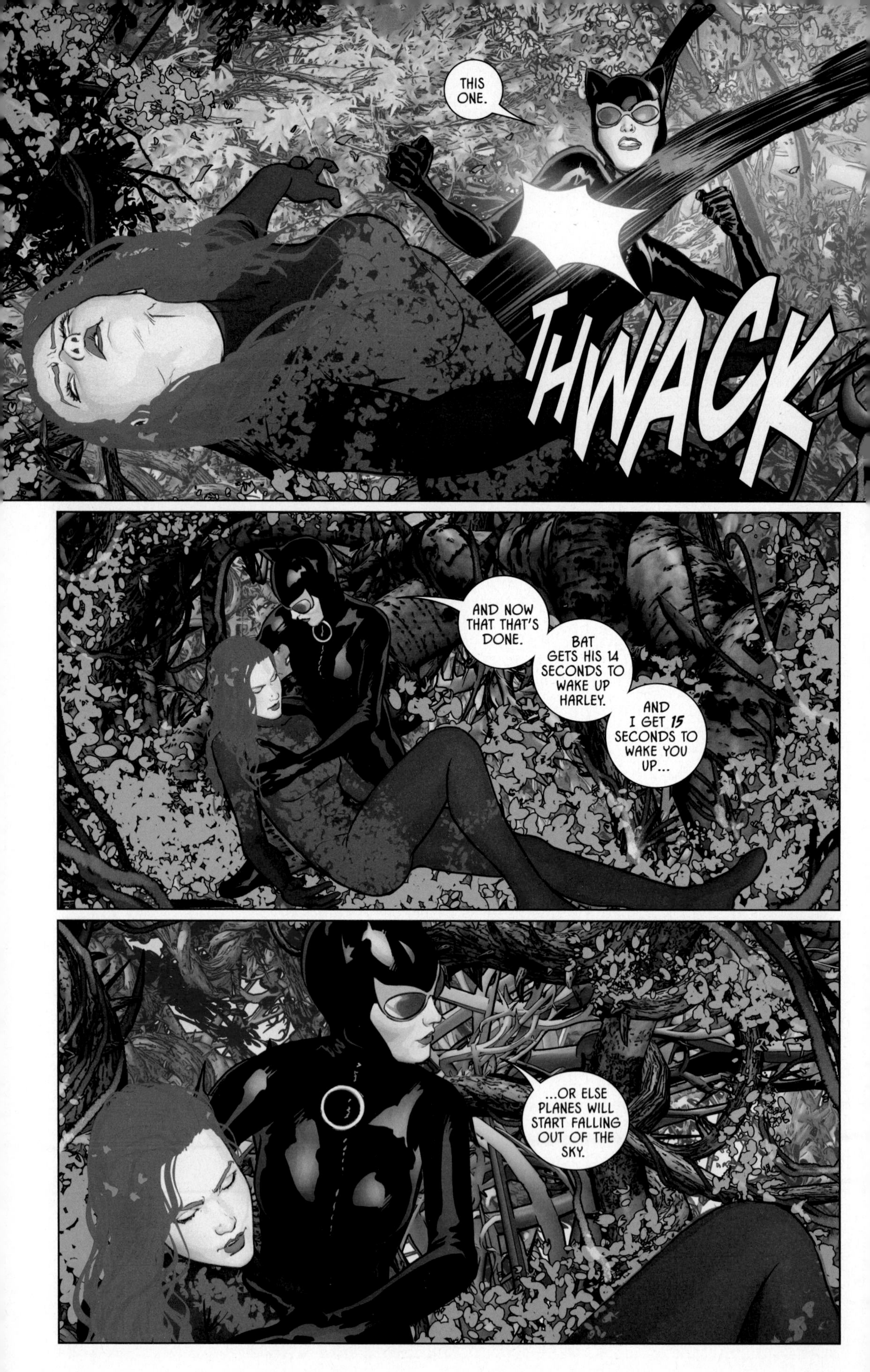
THIS ONE.
THWACK
AND NOW THAT THAT'S DONE.
BAT GETS HIS 14 SECONDS TO WAKE UP HARLEY.
AND I GET 15 SECONDS TO WAKE YOU UP...
...OR ELSE PLANES WILL START FALLING OUT OF THE SKY.

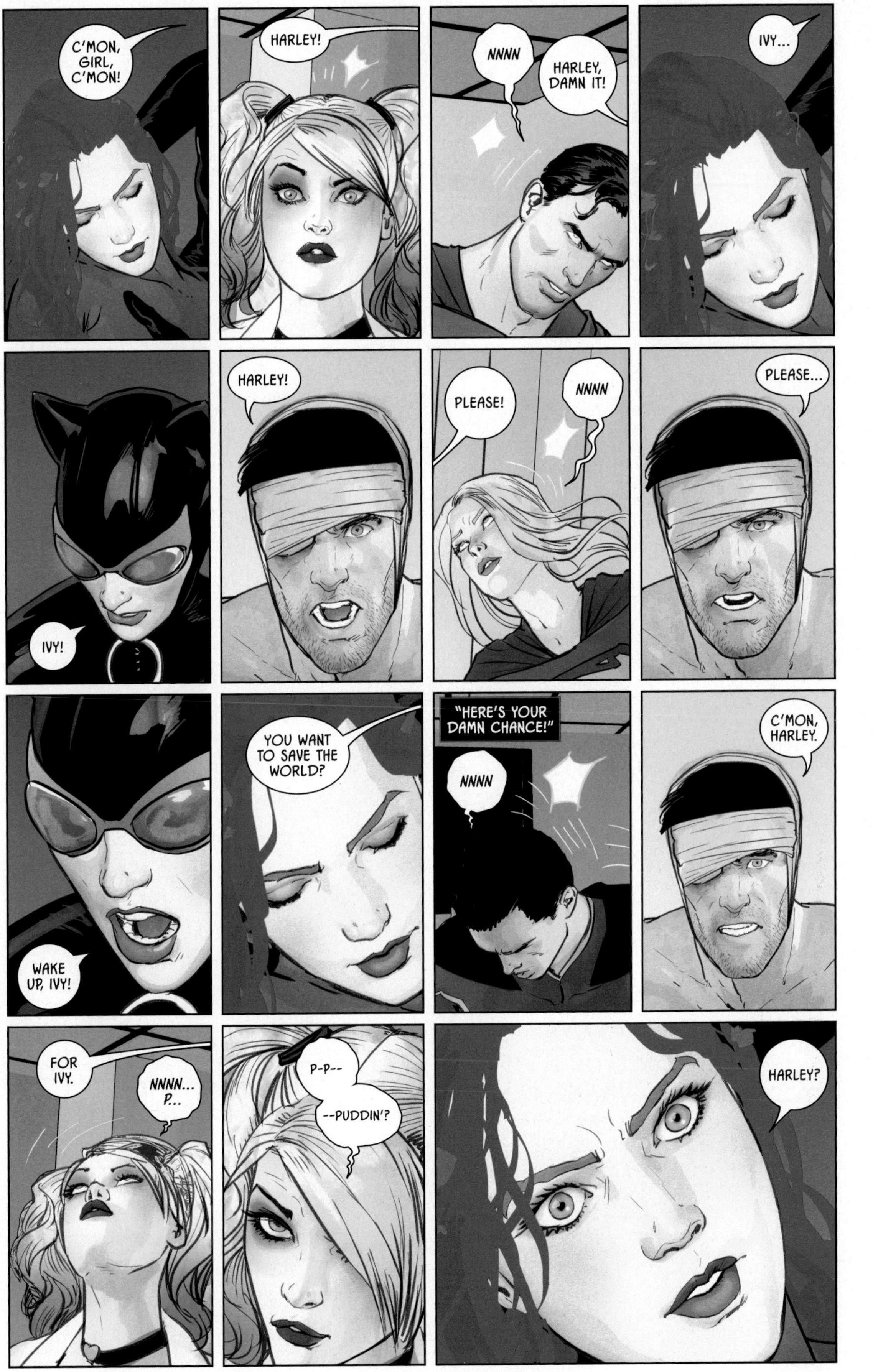
C'MON, GIRL, C'MON!
HARLEY!
NNNN
HARLEY, DAMN IT!
IVY...
IVY!
HARLEY!
PLEASE!
NNNN
PLEASE...
WAKE UP, IVY!
YOU WANT TO SAVE THE WORLD?
"HERE'S YOUR DAMN CHANCE!"
NNNN
C'MON, HARLEY.
FOR IVY.
NNNN... P...
P-P--
--PUDDIN'?
HARLEY?

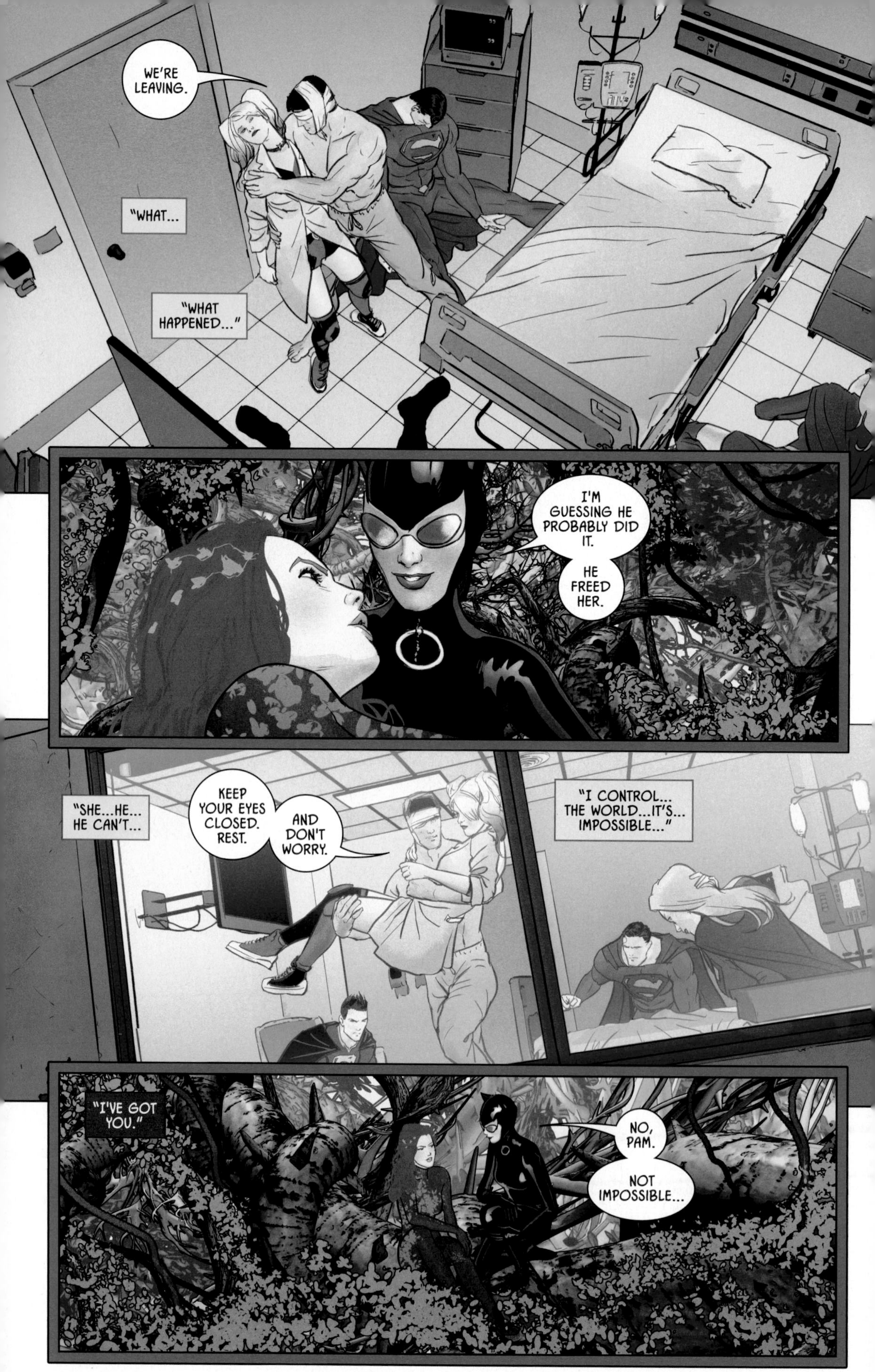
WE'RE LEAVING.
"WHAT...
"WHAT HAPPENED..."
I'M GUESSING HE PROBABLY DID IT.
HE FREED HER.
"SHE...HE... HE CAN'T...
KEEP YOUR EYES CLOSED. REST.
AND DON'T WORRY.
"I CONTROL... THE WORLD...IT'S... IMPOSSIBLE..."
"I'VE GOT YOU."
NO, PAM.
NOT IMPOSSIBLE...

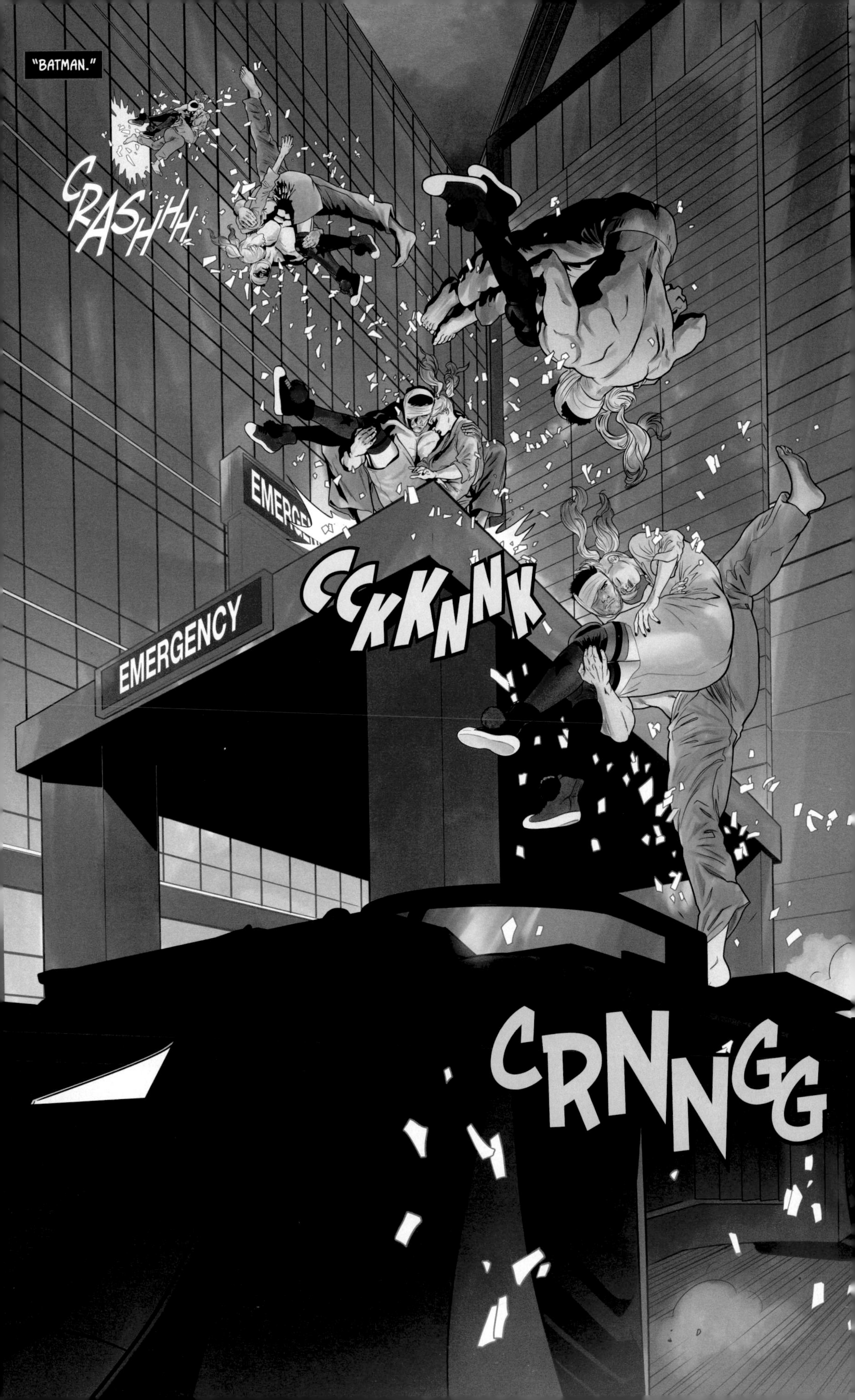
"BATMAN."
CRASHHH
EMERGENCY
CCKNNK
CRNNGG

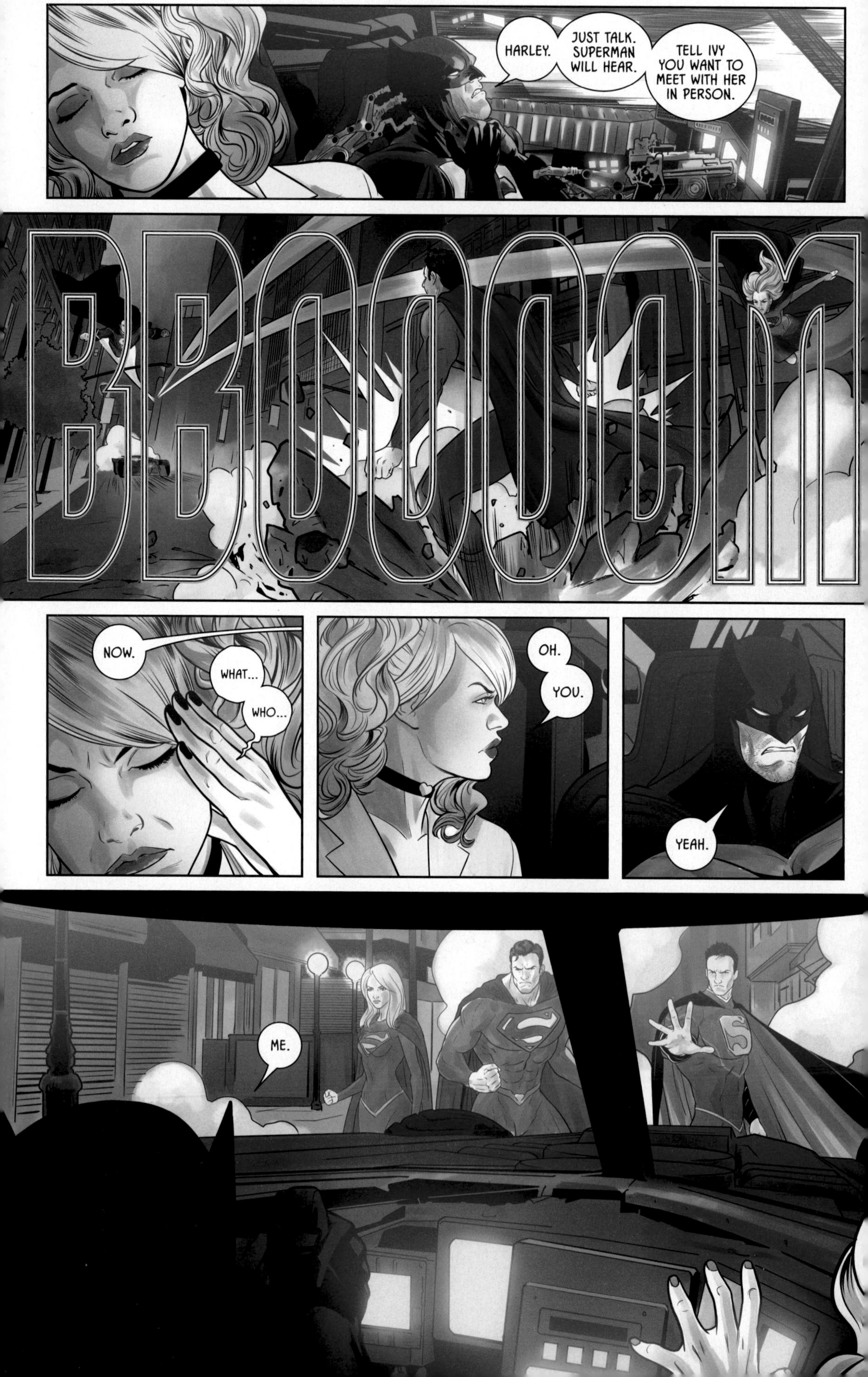
HARLEY.
JUST TALK. SUPERMAN WILL HEAR.
TELL IVY YOU WANT TO MEET WITH HER IN PERSON.
BBOOOOOM
NOW.
WHAT...
WHO...
OH.
YOU.
YEAH.
ME.

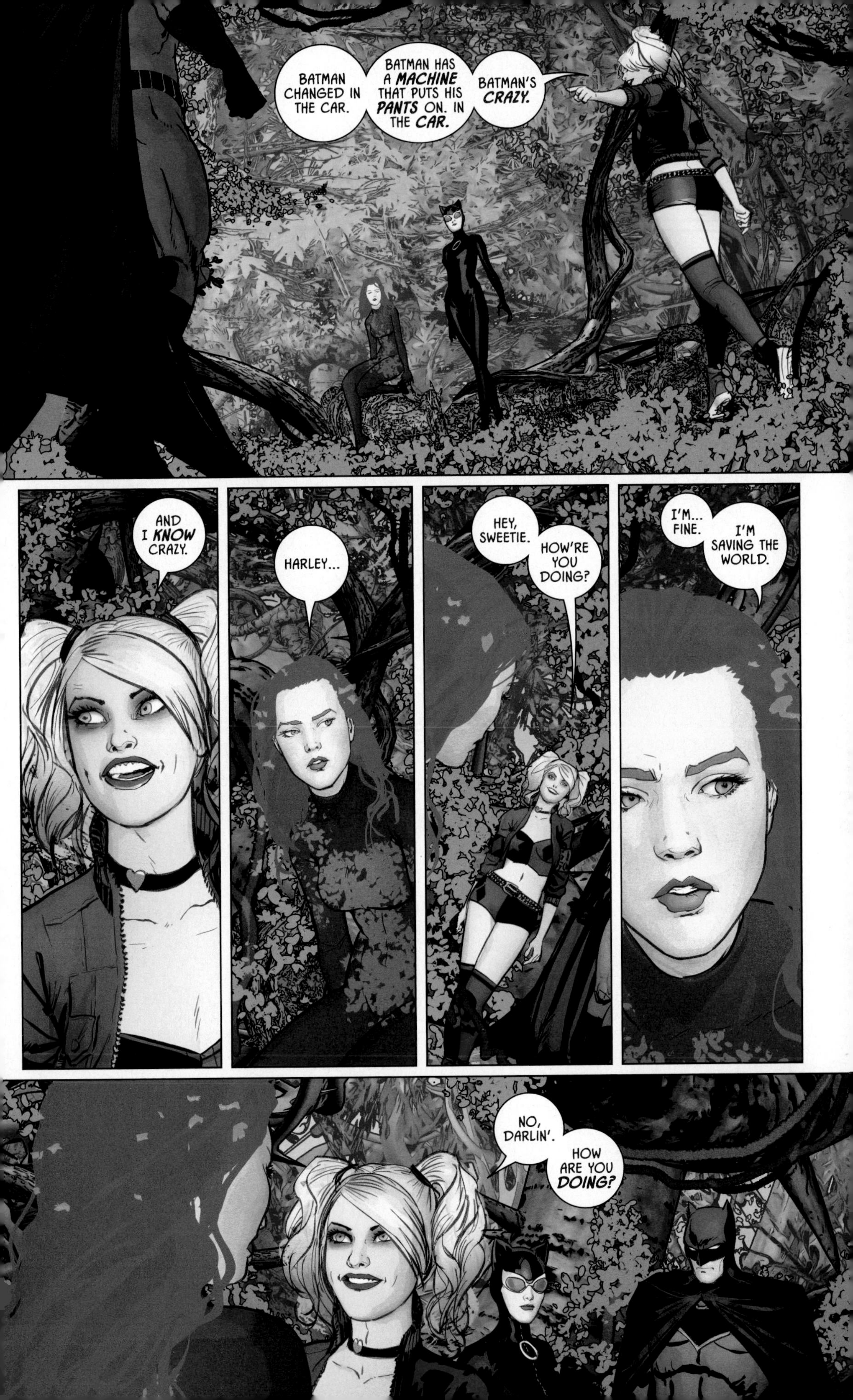
BATMAN CHANGED IN THE CAR.
BATMAN HAS A MACHINE THAT PUTS HIS PANTS ON. IN THE CAR.
BATMAN'S CRAZY.
AND I KNOW CRAZY.
HARLEY...
HEY, SWEETIE.
HOW'RE YOU DOING?
I'M... FINE.
I'M SAVING THE WORLD.
NO, DARLIN'.
HOW ARE YOU DOING?

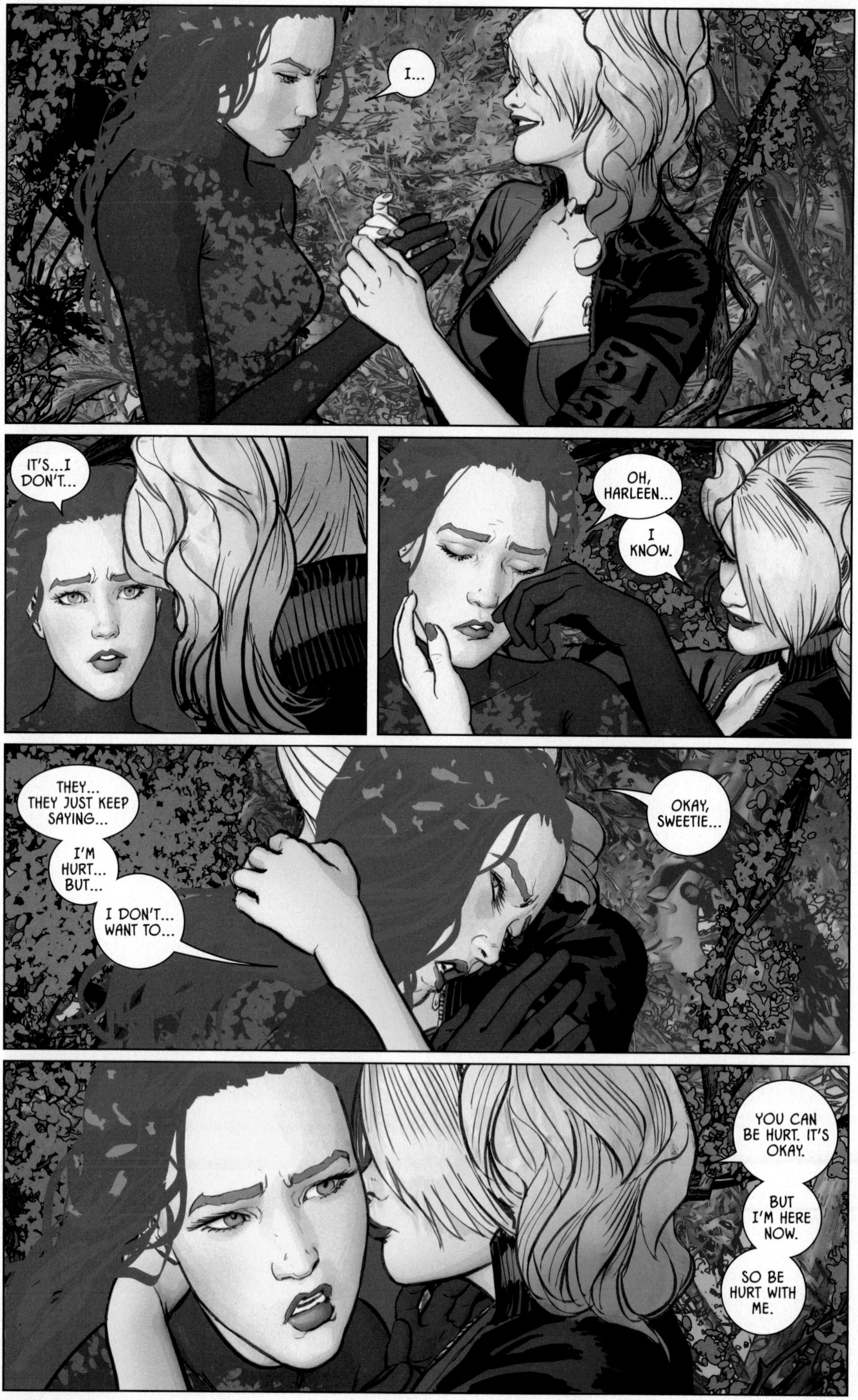
I...
IT'S...I DON'T...
OH, HARLEEN...
I KNOW.
THEY... THEY JUST KEEP SAYING...
I'M HURT... BUT...
I DON'T... WANT TO...
OKAY, SWEETIE...
YOU CAN BE HURT. IT'S OKAY.
BUT I'M HERE NOW.
SO BE HURT WITH ME.

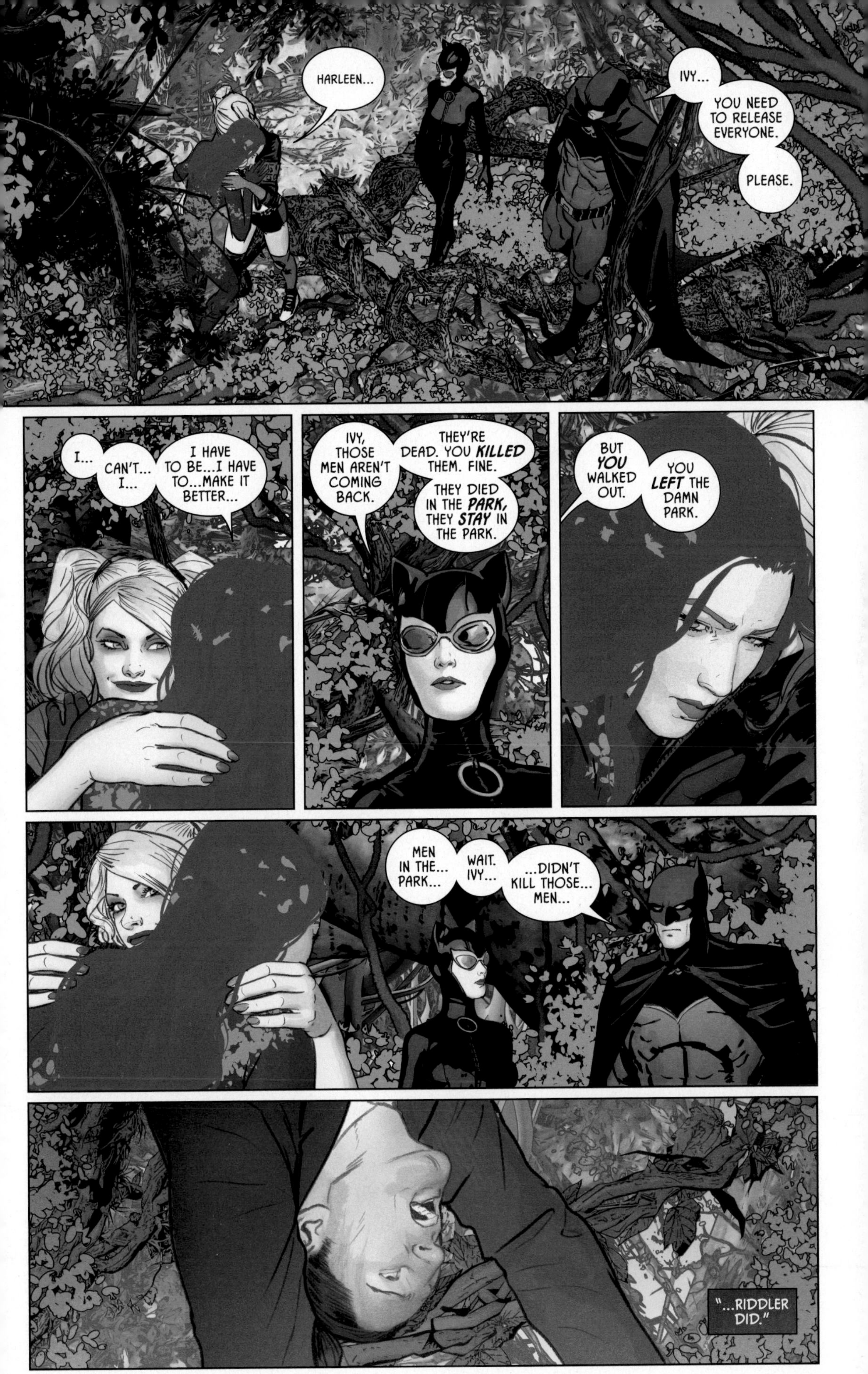
HARLEEN...
IVY...
YOU NEED TO RELEASE EVERYONE.
PLEASE.
I...
CAN'T... I...
I HAVE TO BE...I HAVE TO...MAKE IT BETTER...
IVY, THOSE MEN AREN'T COMING BACK.
THEY'RE DEAD. YOU KILLED THEM. FINE.
THEY DIED IN THE PARK, THEY STAY IN THE PARK.
BUT YOU WALKED OUT.
YOU LEFT THE DAMN PARK.
MEN IN THE... PARK...
WAIT. IVY...
...DIDN'T KILL THOSE... MEN...
"...RIDDLER DID."

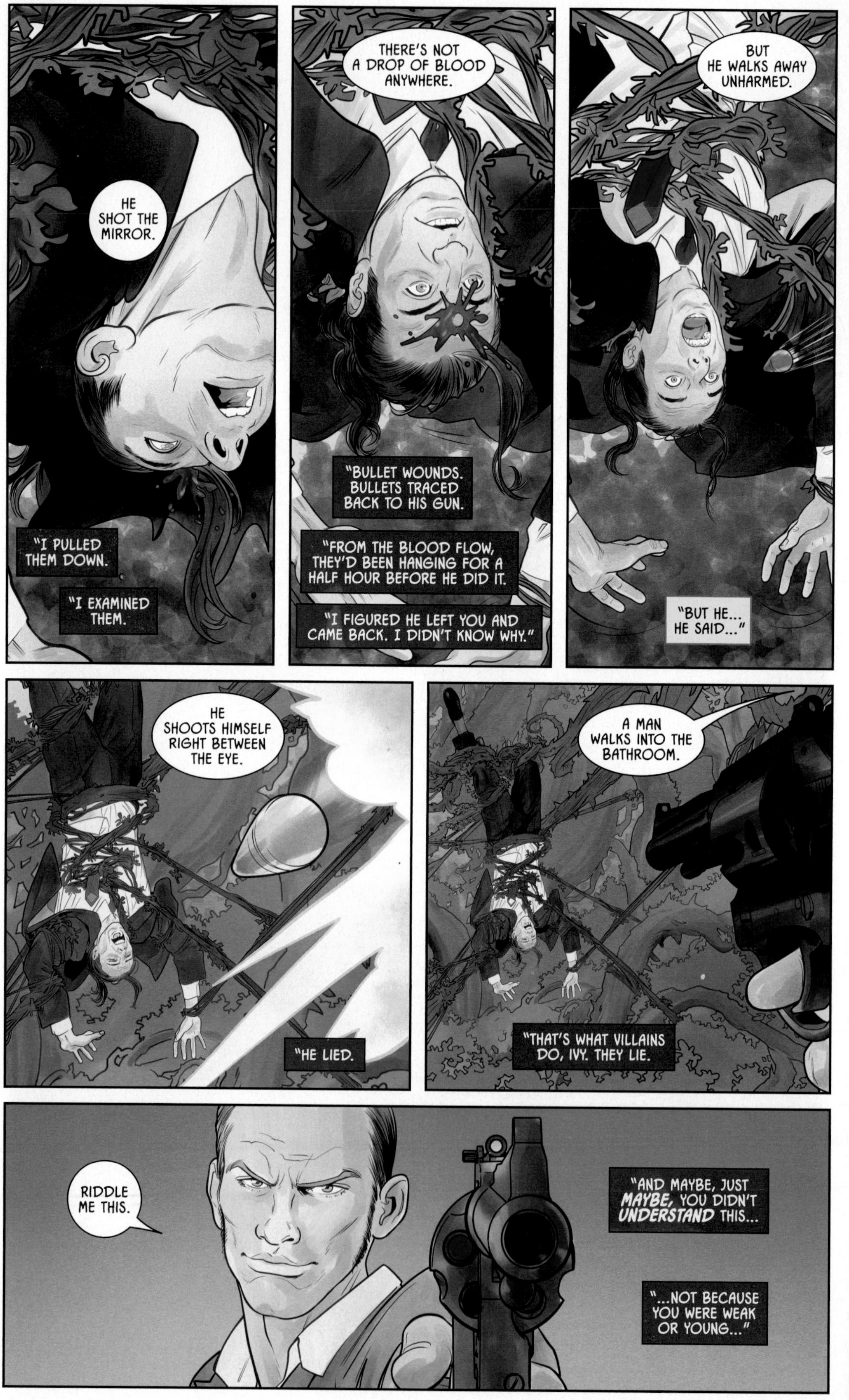
HE SHOT THE MIRROR.
"I PULLED THEM DOWN.
"I EXAMINED THEM.
THERE'S NOT A DROP OF BLOOD ANYWHERE.
"BULLET WOUNDS. BULLETS TRACED BACK TO HIS GUN.
"FROM THE BLOOD FLOW, THEY'D BEEN HANGING FOR A HALF HOUR BEFORE HE DID IT.
"I FIGURED HE LEFT YOU AND CAME BACK. I DIDN'T KNOW WHY."
BUT HE WALKS AWAY UNHARMED.
"BUT HE... HE SAID..."
HE SHOOTS HIMSELF RIGHT BETWEEN THE EYE.
"HE LIED.
A MAN WALKS INTO THE BATHROOM.
"THAT'S WHAT VILLAINS DO, IVY. THEY LIE.
RIDDLE ME THIS.
"AND MAYBE, JUST MAYBE, YOU DIDN'T UNDERSTAND THIS...
"...NOT BECAUSE YOU WERE WEAK OR YOUNG..."

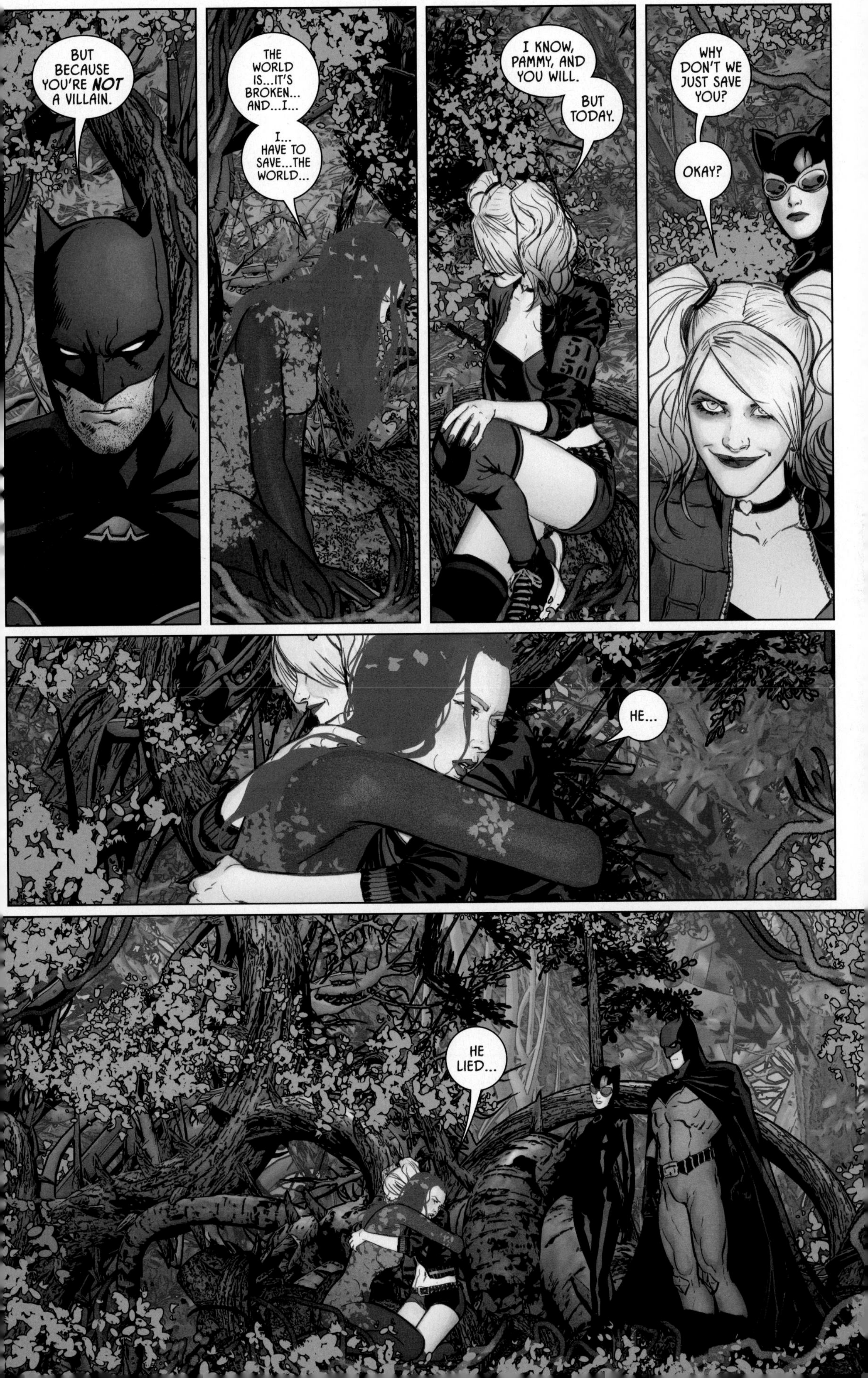
BUT BECAUSE YOU'RE NOT A VILLAIN.
THE WORLD IS...IT'S BROKEN... AND...I...
I... HAVE TO SAVE...THE WORLD...
I KNOW, PAMMY, AND YOU WILL.
BUT TODAY.
WHY DON'T WE JUST SAVE YOU?
OKAY?
HE...
HE LIED...

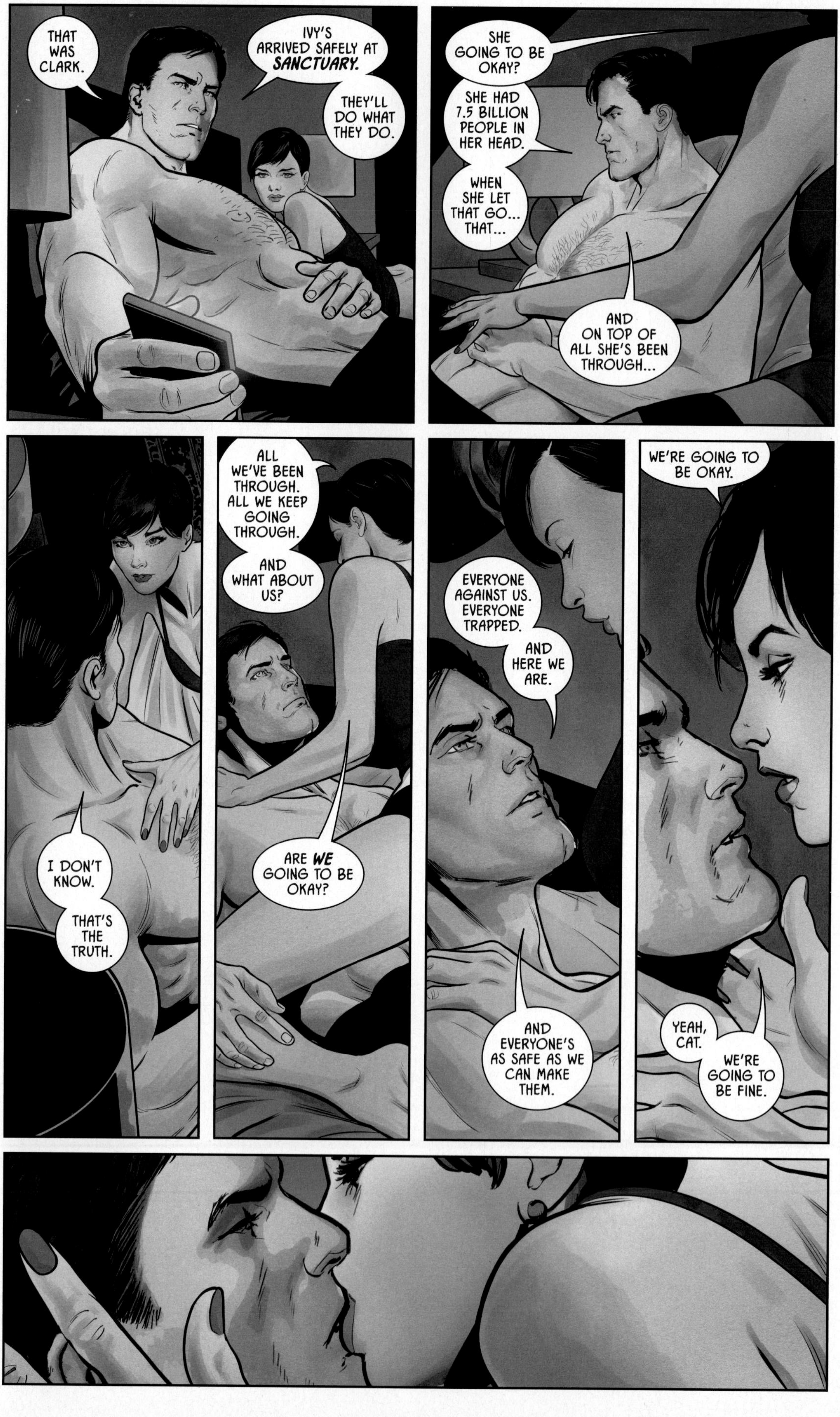
THAT WAS CLARK.
IVY'S ARRIVED SAFELY AT **SANCTUARY.**
THEY'LL DO WHAT THEY DO.
SHE GOING TO BE OKAY?
SHE HAD 7.5 BILLION PEOPLE IN HER HEAD.
WHEN SHE LET THAT GO... THAT...
AND ON TOP OF ALL SHE'S BEEN THROUGH...
I DON'T KNOW.
THAT'S THE TRUTH.
ALL WE'VE BEEN THROUGH. ALL WE KEEP GOING THROUGH.
AND WHAT ABOUT US?
ARE **WE** GOING TO BE OKAY?
EVERYONE AGAINST US. EVERYONE TRAPPED.
AND HERE WE ARE.
AND EVERYONE'S AS SAFE AS WE CAN MAKE THEM.
WE'RE GOING TO BE OKAY.
YEAH, CAT.
WE'RE GOING TO BE FINE.

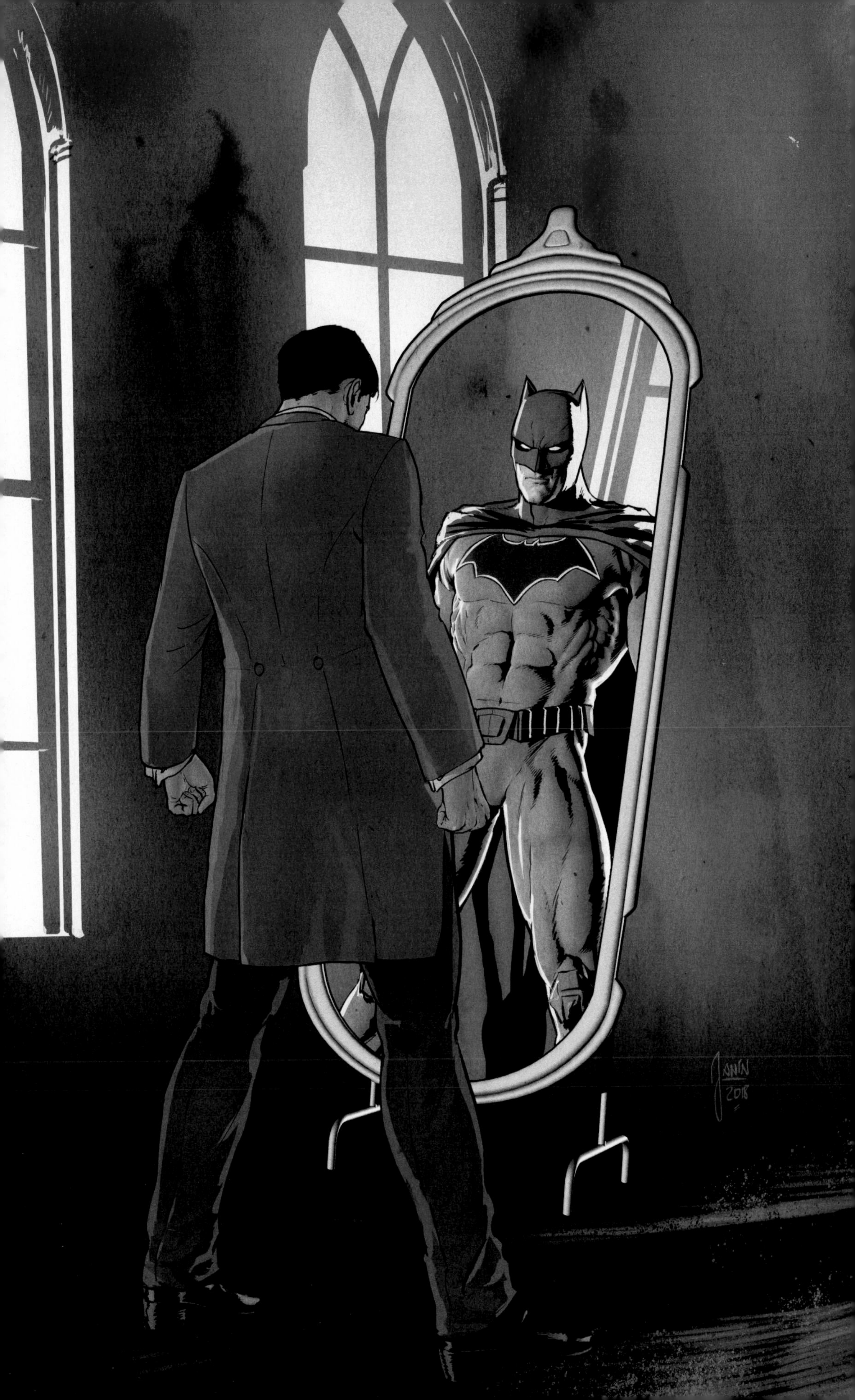
JANIN
2018

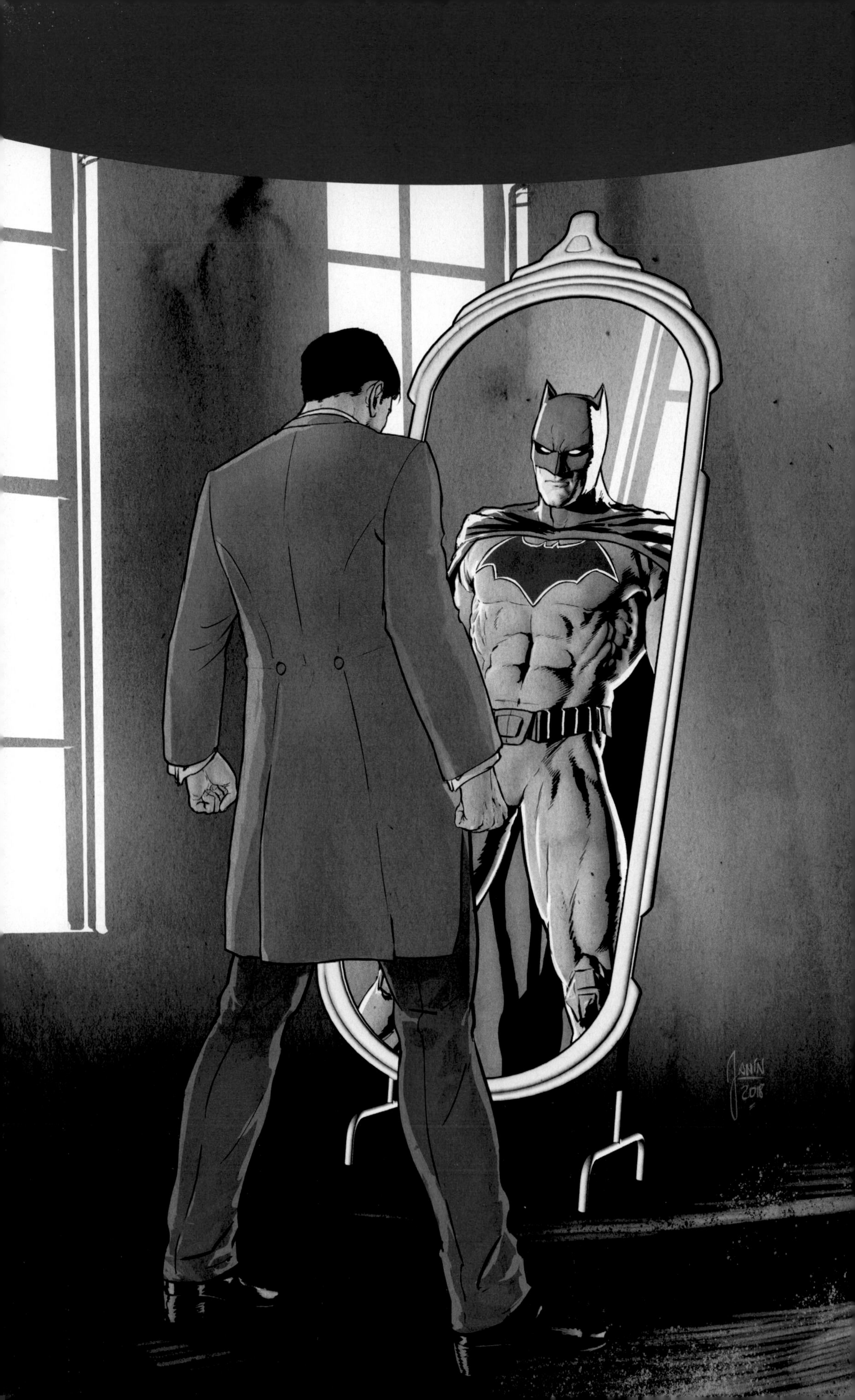
JANIN
2018

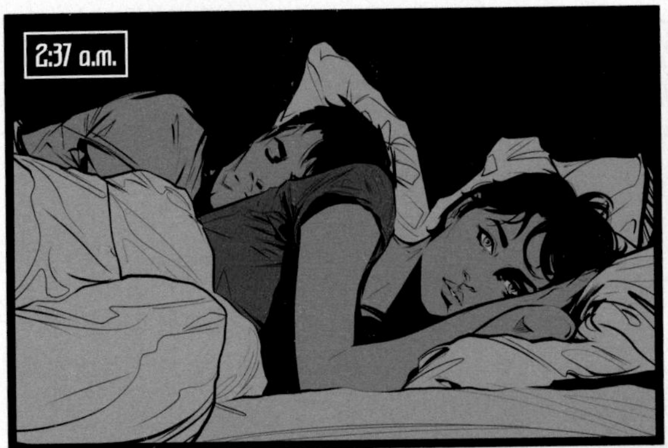
2:37 a.m.
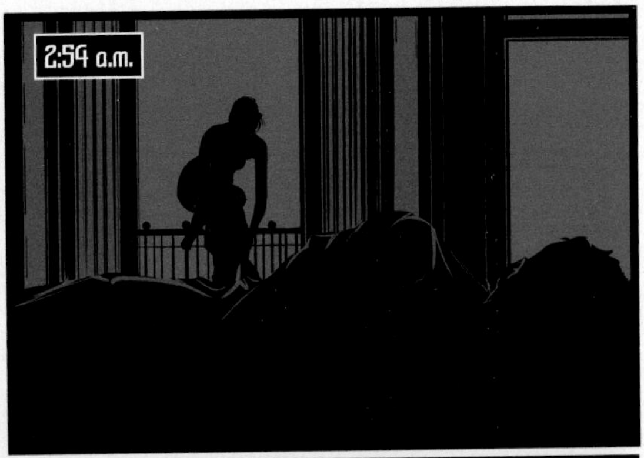
2:54 a.m.
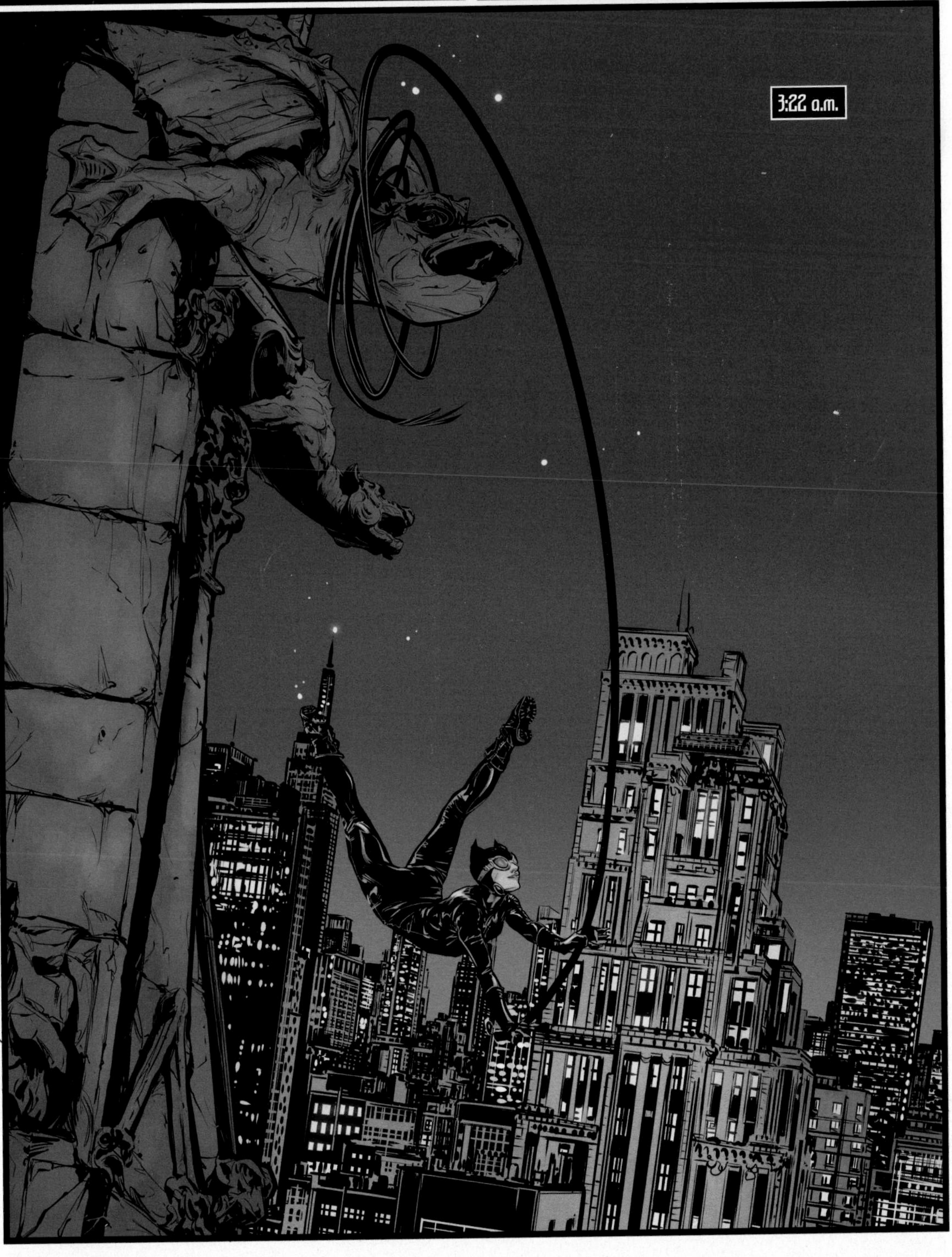
3:22 a.m.

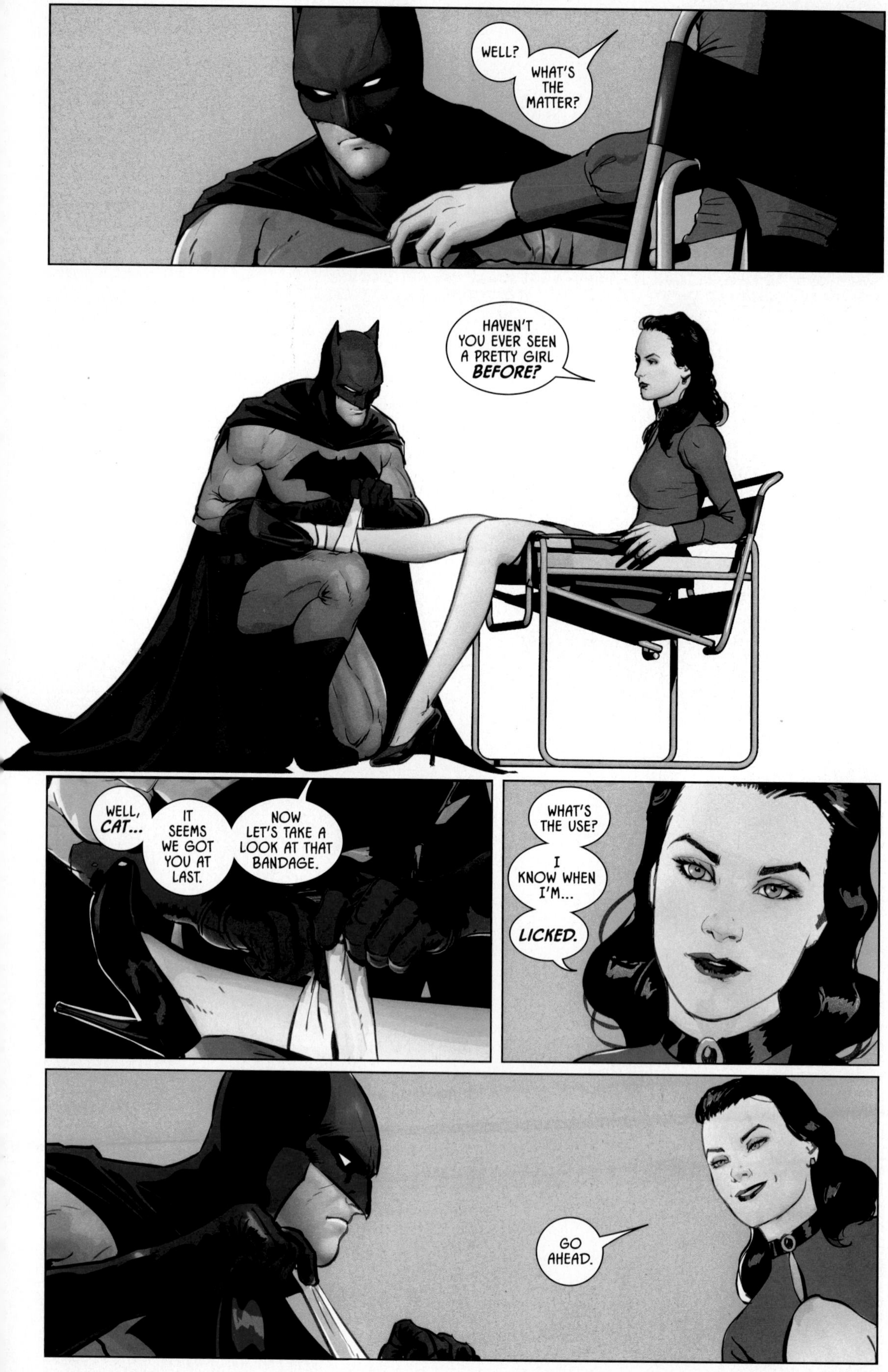
WELL?
WHAT'S THE MATTER?
HAVEN'T YOU EVER SEEN A PRETTY GIRL *BEFORE?*
WELL, *CAT...*
IT SEEMS WE GOT YOU AT LAST.
NOW LET'S TAKE A LOOK AT THAT BANDAGE.
WHAT'S THE USE?
I KNOW WHEN I'M...
LICKED.
GO AHEAD.

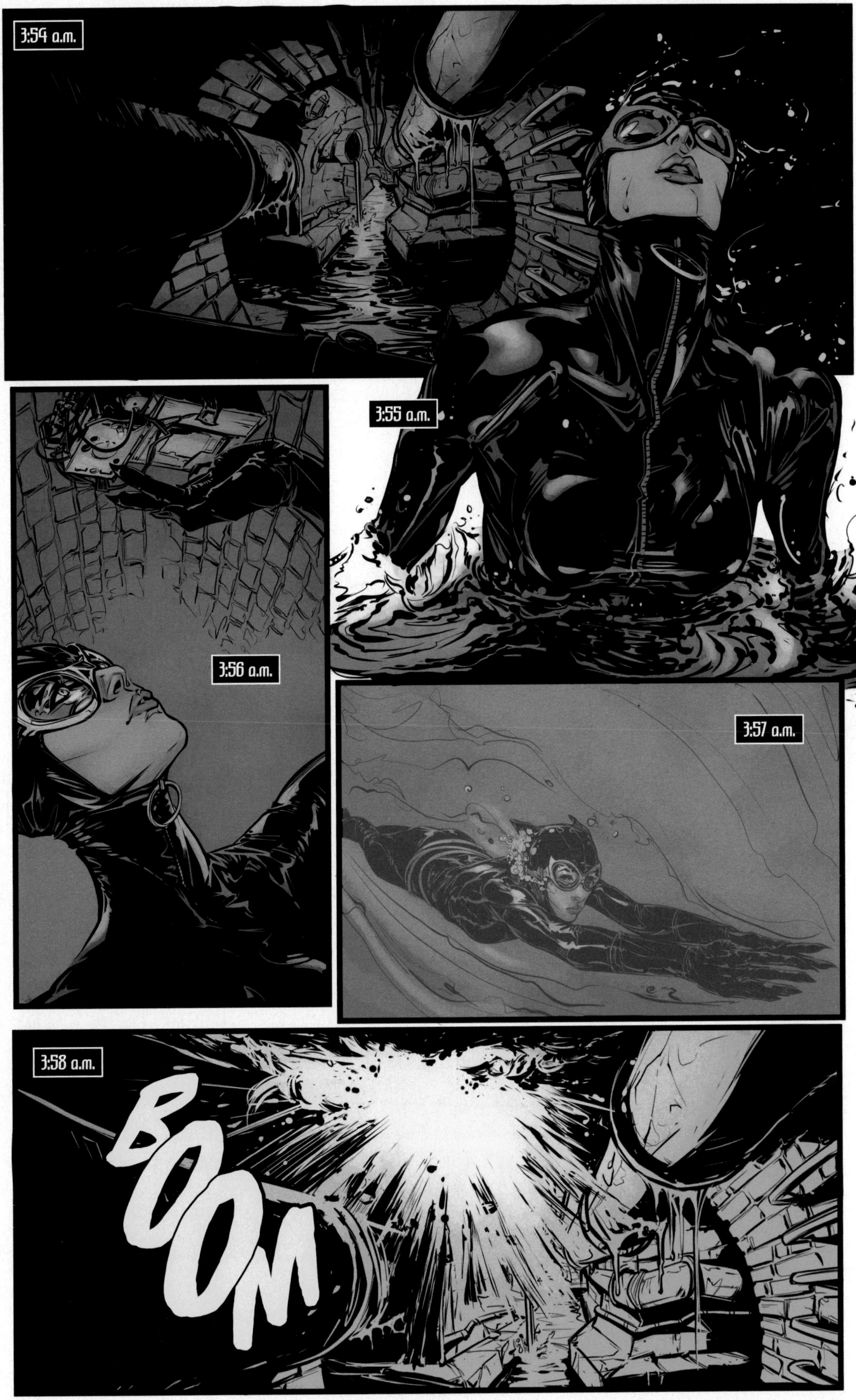
3:54 a.m.
3:55 a.m.
3:56 a.m.
3:57 a.m.
3:58 a.m.
BOOM

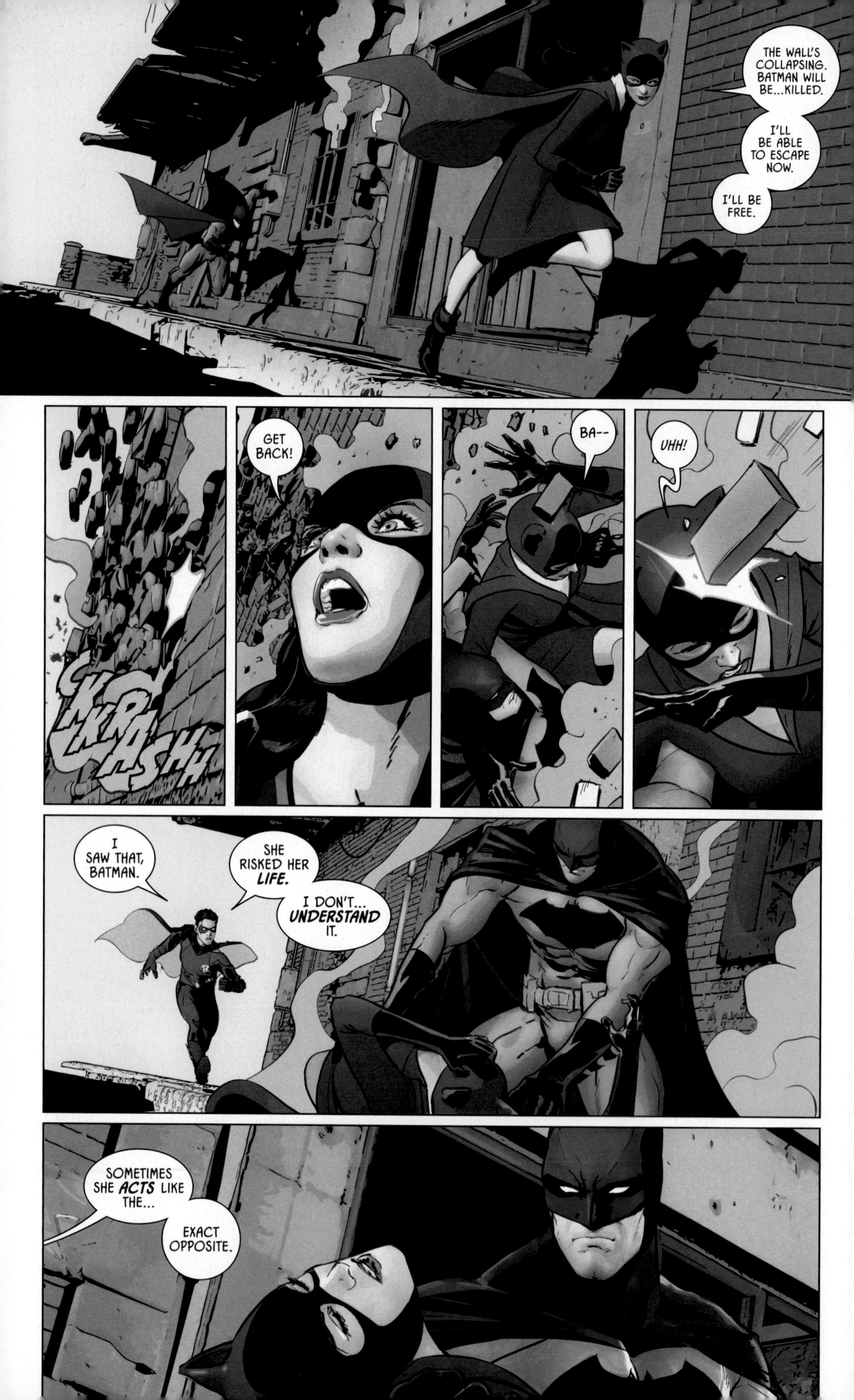
THE WALL'S COLLAPSING. BATMAN WILL BE...KILLED.
I'LL BE ABLE TO ESCAPE NOW.
I'LL BE FREE.
CKRASHH
GET BACK!
BA--
UHH!
I SAW THAT, BATMAN.
SHE RISKED HER LIFE.
I DON'T... UNDERSTAND IT.
SOMETIMES SHE ACTS LIKE THE...
EXACT OPPOSITE.

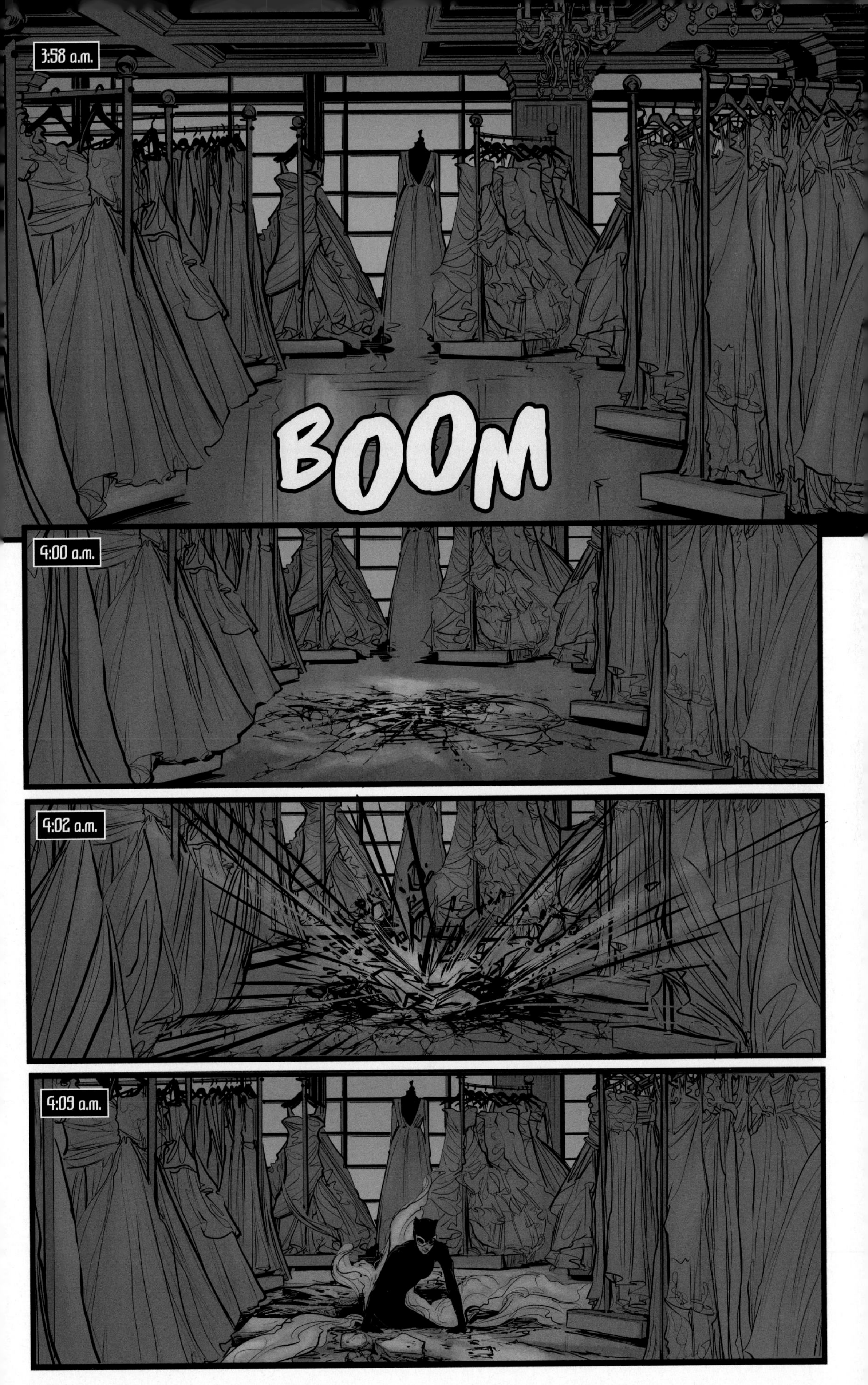
3:58 a.m.
BOOM
4:00 a.m.
4:02 a.m.
4:09 a.m.

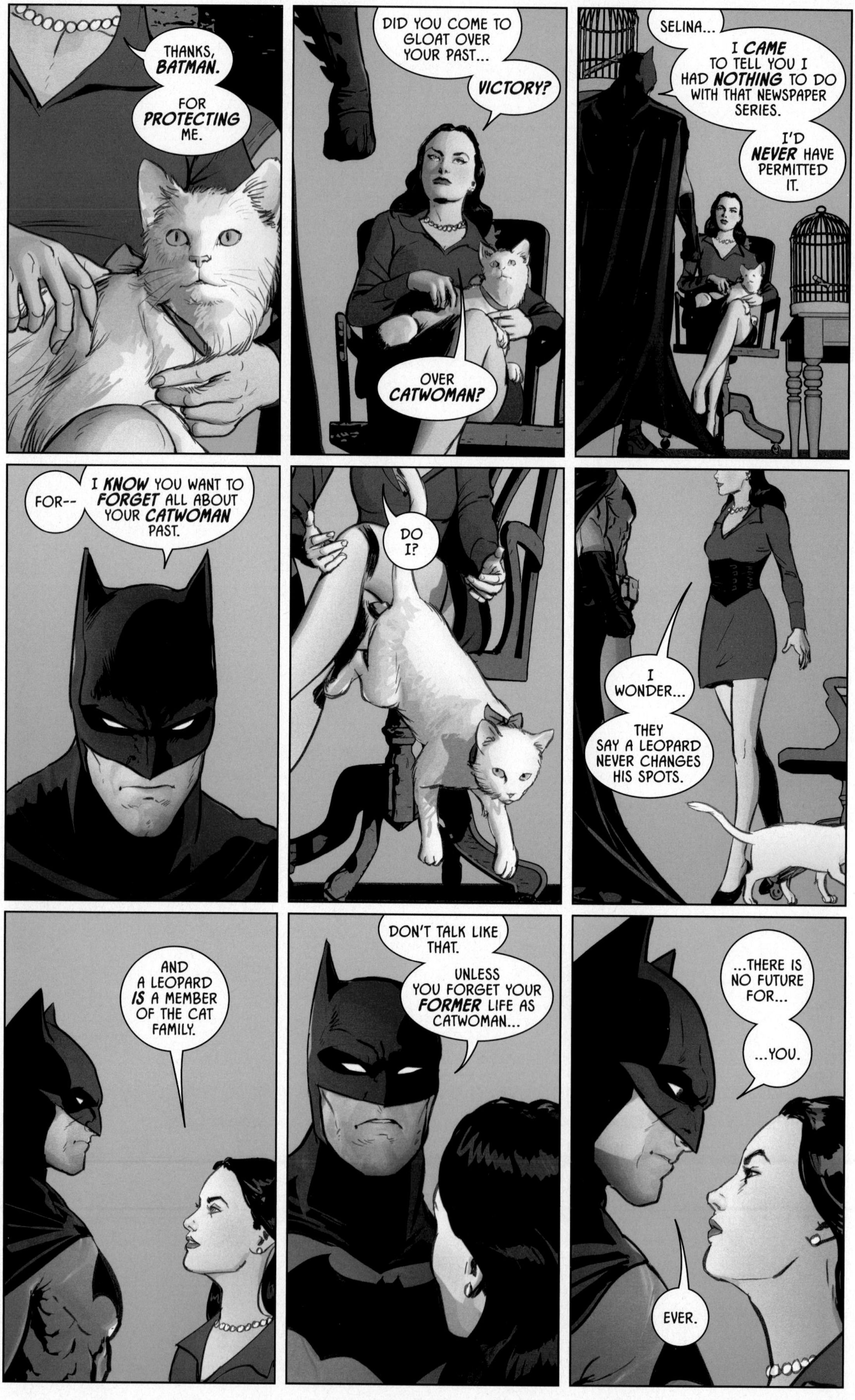
THANKS, BATMAN.
FOR PROTECTING ME.
DID YOU COME TO GLOAT OVER YOUR PAST...
VICTORY?
OVER CATWOMAN?
SELINA...
I CAME TO TELL YOU I HAD NOTHING TO DO WITH THAT NEWSPAPER SERIES.
I'D NEVER HAVE PERMITTED IT.
FOR--
I KNOW YOU WANT TO FORGET ALL ABOUT YOUR CATWOMAN PAST.
DO I?
I WONDER...
THEY SAY A LEOPARD NEVER CHANGES HIS SPOTS.
AND A LEOPARD IS A MEMBER OF THE CAT FAMILY.
DON'T TALK LIKE THAT.
UNLESS YOU FORGET YOUR FORMER LIFE AS CATWOMAN...
...THERE IS NO FUTURE FOR...
...YOU.
EVER.

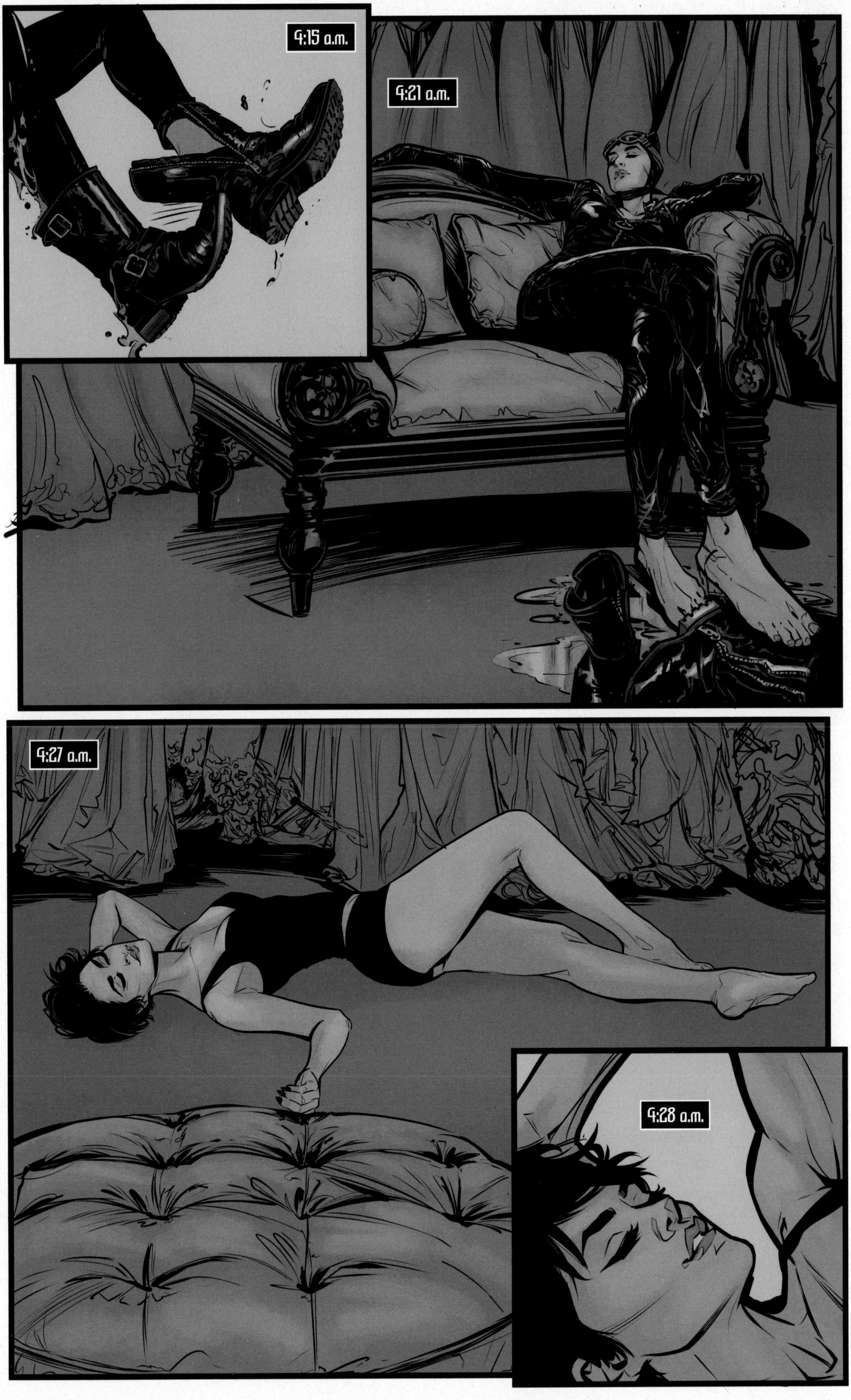

4:15 a.m.
4:21 a.m.
4:27 a.m.
4:28 a.m.

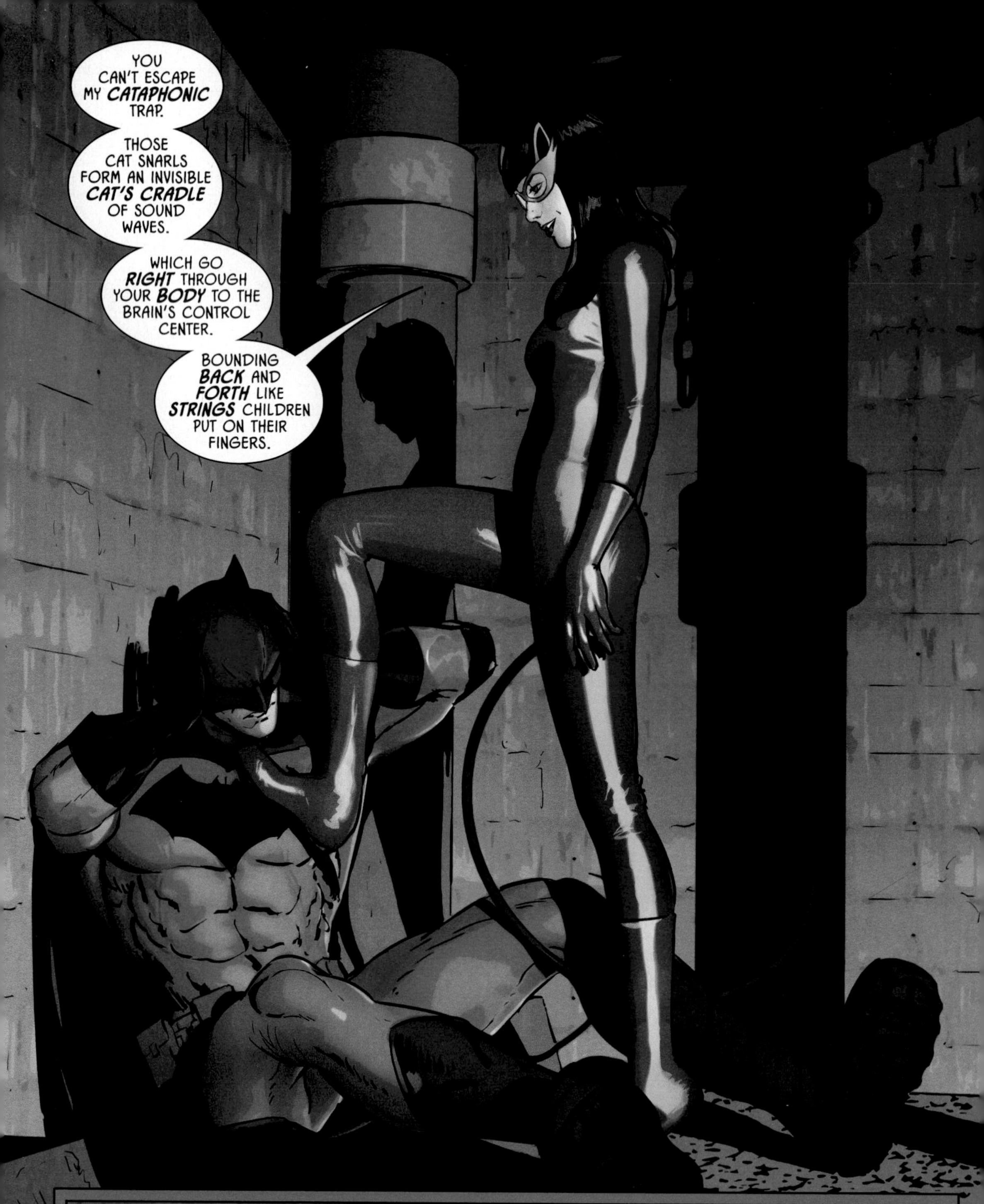
YOU CAN'T ESCAPE MY CATAPHONIC TRAP.
THOSE CAT SNARLS FORM AN INVISIBLE CAT'S CRADLE OF SOUND WAVES.
WHICH GO RIGHT THROUGH YOUR BODY TO THE BRAIN'S CONTROL CENTER.
BOUNDING BACK AND FORTH LIKE STRINGS CHILDREN PUT ON THEIR FINGERS.

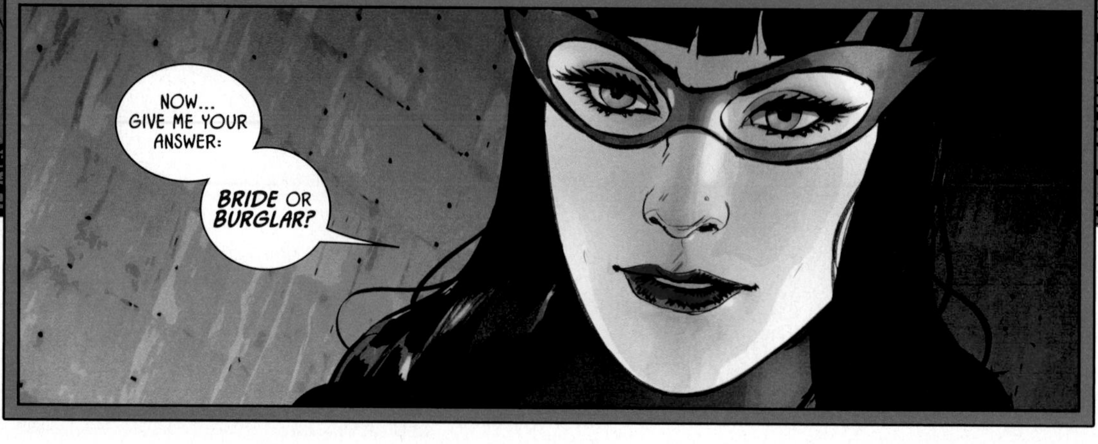
NOW... GIVE ME YOUR ANSWER:
BRIDE OR BURGLAR?

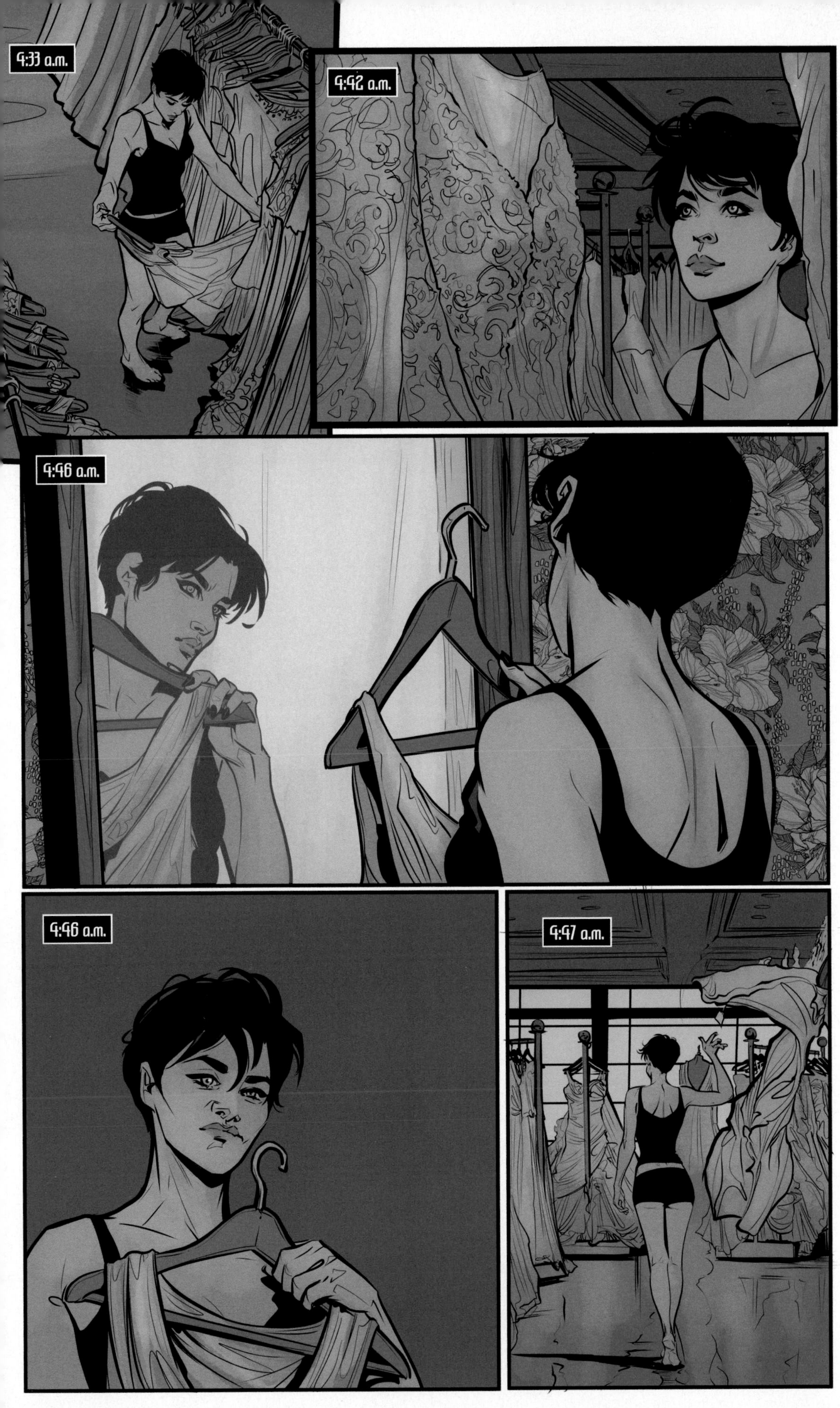
4:33 a.m.
4:42 a.m.
4:46 a.m.
4:46 a.m.
4:47 a.m.

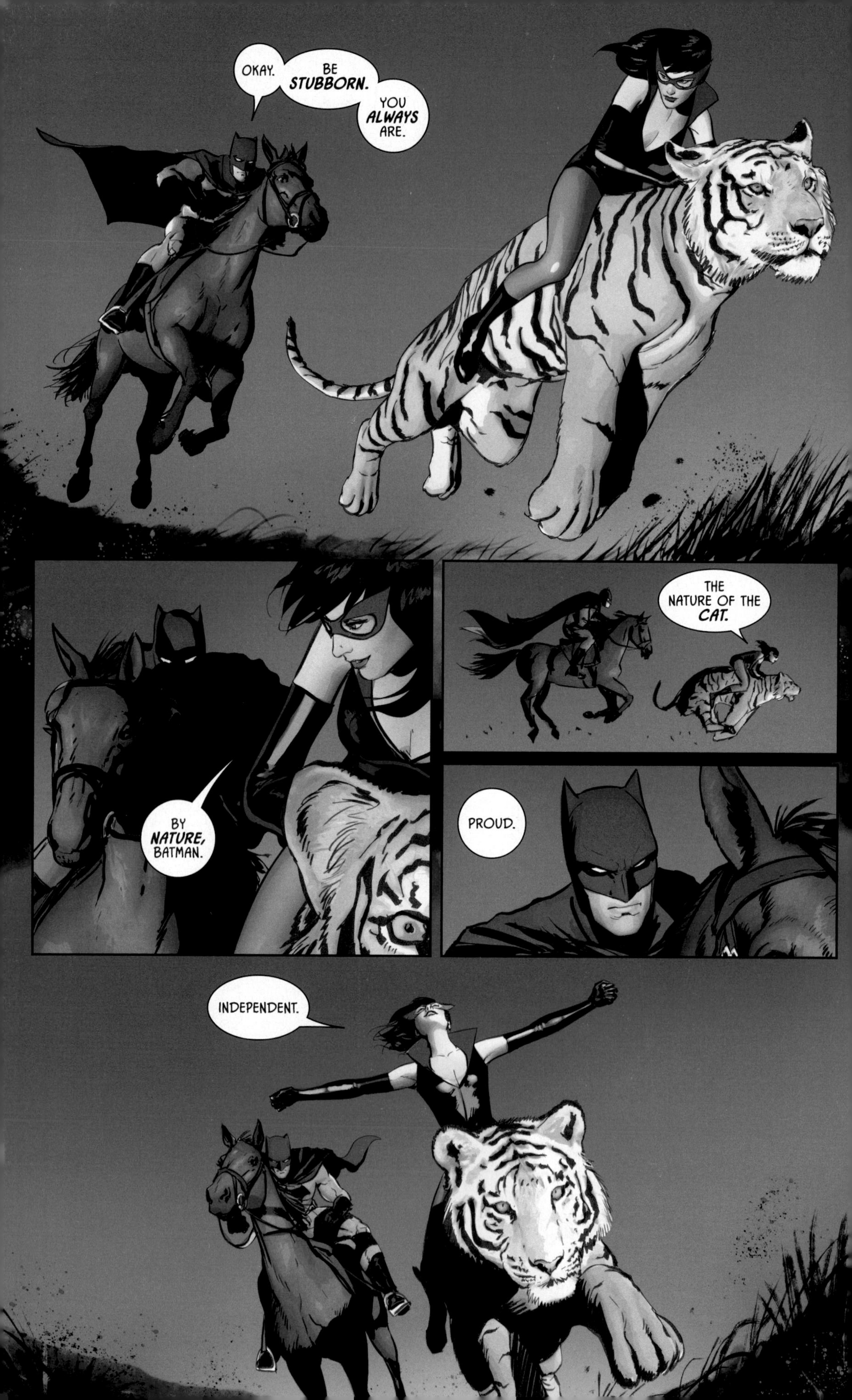
OKAY.
BE STUBBORN.
YOU ALWAYS ARE.
BY NATURE, BATMAN.
THE NATURE OF THE CAT.
PROUD.
INDEPENDENT.

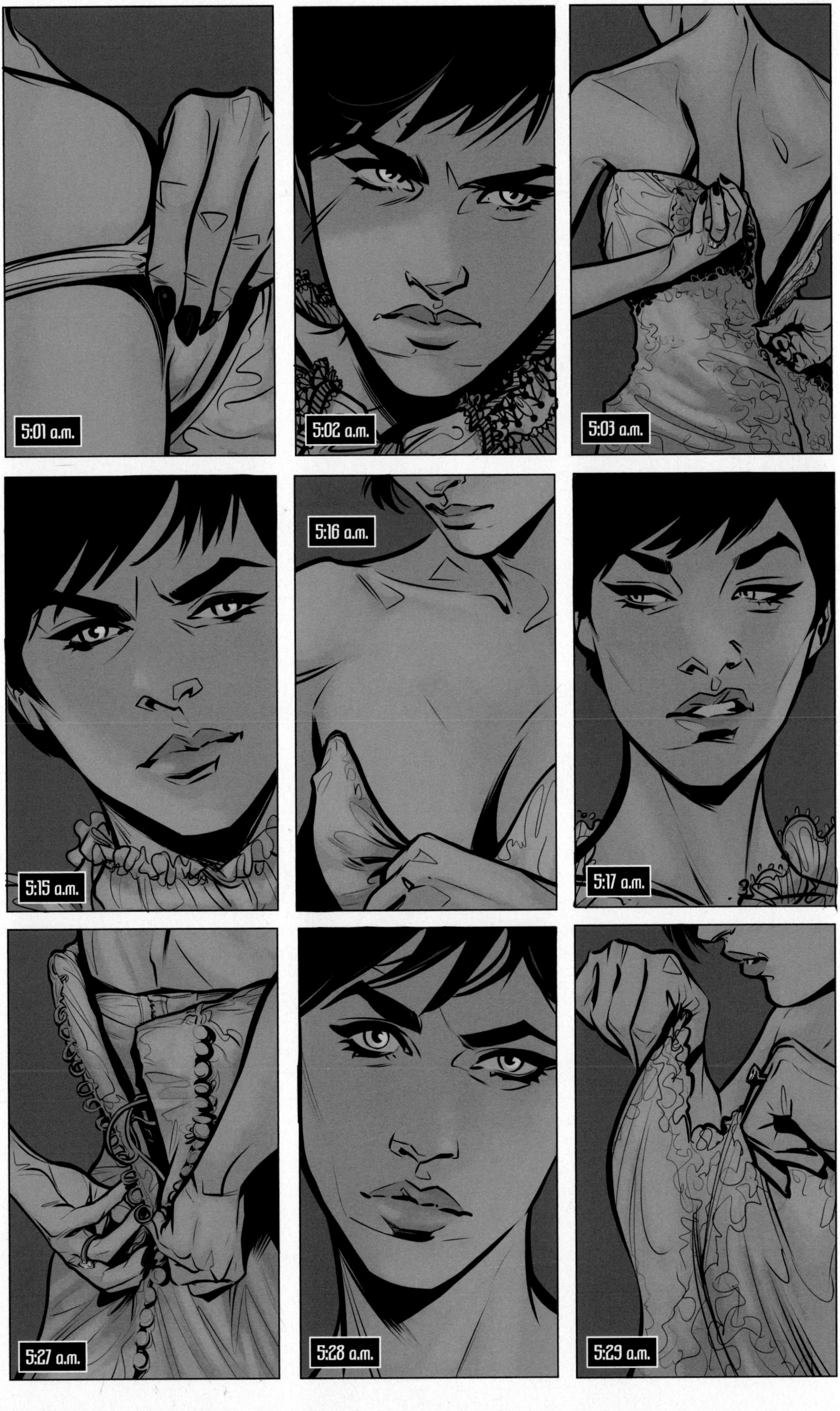
5:01 a.m.
5:02 a.m.
5:03 a.m.
5:15 a.m.
5:16 a.m.
5:17 a.m.
5:27 a.m.
5:28 a.m.
5:29 a.m.

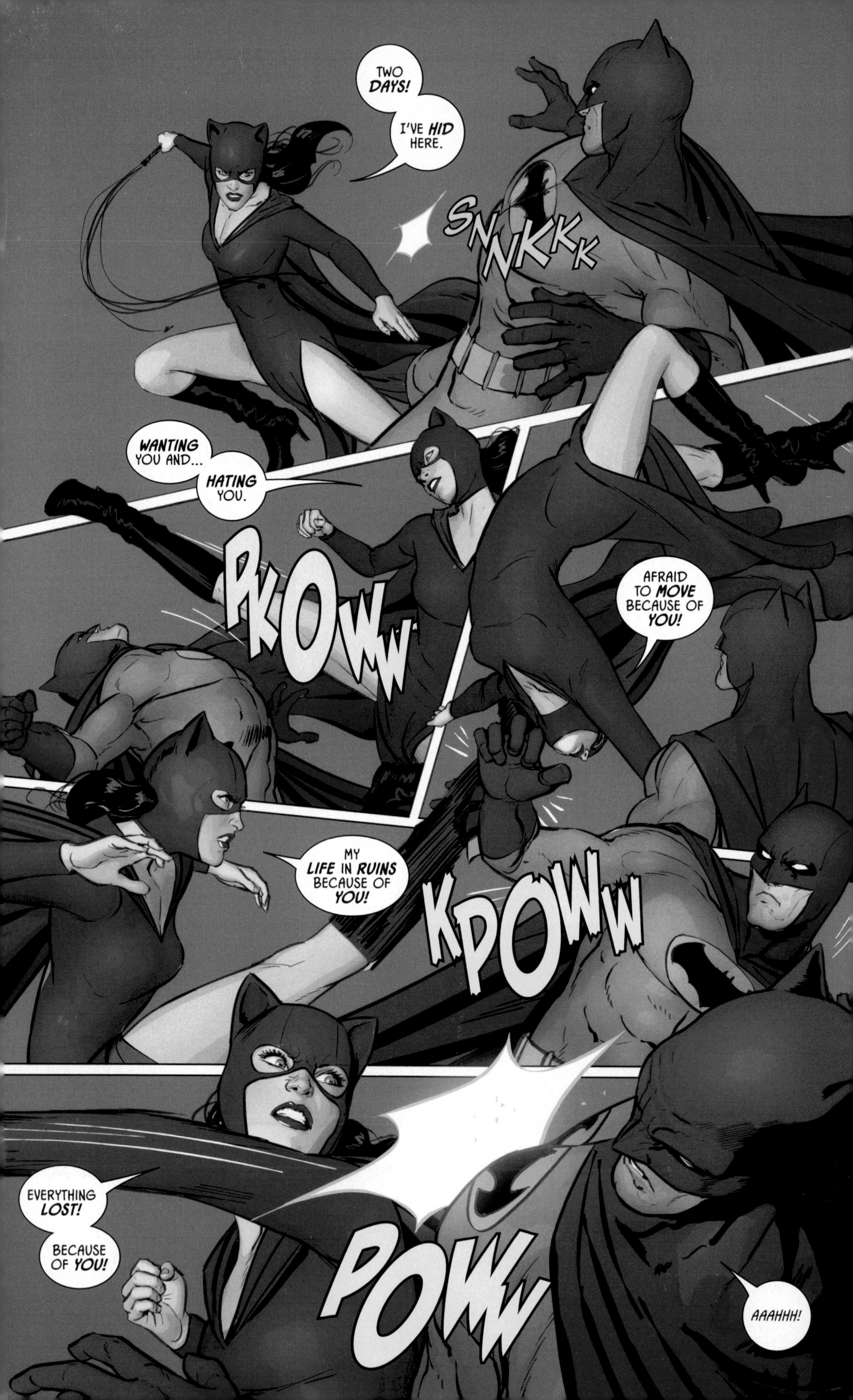
TWO DAYS!
I'VE HID HERE.
SNNKKK
WANTING YOU AND...
HATING YOU.
PKOWW
AFRAID TO MOVE BECAUSE OF YOU!
MY LIFE IN RUINS BECAUSE OF YOU!
KPOWW
EVERYTHING LOST!
BECAUSE OF YOU!
POWW
AAAHHH!

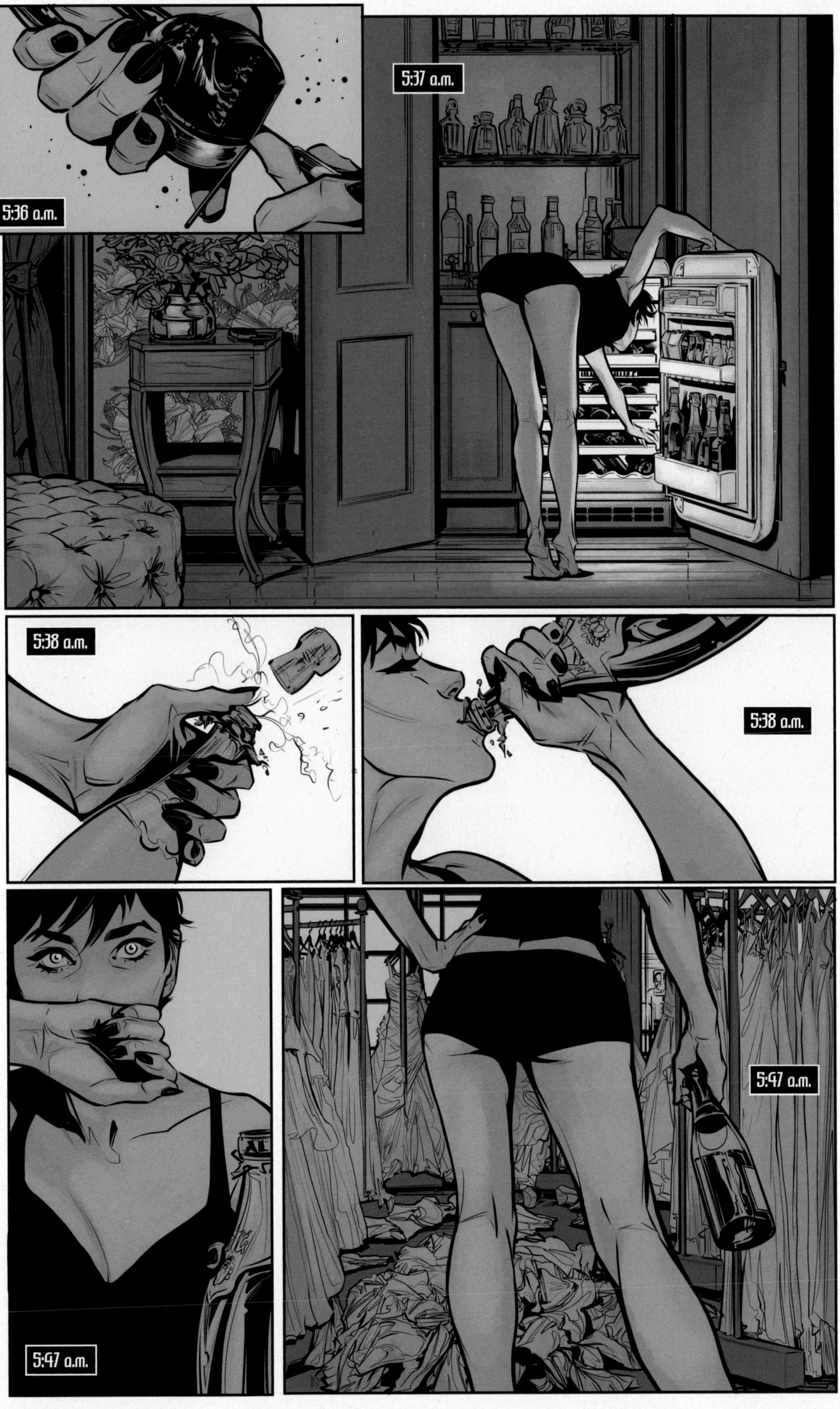
5:36 a.m.
5:37 a.m.
5:38 a.m.
5:38 a.m.
5:47 a.m.
5:47 a.m.

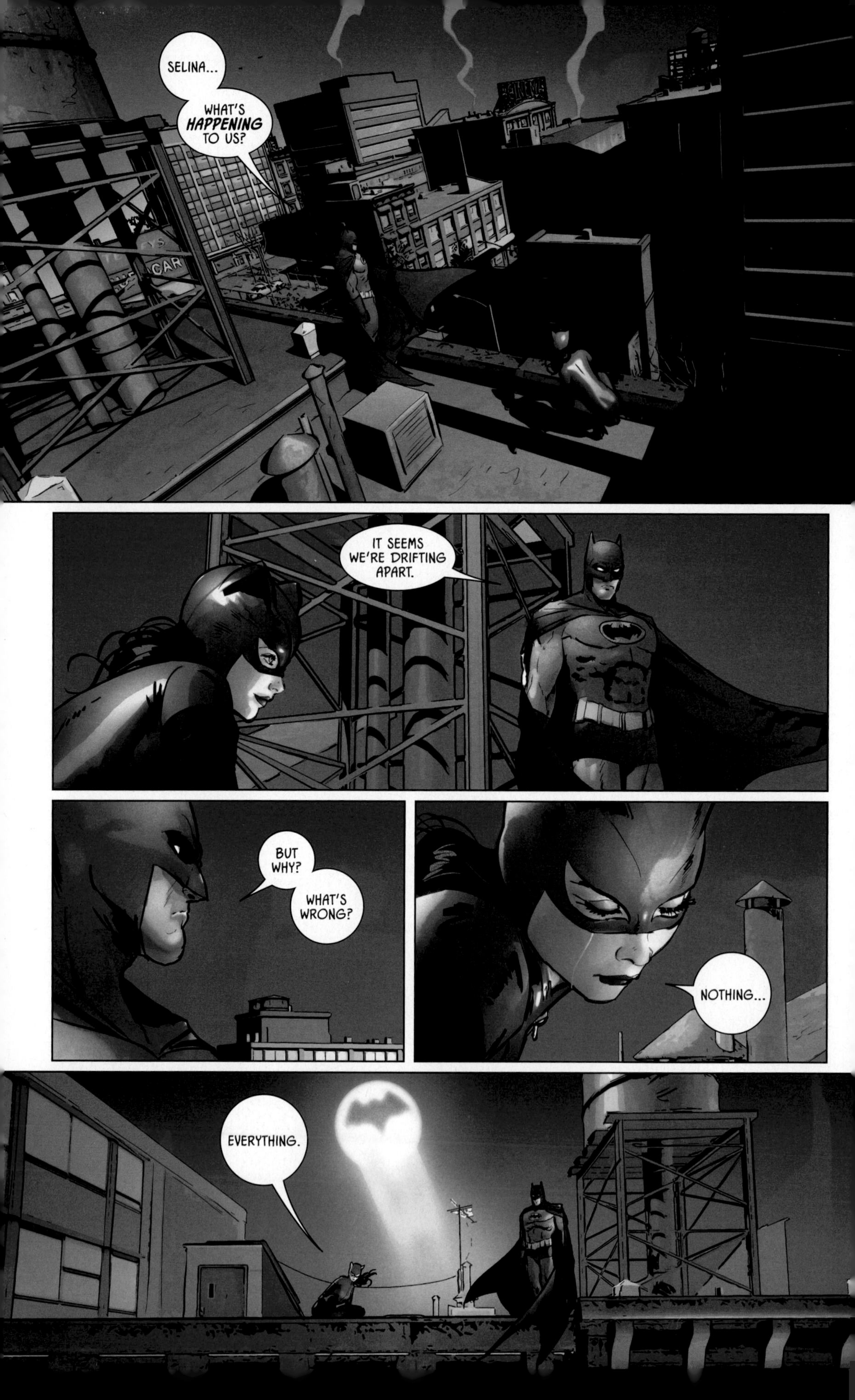
SELINA...
WHAT'S HAPPENING TO US?
IT SEEMS WE'RE DRIFTING APART.
BUT WHY?
WHAT'S WRONG?
NOTHING...
EVERYTHING.

6:12 a.m.

6:26 a.m.

6:26 a.m.

6:26 a.m.

The JJ
Collection
Price $28,000

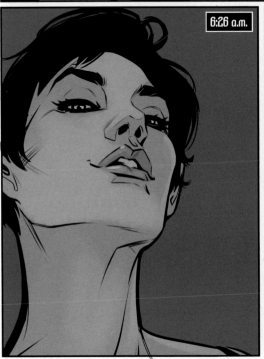

6:26 a.m.

6:28 a.m.

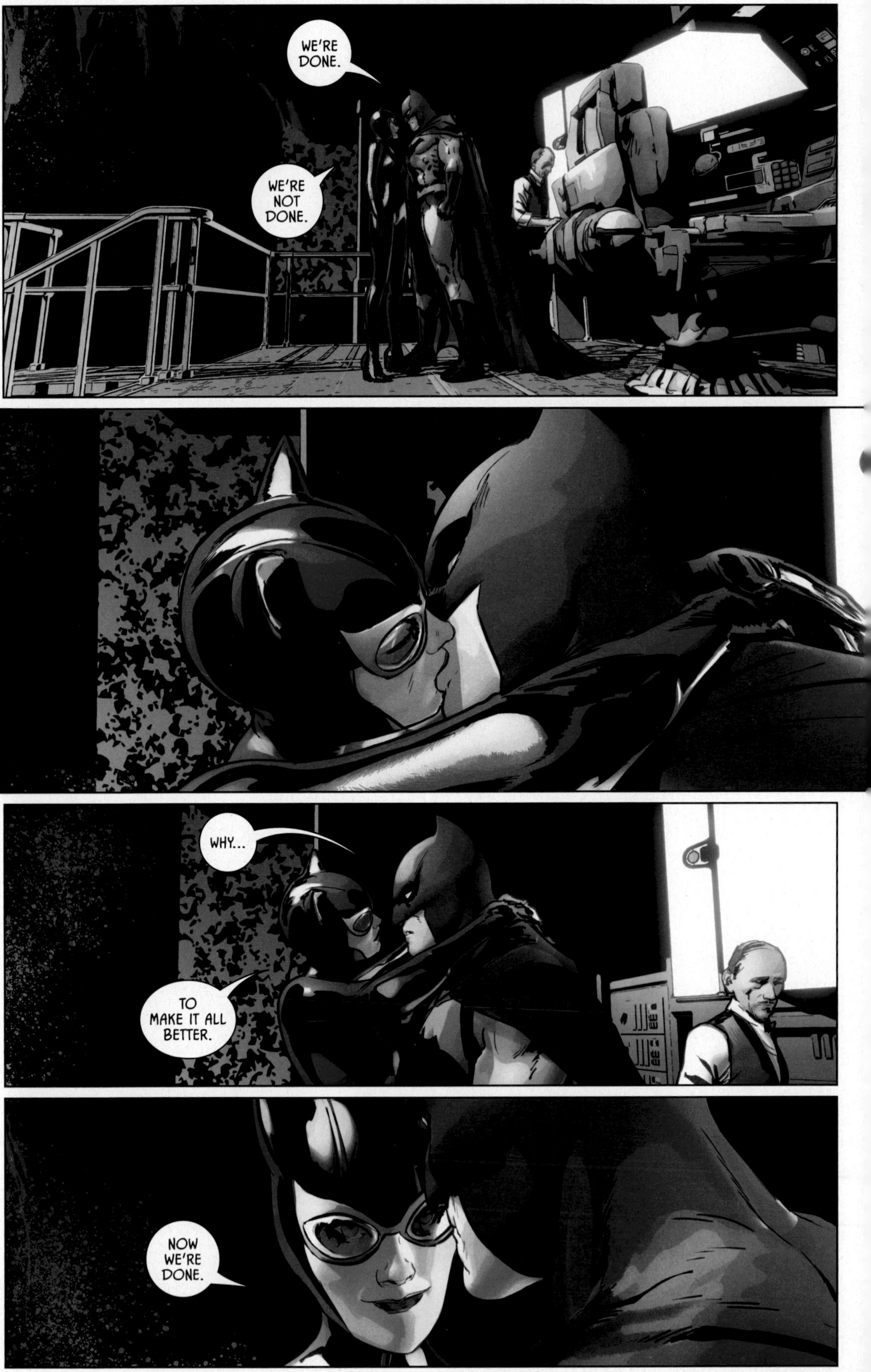
WE'RE DONE.
WE'RE NOT DONE.
WHY...
TO MAKE IT ALL BETTER.
NOW WE'RE DONE.

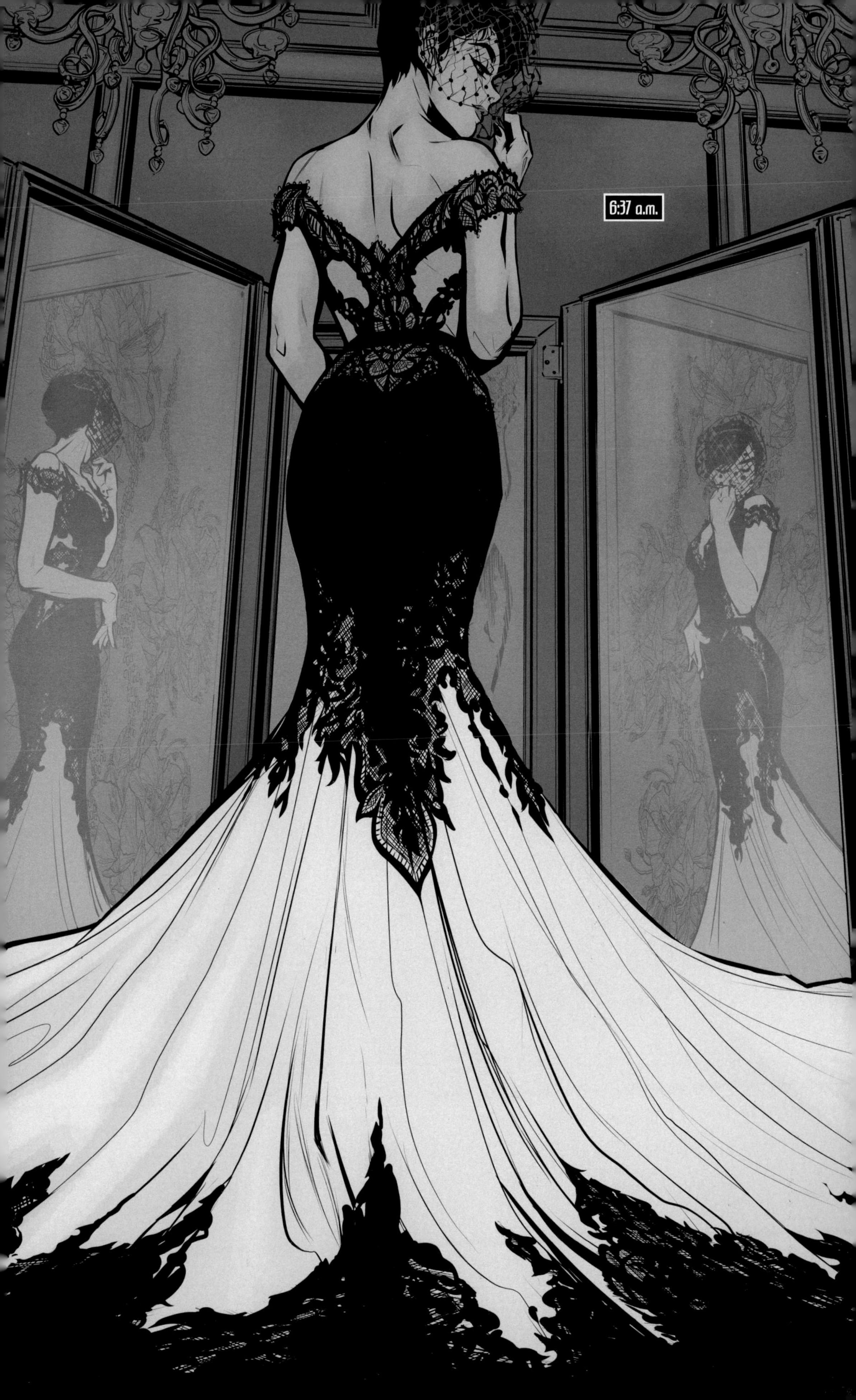
6:37 a.m.

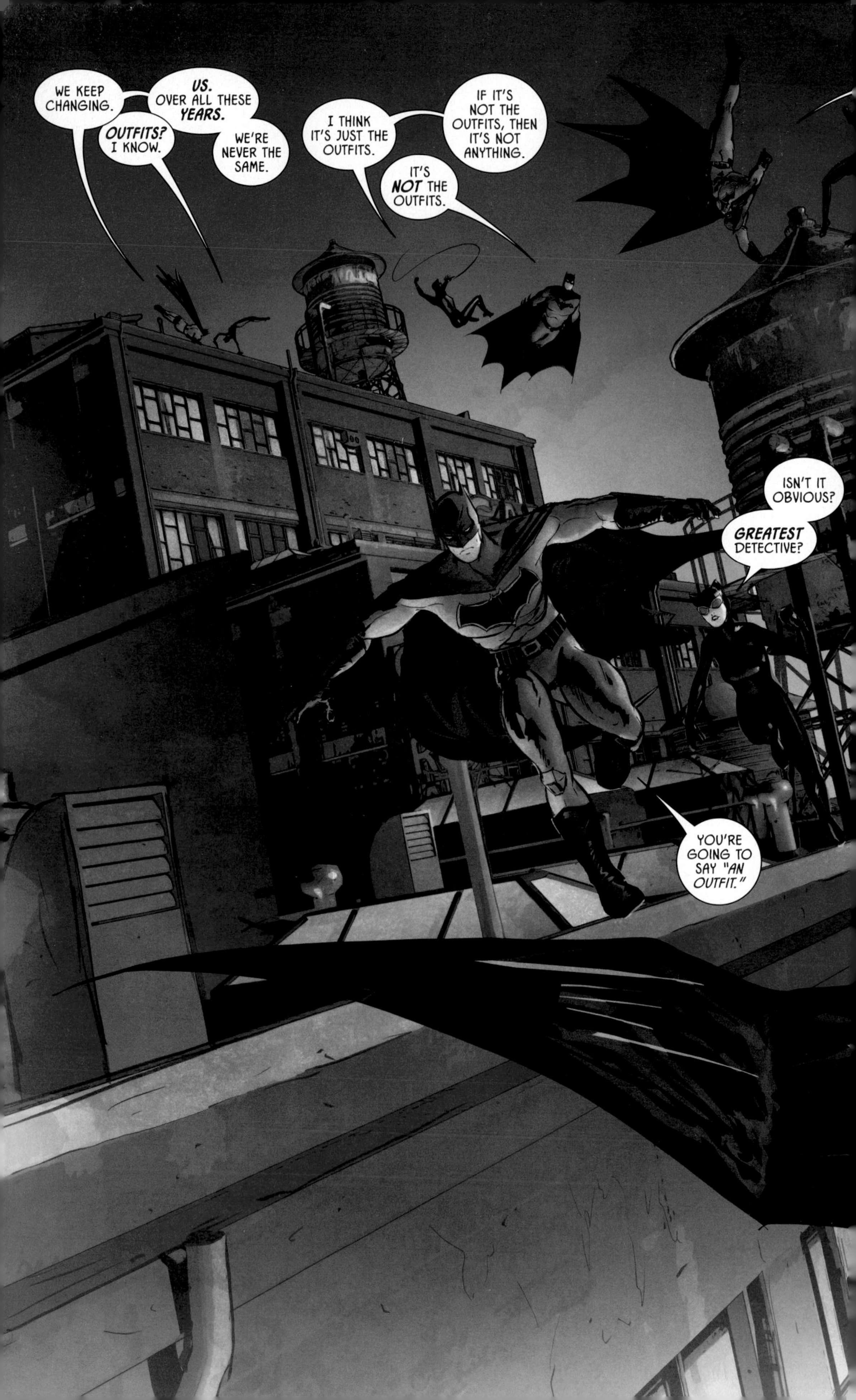
WE KEEP CHANGING.
US. OVER ALL THESE YEARS.
OUTFITS? I KNOW.
WE'RE NEVER THE SAME.
I THINK IT'S JUST THE OUTFITS.
IF IT'S NOT THE OUTFITS, THEN IT'S NOT ANYTHING.
IT'S NOT THE OUTFITS.
ISN'T IT OBVIOUS?
GREATEST DETECTIVE?
YOU'RE GOING TO SAY "AN OUTFIT."

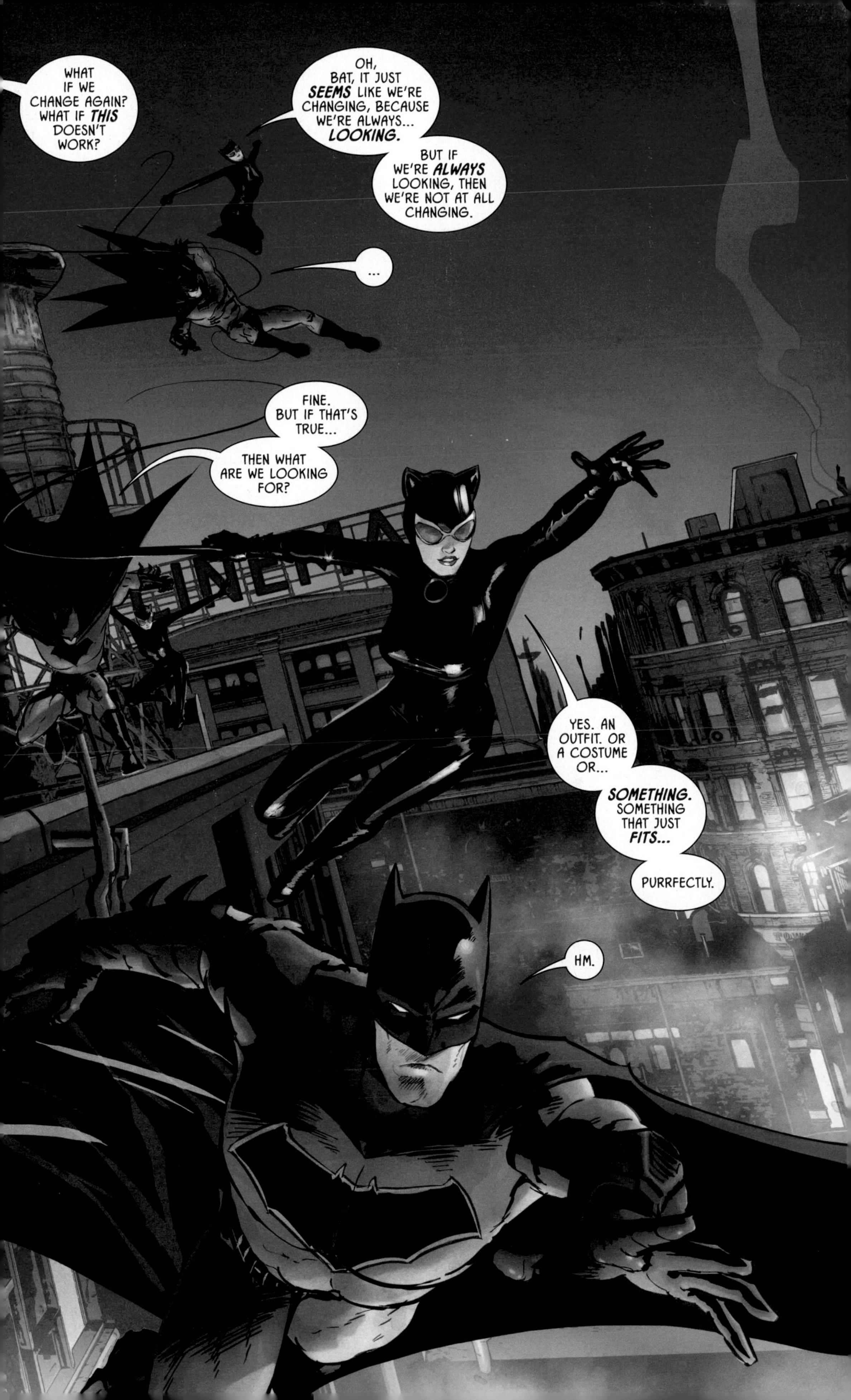

WHAT IF WE CHANGE AGAIN? WHAT IF **THIS** DOESN'T WORK?
OH, BAT, IT JUST **SEEMS** LIKE WE'RE CHANGING, BECAUSE WE'RE ALWAYS... **LOOKING.**
BUT IF WE'RE **ALWAYS** LOOKING, THEN WE'RE NOT AT ALL CHANGING.
...
FINE. BUT IF THAT'S TRUE...
THEN WHAT ARE WE LOOKING FOR?
CINEMA
YES. AN OUTFIT. OR A COSTUME OR...
SOMETHING. SOMETHING THAT JUST **FITS...**
PURRFECTLY.
HM.

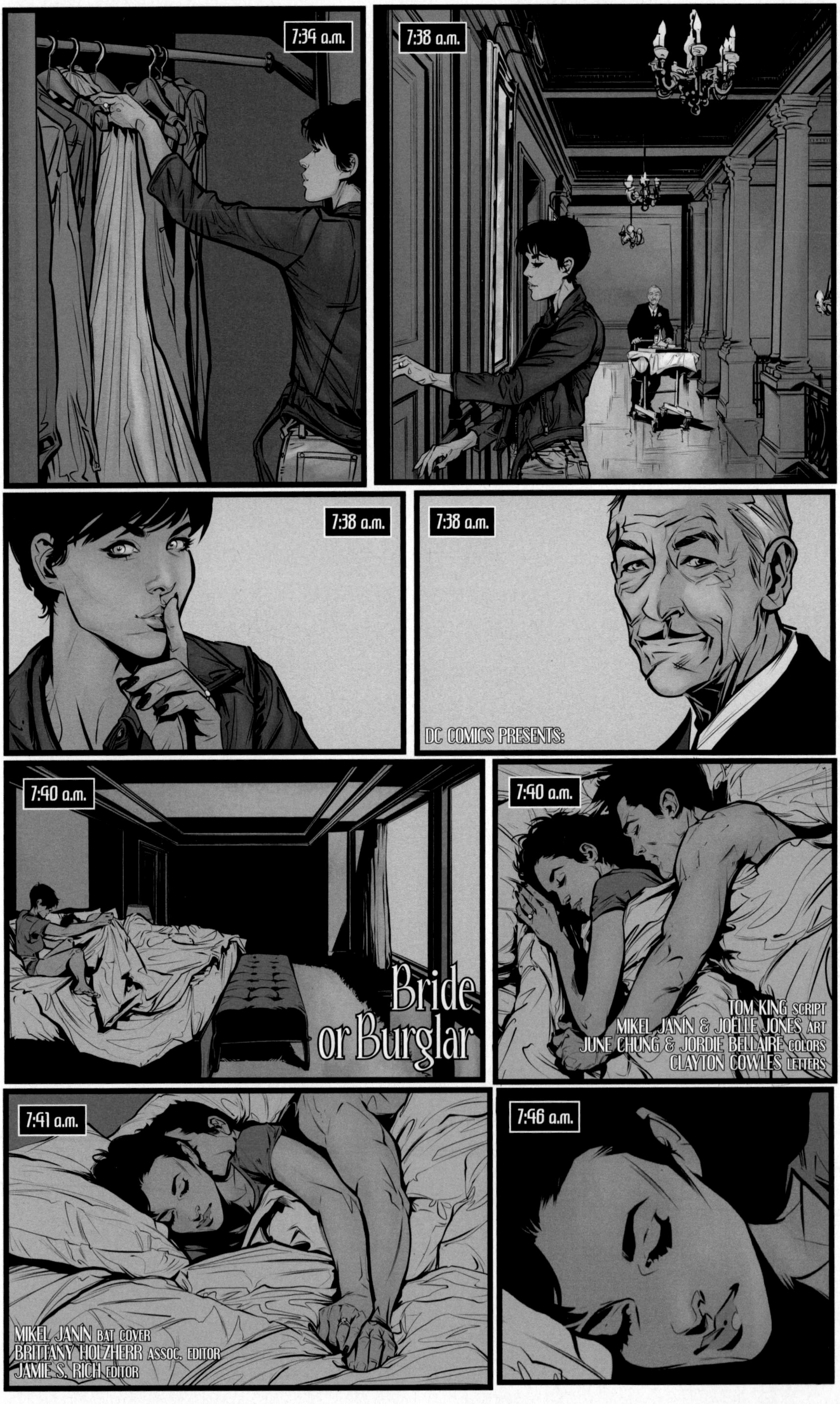

7:34 a.m.
7:38 a.m.
7:38 a.m.
7:38 a.m.
DC COMICS PRESENTS:
7:40 a.m.
Bride or Burglar
7:40 a.m.
TOM KING SCRIPT
MIKEL JANÍN & JOËLLE JONES ART
JUNE CHUNG & JORDIE BELLAIRE COLORS
CLAYTON COWLES LETTERS
7:41 a.m.
MIKEL JANÍN BAT COVER
BRITTANY HOLZHERR ASSOC. EDITOR
JAMIE S. RICH EDITOR
7:46 a.m.

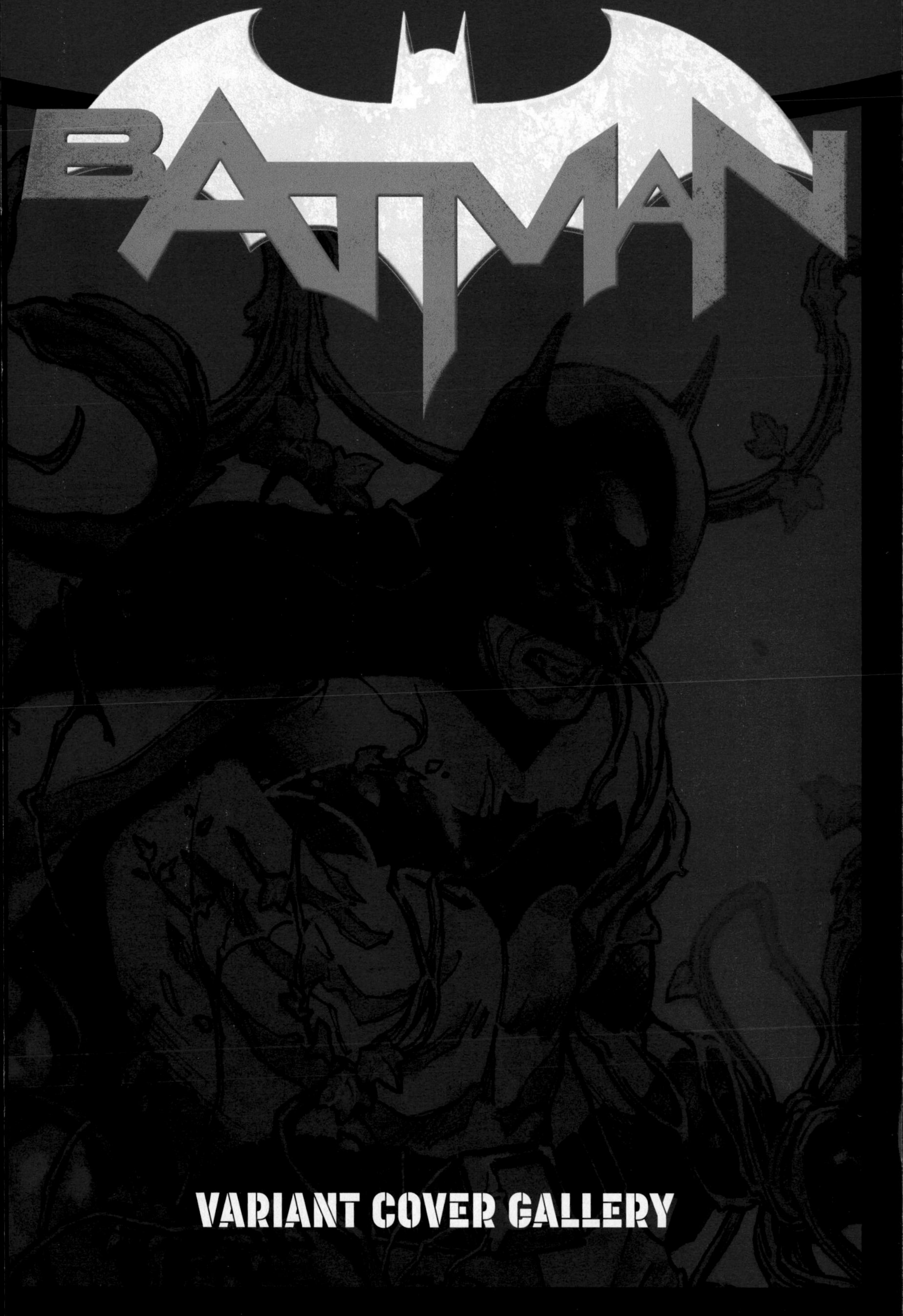
BATMAN

VARIANT COVER GALLERY

BATMAN #38 variant cover by OLIVIER COIPEL and DAVE STEWART

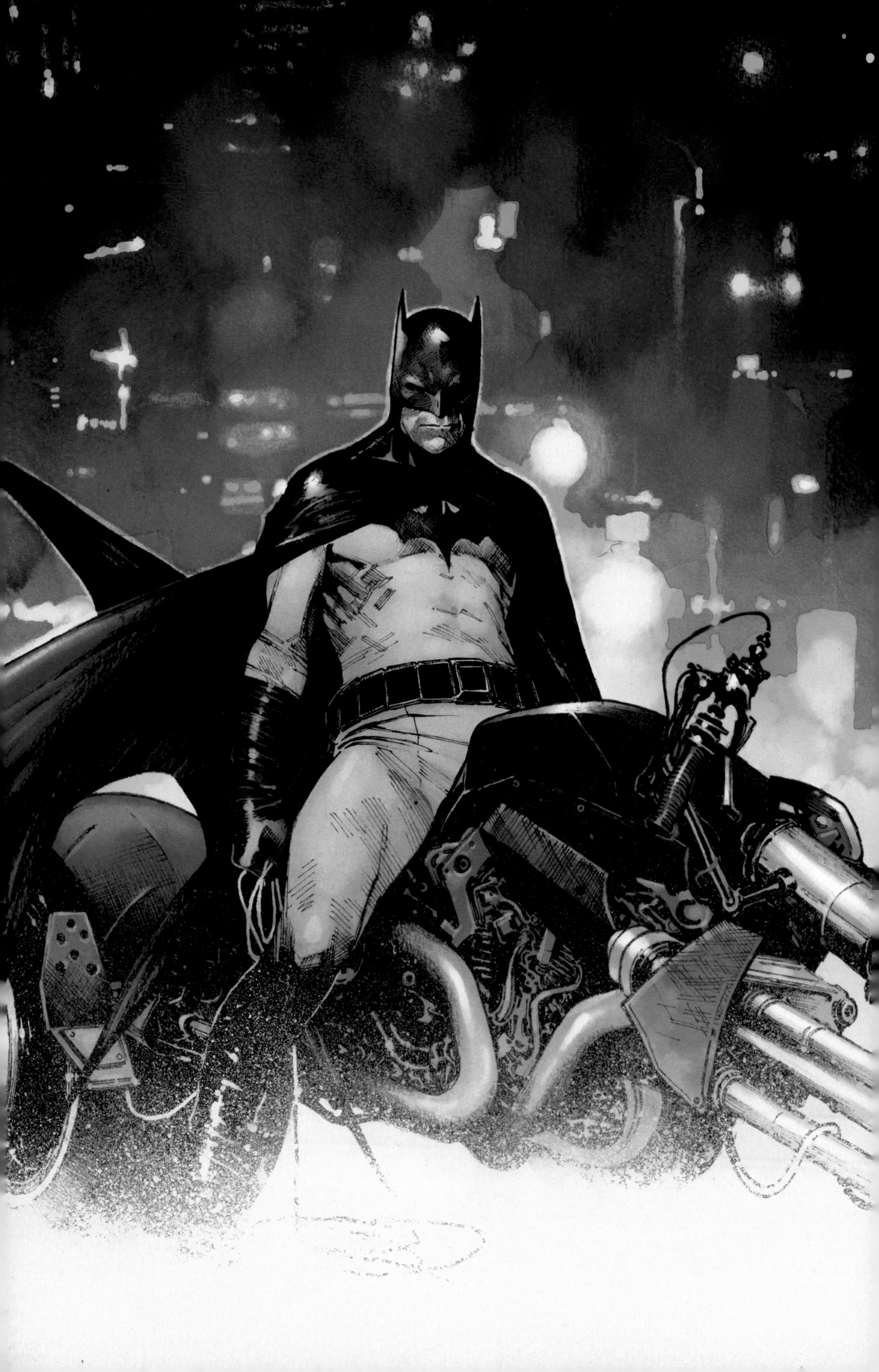

BATMAN #39 variant cover by OLIVIER COIPEL and DAVE STEWART

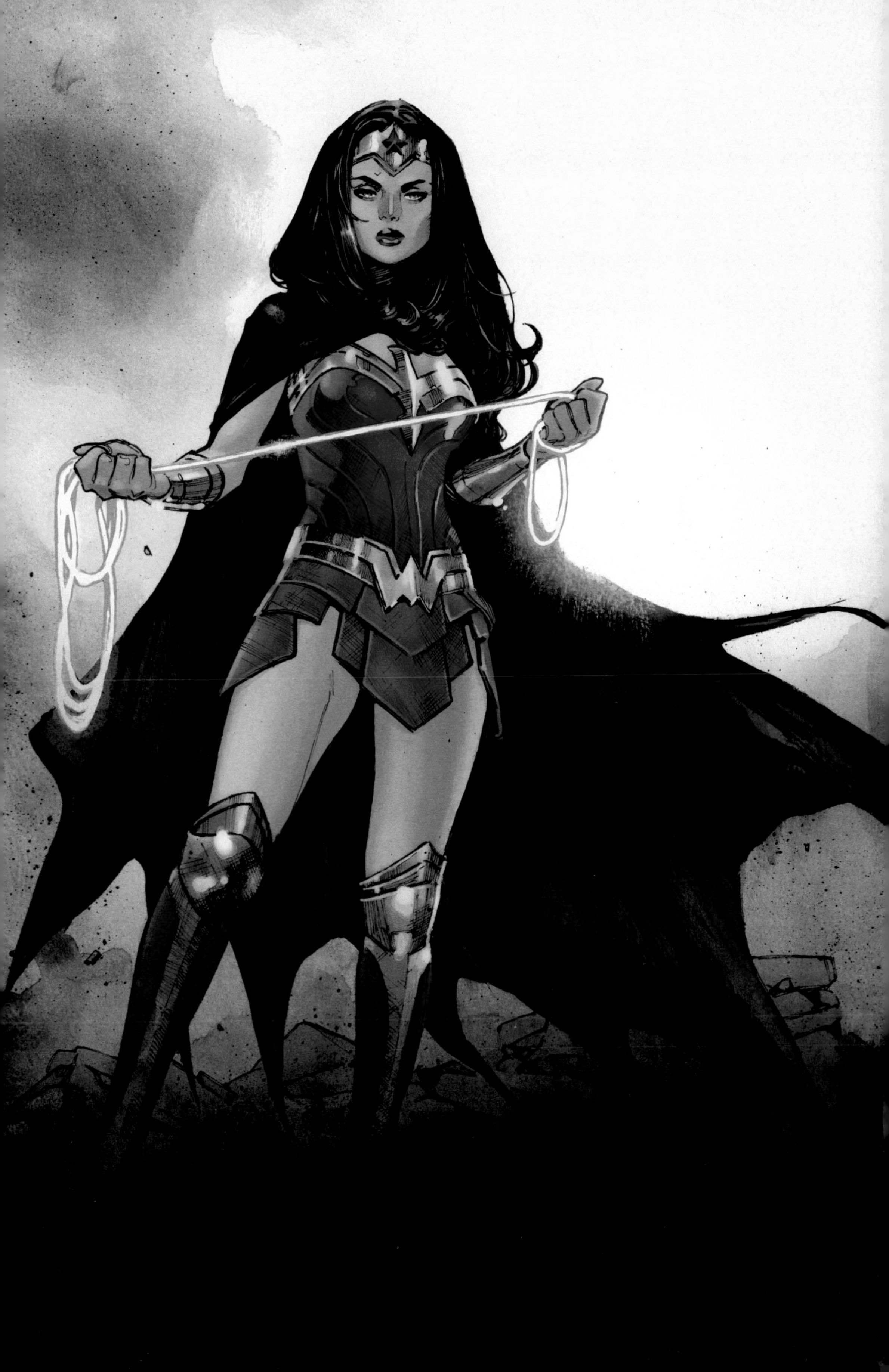

BATMAN #40 variant cover by OLIVIER COIPEL and DAVE STEWART

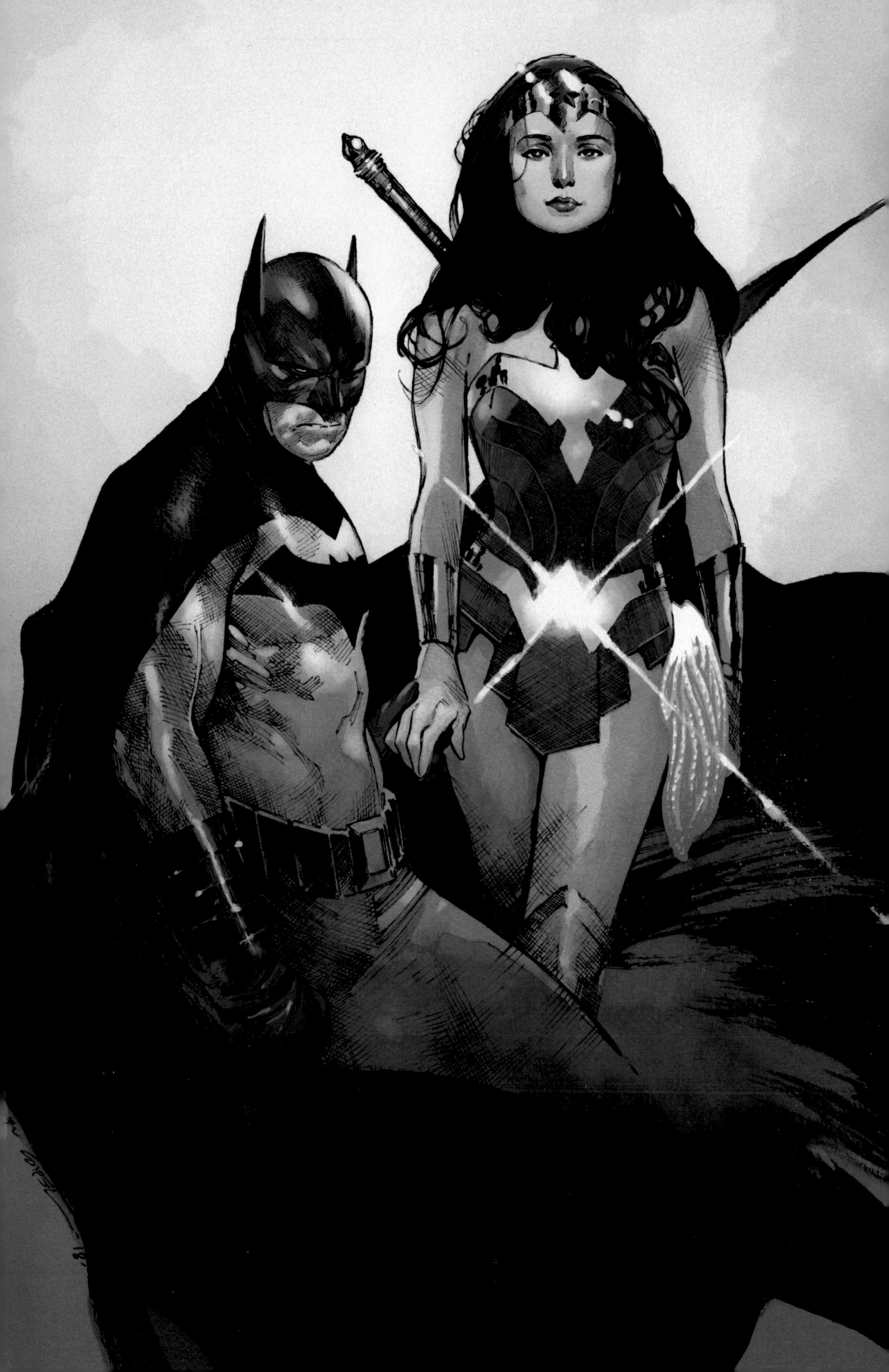

BATMAN #41 variant cover by OLIVIER COIPEL and DAVE STEWART

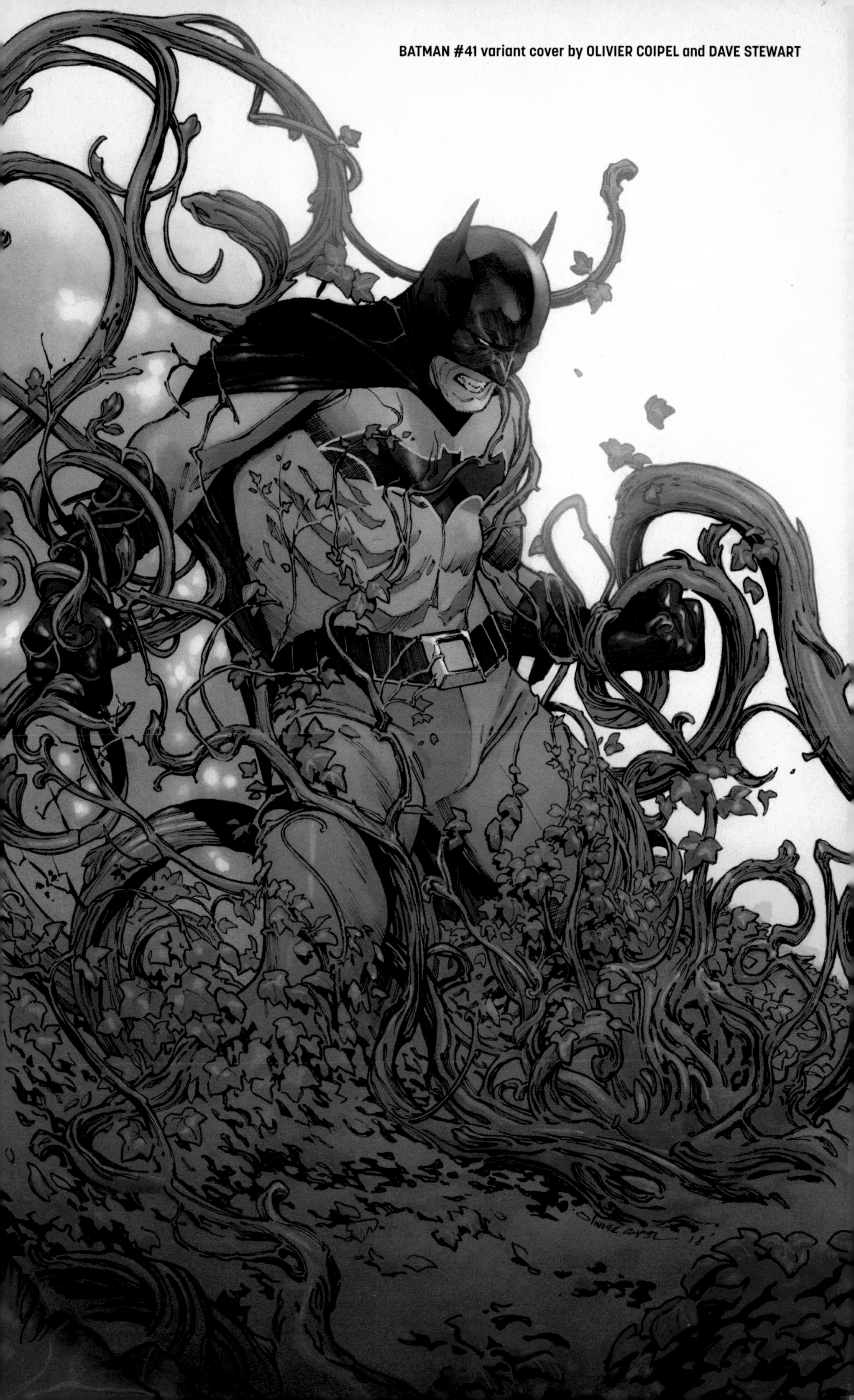

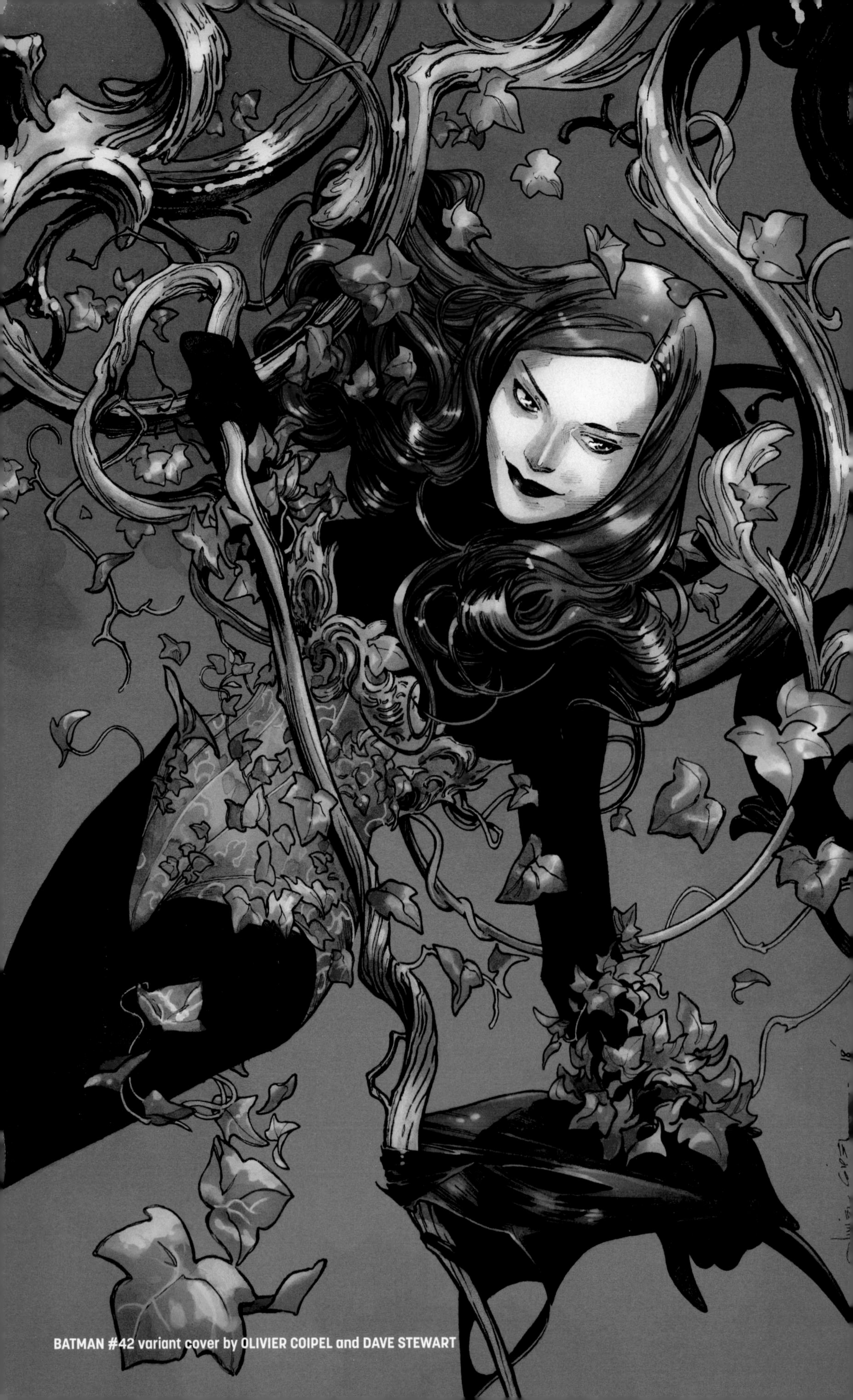

BATMAN #42 variant cover by OLIVIER COIPEL and DAVE STEWART

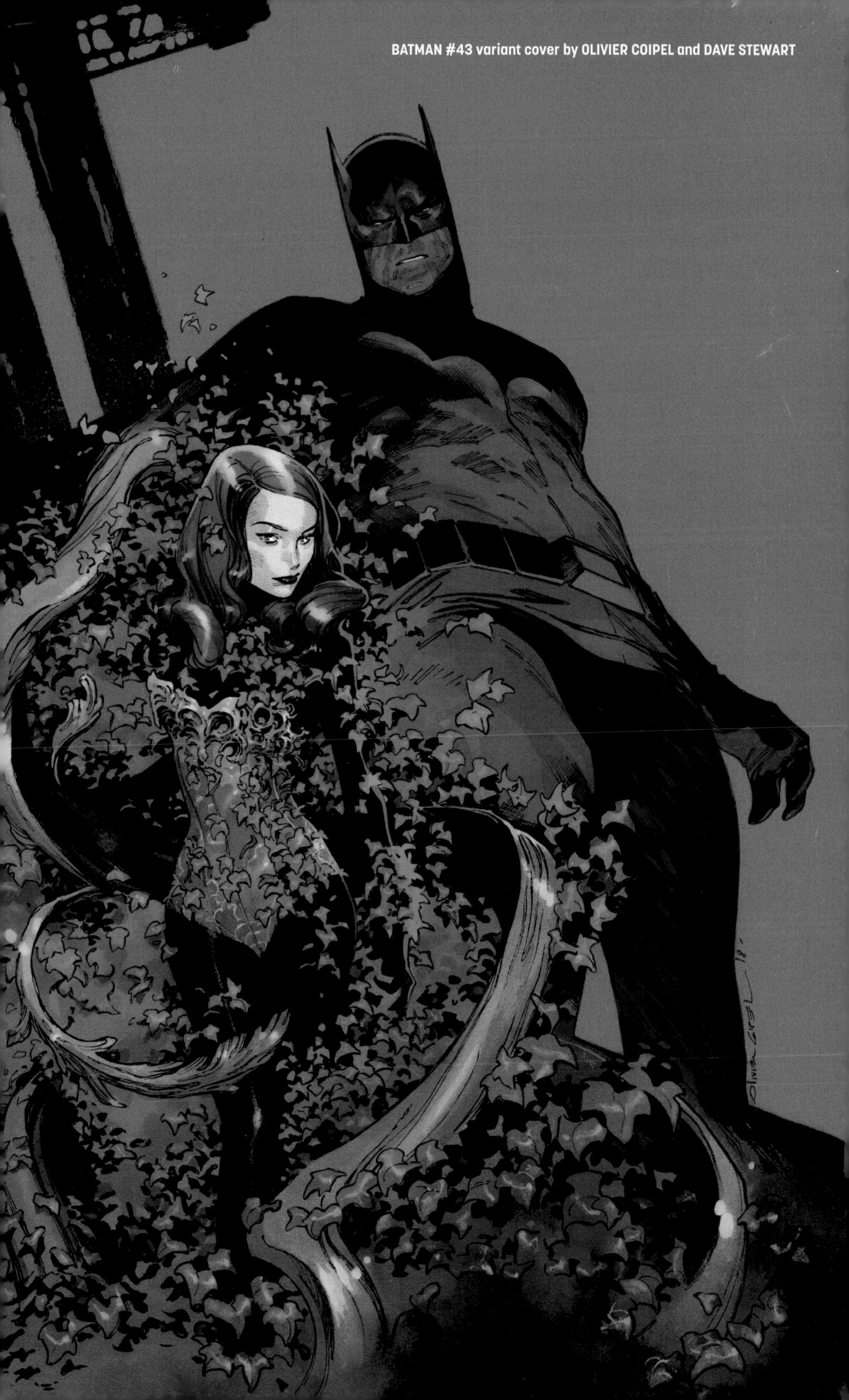

BATMAN #43 variant cover by OLIVIER COIPEL and DAVE STEWART

MAN #44 variant cover by JOËLLE JONES and JORDIE BELLAIRE

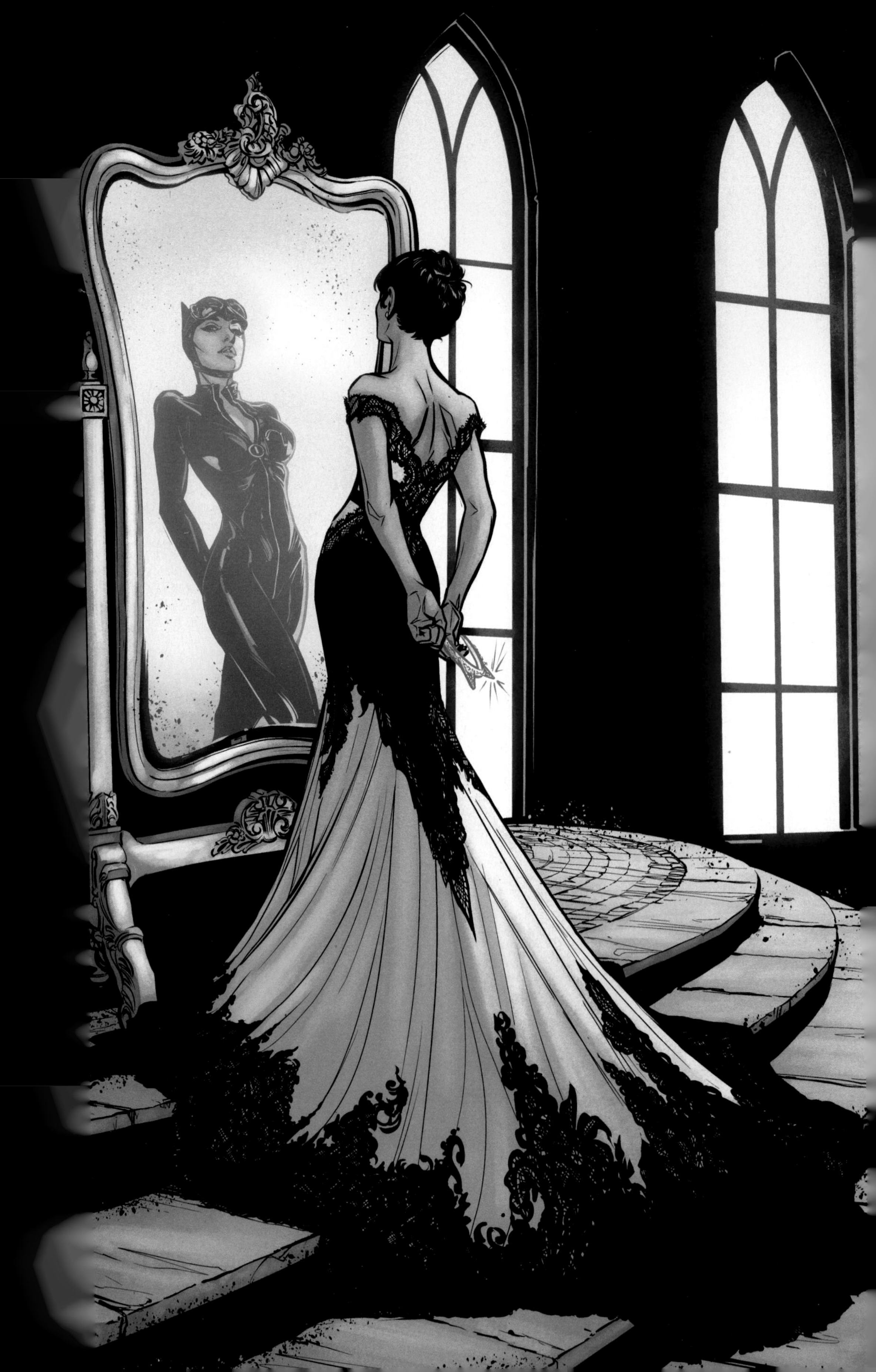

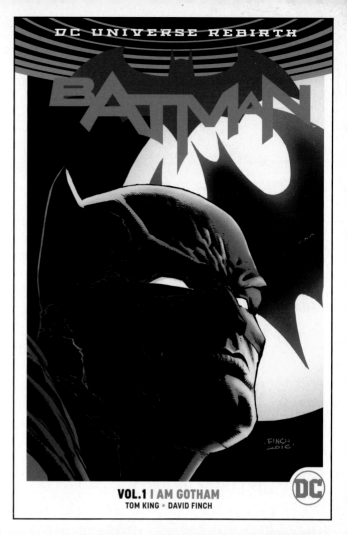
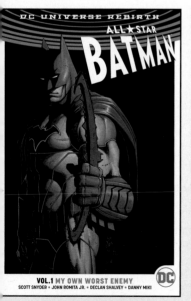

"[Writer Scott Snyder] pulls from the oldest aspects of the Batman myth, combines it with sinister-comic elements from the series' best period, and gives the whole thing terrific forward-spin."
– **ENTERTAINMENT WEEKLY**

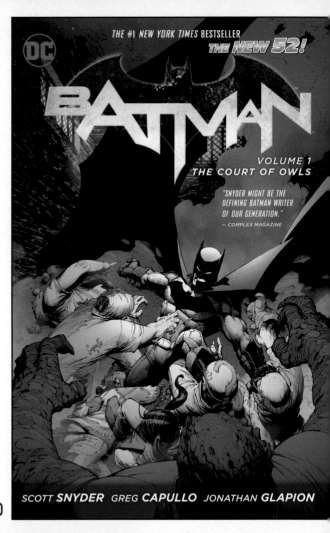

START AT THE BEGINNING!

BATMAN

VOL. 1: THE COURT OF OWLS

SCOTT SNYDER with GREG CAPULLO

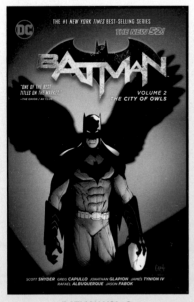

BATMAN VOL. 2:
THE CITY OF OWLS

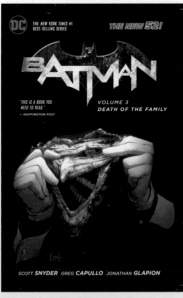

BATMAN VOL. 3:
DEATH OF THE FAMILY

READ THE ENTIRE EPIC

BATMAN VOL. 4
ZERO YEAR – SECRET CIT

BATMAN VOL. 5
ZERO YEAR – DARK CIT

BATMAN VOL. 6
GRAVEYARD SHIF

BATMAN VOL. 7
ENDGAM

BATMAN VOL. 8
SUPERHEAV

BATMAN VOL. 9
BLOON

BATMAN VOL. 10
EPILOGU